IMPROPER BOSTONIAN:
EMILY GREENE BALCH

IMPROPER BOSTONIAN
EMILY GREENE BALCH

Nobel Peace Laureate, 1946

by

Mercedes M. Randall

Eh bench' il fin bramato non consegua,
E 'n tanto studio l'alma si dilegua,
Basta che sia si nobilmente accesa!
—Giordano Bruno

TWAYNE PUBLISHERS, INC.
NEW YORK 3

Copyright © 1964 by Twayne Publishers, Inc.

Manufactured in the United States of America
Library of Congress Catalog Card Number: 64-25058

To the Memory of

Johanna Hart

Born, December 7, 1899, in Boston—the Cradle of Liberty
Died—circa 1943, Auschwitz

Foreword

The career of Emily Greene Balch is largely unknown to her fellow countrymen. If they were asked to name the only two American women ever to receive the Nobel Peace Prize, they might be at a loss for the answer—Jane Addams in 1931, and her close friend and collaborator, Emily Balch in 1946. In certain circles, however, the achievements of Emily Greene Balch are known and admired—in the peace movement both in the United States and abroad; among Quakers, Unitarians, American historians and economists; and among advocates of international organization.

The major part of this history treats of Emily Balch and a band of women who early in World War I attempted to do what had never been done before by women acting together as women: to enter into international political activity, bringing to birth a new spirit, a new approach, generating a new reconstructive force in the world. They were the first in 1914 and 1915 to *think internationally*. "Lovers of our own lands, we are citizens of the world, conscious partakers in the sacrament of all human life or more truly of all sentient life."

As early as 1916 Emily Balch was writing in prophetic criticism that the new age must be "a social age, an age of fraternal relations between men, an age in which exploitation of class by class, of rivalry of nation with nation is outgrown, an age in which the unlikeness of other races will be conceived as much of an asset as the unlikeness of wind and string instruments in a symphony." She believed, heretically for that time, that there was much to unlearn before we could teach. We must unlearn nationalism and patriotism, retaining "only that patriotism you can carry into Heaven with you." She believed in an "Americanism which holds the future of our people as its pledge. This Americanism breathes a spirit of universal and disinterested good-will; it is based on individual liberty, enriched by a sense of social duty."

7

At the onset of the Hitler era, Emily Balch and her European comrades fought to preserve liberty and freedom from forced uniformity, "that rational, reciprocal, life-giving, world-building freedom in which we believe." What totalitarian powers thought is shown by their bitter persecution of the peace people in Europe. "Not only the artist, the poet, the philosopher," she said, "but the crank, the oddity, the natural heretic and rebel have their place in the social scheme." And who but Emily Greene Balch could include in her program for democracy one other freedom? "People must be trained to respect others, all others, including the weak, the dull and the disagreeable. They must learn to give others the liberty that they ask for themselves."

If you like biographies of complicated, colorful personalities with tangled dramas in their lives, this story of Emily Balch and her group may not appeal to you. Two voyages of women over the Atlantic are described in these pages, but they are hardly the voyages of a Ship of Fools. If you are prejudiced against people who have achieved self-discipline and are as "good" as they are intelligent, witty and original, this book may not be grist for your mill. If you scorn those who after two world wars in this twentieth century still retain in their vocabularies such words as "love," "dynamic good-will," "conscience," and "hope"—who have not taken refuge in philosophies of cynicism, despair, meaninglessness, and emptiness—you may prefer to leave these pages unturned.

This book was written because Emily Balch needed a biography. She was a remarkable woman who belonged to perhaps the most remarkable generation of women in modern American history. I first met Miss Balch, as she was always called, when I was a student, in the course of what she described as her "too notorious effort to try to prevent the United States entering the first World War." We knew her as a distinguished sociologist, a professor of economics at Wellesley College, and a warm supporter of the pacifist efforts of young people. In fact, some of us rather thought *we* were waging the campaign, and that Miss Balch, Miss Addams and the others were *helping* us. In the uneasy 1930's I met her again in the Women's International League for Peace and Freedom, and in spite of the disparity in our ages I became one of her legion of friends. I visited her time and again at the Domichek in Wellesley, generally to work on various projects, and she came often to us at Morningside Heights in New York and to our hilltop farm in Peacham, Vermont.

Before her death, Miss Balch turned over to me all her private papers, letters, diaries, journals and unpublished manuscripts, making me her literary executor. The Balches always lived in large houses and seem never to have thrown anything away. She left a number of autobiographical fragments about various phases of her three careers. Unless otherwise indicated, her words in the text are taken from these "recollections." Many passages, quotations, and letters, ordinarily set off as extract materials, are here run into the text in order not to impede the flow of the narrative. The ironic qualities in some of her personal reactions should not blind a reader into thinking that Miss Balch was in the habit of deceiving herself. I have not found it necessary to withhold anything except some of her trenchant and amusing oral comments on personalities. I have tried neither to extenuate nor enforce. In writing this historical biography I have hoped to contribute to that larger peace movement in which she pioneered.

Her philosopher friend William Ernest Hocking wrote of Emily Balch in 1946: "No other life known to me has been so consistently and almost exclusively devoted to the cause of peace and with such pervasive good judgment and effect. . . . Her own thought was recognized as responsible in the best sense, and without self-advertisement won its way to the minds of those who were making decisions. It will be long before the sum of her labors can be gathered; but when it is done, its achievement will be recognized as the more remarkable because its methods have been so much the quiet ways of friendly reason."

The quiet ways of friendly reason!

Mercedes M. Randall

Acknowledgments

Many thanks for vividly recounted memories and for appraisals of Emily Balch are due to Marion Balch (Maidie), who lived to read a good part of the book; to Alice Balch Stone; to Francis and Pauline Balch; and to such long-standing friends as Helen Cheever, Mary Kingsbury Simkhovitch, Vida D. Scudder, Dr. Sarah Stowell, Oswald Garrison Villard, Paul U. Kellogg, Henry and Lydia Cadbury, and Dr. Alice Hamilton.

To those who commented on the entire manuscript I am deeply indebted, especially to Professor Merle E. Curti of Wisconsin, who was the first to give me his warm encouragement; to Professor Mabel Foote Weeks of Barnard and her sister Lizzie Green Weeks; to Professor James Gutmann of Columbia; and to Emily Parker Simon, international vice-president of the Women's International League. Professors William E. Leuchtenburg of Columbia and Arthur S. Link of Princeton, editor of the Woodrow Wilson Papers, read chapters 5 through 10, which cover the period of World War I. Professor Marjorie H. Nicolson read the first twelve chapters, and Professor Richard Hofstadter read chapter 11 on wartime hysteria and the academic freedom case.

Three critics who exceeded the claims of loyalty and friendship in their careful reading of the manuscript were Professor Frederick B. Tolles, Director of the Friends' Historical Library, Swarthmore College; Frederika Neumann, who gave me the benefit of her knowledge derived from her long experience in practicing social work; and Professor Gertrude C. Bussey of Goucher College. Professor Bussey spurred me on while she was writing her history of the Women's International League for Peace and Freedom, a work interrupted by her sudden death in 1961. Her insights as a former International Chairman of the League and her friendship with Emily Balch made her comments particularly valuable. The Curators of the Swarthmore College Peace Collection, Mrs. Marjorie Edwards and her predecessor Mrs. Mary G. Cary, were more than kind and painstaking, as was Mrs. Elizabeth Tapper while I was examing the Archives at the Maison Internationale in Geneva.

The many facets of Miss Balch's personality were brought out through interviews and letters from W.I.L.P.F. leaders: Mildred Scott Olmsted, Dorothy Detzer (Denny), Gertrude Baer, Andrée Jouve, Edith Pye, Marie Lous-Mohr, Helene Scheu-Riess, Bertha McNeill, Kathleen Lowrie; and former Wellesley colleagues and students of Miss Balch. Others who were helpful were Dr. John K. Wright, Louis P. Lochner, Marjorie La M. Thompson, Harry J. Carman, Charles H. Kahn and his wife Dénise, Tracy Mygatt, Frances Witherspoon, Sidney Moritz, and Dorothea Lefkoff. Joan Sedgwick of Twayne Publishers brought consistency and order to an unruly manuscript. Margaret Wilson and Linda Nash typed with devotion the several drafts of the book. In a most literal sense this biography could not have been written without the intellectual, moral, quizzical, and financial support of my husband, who made possible all the travels incidental to writing a biography, including a trip to Geneva.

Grateful acknowledgment is made to the following publishers for permission to quote: E. P. Dutton and Co.; The Macmillan Co.; Harper and Row; Harcourt Brace and World, Inc.; Russell and Russell, Inc.; Harvard University Press; Houghton Mifflin Co.; and to Mrs. Rachel Baker Napier for permission to quote from *The Life and Letters of Woodrow Wilson* by Ray Stannard Baker.

M. M. R.

Table of Contents

LIST OF ILLUSTRATIONS

The sketches heading the chapters are by Emily G. Balch.

PRELUDE

An Artist in Human Relations

It is not often given to an individual to exhibit an inner unity of purpose visibly running all through life like a design in a textile. But so it was with Emily Greene Balch. From the very beginning she was interested in better relations between human beings. In *Howard's End* E. M. Forster makes one of his characters say, "I know that personal relations are the real life, for ever and ever." And the other character replies, "Amen."

Emily Balch's concern for personal relations began when she was a child in the home. In time it widened out to embrace the whole planet. In a large and close-knit family consisting of a brilliant, gentle, uncontroversial, too selfless father, a vital, witty and loving mother, a brother and four sisters of varying temperaments and talents, Emily developed from those first affections the delicate and difficult art of cooperation between complex human personalities. She learned to discriminate the things that for her came first and to choose between loyalties. The only two times she missed an international congress of her beloved Women's International League occurred when her cherished elder sister Annie was ill.

In her early schooldays, according to her classmates, Emily managed to answer all the questions correctly without appearing "smart." Later, as a pupil in Miss Ireland's school for girls in Louisburg Square in Boston, she was at the top of the class and still retained her popularity.

As we look back over Emily Greene Balch's ninety-four years, we see that everything she did sprang from a definite conscious purpose which integrated her life and gave its events a certain logical sequence. She started out with a vague general idea of

15

trying to do right. In her post-Civil War childhood in Boston, among the socially and intellectually privileged group to which she was born, a strong sense of "mission" prevailed. The atmosphere was permeated by what she called "neo-Puritanism without its rigors, narrowness, or introspection, but colored and controlled through and through by a complete acceptance of the rule of conscience and by a warm and generous sense of the call to service." This ideal was exemplified for her in the personality of Charles Fletcher Dole, the Unitarian minister of her church in Jamaica Plain. In his warm faith in righteousness, his liberal theological views, his passion for peace, he was one of the chief influences that played upon her life.

By the time she had finished college, her increasing interest in fostering more just and fruitful human relations caused her to turn from the classics and literature, in which she was highly gifted, to the study of practical economics. With unconscious artistry she pursued these same aims in her three successive careers, social work, college teaching, and pioneering for peace.

At Denison House, an early settlement house in Boston, of which she was the first head worker, this young woman from a sheltered environment came to a realistic understanding of the lives of the underprivileged and the disadvantaged. Though it was her fate to be reared among proper Bostonians, it was her choice to mingle with many improper Bostonians, prisoners, prostitutes, paupers, neglected children, juvenile offenders and, worst of all for her later professional reputation, labor leaders, strikers, and pacifists, with whom she made common cause.

Emily Balch turned to teaching, which she felt to be her true vocation, because she became convinced that if she could help young people feel their responsibility for social conditions, for the creation of fruitful relations between employer and employed, for a juster social system, her own contribution would reach further.

In her teaching she was never very academic. To her, teaching was a sharing of ideas. She took to heart what her father wrote to her when she was a girl in college, "I think the pleasantest relations presume that the teacher is only a student a little further on the same road." In many ways she was a poor teacher, absent-minded and unsystematic. But as many of her students have attested, she was an inspiring one.

In her scholarly work she always had a human, almost a feminine approach. Her *magnum opus* was a comprehensive study of a great stream of immigration, *Our Slavic Fellow Citizens.* She spent two years in the field in America and Europe doing research at her own expense. At the beginning of Part I, called "Slavic Emigration at Its Source," she placed the caption, "Über den Bergen sind auch Leute" (Beyond the mountains there are people also). The second part, "Slavic Immigration in the United States," begins with a quotation which shows her compassionate understanding of immigrant yearnings, "Ubi bene, ibi patria" (Where it is well with me, there is my Fatherland). In the scholarly appendix, full of statistics of population, of Austrian taxes, of the wages of unskilled laborers, she inserted charming sections on "Some Bohemian Nursery Rhymes," "A Ruthenian Poet in Canada," and a "Story of a Peasant Millionaire."

When her professorship at Wellesley College was terminated in 1918 after twenty years of teaching, because of her pacifism in World War I coupled with her radical economic views, some of her colleagues issued a statement ending with the words: "Even when differing from her in opinion or action we have respected her essential fair-mindedness, her courageous and conscientious regard for truth. We feel we have had in our midst a person of rare distinction and nobility."

At the age of fifty-two, in a period unfriendly to dissenters, she was left without a profession and without a pension. The way she bore this injustice illuminates the quality of her character. She harbored no bitterness, uttered no recrimination. Although it was a clear case of violation of academic freedom, this is the way she put it: "Much as I grieved that the well-known liberality of Wellesley College should have been over-strained by me, I could not be surprised, when after much discussion and much friendly advocacy of my reappointment, the Trustees decided against it." By her attitude she increased her own stature and elevated Wellesley.

Up to 1915 her thoughts had been mainly of economic improvement as a means to a larger end, as tending to produce more brotherly relations and also as likely to result from better relations. "Suddenly," as she said, "war broke up the whole network of human relations, disastrously dividing one world into two, destroying, purposely, scientifically, the ancient heritage of beauty and the crops in the field." Her thirty years of pioneering work for peace were about to begin, and her day-by-day labors within the companionship of the Women's International League for Peace and Freedom. To this third career, for which she was to receive the accolade of the Nobel Peace Prize in 1946, she brought the same delicate artistry.

It is hard to put into words the manner in which she influenced the thinking of the people she talked to, how she molded without attempting to mold, how she could change the tenor of a meeting, or shift its tone, by the way she handled it. When an American Legion member tried to disrupt a peace meeting by his abuse, she looked him full in the face and said with feeling, "Oh, I know so well what you must be thinking." When in W.I.L.P.F. councils heated discussion of a policy or principle came to an impasse, Emily Balch, who during the whole time had been quietly doodling, was often able to evolve a way out, not a compromise, but a "third way" satisfactory to all. She was a creative apostle of reconciliation.

She loved the arts, the great painting, sculpture, and architecture produced by men of genius; but even more she loved the handicrafts, the things that ordinary people make and create—pottery, furniture, weaving. Her great pride was the beautiful and colorful collection of Slavic textiles she had gathered in 1904-1905, during her year in Austria-Hungary. She cherished and wore thin a handmade silver peasant necklace she had bought years before from a peasant woman at Ischl.

Unlike many who appreciate the arts, she also had gifts of creation. What she herself made gave other people much pleasure: her sensitive, delicately colored pastel drawings of European and New England landscapes; her exquisite doodles; irises and reeds on a river bank; a clump of ferns; acorns, flowers, pine cones, snowflakes out of a faery world. One gift she did not have—an ear and mind for the world of music. But the music of poetry was hers to appreciate and to communicate.

But above all, she loved human beings with a deep, warm, personal love, whether they were great social statesmen like the Mary Morton Kehew of her youth and the Jane Addams of her maturer years, or plain ordinary people like the "seamstress friend" of her diary.

Her love for people expressed itself in an exquisite courtesy towards her fellows. This trait she had in common with her father. It was more than a graceful consideration for others. It was "corteseye" in the sense in which Chaucer uses it, setting it on a pedestal with "truth, honor, freedom." It was part of her inner spiritual structure. She was courteous to children, to tradespeople, to cleaning women, to obscure young colleagues, and to people to whom others sometimes gave short shrift. She had the happy faculty of giving people her complete, sincere, and undivided attention, a gift as rare as it is ingratiating. A younger friend who sometimes had occasion to observe Emily Balch in her home unawares, saw that her manners even when she thought she was alone were distinguished. Like the Archbishop in Willa Cather's novel, she had a courtesy even to herself, when she was watering her begonias in her sunny window at Wellesley or shifting her mountain of mail from her desk to her card table, and back again, with a half-rueful, kindly smile.

Her tolerance towards others she extended also to herself. Long before Freud, her insights into the workings of the subconscious led her to forgive herself when she thought she had fallen from the standards she had set herself. As a girl she wrote in her diary, "Don't be unreasonable with self when a day proves to be wasted without own fault or when results are unapparent. Do as well as can and then accept imperfections as not responsible for." Later she resolved to "be patient with myself; be fair to myself." This intelligent self-acceptance prevented the rise of inner conflicts. It contributed to a harmony of her whole personality. Perhaps it was this harmony, this union between the inner and the outer, that gave her countenance such nobility (a word regrettably gone out of use today), and made her voice so quiet and musical.

Her love extended to all things living—to birds and plants, to wild flowers, which she could name and knew intimately, to ferns, lichens, insects, and to inanimate objects like pebbles, rocks, and sea shells. Never did a nearsighted person see so much in the natural world. A country walk with her was a revelation of the richness of life.

She loved the languages which express man's ideas and hopes and aspirations. She had studied Latin and Greek, she spoke French, German, and Italian, and she had a knowledge of Dutch, Russian, Polish, and Czech. She loved words; she could use them beautifully and simply. Most of her figures of speech were drawn from the familiar features of the natural world. Thus in her brief welcoming address at the Luxembourg Congress in 1946, she could say: "Human nature seems to me like the Alps. The depths are profound, black as night and terrifying, but the heights are equally real, uplifted in the sunshine. It is not realistic to concentrate our attention on the recent revelations of the depths of evil to which human nature can descend. To do so leads to stumbling feet, weakness and discouragement." Again, in describing Jane Addams, Emily Balch put it, "It is as impossible to evoke her for those who did not have the happiness of knowing her as to evoke the fragrance of a ripe strawberry or of a water lily for someone who has never smelled one." And of the staggering task of working for peace she could say: "We are doing all we know how to create a spirit among all peoples which will make future wars impossible, and although the disproportion between our object and our ability is so vast, I think of the infinitesimal and evanescent snowflakes which can yet in time arrest an express train running at full speed."

If the reaction of Emily Balch to her individual fellow creatures was sensitive and illumined by love, her relation to the earth as a whole was one of kinship. Nothing human was alien to her. She expresses this throughout her little volume of poems issued in 1942, especially in lines which have given solace to more than one refugee:

> Dear to me, beyond words dear to me
> Is the Earth:
> Wherever I pass, I am at home.

The girl who was born and bred New England of New England became in time a forerunner of what she was to call a "planetary civilization."

Emily Balch was in the habit of jotting down at odd minutes on scraps of paper her random thoughts and reflections. Here is a revealing piece that might be called "Hymn to the Earth":

"Every night before I go upstairs to bed I step out of doors and look up at the sky. It is partly to see what the weather promises to be, but it is much more than that. It is like drawing a line under one more day and turning to night and sleep. . . .

"The stars are remote, innumerable, incomprehensible. I remember with something approaching desolation that not one, so far as we know, is inhabited or can be inhabited. Those points of lights are lifeless masses, with no green leaf or moving creature in all that inconceivable expanse.

"My mind returns as a bird to its nest to the familiar earth. The stars are alien to me but no spot on earth is alien to me—the earth is my home. It is my fatherland and motherland, my birthplace. To it my body will return wherever I die by land or sea. I cannot be expatriated or exiled, alive or dead. Where there is grass or a tree, wherever there is a dog or a cat or a bird, I am at home. Above all, wherever there are men I am indeed not only at home but among my own. I am no alien, no outsider; this is my dear familiar family.

"Deeply and happily I feel myself a citizen of the world. I am at home wherever there are people. Wherever I go, I know I shall find cruel, sly, dishonest, unpleasant people, and everywhere I shall find magnanimous, generous people, with keen minds, friendly, honest, open, serviceable.

"Last Sunday I was seeing a moving picture of New Guinea. Primitive peoples with black skin and fuzzy hair considerably given to cannibalism. But such nice people! The giggling girls, the radiant mothers, the serious and careworn fathers, the keen sportsmen, the women intent on their weaving, they were all perfectly familiar types. Yes, I am at home there too. Wherever people build homes or rear children or have work to do, I quite understand what it is all about.

"I am a patriot and my fatherland is this dear, dear earth, sole home of life in infinite space."

If there is anyone in contemporary history whom Emily Greene Balch resembles, it might be the English humanist writer and pacifist, G. Lowes Dickinson of Cambridge, with whom Emily had an unforgettable meeting in England shortly after the Hague Congress of Women in 1915. Both shared the same profession and similar social aims; both were scholars and had original and seminal minds; both were pacifists. Each one placed a premium upon personal relationships and made an art of them in a world of injustice, brutality, and war. They were not blind to the fact that whether the relationship was personal, industrial, or international the other participant might let one down; but they were the more determined not to let their own lights be extinguished. That is why, in the darkness of their times, their lives shine out like stars.

The biographer of Dickinson, a foremost English novelist, E. M. Forster, describes him in words that might well fit Emily Balch:

"My friend was beloved, affectionate, unselfish, intelligent, witty, charming . . . These qualities were fused into such an unsual creature that no one whom one has met with in the flesh or in history the least resembles it, and no words exist in which to define it. He was an indescribably rare being, he was rare without being enigmatic, he was rare in the only direction which seems to be infinite: the direction of the Chorus Mysticus. He did not merely increase our experience; he left us more alert for what has not yet been experienced and more hopeful about other men because he had lived."

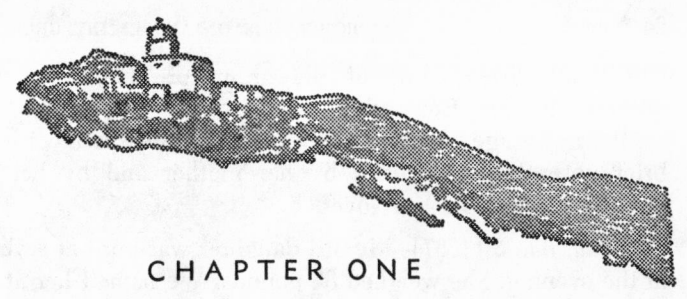

CHAPTER ONE

The Neighborhood of Boston

Emily Greene Balch was born just after the Civil War, on January 8, 1867, in Jamaica Plain, then still a small community in the neighborhood of Boston. She was descended on both sides from old New England stock. Her first American ancestor, John Balch, had arrived on the coast of Massachusetts from England in September, 1623, three years after the landing of the Pilgrims.

Her father, Francis Vergnies Balch, was a Boston lawyer of distinction, son of a wealthy marine insurance merchant. By birth and training he was a proper Bostonian, though scarcely of the inmost circle. Shortly after his graduation from Harvard College in 1859, he had served for a time as secretary to Senator Charles Sumner, the great abolitionist and early protagonist of peace. During the Civil War, at the age of twenty-four, he had married his first cousin Nelly (Ellen Maria Noyes), the vivid and fascinating daughter of a fascinating and vivid father, Dr. Francis Vergnies Noyes of Newburyport, Massachusetts, some forty miles north of Boston. The identical first and rather uncommon middle names of the father-in-law and son-in-law underline the close family relationship. Francis Vergnies Balch's mother, Anne Lathrop (Noyes) Balch, was an elder sister of Dr. Francis Vergnies* Noyes and had named her younger son after his uncle, her much admired dynamic brother. He in turn had been called after a loved doctor

---

* The name is completely anglicized in pronunciation, being called "Verns."

and family friend, one of the group of Huguenots who had migrated to New England.

It was an age of diaries. Emily Balch's birth is recorded in two brief unsentimental entries by her mother and by her mother's sister, Catherine Porter Noyes.

Tuesday, Jan. 8 [1867]—My 3rd daughter was born at seven o'clock in the evening. She weighed 8½ pounds. We named her at once for Emily Greene [a bridesmaid of Mrs. Balch]. (E.N.B.)

Tuesday, Jan. 8—Little Emily was born at about seven in the evening. Nice dark hair and a tolerable face. (C.P.N.)

Emily herself was to keep these compact little leather diaries in an almost unbroken succession from the time she was nine years old, in 1876, to the end of her life, eighty-five years later—a boon to a biographer. The earliest ones, small black leather volumes, the paper unyellowed by age, gifts from "Mama," had the back cover with a seductively lined pocket folding over the front cover in a neat flap, enhancing the privacy of the innocent enough notations.

Jan. 1, 1876 Both my rabbits got away

Jan. 2, 1876 My rabbits got away again

Jan. 4, 1876 Papa and Mama engaged house for next summer in Manchester.

June 18, 1876 Papa to the installation of Mr. Dole [the Unitarian minister at Jamaica Plain who was to have a controlling influence in shaping Emily's life].

July 4, 1876 We each had a package of torpedoes and firecrackers. We fired them on a rock because they bothered Auntie. We sat up till ten o'clock. I saw fire works.

Aug. 18, 1876 Papa came home early to read Daniel Deronda to Mama.

Emily early formed the habit of writing, and she wrote endlessly—diaries, journals, letters, fairy stories, poems. She never threw away a written word. In later years she filed these papers away in manila envelopes slit on the long side, which she labeled "Scripta." She even kept scraps and jottings thriftily written on torn pieces of papers or leaves of ledgers; she kept random notes; notes for speeches; ideas on religion, economics, aesthetics; evocations of remembered scenes and moods; lists of books to be read (filed under "Legenda"); autobiographical fragments. Even in the busiest periods of her life when preoccupied with international affairs, she found time for these jottings, sometimes on refreshingly unexpected subjects.

Although a Bostonian, Emily Balch rarely spoke of her ancestors. Throughout her life her habit was to face not the past but the future. But to understand Emily Balch one must understand the genius of New England and how it had flowered and ripened in the middle of the nineteenth century without betraying its roots. First peopled by pioneering Puritans from England, hard-working, God-fearing, thrifty men and women who took life and religion and politics seriously, the Bay region of Massachusetts had by the time of the Revolution achieved a comfortable prosperity based largely on trade and shipping. The older Calvinist faith with its distrust of unregenerate human nature had for the favored minority given way to a high-minded Unitarianism. But though the Boston merchants now looked more hopefully to the powers of man, their liberalized and humanized religion retained the intellectuality, the respect for reasoned thinking, and the sense of election and mission that had marked their earlier faith. They now realized that the Lord had called them to practice human goodness rather than the holiness of grace, but they still felt deeply the high responsibility to show this goodness in their own lives and above all to help others less favored to achieve it and its conditions.

According to family tradition, Emily's first American ancestor, John Balch, belonged to an ancient family from the county of Somerset in the west of England. In the summer of 1623 he accompanied an expedition to America under the leadership of Captain Robert Gorges, son of Sir Ferdinando Gorges of Somersetshire, who had obtained with others a generous territorial grant covering a large part of the New England coast. Captain Robert Gorges was not an earnest Puritan seeking religious freedom in the New World. He was a gentleman adventurer—a man of the court, a man of the Church of England, and a soldier. He hoped to establish a little aristocratic English principality with English customs and forms on the rough soil of the New World. The colonists, who were farmers, mechanics, and traders, as well as "gentlemen" and "divines,"[1] arrived at Wessaguset (now Weymouth) late in September when the days were forbiddingly short and the nights chilly. But the following spring, 1624, Gorges with some of his followers returned to England, "not having found the state of things here," wrote Governor Bradford of Plymouth, "to answer to his quallitie and condition . . . having scarcely saluted the countrie in his Governmente." [2]

However, a "few men of sterner stuff" remained. One of them was John Balch. He found his way to the settlement of Cape Ann near the present Gloucester. He was joined there by Roger Conant, a disaffected member of the Plymouth colony of Independents. When the enterprise at Cape Ann too, went to pieces, four "prudent and honest men" [3] were left to carry on—John Balch, Roger Conant, Peter Palfrey, and John Woodberry.

Led by Roger Conant, a man of leadership and force, the four went south and west from Cape Ann, in order to plant an agricultural settlement that might shelter the Puritans. In 1626 they settled at a place called Naumkeag by the Indians. Here they cleared the woods for their first homes and so became founders of the town that was to become famous as Salem, center of witchcraft obsession and birthplace of Nathaniel Hawthorne.

These pioneers, or "Old Planters" as they were called, showed a religious toleration unusual for the times. Not one of them is said to have taken part in the subsequent persecution of Baptists, Quakers, and witches. Woodberry's son Peter dared make his home an asylum for those charged with witchcraft, and tradition has it that in his barn he kept a horse saddled and bridled, ready to carry to safety those who came to him for help. With Roger Conant, John Balch and his wife Margery helped found the first church in Salem in 1629. Balch was among the first in Massachusetts to take the oath of freeman in 1631 (only church members were freemen, which meant that the church practically governed the town). He named his third son, born in that year, Freeborn.

John Balch held various offices of trust and frequently acted as arbitrator. When the Massachusetts colonists believed themselves threatened by the excesses of the adventurer Thomas Morton and his crew at Merry Mount (episodes made famous in literature by Motley's novel *Merry Mount* and by Hawthorne's story *The Maypole of Merry Mount*), the heads of the various plantations arranged a meeting in the spring of 1628 to consult for the common safety. It is recorded that Conant, Balch, and Palfrey from

Salem as well as leaders from other areas around Massachusetts Bay participated. In Hawthorne's story Peter Palfrey actually appears as a character, accosting the revelers and playing a role secondary only to the "grim Puritan of Puritans—Endicott."

John Balch continued to live in Salem until he and four other "Old Planters," Conant, Palfrey, Woodberry, and William Trask, were given a tract of one thousand acres on the Bass River. Today this tract is part of the town of Beverly, Massachusetts, birthplace of Lucy Larcom, the mill-girl "poetess." The town is lovingly described in her charming idyll *A New England Girlhood*. Here, in 1636 or 1638, John Balch built his house. It is still standing, and is said to be the oldest house in Massachusetts with a written record. John Balch died in 1648.

John Balch's son Benjamin seems to have inherited much of his immigrant father's spirit of toleration and independence of thought and action. He was arrested and fined "for entertayning forayners," [4] without the approbation of the selectmen. In a day when religious doctrines were rigorously upheld and parental authority unquestioned, he forebore any insistence upon the baptism of his thirteen children and left the matter to their own convictions and desires.

Benjamin's son, Freeborn Balch, was a farmer and had the finest apple trees in Essex County. The apple orchard was bequeathed to his son, the Reverend William Balch of Bradford, Massachusetts, who was in later years thought to be an Arminian.° His Yankee thrift, a dominant genetic trait not skipping Emily, did not desert him with his lapse into heresy, and he continued to run the cider mill near his orchard after he had moved away from Beverly. The product, which brought a very high price in the market, was called by the customers "Arminian cider."

By the nineteenth century the Balches had turned to the commercial pursuits of the thriving trading community. Emily's grandfather, Joseph Balch of Newburyport, later of Boston, "a rather severe and reticent man," according to Emily, was the much respected and wealthy president of a marine insurance company. He was twice married, having first a family of five daughters and one son, then by Anne Lathrop Balch, grandmother of Emily,

---

° Adherent of doctrines of Jacobus Arminius. These doctrines liberalized Calvinist doctrines of freedom of the will and of unconditional predestination.

three more children, a daughter Eunice Ann (Aunt Nannie), and two sons, John Balch and Francis Vergnies Balch, Emily's father. In the 1830's, Joseph bought a summer home in Jamaica Plain, with a garden famous for its roses, "Rosebank," and here they lived in a "fairly sumptuous setting," wrote Emily "for those simple times."

The pre-Civil War society to which these prosperous forebears of Emily belonged was close knit and consolidated. In politics they were Whig; in faith they were mainly Unitarian and Episcopalian. "Its older wealth had come from foreign commerce, from ships returning from distant seas," wrote E. L. Pierce, the biographer of Charles Sumner, "later from mills established on the Merrimac. Its prosperous citizens were men of good stock, enterprising, self-poised, and large-minded. They educated their children in academies and colleges. They were careful in the training of their daughters. They had Harvard College nearby, which has at all times diffused the academic spirit in the city and its suburbs, and raised up scholars and intellectual guides. . . . Their style of living was sober but generous. . . . They were as a class, in private and in business life men of high integrity, interested in public works. . . . They were highly conservative; took a harmless pride in their social standing; received consideration from the masses something like that accorded to an English lord or squire; were accustomed to having their own way. They were English in thought and habit as in blood." [5] They had on the whole, little interest in social reform.

Emily's ancestors on her mother's side came from England about 1633 and settled at Newbury, Massachusetts, now Newburyport. There were two brothers, James and Nicholas Noyes, one a

---

* One of Emily's maternal great-grandfathers, William Bartlett (1748-1841), "a distinguished merchant and a liberal patron of theological learning," was fairly representative of this society at the turn of the century. He was naturally shrewd and enterprising. He became owner of a large fleet of merchant vessels and of numerous wharves and warehouses and was one of the first in New England to undertake textile manufacturing. In 1798 he erected a three-story brick mansion on Federal Street in Newburyport. The money which he accumulated through thrift and wise investments he devoted largely to philanthropic projects, especially to Andover Theological Seminary (opened in 1809), to which he gave more than $160,000. It is recorded of him that "he combined frugality in small matters with lavish generosity where his emotions were concerned." [6]

minister of the Church of England, the other an Independent. Two facts were recorded about the latter—that he was fined for nonattendance at church and that he once walked from Newbury to Cambridge to protest the passage of some law with which he disagreed. This act was paralleled some three hundred years later by his descendant Emily, when, in her old age, during World War II, she made the trip from her home in Wellesley, Massachusetts, to the Labor Temple in New York City for the express purpose of dissenting in an allotted ten minutes from a certain group of her fellow pacifists who were opposing the formation of the United Nations.

Certain traits on the Noyes side of the family, running back to early ancestors and reappearing in Emily, as well as in her mother and her doctor-grandfather, emerge almost as family characteristics: vividness of personality, vigor of intellect and body (often to extreme old age), originality, many-sidedness, independence of thought and action, and a New England wit, dry and salty.

Perhaps her most picturesque and original ancestor was her mother's great-grandfather, Nathaniel Niles (1741-1828), the pioneer settler of Fairlee, Vermont, "inventor, theologian, preacher, politician, with a somewhat less happy dash of the poet" * Like his father and grandfather, he was sent to Harvard, but he graduated in 1766 from the College of New Jersey, now Princeton University. He studied medicine, then law, and finally turned to theology, though he was never ordained. He invented an improved type of wool card and a new method of drawing wire from bar iron. He also found time for politics, serving in the Connecticut legislature, in the Vermont legislature, and in the Unitel States House of Representatives. He was a member of the Supreme Court of Vermont, hence he was known as "Judge" Niles.

Towards the end of the Revolution Judge Niles bought a large tract of land in Orange County, Vermont, and moved with a small colony of friends into the northern forests. Once, when he was preaching in Fairlee, a message was brought to him. He excused himself, saying he would return shortly. His wife had notified him that the bees were swarming. Nobody but he could hive them. The bees safely gathered in, he returned and went on with his sermon,

---

* *Dictionary of American Biography* (New York 1943), Vol XIII, p. 523.

an exhibition of aplomb that betokened complete security of personality and a combination of the spiritual, the intellectual and the practical that later characterized his great-great-granddaughter Emily. "His position as the largest proprietor in the neighborhood, his undoubted intelligence, his positive and democratic ideas, his forceful and aggressive character, all contributed to his success in politics." * He fought against slavery and the banks; he gave vigorous support to the second war with England. In 1793 he was made a trustee of Dartmouth College (till 1820), and he soon headed the opposition in the controversy with the president of the college, John Wheelock.

His one known attempt at poetry, an ode called "The American Hero," written in celebration of the Battle of Bunker Hill, was not so long ago included in an anthology *War and the Poet.* ** The ode was set to music and gained wide popularity during the Revolutionary War. However, the author of the article about Judge Niles in the *Dictionary of American Biography* adds: "Posterity will not regret that thereafter Niles turned his talents to other fields."

The life of Emily's mother, Ellen Maria Noyes (1837-1884), reveals her as the warm and loving center of the large family in which Emily grew up, a group with varying and decided talents, interests, and personalities. Besides five sisters, a brother, and an overworked and delicate father (Francis Balch was so frail he could not have his life insured), the household also included Nelly's sister, Catherine Porter Noyes, the loved and cherished "Auntie" of Emily's childhood, and the servants who, in the custom of that time, received microscopic wages and usually stayed till they were married. The cook and the "second girl" at first lived in an unheated room in the ell and between them did all the cooking, cleaning and laundry. Each day they brought clean water to every room and carried away the waste. Nurses were engaged from time to time, as the eight children were born in fairly rapid succession. There was also a hired man, Herbert, dour, taciturn, but reliable and faithful. He took care of the garden and the furnace, carried

---

* *Dictionary of American Biography* (New York, 1943), Vol. XIII p. 523.
** Eberhart, R. and S. Rodman, *War and the Poet,* (New York, 1945.)

the coal daily to the kitchen and the parlor, took care of two, sometimes three horses, and did all the family driving.

Nelly Noyes grew up in the country, living at one time at Byfield, near Newburyport, in a very old house that had once been a snuff mill. The house overhung the little Parker River where in winter she loved to take long solitary skates over its frozen surface. She was a healthy outdoor girl and loved swimming and adventure as well as reading and study. The domestic side of her education was not neglected. Her girlhood diary records: "We baked in the forenoon; in the afternoon we sewed. I knit on a tippet." When she was twelve she sent a forthright little note to "Dear Aunt Caty, Will you please accept the little cushion which I meant should have been pretty but somehow or other the corners did not come out right and the top was not the right color and the sides were not sewed up alike so altogether it looked so screwy that I did not want to send it."

"My mother had not only humor but wit," wrote Emily, "and a gift for words. Quick-tempered, deeply loving, a fascinating personality—no wonder my father loved her as he did. She did not spoil us but was as tonic as she was warmly devoted. A tumble was met not with sympathy but with 'Jump and take another, dear.' She was the center of my life and its chief influence as long as she lived. I was a very trying child, careless and absentminded, but to have deliberately disobeyed or defied her in any way would have been unthinkable."

After Nelly's mother's death when the girl was seventeen, she had been exposed to evangelical influences at Uncle Withington's house. This enforced piety gave her a horror of religious pressure. She did not encourage her children to read *Pilgrim's Progress*. Bessie, next in age to Emily, recoiled from the book anyway, but Emily loved it and thought it helped make her aware of the burden of sin. Once Nelly took away from Emily a story about a revival camp meeting.

Nelly and her sister Caty were at one time taught at home by a Mr. Wheelwright, a man who groaned as he talked of the souls in Hell. He was stronger on piety than on humor. He once went to Ellen's father to tell him to be prepared for a terrible shock. Ellen was sadly corrupt. Dr. Noyes was not unduly alarmed but begged to know the worst. It seems that Ellen, asked for the moral of a fable about a cat killed in a rabbit warren, had replied, "Never tell the same lie twice."

For a time Nelly attended the well-known Ipswich Female Seminary, to which the brilliant Helen Fiske* of Amherst, Massachusetts, friend of Emily Dickinson, had gone the decade before. In the catalogue for 1854-1855, Ellen Maria Noyes of Newburyport is enrolled in the Middle Class. She is listed in the Latin class which read Livy and Horace, in the French class which studied Corneille and Racine, and in the German class which took up Schiller's poems and *Mary Stuart, Undine,* Wolff's *Poetischer Hausschatz* and Ollendorf's grammar. She seems to have acquired an affinity for the German language and culture which remained with her to the end of her life and which she managed to communicate to her daughter Emily.

As a young woman, during the Civil War, Nelly went to teach in Mattoon, Illinois, a crude ugly railroad junction where she lived under pioneering conditions in a community harboring the secessionist point of view. Here her journal records her deep and passionate attachment to her cousin Frank (Francis) Balch, two years her junior, his enlistment as a private in the 20th Massachusetts Regiment in August, 1862 ("May God protect him, my love, and give me strength to bear what he may lay upon me. But oh, it is hard, bitterly hard"), the terrible anxieties attendant upon the setback of the Union armies ("it seems as if our cause were desperate"), and the news of Frank's severe collapse and slow convalescence under the care of Farmer Hall at Darnestown, Maryland.

The journal ends in June, 1865, "after almost two years of such content in Frank's love and such happiness in our marriage. I know he does not love me just as I love him but it is quite as truly and quite as well—at least I do not feel any flaw in it and would not change it. This spring has brought us our great sorrow. A year ago in June, our beautiful baby was born [Catie] and in April she died and took our hearts with her . . . and now next month, another little child [Anne] is coming for us to love and guard, if God wills."

Perhaps the dominant influence in Emily Balch's life was her father, Francis Balch. Of all his children Emily resembled him

---

* Helen Hunt Jackson, author of *Ramona.*

most closely. Her girlhood spanned an era of great change in the education, the outlook, and the activities of American women. The sympathy, understanding, and companionship of her father prevented the inner clashes that might have been the lot of a young woman destined to go counter to some of the currents of her time and to break ground in so many fields. It is significant that so many of that notable group of women, Emily's friends and contemporaries, who in the last generation lent distinction to American public life, also received such encouragement while growing up. Jane Addams and Julia Lathrop of Illinois, Florence Kelley of Pennsylvania, Mary Kingsbury (Simkhovitch) of Massachusetts, Alice Hamilton of Indiana—all had fathers of brilliance and forceful personality, and all, like Emily, acknowledged their intellectual indebtedness to these farsighted parents.

Francis Balch was a lawyer of great learning, identified with the best of New England life. In character he was gentle, modest, affectionate, sympathetic, humble, "even deferential to his inferiors." [7] But he had an iron will when it came to what he believed to be his duty. He had unusual powers of prolonged intellectual concentration and of rapid and accurate work. He read inexhaustibly, keeping pace with all the best of contemporary literature as it appeared. "To work hard was his nature," said a college classmate, John Grey, "it was not a burden to his gentle and serene spirit. If he had been more self-assertive, it would have been better for himself and others. His worst fault was too great unselfishness." [8]

His legal practice was almost exclusively that of a "conveyancer." Beginning with the examination of small titles, he gradually came to deal with questions concerning large properties, great estates, and corporate interests involving grave responsibility and wide and accurate knowledge of the law.

Francis Balch's personality had an extraordinary effect on all who met him. Mary Kingsbury (Simkhovitch), of Newton Center, Massachusetts, a fellow student with Emily at the University of Berlin, wrote: "Once Emily took me to an unforgettable luncheon with him at the Parker House in Boston. It seemed to me that they were much alike in intellectual penetration, in generous courtesy for their fellow-men, and in a personal taste for simplicity." Intellectual penetration is not uncommon but it is not so often combined with an exquisite courtesy.

Francis V. Balch was born in Boston, February 3, 1839, and died in Jamaica Plain fifty-nine years leter, almost to the day, on February 4, 1898. He was graduated from Harvard College with the class of 1859, of which he was the "first scholar" and "class orator." His college friend, George Chaney, years later remembered that he deliberately tried to lower his rank so that he might not carry too many honors and be also class valedictorian on Commencement Day. He was one of the fortunate few who went to the study of Professor James Russell Lowell, the poet, at his invitation to read the *Divina Commedia* with him in Italian. Lowell presented each student with a copy of Giotto's portrait of Dante and left them all a memory of the Harvard poet at his best.

Eighteen months after his graduation, Francis was admitted to the bar in Massachusetts (April 9, 1861). Most of his friends, however, were joining the army as officers. In spite of delicate health, in August, 1862, he enlisted in the 20th Massachusetts Regiment, characteristically as a private rather than with a commission. His brief military career was heroic rather than effective. He fainted repeatedly on the march and was finally left on the roadside, in an apparently dying condition, to be taken in by the family of a farmer, John Hall of Darnestown, Maryland, of Confederate sympathies. For several weeks he was very ill; they nursed him back to health while the terrible battle of Antietam was raging nearby. By December he was discharged from the Union Army, and he returned to his mother's home at Jamaica Plain to convalesce further.[*]

During two of the war years, 1863 and 1864, after his marriage to Ellen Maria Noyes, Francis Balch was secretary in Washington to United States Senator Charles Sumner, the outstanding leader in the political opposition to slavery. For his views Sumner had been brutally assaulted in the Senate Chamber by Preston Brooks of South Carolina. As Sumner's secretary, Balch served as clerk to the Senate Foreign Relations Committee. He also made the

---

[*] See Lt. Col. George Anson Bruce, *History of the Twentieth Regiment of Massachusetts Volunteer Infantry* (Boston, 1906), p. 139. "With a slight and very delicate physique, but with a heart full of unselfish patriotism, this noble but modest man, thinking himself unfit for a commission, enlisted from a pure sense of duty as a private under his friends in the Twentieth. . . . But his frail body was too weak for the duty imposed by the noble soul, and he was obliged to fall out on one of his first marches down the peninsula."

first effective suggestion of civil service reform in this country: he drew up for Senator Sumner the first bill for that purpose. When young Balch resigned in 1864 to enter the legal profession, Sumner made him manager of his funds and afterwards sole executor of his will. At Charles Sumner's death, he became with Henry Wadsworth Longfellow and E. L. Pierce (Sumner's biographer) Sumner's literary executor. So unreserved was Sumner's trust in him that he was reported as saying, "If Mr. Balch should go to the end of Long Wharf and throw my papers into the sea, I should think it was all right." [9]

For his part, Francis Balch never wavered in his faith in Senator Sumner's true greatness. His description of Sumner is as interesting for what it reveals of himself and what he learned from Sumner as for its estimate of Sumner:

"I was just out of college, immature and inexperienced. The relation was most confidential and close. It is my belief that he had absolutely no secrets from me.

"Mr. Sumner was a man not ready to yield to his equals; domineering is a strong word, but he felt a superiority which really existed and his manner asserted it. To his subordinates, no one could be more considerate, more generous. Never was he impatient or inconsiderate. Working himself to an extent to me before unimagined, sitting at his desk till late in the night, and sometimes the morning, so that a change of linen stood to him in place of a night's rest, he was careful not to overwork those about him. He was never arrogant, but always ready to listen to objections or suggestions.

"I was brought up a Conservative Whig, and of course was far from agreement with Mr. Sumner's views; but again and again I found myself pulling up my conservative stakes and planting them nearer his position until it was only a question of time when I should be brought into entire agreement with him.

"His familiarity with history, with letters, with society, with art, was to me simply astonishing. Of his style I am not an admirer. He was not religious, in the sense that religious ordinances entered much into his life, but he had the essence of the matter. He seems to my memory a giant, and I see no more of his kind." [10]

With characteristic charity, Balch omitted to mention Sumner's complete lack of a sense of humor.

In a fragmentary sketch of her father, Emily recognizes that a man is much more than the sum of his qualities: "So much the most precious thing that we know of is *personality*, that apart from the instinct of affection to treasure and maintain what it has held dear, those who have had the privilege of intimacy with a rarely beautiful spirit long to share their memories with kin of the next generation and with strangers who may chance to recognize a kinship of spirit. This longing is especially strong when there is a sense that the life has not permanently or even fully expressed the person, that the significance of the life is more than only one aspect of the activity or even all the aspects together."

A famous novelist who is also a biographer, E. M. Forster, has said that Mephistopheles should inhabit a cranny in every biography to ask disconcerting questions. But the spirit who denies should not be permitted to carry the day. We can confront Mephisto with a photograph of Emily's father from the old family album showing the delicacy, sensitivity, and strength of "the fine still face which told so well the worth and nature of the man."[11] We can take him back to March 26, 1898, to the Supreme Judicial Court Room in Boston where the "Brethren of the Bar" were meeting to pay a series of extraordinarily sincere and personal tributes to their late colleague Francis V. Balch. In reading these tributes and the obituaries in the old Boston newspapers we can come to understand how, with such a father, Emily Balch came to be what she was. The words of Felix Rackemann, one of Francis Balch's legal partners, would apply with equal force to her.

"Mr. Balch's life was singularly round and singularly beautiful. He was not an advocate and not a fighter. It was not in his nature to fight. It was his nature, however, to be and act the part of a peace-maker, and if a man had a cause which he desired adjusted upon its merits, Mr. Balch was pre-eminent, perhaps, in the fact and the faithfulness and the earnestness with which he would try to bring about some adjustment (upon its merit).

"He was not 'humble' in the Dickens sense; but he was meek in the true scriptural sense. He was a tolerant man. . . . His pity went out to the wrong doer. He had the power of feeling intense condemnation of a wrong without being merciless to the wrong doer. He rarely spoke harshly of anyone."[12]

If Emily was fortunate in her choice of parents, she was equally
fortunate in choosing to see the light in New England. A generation earlier Lucy Larcom had confessed, "I am glad that I was
born a New Englander; and I surely should have chosen New England for my birth place before any region under the sun." If Emily
herself did not echo this sturdy pride, it was because she was the
child of a riper age and her temper had come to find it more
congenial to exclaim:

> Dear to me is the earth,
> Wherever I pass upon the earth I am at home.*

She was to look beyond local loves and patriotisms to a cosmopolitanism embracing two hemispheres, and in time to achieve a
"planetary" consciousness. But she was to be a more picturesque
"citizen of the world" and a more flavorful figure on the international scene just because she looked from her native soil, because
her local attachments were so strong and because she had her
roots so deep in Puritan New England.

The New England mind formed the air she breathed. Emerson,
Longfellow, Whittier, Lowell, and Holmes were still living and
writing while Emily was growing up, aptly quoted in every household. Hawthorne and the dissenting Thoreau who had urged the
duty of civil disobedience were familiar teachers. Emerson for his
generation had the answers to the larger questions; Longfellow
had been an abolitionist, and the Quaker John Greenleaf Whittier
and James Russell Lowell had harnessed their Muse to "the winged
Hippogriff Reform" and had written "burning poems" on abolition,
peace, and freedom.

Though Emily's own family, in the main Whigs and followers
of Daniel Webster, had before 1861 held to the party of tem-
porizing conservatism and compromise in the great antislavery
conflict, the moral passion and power of the great Abolitionist
leaders—Theodore Parker, William Lloyd Garrison, Wendell Phillips, Edmund Quincy, Lydia Maria Child—had burned itself into
the consciousness of even such Massachusetts citizens, to flame
forth with the outbreak of war.

---

* Emily Greene Balch, *The Miracle of Living*, Island Press, New York, 1941.

In Emily's household certainly, the words of Senator Charles Sumner, who brought the slavery question into politics and whom Theodore Parker had admonished to remain in morals although in politics, were familiar as to few other Bostonians: "Our cause is nobler than that of our Fathers, inasmuch as it is more exalted to struggle for the Freedom of *others* than for our *own*."

Added to all this, the very face of New England awakens deep attachment. Emily had the great good fortune to live in a region of unusual loveliness, to return again and again for solace and refreshment to that cluster of states which she was to know so intimately and to love: the villages and towns of her native Massachusetts with their stately merchant's houses and small Cape Cod cottages sitting sedately under wineglass elms and fronting smooth green commons; the white steeples of the immaculate white churches rising among the green hills of Vermont; the granite beauty of the New Hampshire mountains with their softer intervales laced with birch trees; and perhaps dearest of all, the spruce-clad slopes, salt inlets, and spice-breathing air of the coast of Maine.

How did this background and home and heritage appear to Emily herself? Fortunately we have a number of her autobiographical fragments and recollections which, a bit here and a bit there, reconstruct for us in her clear, unaffected and beguiling language something of that post-Civil War childhood.

"The remembered experience of childhood and near infancy may not have for one the mystic beauty that it had for Wordsworth or Traherne but very usually it has a tender and unique charm. Yellow crocus unexpectedly opening on the grass, moonlight so white as to be mistaken for silver, sea water oozing into one's beach-dug well, the nursery fire with mother singing Scotch ballads to the baby—these are not interesting to any reader but dear to recall.

"We lived at first in 'the old house' on Lowder's Lane where blackberries grew along the wall and the red cedars had twisted stems. Here Annie and I and Elizabeth were successively born. Mine was a simple happy suburban home. Grass underfoot and a sky overhead were part of my birthright. It was a shock to me when I went through settlement experience when I realized that many children have never spent a night in the dark—have never spent a night in silence. I had never failed to be surrounded by love and tender care, nor to live without comfort, plenty and essential security. I only gradually realized that these things were not universal."

The Civil War still overshadowed life. Emily's memories of her early years caught its echoes. She was thrilled as artillery pounded past in a June parade in which General Burnside marched. At Mrs. Walker's and Miss Seegar's school, she and her schoolmates sang with gusto "Marching Through Georgia" and with "tingling nerves" Julia Ward Howes's "Battle Hymn of the Republic."

"It was somewhat later," Emily goes on, "that tramps in a world which demobilized its soldiers with no thought of social responsibility, became a plague. My father's health, never good (he had his nurse always with him until he was thirteen, I think) had been shaken by his army fever when he was a new volunteer recruit. The one-armed soldier who peddled at our door, Mr. McNally, an honored army-mate of my father's who had marched beside him in the ranks, was a friend he never forgot. He had been rewarded (modestly) for his brave war service by the right to wear the uniform of a soldier-messenger and to frequent the old Providence station as such." Accustomed to being held responsible for the effects of careless tumbles and bumps, Emily proudly informed Mr. McNally, " *My* papa was a careful soldier." As a matter of fact he was not, as his not-too-wise enlistment made clear.

"The summer I was four and a half," continues Emily, "the family moved to an unattractive but larger house on Burroughs Street, near Jamaica Pond. The day of the moving we noticed two pretty little girls across the street. Carrie Ticknor became my great pal and Bessie and Edith [Ticknor] were the twin braves. We played mostly in the 'yard,' the usual name then for the land around a house. Carrie* was active and ambitious and we were rivals in tree climbing and other adventures. I once told my mother that I did not like her because she always wanted to be first. My mother looked at me and said, 'Is it because you want to be first

---

* Caroline Ticknor, granddaughter of William D. Ticknor who founded the publishing house of Ticknor & Fields. Caroline Ticknor later wrote *Hawthorne and His Publisher, Dr. Holmes' Boston, etc.*

yourself?' This was my first act of conscious self-recognition."

"Our father took us for occasional long walks searching for flowers. He was a passionate lover of 'botany' in the mode of the time. He had studied under the great classifier Asa Gray and tramped the country-side for the rarer or more highly prized flowers. He seldom 'pressed' or even picked them but he could find them in places where not even local botanists knew of their habitat. A yearly delight was to walk with him to Putterham woods to see the first hepaticas, the first brown-winged butterflies drinking from roadside puddles, and to eat the winy barberries that had frozen and thawed and frozen again all winter on their thorny bushes."

In the Burroughs Street house three more children were born, little Ellie; Francis (Noyes Balch), who became a Boston lawyer with scientific hobbies, the only son in a family of five girls; and Alice (later Mrs. Robert Bowditch Stone, a painter and sculptor of considerable talent). Ellie died in 1874, at the age of three, "a lovely girl-baby, with yellow curls, blue eyes and rosy cheeks—deeply mourned." Her death was a revelation to the older children, Annie, Emily, and Elizabeth, of how "grown people" could suffer.

In this early post-Darwinian period, when even the older Unitarian orthodoxies were crumbling, Emily's father and mother "had reluctantly abandoned much that was still dear to them to follow the conscience of reason." They were homesick for the older certainties, though on the whole too honest and enlightened to accept them. Nevertheless, Emily's father, some years after the death of Ellie, in a candid letter to his wife in which he deplores his inability to feel as sorry as he felt he should feel on the death of a dearly loved friend and neighbor, says: "There is one thing I have never doubted I was sorry for—Ellie. If I should see her from that peak, I should look glad I know. Somehow with all the loosening of intellectual belief, I have an undoubted assurance of seeing her."

When Emily was twelve her father bought a house on Prince Street, Jamaica Plain, much pleasanter than the one on Burroughs Street, and with more land, land which went down to the shores of Jamaica Pond. Three large rock maples were a joy and pride, and the Balch's liked to believe that the old English elms had been set out when the land was part of the estate of Colonial

Governor Francis Bernard. It was a roomy house with a slate mansard roof and a large porch or "piazza." From the windows of the garret you could see the Blue Hill in Milton and the shine of the sea beyond. In this house the youngest of the Balch children was born, Marion Cesares Balch, or Maidie, the pet of the household, artistic, frail, lovable. In this house Marion lived until her death in 1961, an unusual record of stability for an American household.

The Balch garden path came to an abrupt end in a wire fence and beyond could be seen the old box-bordered labyrinth of the original garden and house on its high bank, hidden by trees. Opposite was the Frothingham land and nearby the land belonging to Francis Parkman, the historian. Alice, who had a retentive memory, recalled him as a "delicate sweet-faced man who rode every day on his horse or rowed in his boat till the water froze."

"We always had 'Irish girls'," continue Emily's recollections, "whether as cook, second girl or nurse. Anne Glancy sang us haunting Irish songs of the famine: 'Only a grain of corn, mother, only a grain of corn,' and what I remember still more clearly, 'Tis the most distressful country that ever yet was seen, They're hanging men and women there for wearing of the green.' Anne Glancy pushed the baby carriage which was properly Bessie's with Annie and me beside her or at her feet. Annie, eighteen months older than I, cried because in picking the sweet English violets beside the 'Cross-Cow Pasture,' I usually pulled the heads from off the stems. Bessie, eighteen months younger than I, who proclaimed herself in her first articulate words 'I Bonnie Bess,' was the pretty one, for Annie with her red curls, lovely skin and blue eyes, was not so much admired then when 'red hair' was rather a reproach."

The Irish girls were almost the only foreign element in Emily Balch's early surroundings. To be sure Bostonians often visited Europe and this wider contact early came home to Emily. Friends of the family and aunts and cousins traveled abroad. A girl who was to become a lifelong friend, Frances Hayward, after an extended sojourn in Italy made her appearance on the scene at Jamaica Plain when Emily was ten. Emily invested her with a romantic aura of foreign travel. But on the whole Emily moved in a homogeneous, closely knit and fairly provincial society. No foreign names appear in her youthful diaries. The Welds, Morses,

Apthorps, Hales, Bowditches, Cheevers, and Frothinghams move through the pages, paying calls on each other, dining together, meeting at church, or on the Boston train, at musicals, picnics, or "assemblies." Emily recalled that she never, to her knowledge saw a Jew till she was about nineteen, when in a horse car, she recognized with a thrill of pleasure, that a bearded man in a broad-brimmed black hat and caftan was a Jew. Like modern children, however, Emily and her schoolmates had been exposed to lessons in religious tolerance. She long remembered an edifying poem in a childhood reader about a little Jewish boy persecuted by a schoolmate for not eating an apple on the Jewish Day of Atonement. It was entitled:

The Little Jew
By the Author of *John Halifax, Gentleman*

Emily's two living grandparents and their daughters played a large part in her life, especially her fascinating and loved grandfather, Dr. Noyes. "My father's mother, Anne Lathrop Balch, lived near us till her death in 1880. As children we often dined at her house, always I think at Thanksgiving. It was her pleasure to serve the youngest at the table first." The grandmother was rigid and dictatorial and regarded as an ultimate authority. Night air was poisonous. No water should be taken with meals. A day was fixed on which winter underwear would be put on or taken off, regardless of weather. Before going shopping the grandmother made up her mind what she was proposing to buy and it was against her rule to buy anything not planned for before starting. She once wrote to her son John (in response to a query, it must be said), "Never differ with the world but on matters of principle and there be as firm as Mt. Atlas." Her dining room was adorned with two steel engravings, one of Cromwell and one of Milton, a choice which Emily regarded as highly significant.

Anne Balch's only daughter, Eunice Ann (Aunt Nannie), had a freer and more inquiring mind which stood her in good stead as long as she lived. At the age of sixty she strove against rusting by renewing her study of algebra and Latin. She took great pleasure in her study of Italian, reading both modern Italian and Dante. It was from her that Emily learned enough Italian to read Dante.

Aunt Nannie was a vigorous personality, original, stimulating, somewhat eccentric, and very active physically.

"My grandmother's eldest son, John," an autobiographical fragment records, "after a brilliant college career at Harvard, lost his mind. My father's attention and loyalty to his case, as long as he lived, was steadfast. I never saw him till after his death [in 1897]. It was a strange experience to see the still face of a man so close to me, so like my father and other members of the family and yet a stranger. I had a feeling that through the long years, there had run, as it were, underground some current of experience, as water runs under ice, and that this had been in some strange way living of an indefinable sort."

The fact that Emily's two surviving grandparents, her father's mother, Mrs. Anne Lathrop Balch, and her mother's father, Dr. Noyes, were brother and sister made the family relationships a close one. Aunt Nannie spent much of her later life after her mother's death with Dr. Noyes, who was her uncle. When Emily was about five, Dr. Noyes purchased a fruit farm at Billerica (pronounced Bíl-ricka) near Lexington, Massachusetts. This proved a hospitable and delightful vacation spot for all the young Balches. Here were gathered the lively and interesting doctor-grandfather, his second wife, the "exquisite and critical Grandma Sara," as well as Aunt Catie and Aunt Nannie. Aunt Nannie had ample rooms of her own there, with her books. She also enjoyed some vigorous gardening at Billerica. One morning she was digging out a garden bed behind a stone wall. The family could see the stones flying. Dr. Noyes, looking over remarked, "An old woman is as tough as a boiled owl."

"Auntie" (Catherine Porter Noyes) lived at the Prince Street household with the Balches till her death in 1924. From an uncle who was an orthodox clergyman, she derived a Sabbatarian exclusiveness which made a family drive on Sunday taboo. At the same time she was an ardent follower of Phillips Brooks and his liberal churchmanship, in which she took great comfort. She found the family Unitarianism rather difficult.

During the Civil War, she went down south to St. Helena's Island, S. C., to teach the children of the newly liberated Negroes. She accompanied a dearly loved cousin, Mary Lambert Allen and her husband, William F. Allen (later Professor of History and

Latin at the new University of Wisconsin). When she sailed south
for the first time, bombs were still bursting nearby and the ship
was chased by what everyone supposed was a Confederate vessel.
It turned out to be a Union boat looking for blockade runners.
Life among resentful Southern ladies and under fairly primitive
conditions was not easy.

When Emily was ten she had scarlet fever and was quaran-
tined for several weeks with her mother, who gave her undivided
attention. She looked back on this as one of the happiest periods
of her life. She always declared her love for her mother had an
"element of passion" in it. "I think I had no jealousy but I always
wanted more of her than I could have as one of a nursery full of
children, often ailing, and with all the demands of housekeeping,
when in spite of a nurse and a cook and a 'second girl' there was
much to be done. She sang to me all my favorite songs, 'Bell
horse, bell horse, what time of day,' the long ballad of Annie of
Lochroyan (all of it) and Belshazzar:

> Belshazzar is king
> Belshazzar is lord
> And a thousand dark nobles
> All bend at his board,

which called up romantic and exotic scenes. I suppose she was no
singer and I had no ear for music but to me her singing was the
best in the world."

Mrs. Balch also gave Emily at this time her first taste of novels.
She read aloud Scott's *Talisman* and *Ivanhoe* and a long story of
Napoleon's retreat from Moscow.

"When I was let out of quarantine the rooms I had been in
were disinfected with burning sulphur and I was left with the
nurse and baby in the nursery and told not to go out of the room
till fetched. Meantime the fumes of the sulphur found their way
into the nursery flue and we began to suffer from them. At that
time the Casabianca ballad of the boy who stood on the burning
deck till death found him because his father had told him to stay
there, was familiar to all children. I felt that this example, however
noble, was not what my mother wanted and assuming authority
for the first time I told the doubting nurse to take the baby and
follow me downstairs. For this exploit I was neither blamed nor

commended—quite as often as for instance if I told the truth when it was hard to do so—there was a lack of praise that I felt would have been not inappropriate. Nevertheless this decision to disobey was a definite step in growing up."

Books, of course, opened many doors to Emily—both when read aloud and when she could read them for herself. The three eldest girls were near enough of an age to enjoy many things together, though Bessie suffered from hearing a good deal that was over her head and unpleasantly bewildering.

"Auntie," writes Emily, "who normally made her home with us, taught me to read before I went to school and after that I read voraciously. We loved both Alice books, then just coming out, and Grimm Brothers' German folk stories; Harriet Martineau's delightful children's stories and even Miss Edgeworth's too moral tales including that exquisite idyll of vanishing peasant life in England, *Simple Susan*. Charlotte Yonge was a treasure house and *The Little Duke* still seems to me a gem.

"The stories of the time were largely built around a heroine who had a mission. In this there was doubtless a good deal of self-consciousness but also a perfectly genuine conviction of the need of purposefulness in living. This theme of the person with a mission which came to be the subject of so much raillery, has also genuine and useful overtones. When I was ten my mother gave me a collection of Scotch ballads in which I delighted. Our cousin, Agnes Balch, more like a sister than a cousin, was a fairy godmother in her epoch-making gifts of books. A little volume of German lyrics was succeeded by French and both came at the happy moment when I could read them while they still had the strange charm of a new and only partly understood language.

"I had a natural taste for language study and only regret that I did not exploit it more. In the course of my life I had studied Latin and Greek, which were my major subjects at Bryn Mawr. I have at times been able to make use of at least a little of Dutch, Swedish and Polish. I attempted a little Russian, enough to help me with newspapers when I was in Russia [in 1915] and to acquaint myself with many common Slavic roots.

"I think it was when I was nine that I made my first attempt to learn a language by myself. Perhaps not wholly by accident, my mother let a pretty little German book fall my way. She also showed me how to use a dictionary. But I quickly gave it up. 'Ich ging im Walde,' I read. But there was no *ging* in the dictionary. It seemed you had to look up *gehen*. This seemed to me not playing the game.

"It was this year that I learned to swim, this year that my sister Alice was born, and this year that I was pastured on grown-up books to keep me occupied. I read successively Prescott's *Conquest of Mexico*, Motley's *Phillip II* and *Rise of the Dutch Republic*. I remember how annoyed I was with a friend of my mother who refused to tell me what 'expulsion' meant (Spaniards expelled from Mexico City). She said if I looked it up in the dictionary for myself I should always remember it. As I never forgot words this sabotage struck me very unfavorably.

"Children were not guarded then as they are today from the horrible. Grimm's stories were a delight to me and a horror to my younger and more sensitive sister Bessie. But while it did not trouble me to read of the old woman rolled down hill in a barrel studded with long nails, I could not endure the story of hazing in *Chatterbox*,* nor an English story of a servant falsely accused of stealing. When it was a matter of what I regarded as injustice, I went out of the nursery into the unheated 'long entry' outside till it was over.

Emily's mother was a famous story teller. Emily found it hard to say whether she liked best her mother's "true stories" of her own or Grandpa's childhood, or the imaginary ones, especially a delightful though psychologically disturbing one about a little girl who joined the fairies for a day and came home to find she had been away for years. In later life when Emily would delight her friends by "saying poetry" from memory a whole evening through, it was an unforgettable experience to hear her recite, with a nostalgic light in her eyes, the long, haunting Scottish poem *Kilmeny* about the girl who vanished to the land of the spirits:

> Bonnie Kilmeny gaed up the glen
> But it wasna to meet Duneira's men,
> Nor the rosy monk of the isle to see,
> For Kilmeny was pure as pure could be.

---

* An English magazine for children, founded in 1866. There was an American edition as well.

> It was only to hear the yorlin sing,
> And pu' the cress-flour round the spring;
> The scarlet hypp and the hindberrye,
> And the nut that hung frae the hazel tree.

Emily went on in a soft musical voice with a rather Bostonian
Scottish burr till Kilmeny came home again:

> "Kilmeny, Kilmeny, where have you been?"
> Kilmeny looked up with a lovely grace,
> But nae smile was seen on Kilmeny's face;
> For Kilmeny had been, she knew not where,
> And Kilmeny had seen what she could not declare:
> Kilmeny had been where the cock never crew,
> Where the rain never fell, and the wind never blew.

Emily's father read aloud to the family; Emily remembered
especially *Gulliver's Travels*. He had a discriminating taste in
books and a flair for pouncing on new appearances. On a holiday
jaunt to Novia Scotia he took along a little book *Plain Tales from
the Hills* by one Rudyard Kipling. He read *Middlemarch* aloud as
it appeared serially in *Littell's Living Age*, *Daniel Deronda*, and
William Morris's *Life and Death of Jason*.

Once he read *Arabian Nights* to the children on a Sunday.
The mother objected to it as inappropriate for a Sunday but in
general there was no Sabbatarian restraint. In her reminiscences,
Emily sketches a delectable picture of Carrie Ticknor, her "ambitious" little neighbor, standing nearby one Sunday while Emily
played in the swing in the corner of the garden by the sandpile
when Carrie was not allowed to use it. It might be labeled "The
Prig" with the interpretation in reverse, as Titian's Sacred and
Profane Love might be. But Emily was redeemed from smugness
by the question arising in her mind "whether this meant that
Carrie's mother was more particular and perhaps therefore in so
far *superior* to mine."

"We did not go to Sunday school," wrote Emily," for my parents
felt that the atmosphere of Sunday schools as they knew them
was conducive to irreverence by making children too glib. Instead
we attended the Bible class of a much loved and respected neighbor, Miss Ellen Morse, who had studied the Bible under Professor

Toy of Harvard. She gave us fairly adult instruction in Bible history interpreted in a liberal and scientific spirit.

"The whole atmosphere was permeated by what you might call Neo-Puritanism without its rigors, narrowness or introspection, but colored and controlled through and through by complete acceptance of the rule of conscience and by a warm and generous sense of the call to service. My mother read to us the Sermon on the Mount and other passages from the New Testament; my father told us Bible stories which were interesting but had no particular religious bearing. Grace was not said at the table unless a visiting minister came to dinner.

"When I was about ten a prosy old Unitarian divine was followed at the Jamaica Plain Unitarian Church by Charles Fletcher Dole.* His warm faith in the force that makes for righteousness and the challenge of his whole conception of Right commanded my allegiance and became, so far as I can judge, the chief of all the influences that played upon my life. He asked us to enlist, if we were ready to do so, in an absolute sense, without limitations or any holdings back, in the service of goodness, and to determine, so far as in us lay, to meet the demands of this service whatever its cost. In accepting this self-pledge (so far as I recall as a purely voluntary inner act without outward sign or sanction) I consciously dedicated myself as genuinely as a nun taking her vows and in spite of endless weakness, wrong doings, blunders and failures, I think I never abandoned in any degree my desire to live up to it. I remember that at thirteen I used to pray to be made an instrument in God's hand, docile and unbreakable. One of my chief lines of reading has been in the history of religion, especially in its living and devotional side—reading pursued for some years after 1910 with considerable system. In 1921 I asked to be admitted to the Society of Friends and have found in my Quaker membership a constant rebuke and challenge and support. The initial conception of my private ethical belief is that the limitations of self-interest must be progressively left behind for a 'dome more vast.'

"My early idea was to try to be absolutely selfless, literally not

---

* Charles Fletcher Dole, 1845-1927, minister of the First Congregational Church (Unitarian) of Jamaica Plain, in Boston, Massachusetts, from 1876 to 1916, and minister-emeritus from 1916 until his death. He was a pacifist during the Spanish-American War and World War I.

to care for one's own pleasure or pain whatever their degree. My father, of whom a friend once said that he was a combination of Abraham Lincoln, Santa Claus and Jesus, was almost if not quite the most selfless person I have ever known, and I should have liked to be the same. In reality, I remained egotistical, self-centered and far indeed from my ideal. But the truth is that I did try, and I think without any conceit or romance about having a mission, though this was the period of that ideal. It was, I think, only gradually that I came to embrace in my theory a sense of the irreplaceable values of each individual self and the rightness of building on that foundation."

Emily's sister Alice, in a charming little memoir of her girlhood, describes a Sabbath evening in the Balch household:

"As we were not a musical family, my parents had early established the custom of *saying* instead of *singing* hymns on Sunday evenings. We sat in a circle and each one in turn recited a favorite hymn. We each had quite a repertory and to this day one hymn means my mother and another my father:

> By cool Siloam's shady rill
> How fair the lily blows,
> How sweet the scent beneath the hill
> Of Sharon's dewy rose.

That is my mother.

> How happy is he born or taught
> That serveth not another's will,
> Whose armor is his honest thought
> And simple truth his highest skill.

That is my father.

"It was a very pleasant custom, but some of us liked to recite poems that were too long, and some of us grew self-conscious as we became older. When it was found that we were embarrassing guests, we gave up the custom. I think this was a pity." [13]

So Emily Balch grew up, New England of New England.

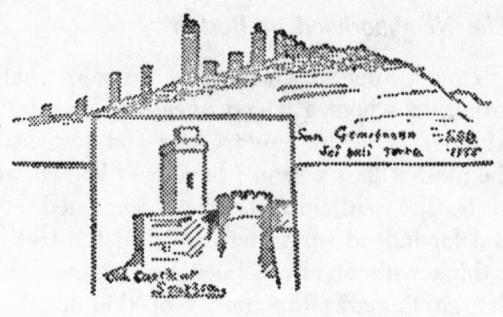

CHAPTER TWO

The Obligations of Education

In the 1880's the idea of women going to colleges was in the air. An older schoolmate of Emily's aroused wonder and admiration because she took and passed the Harvard entrance examinations, not with any "presumptuous idea" of going to college, but just to prove that women could pass such a test. Up to this time Emily had met, and indeed had heard of, only one woman college graduate. A business friend of her father's, William Minot, had married and introduced into an amazed Boston circle an early graduate of Cornell, Elizabeth van Pelt, "and I thought her wonderful," says Emily. Mrs. Minot was the more a curiosity for she had actually delayed her wedding for some weeks to secure her college degree first. Emily James Smith, a close friend of Emily's at Bryn Mawr, and later the first Dean of Barnard College in New York, had never seen a college girl till she became one in 1885. The enthusiastic, gently reared Boston girl, Vida Scudder, who was to become a distinguished colleague of Emily's at Wellesley College, and a prime mover in the Christian Socialist Movement in America, had even wanted to disguise herself as a boy in order to go to Harvard College.

Emily had planned to go to the *Harvard Annex*, as Radcliffe College was then called, with her brilliant young friend from Miss

Ireland's school, Alice Bache Gould. But Alice's father, Professor Benjamin Apthorp Gould, professor of Astronomy in Harvard, objected, and "forbade her," says Emily, "on the ground that he was not willing to have it known among his Cambridge friends that he was disgraced by having a daughter at college." He was induced, however, to consent to a college farther off; and it ended in both his daughter Alice and Emily going to Bryn Mawr College near Philadelphia.

"I decided to go to college," wrote Emily, "when to do so was to feel oneself a marked character in the neighborhood, when returning as a college graduate meant to be constantly met with the would-be amusing protest that people were afraid to talk with me, I was so learned. The same people felt no awe, as I well knew, of a college boy, and I could not see why my very modest undergraduate studies should be more of a barrier than his."

At about the same time similar experiences were confronting a group of intrepid young women, slightly older than Emily, whose paths were destined to cross and intermingle with hers in their later careers. Jane Addams, who from the beginning of the twentieth century till her death in 1935 held the place in national and international esteem later accorded to Eleanor Roosevelt, had been eager to go to Smith College in Massachusetts. But her father, though genuinely sympathetic with her aspirations, wanted for his daughters a school as near home as possible, to be followed by travel abroad, instead of the wider advantages an eastern college was supposed to afford. Therefore, at the age of seventeen, in 1877, Jane Addams entered Rockford Seminary, Illinois, one of the earliest schools for women's higher education in the Mississippi Valley. Jane Addams later recorded in that classic, *Twenty Years at Hull-House*, that many of the first students, conscious of the frontier privations and sacrifices of the founders, accepted this as a heritage and consciously tried to fulfill its obligations. They worked early and late as if they really believed the portentous statement from Aristotle which they got second hand from Boswell's *Life of Johnson:* "There is the same difference between the learned and the unlearned as there is between the living and the dead." [1]

Florence Kelley, who was to become one of the most brilliant of that group of social reformers, wrote: "Entering college was for me an almost sacramental experience. Two long years I had lived for it, since that lonely morning when I found in an otherwise empty waste-basket in my father's study, Cornell's offer of equal opportunities to women. Cornell was the first eastern university to make this glorious offer. Careful inquiry soon revealed that there was no school in Philadelphia equipped to fit a girl thoroughly for college. It was my grotesque experience to be prepared by tutors and governesses not college bred—to enter the freshman class in 1876." [2]

Most ambitious of all was Martha Carey Thomas, ten years older than Emily, and the first Dean of Bryn Mawr College at the time when Emily was a student there. She had come to feel that Vassar College provided a systematic training not much better than that obtainable at a young ladies' seminary. She wanted an education as good as that given to men in the best eastern colleges. and made up her mind that Cornell, a coeducational college, was the place for her. But she encountered strenuous opposition. Her Quaker father, Dr. James Carey Thomas, of a prominent Baltimore family, could not bring himself to approve his brilliant headstrong young daughter's wish. Further education, he argued, might turn her into a bluestocking, and might even undermine her Christian faith. "Many and dreadful are the talks we have had upon this subject," wrote Carey Thomas, as she came to be called. "Father was terribly opposed, and said that never while he lived would he give his consent." Mrs. Thomas, however, backed up her daughter. "Why," argued Mrs. Thomas, "should an advanced education destroy Minnie's faith and not that of her brothers?" The father finally capitulated. When Carey Thomas decided to follow in the footsteps of her young men friends and go to a foreign university (the University of Zürich) for postgraduate work, she had once more to go through the same struggle with her father. A delightful but apocryphal story runs that Mrs. Thomas, seeing that nothing could persuade her husband to change his mind and furnish the funds, remarked to her daughter, "There is nothing for it, thee must cry thyself to Germany." [3] Whereupon they both wept and wept for a fortnight until Dr. Thomas gave in.

On the other hand, Vida Scudder, Mary Kingsbury (Simkhovitch), and Alice Hamilton, like Emily Balch and Florence Kelley, undertook undergraduate and later postgraduate work abroad with the blessing of their families. But, as "the first generation of col-

lege women," in Vida Scudder's words, they felt they must justify
their new opportunities by showing that they did not mean "to
shut themselves up in complacent enjoyment of their advantages." [4]

It was no wonder, then, that so many of the early women
students at Cornell, Vassar, Smith, Wellesley, and Bryn Mawr,
were a self-conscious body of young pioneers on whom the responsibilities of having enjoyed a college education weighed heavily.
They felt their lives were dedicated. In the case of Carey Thomas
it was to scholarship and the higher education of women; for
Florence Kelley and Julia Lathrop to battling for new techniques
of social reform. Jane Addams, Mary Kingsbury, Vida Scudder,
Helena Dudley, and Emily Balch devoted themselves to various
creative movements, such as settlements, resulting from the fer-
ment of ideals and of "compunction" prevalent at the time. In spite
of the classical preoccupation of the colleges in America, the faces
of the young women students, for the most part, were set on the
world of realities and on the future.

What kind of preliminary training was available to this young
Bostonian girl to enable her to take full advantage of the splendid
new higher education for women? Emily's schooling before she
entered college, she used to declare, was "scrappy" and suffered
from discontinuity. But she was rather apt to spread a veil of
deprecation over the more favorable circumstances in her life.
She lived at home in the midst of a large and hospitable family,
where each member was free to bring home guests for longer or
shorter periods, and she sometimes sat down with distinguished
guests to a table of twenty. All this was an education in itself. Her
father was an overseer of Harvard College. In his legal profession
he had a gift for sustained work, both swift and exact, which he
learned perhaps from Sumner, and certainly passed on to his
daughter Emily.

When Emily was eight, she attended a good private school in
Jamaica Plain run by Mrs. Walker and the patriotic Miss Seegar.
Here she had French and German teaching and some Latin. One
of the pupils was Robert A. Woods, later the settlement worker
and author of *English Social Movements,* the first American interpretation of British humanitarian thought. Miss Seegar, remembered through the years by Emily as a sarcastic, tonic personality,
supplemented what Emily's father had taught his children, to know

and to love the wild flowers of wood and field and swamp, and to
look for lichens, ferns and mosses. At this school, when she was
ten years old, a new natural world opened unexpectedly to Emily.
She was fitted with glasses to remedy her nearsightedness. The
stars became small bright spots instead of blurred large ones; she
could see each separate leaf on the apple tree. Whether her elders
deplored spectacles for a personable little girl who like the rest of
her Boston circle was intended to go to Papanti's dancing classes,
to "come out" in society and to go to parties and "assemblies,"
Emily does not record.

After a short period with Annie at Miss Chase and Miss Gib-
bons' private school in Boston, Emily went at the age of thirteen
to Miss Ireland's school in Boston, where she remained till she
entered Bryn Mawr College. This school was situated at 9 Louisburg Square, a part of Beacon Hill that is today still one of the
most picturesque bits of old Boston. A row of quiet, red brick
houses with Bulfinch fronts extends on either side of a narrow,
rectangular iron-fenced park with a small statue at either end.
One is of Aristides the Just, the other of the youthful Christopher
Columbus; both are said to have found their way to the port of
Boston as ballast in ships from Italy. In Louisburg Square and
along the steep side streets, Miss Ireland's girls used to walk during
their midmorning recess, munching the prized buns that were a
specialty of a Charles Street bakery, wishing on hot days that they
could get into the locked enclosure with its cool green grass and
shady elms. The square so much resembled a small London square
that when Minnie Maddern Fiske in 1915 was making a film version of *Vanity Fair*, Louisburg Square was chosen as the setting
and the steps of No. 20 Louisburg Square served for the entrance
to the Sedleys' home and for the arrival of Becky Sharp and Amelia
Sedley from Miss Pinkerton's school after the dictionary-flinging
episode.

The school was informal for its time. Preparation for college
did not enter into its curriculum till later. It provided a very
personal, very inspiring teaching by a group of exceptional men
and women, of whom Miss Ireland, outstanding as she was, was
only one. Especially popular was Miss Elizabeth Simmons, who
taught mathematics and Latin. As the original of Louisa Alcott's
"Old Fashioned Girl" she provoked an added interest in her

charges. Another effective teacher was Fraulein von Seckendorf, who quickened a love of German literature among her pupils, a love that had already been awakened in Emily by her mother.

Though Emily left Miss Ireland's school for a college of the first rank, she often declared that much of her work in college seemed immature and elementary compared to the work done at Miss Ireland's. To her pupils, Catharine Innes Ireland, whose life overlapped that of Emerson and Thoreau, Hawthorne, Longfellow, Lowell and Oliver Wendell Holmes, and who had herself studied under Louis Agassiz at Pekinese Island, shared in the glamor of that golden day in American culture of which she was a first-hand exemplar. It was not only her teaching, especially of literature, but her relationship to her students that her impressionable pupils cherished in their memories. Everything about her seemed full of charm and interest and "personality," that word so dear to schoolgirls. She was thin and spare, with red hair and quick friendly eyes beneath the familiar pince-nez. She was not a New Englander but a New Yorker. Her father's ancestors had been early settlers in Long Island and her mother came from the French Huguenot family of Guion. The family had fled for freedom to New Rochelle bringing their Bible concealed in a loaf of bread. Miss Ireland's voice had taken on the quiet musical cadences common to many cultivated Bostonians, a speech at once precise yet totally unaffected and simple. Her hands were dainty and flexible, always under perfect control. She was quick to respond to humor and would often wipe tears of amusement from her eyes. She was no less lovable for having a quick temper, sudden to rebuke, quicker to forgive. The girls stood in considerable awe of her.

She kindled her pupils by her own admirations—an Adirondack scene, an Egyptian discovery, an Italian painting, an actor's art, a new book of poems, a little kindness. "Her power of taking in," says Emily, "was equalled only by her passion for giving out."[5] Perhaps it was from Miss Ireland as well as from her own father that Emily caught some of that spontaneous and unconscious entering of her whole personality into the feelings and situations of other persons, however different in temper and outlook.

After their graduation from "Miss Ireland's," Emily and a group of girls met at Helen Cheever's summer home at Cohasset and banded themselves into an informal club "Erin Go Bragh"

(Ireland Forever). They continued to meet annually for luncheons, sometimes oftener, under a presiding officer called the "Charwoman," for more than sixty years. Alice Gould, Lena Fabens, and Cora Bowditch, as well as Emily and Helen Cheever, were among this group. Lena Fabens, "lovely looking, delicate in coloring, with curly brown hair and a great sense of fun," lived in Marblehead in a beautiful house owned by her sea captain father. Alice Gould, brilliant, erratic, craving affection, destined to be much alone, was to live for many years and to die in Spain. "I'd give all I know to be as popular as you are," she had declared to Emily at Miss Ireland's. Helen Cheever, who with Frances Hayward remained intimate with Emily into their nineties, was perhaps the most constant and devoted and admiring of Emily's friends.

When Emily was twelve, the Balches spent the summer at the seaside at North Cohasset, near Boston. In 1881 they moved into a delightful unplastered three-story house Mr. Balch had built on a great headland at Quarry Point, Cohasset, not far from the Cheever's summer house. At Cohasset, the Balch family spent seventeen halcyon summers, generally going early in June and staying till October. "The place is undeniably one of the most beautiful in the world," wrote Emily's sister Alice. "There are granite headlands of every hue from dark red-brown through yellows and pinks to snow white, with green lichens on the most sheltered spots. There are pools deep enough to bathe in, islands, peninsulas of rock with quiet deep lagoons at high tide, and sea weeds, starfish, sea anemones, sea urchins, crabs under all the stones, pebbly beaches, pure sand beaches with fine wimpled sand and islands of yellow rocks over which the tide crept slowly.

"The water, at that happy time uncontaminated by oil, was so clear one could look through it to the bottom. To sail one had only to scramble down a steep foot-wide sandy path edged by cat brier, bayberry and low bushes to the rough white granite shoulders below to where the end of our landing stage was fastened with iron posts drilled into the rock.

"The sea was a soft clear blue and the distant schooners pink-sailed and barely moving. There was no sound anywhere unless a catbird called in the sassafras trees, or the sea-moss gatherers, who in my day, sculled quietly among the reefs." [6]

The days went by with events outwardly as quiet as those in a

Jane Austen novel. The family held picnics with friends from far and near. In the afternoons there were drives, horseback riding and for the younger ones, rough games with the boys. The older ones sat on the shady part of the piazza, sewing and reading aloud. Emily read prodigiously and wrote a long series of fairy tales which attest to her literary industry, if not to her talent in the direction of fantasy. In the mornings, as near as possible to high tide, the family went together to the beach to bathe, the women and girls in dark blue swimming suits, skirts to the knees, full bloomers beneath, and black cotton stockings. In the afternoon, after the one-thirty dinner, the beach was sacred to the servants of the summer colony. They bathed, and sat around barelegged. Alice remembers that instead of envying them their freedom she felt disgusted at the sight of the white legs of the Irish girls.

In the summer of 1883, Emily's father, worn out with overwork, was persuaded by his wife to go to Europe with Annie. Mrs. Balch, in a letter to her "two unspeakably dear ones" abroad, has a little vignette of the Prince Street household on a hot June afternoon: "It is a very warm afternoon. We are all scattered about the piazza and parlor, reading and playing, with our fine tall agapanthus and the orange tree promoted to the front piazza. Alice and Maidie are in white, Frank in his white waist and blue trousers, Bessie in her plain pink satin, Emily in her linen lawn, Auntie in her batiste with the blue ribbons and I am in blue linen lawn. Opposite are a fanning group of Frothinghams and everything goes on in the familiar round."

Much of the social life in Jamaica Plain in winter time, according to Alice, centered on skating on Jamaica Pond. People came from Brookline and Boston. The pond represented a Currier and Ives picture of graceful girl skaters with long swinging skirts, slender young men swaying in curves on the outer edge, and on the shore other skaters kneeling to clamp their skates on their high-laced boots. Mrs. Balch, who had loved skating from her Byfield days, had wanted her children to experience the same joy. She spent hours with cold feet teaching her children to skate, for a knee trouble prevented her own skating. Also, to her great grief, she became very heavy in her forties. Her diary records her chagrin at weighing 203 pounds. She liked young people to have a good time and spared no effort for their entertainment.

As the children grew older, theatricals and impromptu charades enlivened the Prince Street household. One end of the long parlor was shut off by curtains strung on wires with a row of candles as footlights. "Dramatizations from the Alice books were a great success," wrote Alice. "I was always the Red Queen or the Hatter, nor was I wholly flattered on being praised for my fine rendering and looking exactly like the Hatter. I knew my Tenniel too well for that. O what fun it all was, and how tired everyone was afterwards, and how flat life seemed next day when the guests had gone and the curtain was pulled down. On looking back, our life seems very good to me. I know it also seemed so at the time, so the opinion is not the effect of nostalgia.

"We had our major catastrophes. The death of our wonderful mother when I was only eight years old was the greatest. Many years later we lost our gentle brilliant father."

The death "of our wonderful mother" left a stunned incomprehension. Ellen Balch was only forty-seven years old. In the summer of 1884 she became ill with Bright's disease in the Cohasset home by her "beloved sea," and she died on September 14. She was at the height of her vitality and usefulness, the center of the universe for her husband and six children, a magnet of attraction for a wide circle of friends, relatives, neighbors. With her going something intensely vivid and alive was snuffed out.

Emily was seventeen years old. With characteristic reticence she did not confide her grief either to her journal, where there was a long gap, or to her friends. During the weeks of July and August while the mother lay ill and dying, a situation rendered doubly painful for the older daughters (the younger children had been sent away to relatives) because of the thin partitions of the unplastered house, the faithful Helen Cheever came every morning in her phaeton to take Emily for a drive. She remembered that on these drives, Emily did not speak a word.

Miss Ireland wrote Emily from Louisburg Square: "It is hard to connect anything painful with your mother. Her face, whenever I have seen it, has been so serene and sweet and strong that it has given me a great sense of peace and power." Mrs. Grace Herschel, a close friend of Nelly Balch who was to become half friend, half mother to Emily, wrote to Emily: "Whenever I was in trouble, your Mama was always on hand with help of all kinds, for the body, the mind, and the heart."

On Annie, nineteen years old, fell, prematurely, the burden of managing the large and by no means easy household and of bringing up the younger children, Francis, aged ten, Alice eight, and Maidie, five. In this complicated task she had the unstinted and loyal cooperation of the two sisters next in age, Emily and Bessie, as well as of Aunt Nannie and Auntie and of Cousin Agnes Balch who occasionally took over the reins of the housekeeping to give Annie a vacation. Annie, gentle, loving, gifted in painting and drawing, "in many ways the nicest of all the Balches," became Emily's close friend and confidante. Her breakdown in 1920, followed by repeated illnesses throughout the years, bore heavily on Emily and the close-knit family circle.

Mrs. Herschel assumed the maternal solicitude that the two unmarried aunts, loving and interested as they were, could not provide for the three older girls. She carried on an intimate correspondence with Emily urging her "to enjoy her youth," "to go to parties," "to meet young men." This, Emily was wont to declare later with a shrug of her shoulders, "was beyond me." One piece of Mrs. Herschel's advice was more successful. "When I was a little girl," wrote Emily, "a very interesting friend of my mother's and of my own girlhood, Mrs. Grace Herschel, said the ugliest sight in the world was a person trying to be good. This was so contrary to my own conceptions to which the effort to be good was dominating—that it led me furiously to think, and tended to correct any tendency to self-conscious self-cultivation."

With Mrs. Herschel too, Emily always felt free to discuss the religious questions that interested her so deeply, both personally and intellectually. This religious concern was unguessed by many of her later colleagues, since she never obtruded it in conversation unless she was sure of an answering interest. "When I was a little girl," said Emily, "I read a banal story in St. Nicholas Magazine which affected my practice, whether advantageously or not. A little girl had gone away from home to visit relatives. In her own home religion was never talked of, though her parents belonged to church and were religious people. The relatives she visited talked a good deal of religion, as one of the things they were

interested in, naturally and simply. This appeared to me reasonable. Religion seems to me one of the most interesting things in
life, one of the most puzzling, richest and thrilling fields of human
thought and speculation. While like human affection it implies
reticences, and while speech can be a profanation and a painful
disloyalty to deeply sacred intimacies, religious experience and
thought need also a light of day and sunshine and a companionable sharing with others of which it seems to me there is generally
too little. I am quite ready to admit that I may make the mistake of
talking about religion too easily and too much—but I am convinced it may be possible to talk of religion too little and too
seldom and thereby lack a very beautiful type of communion
between persons. The Quaker worship at its best seems to me to
give opportunities for this sort of sharing without profanation.
What is said in meeting is at once public, deeply private, and
intimate as the confessional."

In 1885, the year after her mother's death, perhaps to help
soften Emily's grief, her father put a priceless experience in her
way. On April 6 Emily writes in her diary: "Suggested I should
go abroad"; on April 7: "Decided": and on April 11, "Sailed from
New York on the *Archimede* of the Florio-Rubatino Line about
one." Professor William Allen, with whom Auntie had gone to St.
Helena's Island in 1863 to help with the education of freedmen,
was taking his seventeen-year old daughter Katie and another
young girl abroad for a four-month's grand tour. It was arranged
that Emily should travel with them. They were to sail for Gibraltar,
the most beautiful of all approaches to Europe.

To an eager sensitive girl of eighteen, steeped in English literature, a first trip abroad, to Sicily, Italy, Switzerland, Belgium,
Holland, England, and Scotland, was to open one magic casement
after another. "If we could have chosen one girl to go," wrote Lena
Fabens to her, "*You* were the one we should all have chosen. You
are best fitted to appreciate and enjoy everything." But it was to
be more than a literary pilgrimage. It was the beginning of her
international education and experience. One incident made a great
impression on her. To her brother Frank, aged twelve, she wrote
of a threatened war between Russia and England that never
materialized. Emily's party had been to Tangier, which she recalls

as so little modernized that she did not see a single person in European dress. They had returned to Gibraltar to wait for the Peninsular and Oriental steamer that was to take them on the next lap of the trip to Malta. In Gibraltar there was considerable excitement. *Galignano's Messenger* was full of the tense international situation and predicted that war with Russia would break out within twenty-four hours. Professor Allen's party found the vessel full of British officers, on leave from fighting Zulus and Afghans, who had been hurriedly ordered to rejoin their commands in India. Besides the three girls in Mr. Allen's party, there was only one other woman passenger. The boat buzzed with talk. Russian vessels had been sent to the western Mediterranean and as the Peninsular and Oriental ship *Cathay* was loaded with specie for India, she was quite a prize. The captain, at whose table they sat, said that his orders were not to resist if attacked, but to try to run for it. "We wondered how soon we might all be cooling our heels in Moscow." When they reached Malta, things had taken another turn and "The war with Russia that was believed to be immediate in April 1885," Emily wrote [in 1951], "has not yet taken place." This episode of an "inevitable war" that failed to come off, kept her unruffled and unalarmed during the numerous "war scares" she was destined to live through in later life.

To her sister Maidie aged six, she wrote in different vein: "Dear Little Sister:

. . . There was another thing there [at Basel] which would have amused you and that was a clock. Wait till I tell you about it. The city is built on both sides of the river Rhine, and in old times the people on the opposite banks hated each other very much, and one side, to plague the other, set up on the river bank a clock with a man's face above it which all the time kept putting out its tongue at the people opposite. We saw it among a great many curious old things in a sort of museum behind the beautiful cathedral. It keeps sticking its tongue out a little way and rolling its eyes (of course by machinery inside) and at the end of every minute it ran it out so far that I almost thought it would never stop till it reached Jamaica Plain. It is called The Laller-König or King."

Emily returned to Boston in August for a last year at Miss Ireland's school. Before the death of her mother, Emily had shown no particular inclination to go to college, though her father had noticed his daughter's aptitudes and had often suggested that she study law and work with him.

When the Harvard Annex was closed to Emily and Alice Gould by the objections of Alice's father, their thoughts turned to the recently opened Quaker college for women at Bryn Mawr. Emily and her father took a trip to Philadelphia in August, 1886, to look over Bryn Mawr (Welsh for High Hill). Bryn Mawr College did not then have the opulent beauty of later years, with its groups of buildings in collegiate Tudor (bastard Gothic, Roger Fry called it) set in a beautiful campus of smooth green lawns, shrubbery, and trees. In 1886, in Quaker simplicity, the grey stone walls of Taylor Hall, the first academic building, and Merion Hall, the first living quarters for the students, rose gaunt and even ugly.

Bryn Mawr had been founded by Quakers in 1885 to give women an education as good as that offered their brothers at Harvard and other men's colleges of the first rank. The early Bryn Mawr students for the most part regarded themselves as pioneers in what they thought was the final step in achieving equality with men—an education equal to the best. So high were the intellectual standards set by the first president of Bryn Mawr, Dr. James E. Rhoads, and the first Dean, Carey Thomas, that Bryn Mawr hoped in time to take its place in the forefront of all colleges, men's and women's. Hence arose that attitude of quiet superiority associated for many years with the students of Bryn Mawr College, an attitude that gave rise to many anecdotes and pleasantries. At any rate Bryn Mawr became a mecca for the more intellectual of the first generations of college women.

In the autumn of 1886, Emily and Alice Gould, both regarded as highly gifted students in Miss Ireland's school, were entered as members of the class of 1890. But they spent only three years there, both graduating with the class of 1889, the first graduating class, of which Emily James Smith (later Mrs. George Haven Putnam) was an oustanding member, as well as Alys Pearsall Smith (later the first Mrs. Bertrand Russell) and Helena Dudley, soon to be a member of the pioneer group responsible for the first social settlements in America.

"It was a disadvantage" wrote Emily "to everything but my

vanity that I squeezed so much into three years, utilizing vacations for study, dislocating my class relations, and losing the fourth and most important year of undergraduate study. My work was mainly in the classics, but this was really as I see now curiously against the grain. Much as I owe that great Platonist, Paul Shorey, his teaching never got inside my skin.

"History, which as I look back, would have naturally been my favorite study, took little of my scant three years. I had intended to take Professor Woodrow Wilson's course in my senior year, but, alas, I missed the opportunity as the young professor who was so much admired left Bryn Mawr before my last year.

"Edmund B. Wilson, a pioneer in the fruitful early days of biology and his specialty cytology, was a great teacher, a revealer. I saw that I was no scientist myself, but I understood something of what scientific method was and of what scientific method involved. I was interested not in the laboratory nor in details but in the implications of theory. Evolution was then suspect to the orthodox. Professor Frederick Lee, the physiologist, Wilson's colleague, asked me, to test as I felt sure, my reaction, what I personally concluded about evolution. I said that I was convinced of the truth of natural selection in the Darwinian sense but could not believe that it was the whole explanation of evolutionary change. I remember I felt it difficult to conceive that every step in the change that resulted in a cypripedium could be sufficiently valuable for survival to insure its selection and transmission. This strikes me as clear-sighted for a college freshman as I then was."

Through Dean Carey Thomas' genius for selection, in its opening years Bryn Mawr had on its faculty an immensely gifted group, very young and fresh from their university or foreign training. There was one full professor, Carey Thomas, twenty-eight years old, who held the chair of English as well as the deanship. Among the associate professors were Charlotte Angus Scott, British mathematician, senior wrangler of Girton College, Cambridge, and Doctor of Science from London University; Edmund B. Wilson, professor of biology, Paul Shorey, associate in Greek and Latin, and Woodrow Wilson in the department of history and political science. Indeed, the group was so outstanding that many of them were soon drawn away to high positions in the universities: Edmund Wilson left in 1890 to go to Columbia University; Paul

Shorey in 1892 went to the newly formed University of Chicago;
and Woodrow Wilson resigned in 1888 to go to Wesleyan
University.

The number of students was small enough for the girls to be
taught in small classes by these unusual people. Emily James Smith
later wrote: "I took for granted the heady brew that was my daily
drink, and supposed, until further knowledge of the university
world showed me otherwise, that all freshmen were taught in
small classes by teachers of the first order of distinction."

The young dean, Carey Thomas, had a brilliant reputation as
one of the very first woman students to receive her doctorate (in
philology) from Zürich University, with a *summa cum laude*, rarely
given even to men. Her life exhibited an insistent unity of purpose—the education and advancement of women and the glorifica-
tion of the intellectual life. To these two goals she was willing to
sacrifice everything else. In achieving them she was aided by
family background, undeniable beauty, and an invincible will.
Every student who ever came in contact with her was to feel the
effect of what she had written in her dairy in 1871 when she was
only fourteen: "If I ever live and grow up my *one* aim and concentrated purpose *shall be* and *is* to show that women *can learn,
can reason, can compete* with man in the grand fields of literature
and science and conjecture that open before the nineteenth century, that a woman can be a woman and a true one without having
all her time engrossed by dress and society."

When Emily entered college, literature, including the classics,
was what interested her most. As was required she took Dean
Carey Thomas' two-year survey course in English language and
literature five times a week. She read *Chanson de Roland* in Old
French (reading also the modern French translation when she
seemed to be losing the general sense), Boethius' *Consolations of
Philosophy* in Latin, and Dante's *Vita Nuova* in Italian.

Emily found this course "very interesting," she said lukewarmly.
She does not seem to have succumbed like so many of the Bryn
Mawr students to the spell of Carey Thomas' sparkling and magnetic personality. Perhaps it was because Emily was never to
respond emotionally, as so many women of her generation did, to
the appeal of other women. Perhaps it was because by temperament Emily and the young Dean were at opposite poles. Carey

Thomas admired physical beauty, Emily Balch loved also the beauty of the inner person; Carey Thomas had assurance and high spirits, Emily was inclined to be deprecatory and to lean to quietness; Carey Thomas moved at a quick, impatient pace, Emily, like her father, even in college contrived an infinite leisure; Carey Thomas, though a birthright Quaker, had a Renaissance exuberance, love of lavish living, rich materials, strong colors and contrasts; Emily, like the Greeks, was a "lover of beauty with economy," like the Quakers she loved plain words and simple ways, and like the proverbial New Englander, she tended to restraint, reticence, and understatement.

Paul Shorey was another great teacher who somehow failed to strike fire with Emily. "Some fabrics take the dye, and some don't," she remarked dryly, "and I didn't." Something in her democratic soul revolted from what she thought were the aristocratic ideas of Shorey's beloved Plato. Like Jefferson, she felt an instinctive antipathy for what Shorey presented as Plato's closed society.

Emily James Smith ("Jim" Smith), the outstanding classical student, felt and thought otherwise. When as a senior, she translated in Shorey's class the closing passages of Plato's *Republic*, she felt that she had shut her book on what was surely the greatest prose ever written by man. "I felt I had come in sight of a solution of the riddle of the world. My sense of obligation to Shorey crystalized at that moment and has never dissolved." [7]

But, in common with all Shorey's students both at Bryn Mawr and later at Chicago, Emily derived from Professor Shorey the sense of humanism as a continuing tradition. Greek and Latin were not only the vehicles of a great literature, they were the origin of all the great literature of Europe.

During her three years at Bryn Mawr, Emily experienced for the most part the normal life of an undergraduate today except that it was more monastic. A fire in the college and a wind that blew down the chimney into Alice Gould's half of the room in the famous "Blizzard of '88" diversified the academic routine. Emily had her first insight into Quaker ways and thought. She attended Quaker meeting at neighboring Haverford and during the silences, as she listened to the sound of squirrels pattering on the roof, she thought deeply and felt herself drawn to the Quaker form of worship, its creedless faith, and its testimony for peace.

Above all, Emily learned from the highly selected group of girls Bryn Mawr had attracted. There was Emily James Smith who had a "rapier-like mind" and an amused detached sophistication. She was one of the first American women to study at Girton College, Cambridge. There was Alys Pearsall Smith of Germantown, Pennsylvania, who was frank and unconventional. Alys was a first cousin of Carey Thomas; her mother was the redoubtable Quaker preacher and writer, Hannah Whitall Smith; she was the sister of the lovely Mary, who was to marry Bernard Berenson, and of Logan Pearsall Smith, the expatriate writer. Alys spent much time abroad with her family. In one of her undergraduate absences she wrote to Emily from the Riviera: "I think Parliament is doing very badly. Why don't you brace it up, Emily? I consider it a very valuable and important thing for the girls."

Another classmate, Louise Elder, converted a rather reluctant Emily to belief in woman suffrage, a "change to an opinion which was wholly against my taste and associations," as she confessed in her journal. Emily, like Jane Addams, was strongly committed to the idea that woman's full capacities should be used. But she was at no time primarily a suffragist, like Carrie Chapman Catt. Not the advancement of one sex or class, but better relations between human beings, interested her from the beginning, and the desire to provide a fair chance for all people "to grow to full human stature." Unlike Lucy Stone, Susan B. Anthony, Lucretia Mott, Julia Ward Howe, and the pioneer feminists who belonged to the nineteenth century, Emily Balch, Jane Addams, Florence Kelley, and Alice Hamilton definitely belonged to the twentieth century and are recognized as modern Americans.

With the brilliant Alice Gould, Emily remained on intimate terms, receiving mental stimulus from Alice's original mind, and learning from Alice's knowledge of mathematics, science, and history. Alice, shy and awkward in her earlier years, plain except for a pair of fine large brown eyes, demanding much of others, exacting more of herself, perpetually disappointed, needed just such a stable friend as Emily in college. In Emily she found a confessor and savior in her more distressing moments. Alice had had a shattering experience when she was only six years old. In Cordoba, Argentina, where her father, the astronomer Benjamin Apthorp Gould, was living, with his family, while he was charting the stars of the Southern hemisphere, Alice had seen two older sisters drowned in a lake before her own eyes and those of her mother and a nurse. Alice, the third child, thus became the eldest of three children. When Alice was not in Argentina with her parents she lived much of the time in her grandfather's home at Quincy, Massachusetts.*

Helena Stuart Dudley, a biology student, was several years older than the rest of her Bryn Mawr classmates, maturer and more experienced. When Jean Fine (later Mrs. Charles B. Spahr) came to Bryn Mawr to describe to students the plans for a settlement of college women on Rivington Street, in New York City, Helena with her humanitarian leanings joined Emily Balch as one of the first to be aroused. It is interesting to note that the inspiration for this settlement (largely initiated by Vida Scudder and a group of young Smith College alumnae), was not scientific nor even purely philanthropic. It was motivated by the desire of these young women to share the recently-granted privileges of a higher education they could not yet take as a matter of course. Vida Scudder, to whom "privilege unshared was a fret that would not heal," formulated this motive into a sort of College Woman's Manifesto: "Into this world, . . . bent as no other age has been, in the analysis of social evil and the right of social wrong—into this world we are born—we, the first generation of college women. We represent a new factor in the social order. . . . Our lives are in our hands. . . . What is the relation which these lives should bear to the needs and demands of the time?" [8]

A Bryn Mawr photograph of Emily at about this time, in academic cap and gown, standing by some shrubbery, reveals a tall slender young woman, with a thoughtful face, long graceful fingers holding a book. The book was no mere photographer's pose. All her life Emily had an affinity for the printed word. She could not pass anything written without looking at it. She always said, "It was not an apple but a book that did the mischief." She was, however, by no means a blue stocking. She loved long

---

* Alice Gould spent most of her working life in Spain, doing research on a single subject, the makeup and character of the shipmates of Christopher Columbus on his first voyage. She discovered that, contrary to popular belief, "only four of them had been in jail." In 1927 she received from the Spanish Government the Cross of Alfonso, and in 1951 the Cross of Isabella the Catholic.

country walks, horse back riding, bicycling, and some forms of athletics. In college she excelled in pole vaulting, her thin spare form hurtling over the bars. When she was a well-known professor at Wellesley College she convulsed her students and the faculty by her sprightly execution of the Highland Fling.

For all her balance, she had a quality of eagerness which, retained to extreme old age, kept her always from seeming to be an old woman. At Bryn Mawr she had plenty of college-girl enthusiasm. One weekend she visited Alys Pearsall Smith at Germantown. The Smiths always knew interesting people. Alys and Emily were to visit Walt Whitman at Camden. Emily remembered how she set out "in the flush of youth and joy" and expectancy to call on the famous poet who was such a controversial figure. The visit somehow fell through. Walt Whitman was not at home. At another time, Emily arranged a rollicking skit on the *Return of Agamemnon* and acted the part of Clytemnestra.

Few of her letters or diaries remain to show what went on during this maturing period. Here is a snatch:

January 1, 1888. As I look back I see the last year a very happy one. Grandma Sara better, Alice Gould better. A year of happy work, a happy summer at home and with my friends. I wish I dared think I have gained as much as I enjoyed.

Began the New Year with service at Trinity. I long for reverence, humility, purity, truthfulness, simplicity, strength, wisdom, love, providence, gladness, regularity.

I have been thinking about luxury.

During the year I have written two essays, one on Gray and one on Epics, a few verses, one story and many wretched letters.

January 7, 1888. I come of age tomorrow and will try to put away childish things.

I should like to be in bed at 10:30, have fifteen minutes a day at least for uninterrupted reading and be much more careful in personal habits and manners including buttons of all sorts.

I hope I shall not get lost in study or pursue it for pleasure beyond its best measure for my purpose, unknown to me as yet.

The essay on Thomas Gray and the one on Epics were the only pieces of writing required of Emily during her years at Bryn Mawr. As she felt she had not been sufficiently trained in writing as a tool, the year after leaving college she took private composition lessons from Miss Heloise Hersey of Boston, who later had a reputation as "the dean of women reviewers."

For further practice during this period, Emily had been in the habit of writing into a little notebook informal reviews and criticisms of books she had read. Many a dutiful student of English literature will echo her honest cry on reading Izaak Walton's *The Compleat Angler:* "I am afraid I am not cultivated enough to appreciate old Izaak. If I did not hate fishing so much I should like it better, I suppose." On *Discours sur la Méthode* by Descartes, she begins: "After trying for four years and never passing 'cogito, ergo sum' I have at last finished this wonderful essay." and ends with "I wish I ever had time, courage, energy or power to think." Machiavelli's *The Prince* naturally puzzled the disciple of Charles Fletcher Dole. "A fearful weapon he offered to those who had not in their veins a drop of human kindness." The following passage on Gogol's *Taras Bulba* was written before the era of Freud, so fortunately it is not necessary for this biographer to interpret it:

"Oh, to be a wild Kossack! Fight hard and drink hard and ride hard. Out in the wide steppes or wilder Setch. A new world is opened to us, a new life, a new nation, a new time. All this was here and I never heard of it till now. Have I been dreaming? Our clothes grow strait. Oh for a horse between the knees, my blood boils, I want to fight, strain, wrestle, strike. Not a nice time for women then. Never so good a time as now. I must have some Indian or Gypsy blood I have such a longing for wild life at times and this strange wonderful book wakes it all. To be brave and have it all known, to surpass and be proud, oh the splendour of it!

"This is a nice sensible book review, isn't it?"

In her senior year Emily struck out into a new path. Though her major concern had been literature, she now began to feel that to devote herself to this was "pure self-indulgence and that it led nowhere since I had just enough sense, but barely enough—to know that I was not fitted to be either an original writer nor a critic." Emily took up economics under an "inspiring and original teacher," Franklin H. Giddings. He first presented contrasting schools, William J. Ashley's historical approach and that of the orthodox classical theory. Professor Giddings thought well enough of her

capacity and originality to want her to go into that field, then not a
usual one for women. "I have never regretted my decision to do
so."

"Social compunction was in the air," wrote Emily. She became
disturbed by the literary revelations of bad labor conditions, especially the sweating system. These revelations had been publicized
earlier in England by the Christian Socialists Charles Kingsley
and Frederick Denison Maurice. They challenged the laissez-faire
system and advocated a cooperative instead of a competitive economic system. Emily, often influenced more by books than by
people, was deeply moved by reading Charles Booth's monumental
study of conditions in London, *Life and Labor of the People in
London;* Sir Walter Besant's novel, *All Sorts and Conditions of
Men,* a stirring story of the East End in London; Charles Kingsley's *Alton Locke,* against the sweating system; and later Jacob
Riis's *How the Other Half Lives.* She was also influenced by the
Fabian Essays and by the "ringing lines in Tennyson's *Locksley
Hall.*"

"All this had a repercussion on me," she wrote, "and I felt that
this was no time for 'idle singers of an empty day' but for efforts to
study and better conditions. This is interesting not as the development of one young woman but as characteristic of my generation."

The greatest honor Bryn Mawr could confer at that time was
the European fellowship, to be awarded to a senior for a year of
study abroad. It was to be given first in 1889. Ironically enough, it
was owing to Paul Shorey that the fellowship was awarded to
Emily. Emily, deprecatory as always, immediately wrote home to
her family that Jim Smith, not she, had deserved it. After a tussle
with her conscience she went to President Rhoads and Dean
Thomas to say that she yielded in favor of Jim Smith. According
to Emily the reply was that if she did not accept it, the fellowship
would not be conferred. She adds that she and Jim Smith sat down
and wept together.

When Emily accepted the Bryn Mawr Fellowship for European
study, she felt she was not adequately prepared for advanced work
in her new field. So before leaving for Europe she decided to spend
a winter at home, reading and studying under the direction of
Giddings. She was delighted when her school friend Lena Fabens,

wishing for an opportunity to spend a year abroad, decided to accompany her.

In the minutes of a Bryn Mawr Faculty meeting, April 12, 1889, there is a recommendation to the Trustees: "that the Bryn Mawr European Fellowship be awarded to Emily Greene Balch who has been nominated by the Faculty. Emily G. Balch entered college three years ago with advanced standing. She is twenty-two years of age, a woman of unusual ability; of extraordinary beauty of moral character, of great discretion and balance of judgment, very unselfish and in every way fit to be a representative of the college and to engage in study in Europe."

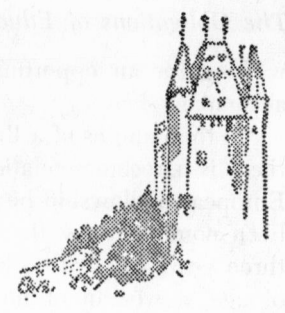

CHAPTER THREE

Discovering the Wider World

And so, on September 6, 1890, on the S.S. *Volendam*, Emily, accompanied by the gay, lively, and companionable Lena Fabens, sailed for France for her year of graduate study. In Paris they settled temporarily at the apartment of an American friend, Mrs. Van Pelt, to get their bearings and look for living quarters with a French family where no English or Anglo-French would be heard. Professor Giddings had written Emily the previous winter: "I am pretty well satisfied that the place for you to spend most of your time is in Paris. Not only are women better treated there than anywhere else, but the opportunities are almost immeasurably greater." What did Emily, the first Bryn Mawr European Fellow, expect from her *Lehrjahr?* "I was always greedy," she wrote home, "and now I want to swallow France whole in one year, to study not only Political Economy but to learn French, read French literature, get abreast of French thought, understand French politics, know French art and artists, all in one year."

Soon Emily and Lena settled for the month of October with a French family, Mme. de Hénaut and her daughter, near Passy, out by the Bois de Boulogne. "I am sure we shall know Paris better for seeing it from this side though I like the Latin Quarter best. The family is charming, especially Mlle. de Hénaut, who talks very well and is interested in everything. The table is extremely nice and ample. I wish you could look in on us and see us with all our Penates around us and on the hearth a jolly little wood fire."

In her recollections Emily briefly sums up her French experiences as follows: "In this Victorian age, when modern youngsters imagine us to have been so chaperoned and hedged in, I went, a girl of twenty-three, who knew nothing of the world, had never come out in society or acquired any human experience, to enjoy complete independence. As a woman student I was something of a curiosity, and I found no appropriate courses available, though I followed some evening lectures which took me alone, across the city to come home by a lonely street in the Étoile quarter at eleven o'clock at night. It ended in my doing a mild piece of historical research on Public Assistance of the Poor in France,[*] rewritten after my return with the footnotes and apparatus that Professor Emile Levasseur, who with infinite generosity directed my study, had never suggested. My work was all with books and all with secondary sources. I had only the vaguest idea of what the Monts de Piété (or pawnshops) which figure in this history were like but the idea of visiting one apparently struck M. Levasseur as preposterous. Nor, so far as I can recall, did it occur that I might try to see a *bureau de bienfaisance* as a functioning reality. Nor did I ever visit a slum or see a workingman except as a fellow passenger in a bus. I did try to get for myself the figures of certain taxes levied for public charity. I was scandalized when I learned that the receipts were never published and were known only to the minister whose perquisites they appeared to be.

"At least I had the sense to be dissatisfied and seek actual contact with the problems I had read of in books."

Though Emily did not know it, she was laying the broad foundations in language and international knowledge for the third and most enduring phase of her career, her work for international peace. A packet of her letters, addressed for the most part to "Dearest Papa" in Jamaica Plain, reveal what caught her interest in Paris and describe in some detail her experiences with her mentor, Emile Levasseur. The reader can judge for himself how

---

[*] Public Assistance of the Poor in France, American Economic Association, 1893.

seriously the French professor regarded a student who was both
a woman and an American.

"Yesterday I took my life in my hands and went to Professor
Levasseur. He was in a little study by a hot wood fire, at a table
littered with endless papers. He is quite elderly, tho' not at all old,
grizzled with a smooth-shaven face like a priest's, with a good
mouth. He was very pleasant, asked me about my past work, my
plans etc. Gave me a card to his lectures at the Conservatoire des
Arts et Métiers, told me to get one for de Foville, who lectures
there the hour after, gave me a card to Leroy-Beaulieu who lectures at the Collège de France and is going to speak to the director
of the École Libre des Sciences Politiques—a private institution—
about a jeune fille's going there but doubts if I can as no woman
ever has. This makes me shiver in my shoes a little, and I don't
know whether I hope for his success. Now all this was very nice
but what I wanted most of all was to be directed in some private special work. So I plucked up my spirits and remarked
blandly that though statistics were not my ultimate aim and
what I desired was to be able to reason and understand reasoning from them, I thought that I should get the best general
idea of them by taking up some special narrow application. At
this he beamed and said, 'Ah, you desire to make a special
study; have you thought of a subject?' So I said very deferen-
tially that I *had* thought of the question of the flux of population in great cities and explained a bit. At this he was fairly
radiant, 'Mademoiselle, it is what I am just doing in my second
volume of the Population of France which is now in press. I will
lend the pages to you, but you must return them very soon.' He
then got me the first volume which has an introduction in statistics,
history, methods etc. and told me to come back in a fortnight or
later if I pleased, to read it attentively and ask him if anything
puzzled me and then he would lend me some other works as it
would be better to do a certain amount of general reading on
statistics first. I was delighted of course; for it is almost more than
I dared hope that he would give me this personal direction. Isn't
it very good of him?

"It didn't occur to me till just as the end of the interview that it
had been all in French, and though I know I spoke very incorrectly
I never failed to say pretty easily and apparently intelligibly what

I wanted to. I kept throwing in a deferential *Monsieur* every little while and I tried to thank him and apologized for my poor French and he was very nice about it."

A little later Emily wrote: "At last my lectures have begun in part at least. I have four a week at the Conservatoire des Arts et Métiers, one course with M. Levasseur, one with M. de Foville each Tuesday and Friday evening, both on Political Economy. I have been twice now and found no difficulty at all as I come in the omnibus directly to the door. Mademoiselle de Hénaut pooh poohed the idea of there being any question of the propriety of my going so and Mrs. Van Pelt thinks it is all right.

"I have only been to one (at the Sorbonne) on French literature by Professor Dejob. He was thoroughly in earnest and I liked very much what he said and it was very interesting for me for I find the French disposition and character and what France means in the world and what this next generation is going to turn out a very interesting enigma. He spoke of '70 as did M. de Foville in his lecture on the progress of civilization. I fancy it is very much in their thoughts always. He said it was a great mistake to think a nation went to the wall in a trial like that because of superior science on the part of the enemy. It was the stuff that men were made of and their disinterestedness that told.

"Yesterday morning I went to see M. Levasseur. He says I don't need to know anything in especial of mathematics to study statistics which disposes of my last scare. He directed me to take down the names of some fifteen huge tomes on statistics of different cities, gave me two books to take with me and dismissed me with a 'courage.' I needed that remark sadly for what I am to do I don't know. If he expects me to be able to read all that before next Saturday he is a madman for nobody could do it. He asked me if I had a method and took notes. I said I did but I am afraid I ought to have got him to tell me how I ought to work, but he was in a hurry and perhaps it is just as well to see what I can do by myself this week.

"On my way home I refreshed myself with a little visit to the Luxembourg. I came out refreshed as I always do after seeing pictures and particularly, sculpture."

While Emily was attending lectures and reading population statistics, she found time to ramble with Lena about the various quarters of Paris. If they did not succeed in "swallowing France entire," seeds, pulp and all, they were tasting delicious morsels of at least the rind, of Paris. They had season tickets to the classic matinees at the Odéon. "We went last Thursday, Les Plaideurs and Athalie and a lecture sandwiched between them. Isn't it a funny plan? I think it is a good one except that it does make a very long session. The week before it was a little play of Scribe's and Le Barbier de Seville with a very good lecture on the two authors. Figaro was charming and looked very much like Ethel Atwater in her gymnasium costume.

"The market is Lena's great delight and she comes home laden with spoils such as two sous worth of tiny radishes (a great bunch), three sous worth of cress green and fresh, a couple of yellow pomegranates, or black figs and yesterday the most exquisite little red fruit the size of a strawberry but all rough like a button ball with yellow flesh and yellow in its recesses but with all its little knobs aglow with scarlet. It is the *arbute* which I always wondered about when I met it in Latin."

By the end of January Emily voices strongly to her father her doubts of the value of her studies in Paris. At one interview M. Levasseur had looked at her in surprise and said, "Ah, Mademoiselle, vous voulez étudiez sérieusement!" "I really don't do anything but go to lectures and read stupid books making endless and very pointless notes. Yesterday after a five weeks delay I took back to Professor Levasseur the two books he had given me and came back with a 3 volume 'report' much the size and consistency of a Congressional Record to read at discretion. I have not the smallest idea whether I am wasting my time or not, nor what I am going to do finally; but if I knew where I were steering for it would be a good deal easier to steer. I think there never was more of an idiot than I am in certain respects. . . . Would it not be a good deal more useful to study our own system of public charities than the French system? If I knew all about our ways I could tell when I was getting new ideas. I should like to know something about the *Monts de Piété,* that is certainly something we have not and I should think it a very good thing. I am sleepy and have written too long so that I am writing foolishly but I really have been and am puzzled about my study here. I don't like to think it is because I am incapable of directing myself at all and need to have my work chosen [and] arranged for me like a child but it looks a little like it. M. Levasseur is very good and very eminent but so far I have not got anything to speak from him in the way of advice or criticism. He expects me to bring the initiative and I expect him to perhaps.

"One of the questions in my mind is—should I be better employed studying or trying to study some theoretical question or something practical? I want to know something however small down to the ground as a training in method if nothing else. If I decide what to do before I go it will be a miracle. Meanwhile I am going serenely on, you understand, reading books on public charity and whether I learn anything special or not I am learning a good deal in general and falling terribly behindhand in all information as to what is happening outside of France, and in it too. I have been reading Fourier and perhaps madness is contagious for I am sure this is as mad a letter as even I ever wrote.

"With dear love, dear Papa, with constant love always

Emily"

Emily's letters home were just such letters as a parent and sisters would wish for—frequent, not written with an eye to posterity, detailing both what the family wanted to hear and what interested Emily. The letters evoke the recipient as well as the writer. As in her pen and ink sketching, for which she had a decided gift, her observation was both keen and loving.

Dear Marion, [age eleven]

I wish you could have been with us yesterday when we went to the Jardin de Plantes which means Plant Garden and which is chiefly a menagerie. We did not go into the houses but contented ourselves as we had not very much time, with the animals outdoors. America did nobly and we hailed a Californian sea-lion, buffaloes, grizzly bears as our fellow countrymen and gorgeous cockatoos from South America as neighbors. Perhaps the most interesting place was that devoted to all sorts of birds; the most beautiful pale gray ducks, little woodcocks, gulls, storks, ibises and the most beautiful rose-colored flamingoes. There were four of these and they always went through their exercises together—rise on toes, get out wings (a little hard as they were packed in very close underneath their outer feathers) extend wings, balance to partner, run flapping, fly. It was very funny. Their legs were as thin as a hairpin almost. It seemed as if they could hardly hold them up.

There was a nice little zebra freshly painted, and an Egyptian donkey who sang for a piece of gingerbread in the most remarkable voice I have ever heard, even in a donkey. . . .

Give my love to Pauline and to Martha and write soon again to your very loving sister Emily who would like so much to give you a good hug and kiss this very minute. Emily.

Some time before, the two girls, Lena and Emily, had arranged for a change in living quarters, a move that was to bring Emily an interesting acquaintance.

"We are going to board," she writes to her father, "in a French boarding school, rue de Vaugirard, back and west of the Luxembourg Gardens. I must describe it all to you it is so quaint and foreign and makes me think of Villette only I trust we shall find it without the disagreeable features of Miss Brontë's school. The great street door opens on a good-sized court round which runs the school buildings which are quite low, two or three storys. Behind is a garden, a really big one with grass and walks and rows of trees. On one side of this is a sort of arcade open and sheltered at the same time where the children were playing. They seemed to be having a fine time too only the noise always hushed at our approach to begin again a little louder when we had passed. There were a number of pleasant enough class rooms with scattered groups of girls studying or reading who usually stood up till we had gone. Upstairs were the dormitory, 18 little snowy white beds in one room, which was however light and airy, and single and double rooms. The two we have taken are single rooms. . . . Both open on the garden, giving northwest Lena says from consulting the map. It was charming. The meals are at 8, 12 and 6 with *gouter* if you want it beside.

"Though there are a great many foreign pupils, two American I think, we shall be at a table where there are only French people, so that I hope we shall go on pretty well with our French. I think Lena will be very happy if she can make friends with some of the children."

One of the American pupils proved to be little Dorothy Canfield, who as Dorothy Canfield Fisher was to be a novelist of charm and, through her books, an educator of wide influence in her native America. Emily describes a visit from the Canfields after they had left the school: "This morning Mrs. Canfield and little Dorothy and Dorothy's 'Brother Jim' came to see us. Did I tell you about Dorothy? She is twelve years old and always makes me think of Editha or Little Lord Fauntleroy, she is the same mixture of perfect childlikeness with the considerateness and sense of responsibility of a grown person. When her mother was sick this winter she took all care of their rooms except bringing up coal and things like that, and did all the cooking too, and on such a funny little stove over charcoal. She showed it to me with great pride and said wasn't it just like a baby-house? Then she put on the thinnest little cape and went out to get some little cakes for supper as long as we were there to sit with her mother. It was dreadfully pathetic; she said, 'Sometimes I wish I were lying down too,' and I should think she would have wished so. However her mother is well again now and her beloved brother a nice boy of sixteen has come over and joined them and they are going off on a trip up the Rhine. Lately since her housework is over Dorothy has been making dolls' clothes, and posing [her mother Flavia Canfield was an artist]."

To this chance meeting with Dorothy Canfield in Paris we owe an authentic and life-size portrait of Emily Balch in her youth, written years later by Dorothy Canfield (Fisher) when both were at the height of their fame:

"When I was a little girl, I was taken by my mother to France. She was an artist, and studied in one of the Paris ateliers. I don't know how we came to be taken, my mother too, into a girls' boarding school on the rue de Vaugirard.

"There were two other Americans there, grown-ups, two young women who were studying political economy. Of one of those pioneer Americans I have no recollection. They were really pioneers, for this was more than half a century ago, and as all readers of Henry James know, it was then an adventure for an American woman to go to France save to buy hats and dresses. The other one I have never forgotten, for then, and in the many years since, she has steadily had a great influence on my life.

"She was a tall, slim girl in her early twenties, comely with youth, with a magnificent smooth forehead, and gleaming young hair which she wore in classic simplicity, not tortured into the frizzes then fashionable. Her great eyes were clear, intelligent, calm, as few young eyes ever are. She dressed simply and unobtrusively.

"Now, the French are impassioned creators and followers of fashion. But they also have an instinctive respect for distinction of person, and Emily Balch (Mees Balshe as I always heard her called) had distinction if ever anybody did. The whole school was proud to have her there, from the fat, by-no-means distinguished, but very stylish Directrice, to the littlest girl—that would be me, for I was pint-sized then, as always. She was called 'The Intellectual,' with an accent of warm admiration. And once, a teacher, trying to explain the symbolism of Greek myths to a class of bored little girls, said to us finally, about Athena, 'She was like Mees Balshe, she was the Intellectual.' We understood perfectly.

"My mother was an artist in sensitive, highly strung temperament as well as in talent; and her nervous equilibrium was not very good at that time. Her fatigue showed itself in occasional night-panics, when she started from bed, whispering in terror that someone had shut her down into a ship and she could not get out. Or she would cry that she couldn't find Dolly. (I was Dolly.) I was rather a young child to handle such distressing black moments, but I was never really terrified, for I knew that I was not alone, that always, if things got beyond me, I could run down the corridor in my nightgown and get help from L'Intellectuelle, the good, the kind, the calm young intellectual.

"Some months later, my restless, unconventional mother left the school and took a tiny apartment (all that my father's professor's salary made possible). There Mees Balshe was no longer just down the hall. But she was in the same city. And the thought of her clear, quiet, attentive face gave me the same assurance in difficult moments. I could always at the worst, appeal to her. I never did, actually. She became then, rather than a person, the idea of intelligence and goodness; but an idea that was embodied in human form, palpable enough to cling to in spirit."[1]

At the end of the year, when Emily left Paris, she already realized that her knowledge was one of books only and as she wrote, "completely second hand and unreal. I came home determined to see something of things for myself. I had read much of l'ouvrier but had so to speak never known one to talk with. I put myself as a sort of apprentice to a very remarkable Boston social pioneer, Charles W. Birtwell who was helping Harvard under-graduates to acquaint themselves with what we would call social work, a field at that time entirely unorganized. Mr. Birtwell was the shaper of the Boston Childrens' Aid Society. I met regularly with a little group of Italian children in Boston's then notorious North End in a so-called Home Library. I learned the need of systematic verification, something of filing, recording and library technique. I became, for my sins, the guardian of a little Negro girl, as without morals, poor child, as a puppy in a kennel and less wholesome. I was fond of her and she, as she said, 'buttered me up' but in the end she had to be sent to the school for girls in Lancaster. This school was one of the things to which Miss Lizzie Putnam, one of that extraordinary group of Boston aristocracy of goodness and public spirit, gave herself without stint. It was con-ducted on original and informal and sensible lines.

"I compiled a careful little handbook of laws and institutions in the field of juvenile delinquency and juvenile needs.* Later on [in 1898] I was appointed by Mayor Josiah Quincy [of Boston] to the board of Trustees of an institution for pauper, neglected and criminal children. The old Marcella House was the only home of some hundreds of unfortunate children who had not so much as a separate claim to a single garment, nor, if I am not mistaken to an individual toothbrush. One kind teacher allowed some little girls to keep a doll on their desks. I learned something of the crude facts of *realpolitik*. Mayor Josiah Quincy fed the reformers with one hand and the ward politicians with the other.

"Under Mr. Birtwell's burning and intelligent zeal great changes were made during my single year of service and later. Pauper and neglected children were placed out in homes most carefully chosen and supervised. The correctional institution for truants then in a malarial spot on the Charles River, selected for reasons of graft, was made unnecessary by better methods in the public schools on the one hand and better reform schools on the other.

---

* 1895—Manual for Use in Cases of Juvenile Offenders and Other Minors in Mass. 1895 (revised 1903 and 1908), 72 pp.

"Much that now seems rudimentary was starting at that time and Boston was a leader in all this."

In the summer of 1892 Emily attended a rather portentously named Summer School of Applied Ethics at Plymouth, Massachusetts convened by Dr. Felix Adler, founder of the Ethical Culture Society. "It is a kind of a stimulus I have not had very much of," wrote Emily to her father, "and that I am sure is good—in moderation. Among my gains I count foremost Miss Addams, then perhaps Miss Coman who professes History and Political Economy at Wellesley." These two outstanding women were each destined to give a crucial new direction to Emily's life. Jane Addams, then a young woman of thirty-two, was already a famous figure, though Hull-House was only three years old. From her emanated an atmosphere of gentleness and power, an untranslatable, indefinable magnetic quality which could only be described by its effect upon others. Here also Emily met the ardent and enthusiastic Vida Scudder, a leading spirit of the new College Settlement movement, who later at Wellesley became a dear and intimate friend. Helena Dudley was there, and Julia Lathrop, Jane Addam's friend. Emily's mentor Franklin Giddings was one of the lecturers, and Robert A. Woods, who had just published his book *English Social Movements*, the first systematic treatment of English attempts to achieve social democracy by various humanitarian groups.

"The next winter [December, 1892] a little group of us," wrote Emily, "started Denison House in the South Cove district. We wanted as headworker my Bryn Mawr classmate, Helena Dudley, 'eine schöne seele' if ever there was one, but she was not to be free till the next year. To avoid delay, I accepted the position of Headworker. My friend and former schoolmate Helen Cheever made her cooperation conditional on my doing so. I continued, however to live at home, which was quite contrary to our whole theory and purpose."

Soon after Helena Dudley's arrival at Denison House, the panic of 1893 with its bitter unemployment engaged the constructive talents of the founders. There were then no methods of meeting such recurrent catastrophes. The welfare state was as yet undreamed of in America. The settlement, then, was not only the chief power house of social concern but the frankest agency for focusing the interest of the community on economic needs. Out of a firsthand knowledge of the sufferings of its friends and neighbors, therefore, Denison House induced Boston's mayor to open work rooms. Though relief work was not part of the work of a settlement, Helena Dudley with imagination and intelligence started sewing rooms where three hundred women were employed.

At last Emily had her chance to come in contact with l'ouvrier and his family outside the pages of books. Through her contacts at Denison House, Emily and the other residents, helpers, and visitors were brought into the labor movement and gained a unique acquaintance with the realities of the labor struggle.

In 1892, when trade unionism for men was still economic heresy, a very remarkable Boston woman, one of the founders of Denison House, Mary Morton Kehew, brought to Boston from Chicago a young union bookbinder, Mary Kenney, to help organize the women factory workers. In Chicago, through her activities in a very difficult strike, Mary Kenney had won the warm friendship of Jane Addams. And warm friendship and wholehearted cooperation this rich-natured, humorous, tempestuous, generous young organizer continued to win everywhere in Boston—where she married an equally ardent trade-union crusader, Jack O'Sullivan (John F. O'Sullivan). Jack O'Sullivan was working with the American Federation of Labor, then a new struggling successor to Powderly's Knights of Labor, "with a generous enthusiasm that was very contagious" wrote Emily. "He organized us into a federal labor union in which non-manual workers were allowed to join on equal terms with those who were manual laborers. We took with a rather troubled sense of adventure the obligation or pledge."

Emily's diary for March 3, 1894 records: "Joined Fed. Labor Union under Am. Fed. of Labor to which I promised loyalty. The pledge is a noble one though some clauses were hard to accept on the most obvious construction."

"Both the O'Sullivans," wrote Emily in her recollections, "understood trade unionism not as a struggle for material advantages for a limited class of people but in the same sense in which I understood my teaching at Wellesley College, as a part of a wide-spread and many-sided effort for juster and more humane social relations everywhere. There was a great deal of idealism in the trade union movement of the time as we saw it, and it has been one of the sad experiences of my life that it has done so relatively little for the weakest and most unskilled laborers."

Another item in her diary gives a sample of her interests: "April 11, 1893: Dined at Denison House. Miss Scudder and Mr. O'Sullivan and a labor reporter of the *Globe* to dinner. Talk mainly on Labor topics—unions, antagonism of capital and Labor (I arguing that the identity of interest is deeper and more permanent than the conflict), Homestead strike, Judge Rich's decision etc.

"By the end of my life if it is a long one shall I see this problem of the right relations of employed and society threshed out to any materially advanced point?"

The Denison House friends were especially interested in the shocking sweated conditions, in the underpaid girls engaged in tobacco stripping and other unskilled work, and in the telephone operators. Julia O'Connor, especially attracted them, a clever, public-spirited girl, with a career of usefulness ahead of her. Sunday afternoons Emily and Vida Scudder, Mary Kingsbury, and others attended meetings of the Central Labor Union at the Wells Memorial Institute, a center of intellectual stimulus and free discussion for working people. From their comfortable, often luxurious Boston homes, these young ladies Sunday after Sunday mounted the worn wooden steps that led to the forlorn hall with long wooden benches, where in a smoke-filled atmosphere, they listened to interminable discussions, sometimes keen and brilliant, and to devious wranglings on problems of internal adjustment. Emily was sent to one convention as a delegate of the Cigar Makers' Union.

Emily had early started out with the idea of "being of use." Her activities immediately after her return from Paris had brought her in contact with members of the Boston sociological group whose methods and personalities were to influence her down to the smallest details throughout her three subsequent careers of social work, college teaching, and working for peace.

The reforming activities of this group, which Emily called the "Boston aristocracy of goodness and public spirit," form one strand of American social history. The society by the Charles River presented in essence the social problems created after the Civil War by urban and industrial changes: poverty, slums, sweatshops, disease, crime, prejudice and fear in the face of the new immigrants, strikes, concentrated wealth, corrupt politics, and laissez-faire combined with doctrinaire charity. The "social reformers" then, as always, were the subject of much raillery and caricature. But courage was not the least of their attributes. Emily's close associates from 1891 till she went to study in Germany in 1895, were people of unusual sensitivity and compassions, intelligent and disinterested who, by their social standing, impeccable ancestry, group traditions, and education were able to lead the way.

Of these, foremost in her influence on Emily and a lifelong inspiration was Mary Morton Kehew, whom even at the end of her long career Emily still called "the greatest social stateman I have ever known." Others vivid in her memory were Miss Lizzie Putnam and her brothers Dr. Charles and Dr. James Putnam; Rose and Horace Lamb; Joseph Lee, the "father of playgrounds," who was among the first to see recreation as a social and educational influence and as a preventive of crime; Judge Frederick Cabot, founder of the Juvenile Court, who recognized the absurdity of dealing with boy and girl delinquents by the same methods that were applied to older offenders; Dr. Richard Cabot, who originated medical social work in hospitals, by following up patients in homes where social and economic disadvantages undid the good effects of hospital treatment, and who, in 1905, appointed the first medical social service worker. Not all proper Bostonians, however, were reformers. Some, overcome by what they felt to be the sterility of New England culture, succumbed to despair, pessimism, and withdrawal—notably Henry Adams.

Emily's own family connections furnished impetus and inspiration. Her cousin Anne Withington was one of the group. Her mother's cousin, Mrs. Mary Hemenway (1820-1894), was one of the outstanding women in the Boston of her time. She combined wealth (she married Augustus Hemenway of ample fortune) with the right ancestry so highly prized in Boston.

More than sixty years later, Emily Balch was to talk of Mary Morton Kehew and this circle of innovators from whom she learned so much, with great personal humility. "It was an honor to be associated with them," she said. Though their ideas and reforms spread from Massachusetts throughout the whole country and the world, they worked without thought of future reward and were content to serve faithfully their day and generation.

Why Emily Balch turned from her engrossing experiences in social work to college teaching is best explained in her own words: "I gradually became dissatisfied with my philanthropic efforts and decided that the point of leverage was in teaching social-economic subjects. My first contact with a scholar as a contemporary was with Miss Lucy M. Salmon who was a graduate fellow at Bryn Mawr while I was a freshman. She had said to me that since I was not under immediate economic pressure I ought to hold off from teaching as this was the only door open to many women who must support themselves at once. A woman in my place ought to find new channels unless indeed she had a real vocation to teach.

"I had accepted her advice but gradually came to the conclusion that if I could awaken the desire of women students to work for social betterment and could help them to find the best methods worked out at that time, my efforts however feeble would at least mean getting hold of the long arm of the lever. The time I had put in active social work was of enormous value to me and colored and widened my teaching and gave it most of what value it may have had."

Emily Balch began by forming private classes at the Settlement in what was then called "charities and correction." "The effort to systematize the scattered material and my scattered experience was very valuable to me, and I wonder if I were not in fact the first to create a course of study in this field [social work]. The collection of books and reports accumulated on my bedroom shelves at home led one of my sisters to horrify an unsuspecting friend who wanted to rest there, by exclaiming, 'Oh no, Emily's room is too full of child murder and drunkenness!'"*

If Emily Balch was to teach she had to equip herself with further study. She spent a semester at the Harvard Annex, today called Radcliffe College, and came under the stimulating influence of Professor William J. Ashley. She also studied economic theory for a quarter at the University of Chicago, as well as "the excessively inchoate subject of sociology as conceived by Professor Albion Small. I was (and have always been) a disciple of the

---

* Helen Cheever recounted one family's reaction to their young daughter's social work by their remark, "If you bring home a bedbug, I'd rather have a tiger."

Austrian school with its theory of marginal value. I now attempted to write a theory of distribution on this basis but gave it up as beyond my powers putting the unfinished manuscript away in a folder labelled *The Great Eastern* after the steamship that proved too big to be practicable and was never launched.

"My father whose generosity to me was without bound or limit was willing to have me go for a year's study in Berlin. I told him I would not be away over a year. The thing that was much of a sacrifice for him was to have me or any of his children out of the home. Was I wrong or right in refusing to live in Denison House when I was 'head-worker,' to take more than a year's continuous study in Berlin? I do not regret it."

Emily was now twenty-eight years old. She had arrived at a certain maturity, with a friendly outward poise that gave no hint of inner questionings and doubtings. That her self-discipline was a grace not easily acquired, her diary entry for December 31, 1894, not long before going to Germany, reveals: "I have read through today the whole of this diary covering over five years. This ought to mean a good deal done and growth made. What more critical years than the five after leaving college? Aspirations and failure make the record. If only I can keep the one to at least the same level and diminish the others recorded and not recorded, conscious and unconscious.

"In these years I have had a homestudy year, a wanderjahr with a piece of 'prentice work to show which took two years more to finish, two years of work in the world, one year of study and teaching. Now my path seems pretty well made out in so far as that it lies in the domain of study and teaching in the department of social science. All the questions of unfairly large consumption of the world wealth, of dependence and of compromise still puzzle me."

And she resolves to try:

To be self-respecting and

To control my temper and be actively spontaneously pleasant and cheerful

To be honest

To be discreet

To be more thoughtful

To grow, by God's grace, in the power of living a spiritual life
To be more tenderly and efficiently sympathetic.

Her interest in the personal self is beginning to recede and her interest in the world of men and affairs to increase: "May the New Year help me advance to meet these needs. May the world of men make progress, more right living and good thinking be done in this New Year. May men better understand the conditions of their being. May the new time bring to us the leaders and teachers we need and give us open eyes and hearts to know them."

She was now ready for her plunge into German culture.

"I have been in Berlin a week now and like it very much," she wrote Cousin Agnes, who knew Germany and had lived in Dresden. "The adjective that suits it best is *handsome* I think, not quite beautiful, but everything fine, well planned and fitting if a little heavy."

In Berlin Emily cemented what was to be a life-long friendship with the beautiful golden-haired Mary Kingsbury of Massachusetts, (later Mrs. Vladimir Simkhovitch). "Miss Kingsbury," she wrote home, "is a woman of my own age whom I have known slightly for some time. Last winter she distinguished herself as a graduate student with Professor Ashley and now she is here on a European fellowship of the Women's Educational and Industrial Union.* As her mother is with her I have counted on them quite a little. She is more interesting than I remember and it is great fun to have some one to discuss one's pet ideas with. She is one of those people who look so well and capable that it seems as if you must catch something of both."

In the mornings Emily and Mary would sit in the Tiergarten and read Kant together and talk. "The Tiergarten is heavenly now," wrote Emily in the spring, "though I have not succeeded in hearing any of the nightingales said to inhabit it." Both Emily and Mary were too Yankee ever to wax sentimental about their German sojourn, as so many American students did. But now that the old Tiergarten has been bombed out of existence, it is pleasant to recall these two young daughters of the Puritans, one a descendant of John Balch, the other a descendant of his friend Roger Conant,

* Founded by Mary Morton Kehew.

sitting together reading Kant, "tiring the sun with talking," and to know that the "nightingale voices" of their friendship were to live on beyond their different attitudes to two world wars.

Mary was musical and with her the unmusical Emily often went to the opera. "Dear Papa," wrote Emily early in her stay, "the event of the week was 'The Walküre' Friday evening which in spite of not enjoying the music as anyone else would I did enjoy very much. But what a performance, seven till nearly half past eleven with very short intermissions. In one of them who should turn up but Mrs. Russell (Alys Pearsall Smith now the Hon. Mrs. Bertrand Russell). I was greatly pleased to see her and am going Tuesday to afternoon tea with them."

Toward the end of her German year Emily records a musical advance: "Last night I went to the opera with Mary and Mr. Estabrook and and heard Siegfried. I believe I have a budding germinating though infinitesimal love of music in me. Certainly I have enjoyed more and disliked less of each of the operas I have heard. The Siegfried last night almost equalled the younger Salvini in his impression of 'lebenslustig' youth and strength and daring. There is a great deal of poetry apart from the music to me in these primitive epic dramas. It does not begin to come up to the prose translation of the Volsungen Saga but it is there."

But her contacts were for the most part not with Americans, but with the German and the foreign students at the University of Berlin, especially the numerous young Russians, "so busy with the future." For the first time Emily came in close contact with the philosophy of socialism that was kindling the enthusiasm of young students all over Europe and flooding the minds of working men and women with the assurance of a better world. Only a few years before at the Zürich University, Emily's future friend and coworker, Florence Kelley from the Quaker City of Philadelphia, after her first attendance at a Socialist meeting had exclaimed, "And here was I, in the World of the Future." [2] Emily with Yankee restraint did not allow herself to be carried away, but she was to be deeply influenced.

"Among the Russians in the student body," wrote Emily many years later, "was Vladimir Simkhovitch, later the brilliant professor of economic history at Columbia. He with various others was captivated by Mary Kingsbury. After her return to America, Dr.

Simkhovitch joined her and they were married in America in 1899. She gave herself to settlement work and Greenwich House, her creation, has given almost unequaled service to New York City."

"My year at Berlin (1895-1896)," says Emily in her recollections, "was happier and far more fruitful than my earlier year in Paris. On the advice of John Graham Brooks who was a greater influence then, whose seminal mind had richer results than his writings perhaps suggest, I went first for six weeks to Hildesheim to his friend Dr. Wilhelm Bode to brush up my German and for background. I went to Berlin when the University opened. As it was not regularly open to women students I got permission from the Reich Cultus Minister, the Rector of the University, and separately from each professor with whom I was to study. My friend, Mary Kingsbury and I were curiosities, she the more so because she was so beautiful, to my eye the most beautiful woman I have ever seen. To her beauty was added the charm of her delicious warm voice, her intellectual vigor and originality and her character. We were admitted to the seminars of Adolf Wagner and Gustav Schmoller. Though not over-friendly to one another, they were both what was then called *Katedersocialisten* (socialists of the chair or professorial socialists); that is, they believed in extension of national control of economic processes for social and political ends. I was thrilled by the thought that Fichte lectured in these halls while Napoleon's invading troops beat their drums in the square outside. In re-reading his *Addresses to the German Nation* and his *Closed Commercial State,* I am today startled to see how much of what is basic in Nazi policies existed in principle in the philosopher and in our own teachers.

"As my professors spoke of the State Government as if it were an independent entity, I remembering my American principles would remind myself that it is after all only an instrument to do for the public what the people will. It was only gradually that I began to understand how far this was from being the case in Germany, where the body of expert civil servants constituted mainly the state and were an almost independent more or less self-perpetuating body."

Her letters show that Emily found herself able to participate in student life and to mingle with her professors and their contemporaries more freely and easily than in Paris. Like most Americans in Germany, she was charmed by the friendly warmth and "gemütlichkeit" of the people and repelled by the supreme self-confidence and arrogance of the military officer class. In November, 1895, she wrote. "I am afraid your hair would have stood on end if you had seen Miss Kingsbury and me Wednesday night at that 'Verein.' There is a 'socialwissenschaftlicher' association among the students and we were invited very politely to the first meeting. We, with various other ladies, sat in the gallery of a big hall while on the floor the students sat at tables and drank beer and listened to a speech. At the second meeting at which Professor Jastrow was to speak on the unemployed, a paper I really cared about hearing, we found to our dismay a room full of smoke, beer and students, no gallery, just a plain room. One of the Americans with us went ahead and reported there was a lady there so we went in. We were given seats at the head table opposite the speaker and smoking was stopped, which latter thing Miss Kingsbury and I were sorry for; still it was put on the ground of consideration for the speakers as well as for the ladies. There were three women there besides ourselves and we felt well repaid for going as it was a thoroughly interesting evening. The next time we went we were the only women and the discussion, largely monopolized by the most entertaining and attractive Russian boy, a Socialist, lasted till long after midnight. Smoking was stopped during the speech. We are taken in in this way because we are members of the Seminar. Most of the men at this meeting were fellow students there. It is a real privilege to be able to see the German student thus in his native haunt and one I never dreamed we could have. We could not be taken more simply nor courteously. The paper this time was not very good, though the man was supposed to be a great light and had studied the agricultural conditions in Australia, and all about, on the spot. But when it comes to averaging prices of grain in three year periods over some sixty years and then deducing a natural law from the uniformity that then appears and prophecying from it, it seems as if something were wrong. . . . I would not retail the story of the student gatherings too widely as people would not understand e.g. not at Lakeville Place."

Two German women deeply impressed her. Frau Gnauck, "out and away the most interesting as well as the most attractive

German woman I have ever seen, interested in women's education
and activities and in the social questions," and the equally attractive Fraulein von Dyhrenfurth, who had just published an article
on "Working Women in England" in Schmoller's *Jahrbuch*, probably the first woman to print a paper for a German orthodox
scientific-economic quarterly. Emily also admired a Polish fellow-
student Frau Daszynska, later a labor leader in Poland. "February
16, 1896. Dearest Papa, what do you think we did today? Gave a
tea! At the Kingsbury's! Sent Mrs. Kingsbury's card and mine,
asked something under twenty people. I had Ethel Parrish, Miss
Puffer, a nice American girl student and Frau Daszynska, my
Polish friend—then Mr. Slade, Dr. Breckenridge and Mr. Estabrook, three nice American students, Herr Heckscher and Herr von
Pritsbur (Herr Heckscher has studied in London, been at Toynbee
Hall, wants to start a settlement in Berlin, met him at Mrs. Russells,
Herr von Pritsbur is in Schmoller's Seminar), last but not least a
little Russian whom we see a good deal of, Vladimir Simkhovitch,
clever, high strung, fearfully enthusiastic, really a boy and yet in
some ways a man. There is something so attractive about him and
at the same time very pathetic.

"I was afraid it might be a mixed mess, but people seemed to
find one another highly congenial and I must say there was not a
person who was not truly interesting and most were clever; and it
went off capitally. . . .

"I keep putting off telling you about my work. I have begun,
under Schmoller's advice, a study of "Arbeitsnachweis," i.e., labor
intelligence, registration, employment agencies or what you call it.
Many towns here have lately made it a municipal function. With
better understanding of their language and of [their] standpoint as
well as continued relations, our judgment of the men here has
changed considerably. We now think Schmoller a very exceptional
scholar. He is a good teacher too and very interesting. Simmel is
immensely clever. Paulsen does not improve on acquaintance—he
can be shallow to an undreamed of extent. I dare say he is better
in other courses. Wagner I don't feel yet that I can judge. He is
very tiresome at times and given to truisms but one likes the *man*.
I have heard him only in elementary or popular lectures."

As in Paris, Emily was laying concrete foundations for her
knowledge of European conditions and international politics. "I

don't know when politics has seemed to me so interesting as now—here, in England and at home and above all internationally," she wrote home in February, 1896. "German foreign policy seems to me to lack all the moral element that makes America's and England's (in spite of her grabbing propensity) interesting. The unripe and indifferent cosmopolitanism of Goethe's day has developed, through the Napoleonic oppression, the excitement and enthusiasm of the war of Liberation, and the intoxication of the success of '70-'71, into an enthusiasm for the German nationality which has its bad as well as its good side to put it mildly. Polarization has taken place. The socialists after working with the liberals for constitutional and political reforms were left out in the cold after the success of the joint efforts and this strengthening and embittering the theoretical and generous cosmopolitanism of socialist idealism has given the social-democratic party an antinational color. This and the 'national' idea now antagonize, react on and deepen one another all the time. Meanwhile the socialists devote themselves body and soul (though they deny the latter) to a cause which most of them know can better their grandchildren at best, and bear with wonderfully little bitterness on the whole a great deal of small persecution and taunting, while the nominally religious government and governing classes simply mean to put the (Prussian) empire through to the utmost possible point, to bully and shoulder thought till they stand at the head by virtue of *force, force, force* and they hate England because she is the other big boy and has what they want. They jeer at the idea of other than selfish aims in national policies. Their unshakable belief in English hypocrisy seems to rest on the inability to conceive of seriously wishing for anything unconnected with national aggrandizement. The same thing is true or would be if any conflict of interests arose, as far as America is concerned. It is pitiful—this national misunderstanding and seems less excusable here than in France. I wish the newspapers ever got anything to give the Anglo-Saxon point of view. But perhaps it is unassimilable."

A great experience for Emily was hearing Wilhelm Liebknecht the elder address a general mass meeting. "This form of meeting," she wrote, "was a device for getting around the law forbidding apprentices or women to attend meetings of a political organization. Police sat at a table on the platform with their spiked helmets in their hands. If their helmets were put on the meeting was thereby closed. Liebknecht was then an old man of seventy, had just been sentenced to four months imprisonment for *lèse majesté*, on the principle of 'dolus eventualis,' that is, provisional crime. The judge agreed that the incriminating speech contained nothing derogatory to Majesty, but held he must have known that it would be understood by his hearers in a derogatory sense, this constituting 'dolus eventualis.' There were no chairs and I with the rest of the orderly crowd stood for two hours completely held by the speaker. I admired the skill with which Liebknecht raised a growing enthusiasm and yet succeeded in leaving no opportunity for applause to break out until the meeting was dismissed."

There were plenty of American friends to turn to at holiday times when she needed "homefolk." She had an American Thanksgiving dinner of turkey, cranberries, and mince pie with Robert Woods and his wife and two babies in Charlottenburg. At the Woods' she and Mary Kingsbury were asked to meet a Mr. Willard, who as Josiah Flynt had written articles on tramps and tramp life which he had studied from the inside. This method of field investigation, very novel at the time, appealed to Emily and influenced her future teaching. "He was very small, and boyish, though with a look of having seen a good many sides of life, and was much interested in asking about America. I noticed that the people you want to pump always want to pump you."

At Christmas time she joined Helen Cheever, Helen's two sisters, and a gay party of young people at Dresden. Together they went to art galleries, Christmas shows, bazaars, droshky drives, skating parties, and the theatre. "This is such a different Christmas from last year when I felt so oppressed. [Emily had spent the preceding Christmas at Louisville, Kentucky, with Bessie who, though still suffering from the effects of a bad "nervous breakdown," was teaching there]. This is a belated place to thank you for your pretty Christmas card, the little note with the present of fifty dollars. It seems almost absurd to thank you for anything in particular when I have to thank you for everything. Nevertheless thank you, pretty Sir."

In February and May, Helen Cheever visited Emily at Berlin. In the spring Emily took another holiday—to Munich, Nuremberg, Bamberg, Ratisbon, Freiburg, Augsburg, Ulm, Stuttgart, Cologne, and Weimar. In the freedom of her holiday, Emily's home thoughts from abroad turned to Bessie, who was still far from well. The tie between the sisters was strong.

Köln, April 6, 1896

Dearest Papa, I am rather troubled at what you say about Bessie. . . . I do not think we have any right, really, to expect Bessie to be all right again soon. She got a bad strain metaphorically speaking and recovery is always slow. I know Ida Woods who overworked and had a time of nervous exhaustion told me her doctor allowed five times (I think it was) as long for the going uphill as the going down had taken! We trust Bessie will do better than that and I do not doubt she will, for one thing because she has never let go the reins and been simply the nervous invalid.

I am glad Annie is planning such a pleasant round of visits. Dear Papa, are you lonely with one naughty girl on the continent of Europe and one sick and away from home and one visiting and all depending on you for love and care of every sort and counting on you as they count on the eternal laws, taking all your love and care for granted? Emily.

A letter to Annie in June, 1896, contains a rare criticism of her father. The family sometimes suffered from the defects of Francis Balch's virtues.

Dear Nanny:

I long to hear about Class day. Did Cisco [Francis] get his many theses through all right? Did Alice and Maidie have a good time? . . . I think a good deal about Bessie. Papa says he does not know if she is improving under the massage treatment. . . . Dear child, I hope she will be out of the woods soon. I had a long letter the other day from Mrs. Herschel who seems to be very happy in feeling that she has learned to deal more wisely with this curious problem of personal health of which we must think and mustn't think, and to feel that she could make Bessie a present of her experience and convictions. I don't feel so sure, we have to learn for ourselves and we don't even all learn the same thing. Oh dear if Mama had lived I think we should all have been so much better and it would have been easier to decide. The mixed influence of parental authority, a curious power of making one see his point of view with its distortion through his unselfness almost antiself-ishness, his sometimes sophistical reasoning, one's own inclinations and easy goingness and puzzle-headedness make it hard for Cisco and Bessie and me to find our path—it does not seem to affect you in just the same way. I think Mama would have helped us to judge sanely for ourselves and others.—All this is not apropos of any definite point so much as in general. Kindly read neither to Papa nor Auntie.

I had a letter from Aunt Emily [of Lakeville Place] a while ago about home affairs and myself—I am inclined to think advice from outside the immediate family circle in regard to relations within it is not likely to be very valuable. But how much better we can *talk* about all such things—. Have you missed me? and in what way? . . . I am afraid this is a very horrid letter but it carries lots of love to "our eldest." What should we all do and have done all these years without you? Goodnight dear, Emily.

In Berlin, as in Paris, Emily as a woman student was constantly up against questions of propriety, etiquette, behavior. "We settle them," wrote Emily to her father, "mostly in favor of freedom and doing the pleasant and profitable thing and I trust do the right way. I should be awfully sorry to do anything to make women *personae ingratae* in the University now they are just being let in. The world does move and Wagner as Rector moves his little world in this direction. He was quite funny when he talked with us the other day. Some people thought there was more 'Bedenken' (hesitation, scruple, objection) to admitting women to the seminar than to the lectures. He thought there was less, 'though' (he hastily added waving his hands) 'there is in my opinion no Bedenken in either case.' He also abruptly remarked that he supposed Mill was our God, and that sociology was a favorite subject with Americans—a gratuitous insult as *we* had said nothing about sociology."*

Emily's father, in writing to her about her plans for the future and the possibility of her entering the law firm with him mentioned the approximate annual sum that might come to her on his death.** She was clear-sighted enough to realize that in the field she had chosen she might some day be in need of a material basis for

---

* Mary Kingsbury (Simkhovitch) in her autobiography *Neighborhood* also relates that Wagner was particularly caustic in regard to the "so-called science of sociology." In his seminar he half sprang from his chair and said, "Ja, die Sociologie! Was heisst, aber, die Sociologie? Das heisst, meine Freunde, die Amerkanische Wissenschaft!"

** The sum Mr. Balch mentioned was slightly over $500 a year.

independence in thinking. "I do not want to live on your earnings all my life," she wrote to him, "and hope I shall not but at the same time I feel that it is very possible that I may be in positions where the being not wholly dependent on my situation may be most welcome and make frankness and independence of expression easier. Look for instance at Professor Bemis with wife and children and no special ability, losing his position at Chicago because (I have reasons beside newspaper talk to believe) his views as to labor organization displeased the rich men who have given and give so freely to the University. In Mathematics no such contingencies are probable but it seems to me in these very debatable matters they are more than likely if one is trying to make one's living by writing or teaching, and that therefore a sum, not enough to live on but enough to give one time to turn round, to wait a while for the right place to open, is a thing to be very thankful for."

After the close of the second semester at the University of Berlin, Emily Balch and Mary Kingsbury went home by way of London, where in July, 1896, they attended the International Socialist Workers' and Trade Union Congress for which they both had obtained press tickets. This proved to be the last of the great International Socialist and Labor Congresses, and the two young American students had a chance to see in action some of the famous labor and Socialist leaders of the time, including some of the last generation of original Marxists.

The attendance (800 delegates in all) was very mixed and the opening sessions stormy on account of the decision to exclude the Anarchist element. The meeting was kept in a semblance of order by the vigorous ringing of a huge hand bell. It was fortunate that "Lakeville Place" did not see the two well-bred Boston girls taking in the sessions, which Emily wrote up for a little settlement house review. They missed nothing of the excited speaking, the interruptions from floor and gallery, made worse by widespread shouting for order, and one piece of actual violence when a French interpreter pushed a man off the platform, throwing him over and down the platform steps. The chairman could not restore quiet and declared the meeting adjourned.

In 1896 the proceedings had a still unfamiliar ring. Emily followed keenly the debates advocating political action "apart from all bourgeois political parties," the recommendations for forwarding the socialization of great corporations as well as mines, railways, great iron and chemical works; the condemnation of war; the protests against secret treaties; the resolutions in favor of liberty of speech, press and meetings; of amnesty for political prisoners; of free employment bureaus. It was a surprise to Emily to discover that they were so largely concerned with achieving democratic rights which for her seemed a matter of course, that they were striving, in fact, more for democracy than for Socialism.

"But after all," wrote Emily, "in such a gathering, the human interest is greater than the theoretical. A meeting of the early Abolitionists may have given evidence of as much enthusiasm for humanity, the indignation against injustice, the self-devotion, that made this meeting, with all its faults, so moving, but it could hardly be so rich in contrasts and variety of types. . . .

"It was curious to see how many heads suggested, more or less, types which have been chosen by painters in their attempts to portray Christ, and this, not only in the general character of the head, but in the expression which was marked by the simplicity due to a concern with large and ideal issues rather than with details of actions, and by a look that showed an abiding consciousness of the suffering in the world." [3]

Head and shoulders above the well-drilled battalion of Germans, stood out Liebknecht, Bebel, and Singer. The first, whom Emily had admired so much at the Berlin mass meeting, again displayed, as she noted, "his marked sympathetic quality and power of winning respect. When Monday's tumult was at its height he alone commanded an instant lull and attention to what he had to say. Doubtless the effect of his personality was enhanced by the fact that he was to go back from the Congress to serve a sentence of four months for lèse majesté." [4] Among the French group was Jaurès. Emily met Lafargue, the son-in-law of Marx, a Cuban by birth, "a charming old gentleman, courteous, earnest and humorous." Ferri, the well-known writer on criminology from Italy, was there, and for the first time at such a Congress a Russian delegate elected by Russian workingmen in Russia.

The British made up about one half of the delegates. Emily saw and heard Kier Hardie and Tom Mann of the Independent Labor Party; the Fabians Sidney Webb and Bernard Shaw, "with his inexhaustible flashing cleverness"; Mrs. Aveling, the youngest daughter of Marx, and Mrs. Sparling, the daughter of William Morris, "looking like an incarnation of Pre-Raphaelitism," and others bearing the "influence of Ruskin and of more modern aesthetes, seen in the colors and unconventional and very attractive dress of some of the 'bourgeois' contingents." [5]

The week's congress, Emily wrote to her father, had been preceded by a procession to Hyde Park and a demonstration in favor of peace. Today over sixty-five years later, it is ironical to note that peace was to be brought about through the "abolition of the capitalist and landlord system of society in which wars have their root," [6] and, as a further measure, through an internationally established eight-hour day and universal suffrage. Speakers of different nationalities were to speak from each of twelve platforms. "Unfortunately just at that time the heavens opened and it poured torrents. It was a striking sight to see Tom Mann, the leader of the Dockers in their struggle of '89, speaking bareheaded in the pelting downpour, and his listeners with their drenched banners sticking it out and laughing at his courageously good humored jokes on the circumstances. Lafargue followed with a few words, his grey head uncovered also. The crowd took off their hats, passed the resolution with hearty cheers, then broke and ran for shelter, with the thunder crashing overhead." [7]

Between the absorbing sessions of the Congress, Emily observed the English, particularly in the London scene. She wrote to her father: "I am so struck with the peculiarities and characteristics of the English as I see them now after this long immersion in Teutonism that it is hard for me to generalize or analyze. Could any two men be more unlike than the trim officialized uniformed conductor of a Berlin omnibus and the intensely individualized drawling Londoner who takes your fares and helps you on and off a bus answering your questions with something between friendliness and impudence. . . . Even the police and soldiers look so individual and unofficial that it strikes me as almost indecorous. . . .

"It seems as if the English tend to be divided so very sharply into respectables and non-respectables, the former so smug and self-satisfied, the world so neatly fitted to their pocket plan of it, the others so disgustingly degraded."

Like the young literary Willa Cather who in 1902, at the age of twenty-nine, was to see London's East End for the first time, Emily was revolted by the sordid, dirty, gin-soaked, rasping-voiced London workers she saw there. For her it was not the major shock it was to be for Willa Cather, still fresh from her memories of Nebraska. As a girl in 1885 Emily had seen degraded poverty, and drinking, brawling women, and children paddling in open sewers in Glasgow. In her native Boston she had seen equally cruel, though less indecent sweatshop poverty. Her letter to her father continued: "I passed three girls—I cannot tell—for I am not quick to read such things—if they were prostitutes or working girls showing their finery, but their clothes were loud enough to drown the noise of a steam whistle. Two had intense unmitigated blue gowns; one had three bright purple ostrich feathers in a flaring openwork hat, the other had a bright purple dress and blue feathers in her hat. Nothing but London *can* produce this type.

"Then I see the extreme type of London poverty and degradation, the man sitting on a sidewalk with feet tied up in stained bandages of different sorts worn through and through, ragged, dirty, low in every sense, the drinking bloated women sitting about in groups on benches, the servile cringing boys and impudent boys that sell papers and flowers. It is pretty sickening."

Her last glimpse of England showed the reverse side of the coin, "the stately homes of England." She and Mary had dined at Toynbee Hall and had been invited to join an excursion to Norwich and vicinity. "We drove to see a Jacobean mansion, one of the finest in England, the first big beautiful English place I ever saw. We were shown about by Lady Lothian, the owner, with great courtesy and saw everything—really a very beautiful house—and the most fascinating garden—the kind Bacon dreamed of and that Beatrice and Benedick quarreled and courted in."

Emily returned home hoping to complete the requirements for a Doctor of Philosophy and her thesis at the Massachusetts Institute of Technology. This proved to be out of the question as chemistry was required for a doctorate at the Institute, and Emily had never studied chemistry.

"I returned home from Germany on the same ship with Miss Katharine Coman, then teaching economics single-handedly at Wellesley College. She offered me an opportunity to teach there— a half time position to be devoted mainly to reading student papers, though by the second semester I was teaching a class.

"I saw that after being supported by my father till nearly thirty it was time that I ceased to be an expense to him. The fact that I could live at home as so much desired by my father was one great advantage of the Wellesley offer but in any case it was a Godsend when opportunities for a woman to teach economics were rare indeed. As can be seen, my preparation was very scrappy and my teaching doubtless suffered from this. Nevertheless it was my happy profession for more than twenty years till in 1918 my teaching came to a sudden end."

CHAPTER FOUR

Social Pioneering in the Wellesley Years

In 1906, after a short visit to the United States, H. G. Wells wrote an entertaining book called *The Future in America*. In the chapter "Culture" he describes the intellectual and spiritual Boston he encountered, and a visit to Wellesley College, "that most delightful, that incredible girls' university" set in its broad park with a club house among glades and trees, with its "girl students who were fitting themselves for their share in the great American problem by the study of Greek."

His contention was that culture, as conceived in Boston, made no contribution to the future of America. Over Boston there brooded "an immense effect of finality." Boston tried to remember too much, to treasure too much, and had refined and studied herself into a state of hopeless intellectual and aesthetic repletion. A meeting of bibliophiles gave him the horrible conviction "that the mind of the world was dead and that this was a distribution of souvenirs." To shake off this unfortunate impression he wandered disconsolately about Boston till about midnight he came to a publisher's window full of copies of Izaak Walton and Omar Khayyam, of happy immortals who got in before Boston had locked her gates. There, he discovered a thin small book. He could scarcely

102

believe his eyes. It was *A Modern Symposium* by Goldsworthy
Lowes Dickinson, " a leaf of olive from the world of thought."

Wells then visited Wellesley College, which the Bostonians
assured him would remind him of Tennyson's *Princess*. "I cannot,
for the life of me," wrote Wells, "determine how far Wellesley is
an aspect of what I have called Boston; how far it is a part of that
wide forward movement of the universities upon which I lavish
hope and blessing." In a state of "mighty doubting" he examined
the *Wellesley College Calendar* [catalogue], reading with misgivings the list of courses on Italian art, seventeenth-century French
drama, etc. "On the other hand, there are courses upon socialism
[Emily Balch's course], though the textbook is still *Das Kapital*
of Marx—and upon the industrial history of England and America
[taught by Katharine Coman]. How far, I wonder still, are these
girls thinking and feeding mentally for themselves? What do they
discuss with one another? How far do they suffer under that blight
of feminine education—note taking from lectures?"

Would H. G. Wells' "mighty doubting" have veered towards
"hope and blessing" had he been able to sample the quality of the
pabulum Wellesley College was offering the girl students at about
that time? An Indiana undergraduate of the class of 1910, writing
years later of her college memories, said that two words supplied
the *leitmotifs* of her four college years: the first was aesthetic (the
nightmare of H. G. Wells); the second was altruism. "This brought
me under the influence of a great personality, Professor Emily
Greene Balch. Miss Balch was an utterly unpretentious woman,
spare of figure, unmindful of clothes and fripperies. Beside her
learning, which was broad and deep, she had a very wide personal
acquaintance with civic and humanitarian leaders in Europe as
well as in America, . . . and her teaching was all the better for her
excursions into the buzzing centers beyond the placid college
walls." [1]

Through the influence of Professor Balch, the girl, as a sopho-
more, tore herself from the fudge-chocolate parties of the dormitory, from deep sessions in a Morris chair reading Ruskin, Matthew
Arnold, Cardinal Newman, and above all Walter Pater, to give an
afternoon and evening each week to Denison House in Boston to
help in clerical work on case records (a comparatively new procedure), and to assist in teaching Syrian and Italian children.

When the train brought her back to Wellesley in the evening, the wintry walk through the snow-shrouded campus to the cheery college lights provided a striking contrast to the slums from which she had just come, and the struggling masses of an industrial city. "It gave me furiously to think," she wrote, borrowing an expression Professor Balch often used.*

Three decades later, in the year 1940, the Wellesley Department of Economics and Sociology issued a retrospective survey of its work. In the terse unembroidered manner of a report, it listed the innovations in subject matter and method in the earlier days of the department from 1897, when Emily Balch first became a member: "The special interests of Katharine Coman, head of the department till 1913 when she was succeeded by Emily Balch, made the department a pioneer in the field of economic history. The department always emphasized aspects of economic life in which social factors were involved. Wellesley must have been among the first colleges to offer work in socialism and labor problems [both taught by Emily Balch]. Miss Emily Balch inaugurated work in social pathology, a study of the defective, dependent, and delinquent classes, accompanied by discussions of methods of dealing with each, and was a pioneer student of normal modes of providing for community needs, sanitation, housing, household economy, education, recreation and thrift. A great deal of attention seems to have been given to field work in the early days of the department. We hear of Miss Balch's students in 1901-1902 mapping the North End of Boston. Immigration (1906) was another of Miss Balch's pioneering studies. The special course in Consumption established by her in 1908 must have been one of the first in its field."

There were some other things about Wellesley College that H. G. Wells could not learn in so fleeting a visit. One was that the Wellesley faculty boasted a notable group of women far ahead of their time whom he would have admired because they were alive to what he called "the tragic greatness of the unheeded issues" that cried for solution.

Professor Katharine Coman, head of Emily's department and a close friend of Emily's, grew up on an Ohio farm. She brought a Midwestern vigor and tang into her teaching of economic history.

* Ruth Sapin Hurwitz, "Coming of Age at Wellesley," *The Menorah Journal,* Autumn, 1950, Vol. XXXVIII, No. 2, pp. 226 ff.

Like Emily Balch, she was a pioneer in the college settlement movement, in the Consumers' League, and in identifying herself as friend (and interpreter to the public) of women in industry, especially in the garment trades. Emily Balch had met her at Felix Adler's Plymouth Conference of 1892 and had come to know her more closely in connection with Denison House during the terrible time of starvation which the settlement house neighbors lived through in 1893. Katharine Coman and her wealthy friend Cornelia Warren of Waltham established a cooperative sewing shop to provide work for unemployed "tailoresses." Katharine Coman, the college professor, and Kate Comiskey, the Irish-American Boston "tailoress" from whom the former learned, met on equal and common ground.

"As the time I worked with Katharine Coman as a younger colleague gradually recedes," wrote Emily Balch, "from 1896 till her death in 1915, her figure shines out more impressive and more important even than I realized. It was a very great privilege to make one of the household of Katharine Coman and Katharine Lee Bates* [in Wellesley] as I did for so long. It was Miss Coman's fate, I felt, to miss the full recognition she deserved. Her admirable and most readable *Industrial History of the United States* was eclipsed by the almost simultaneous publication of another book covering the same field which was more suited, I regretfully suppose, for text-book use." Katharine Coman was also widely known for her *Economic Beginnings of the Far West,* and for her studies of various phases of social insurance in such European countries as England, Sweden, Denmark, Norway, and France. Like Emily Balch, Professor Coman had an essentially humanizing faculty which led her to emphasize the human problems of history and economics. Among her richest contributions to her students were her social and personal relations with them. Like Emily Balch, she could lead her students to think for themselves and to deal independently with their materials.

Two other members of the faculty of whom H. G. Wells might have approved were the so-called social radicals—Vida Dutton Scudder of the English Department, author of *Social Ideals in English Letters* (1898), and Ellen Hayes, professor of astronomy

---

* Author of "America The Beautiful."

and applied mathematics. Vida Scudder was a member of the Socialist Party when it was not even considered respectable to be a member of a trade union. President Julia Irvine of Wellesley considered Vida Scudder a "detriment to the institution." [2] Professor Ellen Hayes, a sympathizer with working-class movements, was a nonconformist all her days—dauntless and picturesque. In the 1880's she dared to wear short skirts, in the 1890's she was a staunch advocate of woman's suffrage. In the first decade of the new century she became an ardent Socialist "who dragged the Communist Manifesto into her lectures on astronomy." She, too, was a "thorn in the flesh of the trustees." She retired in 1916. In 1926 at the age of seventy-six she made another appearance in the headlines picketing against the Sacco-Vanzetti execution. And there was Emily Balch, who broke ground in so many fields and who finally, in her own words, during World War I "overstrained the habitual liberality" of Wellesley College.

At the turn of the century, Emily Balch, Vida Scudder and other "radical" members of the Wellesley faculty were much disturbed by the college's acceptance in 1900 of the first Rockefeller gift of money that came from profits of the Standard Oil Company, "tainted money," as it was then called. The trustees of the college were troubled from time to time by protests from the professors. Emily Balch has an entry in her diary on April 15, 1900, "Tomorrow work begins again. I hope to do better than I have done. The facing the possibility of leaving Wellesley in considering the Rockefeller gift has made me realize more the opportunity, and the weariness due to my poorness of standard as well as of performance." People were widely stirred when Ida Tarbell's sensational charges in her famous *History of the Standard Oil Company* appeared in 1904.

When an intellectual or a knotty moral problem arose, Emily had always been in the habit of formulating the pros and cons in writing. Perhaps such intelligent formulation pointed the way to an answer. A stray undated sheet of paper reveals that for her the question of "tainted money" was wholly one of relations of persons, acts, and ideas. It was not in the least a judgment as to character of the money except in a purely metaphorical sense. Therefore, she concludes that money may be accepted regardless of its origin, if no other claim to it can be made or if restitution is impossible, if no other use could be made of it more compensatory in nature, and if acceptance in no way implies cooperation, approval, or lessened criticism. The protesting members of the faculty did not resign, but stayed on at Wellesley, because, according to Vida Scudder, they perceived that short of fleeing into a hermitage, they could not escape the taint of communal guilt.

The sense of social compunction Emily had acquired in her college days led her even as a girl to think on questions of money, income, expenditure, luxury, leisure, and thrift. Most of her life she had been supported directly or indirectly by her father. Her first salary at Wellesley in 1896 for reading papers was $500 for half time. After her salary became more substantial she undertook to live wholly on what she earned and to give away or save her unearned income from the estate of her father, who died in 1898, early in her teaching career. It seemed to her unfair, since she was in a sense in competition with her colleagues, to enjoy a subsidy in addition to her salary.*

"As regards my college work," wrote Emily of her teaching years, "I had my share in the general introductory work dealing largely with fundamental theoretical principles as then taught at Harvard and elsewhere.** As a beginner I had been captivated by those essential harmonies which Adam Smith set forth with too little allowance for the factors which even under a system of the most complete laissez-faire, complicate the economic process. I had been led to realize these both by my personal experience of social facts and by the economic-social writings of the time.

"The lecture course I was asked to give dealt with the *history* of socialism, and to my surprise H. G. Wells in his chapter on Wellesley College criticized this Wellesley course because students were given Marx to read, as if one could discuss that history without doing so. I regarded this course among other things as a

---

* In 1916, she was to go to Stockholm to Henry Ford's Neutral Conference at his expense, but she did not accept the payment he made to members of the conference. She even incurred a financial loss which Louis Lochner tried to rectify. Before leaving the United States for the Ford Conference, she had been directed by cable to engage a substitute, which she did at an expense to herself of $600. Her only comment on the outcome of this, characteristically generous, was, "Owing to a confusion as to who was responsible for paying this sum, it was never refunded."

** She was an adherent of the marginal value school of Boehm-Bawerk, the reigning theory of the determination of value by market price.

valuable training in thinking for oneself in the face of conflicting evidence and arguments, and I was pleased when at its end a student asked what my own conclusion was, as she had not been able to guess from the classroom."

In February, 1909, Emily Balch and Vida Scudder organized in Boston a three-day conference on "Socialism as a World Movement." The spirit of the time was reflected in the statement of the organizers that "membership in this Committee does not imply acceptance of socialism or responsibility for the views of any of the speakers. The Committee simply undertakes to provide a calm and considerate hearing for a type of social unrest which is beginning to make itself felt significantly in nearly all civilized countries." One of the pleasant by-products of the conference for Emily was the personal contact and friendship with men like Morris Hillquit and Victor Berger, both of whom she said "were generously friendly to a half-way ally like myself."

One of the college courses she enjoyed teaching most was economic history, in which she lectured to over a hundred students. "In this course I had had great teachers in Gustav Schmoller and W. J. Ashley. Ashley was a deeply religious man with an awakened social conscience as well as an original scholar from whom I had learned both facts and method."

Emily Balch's concern in economics was, in her own words, "both intellectually disinterested and ethically and practically interested." Her desire was to help women to train themselves in understanding economic problems, to examine critically the social order of which they were a part, to make themselves "serviceable," and, above all, to fit themselves to bear part in any deeper reconstruction—the reconstruction of ideas. In her course on labor problems and labor legislation she tried to give students a chance to learn from sources outside of books, which was not difficult, as she continued to keep in contact with labor. This gave her teaching a firsthand, nonacademic quality which attracted and stimulated students. On the occasion of a bitter strike in the shoe industry in Marlboro, Massachusetts, in which the employers refused to confer with the workers' representatives, the Boston Twentieth Century Club asked the well-known architect, Charles H. Rutan, Professor Spencer Baldwin of Boston University, and Emily Balch to investigate and report on the strike. The workers were very willing to answer questions. The employers refused to talk with the committee. The three investigators did what they could to give a fair account of the situation, but they made it clear that they had not had equal access to information. Sometime afterwards Emily Balch felt free to lend $200 to the union in question. Later she was told by President Caroline Hazard of Wellesley that this loan was the reason that she had been kept on as a mere assistant without normal promotion. Emily Balch replied in a conversational tone, "I consider that reason very creditable." Then, seeing she was not understood, she added quickly, "I mean, very creditable to me." In describing this incident later Emily commented, "This impertinence, if it was that, had no ill consequences I think."

It is a pity that President Hazard had not been able to read the notation of April 29, 1899, concerning the strike in Emily's private diary: "The Marlboro strike report must be got ready this week. The creature in me does hate controversies. That is one reason I believe that I love temper, charity, and truthfulness in arguing. Q.D.A. (Quod Deus Amendet)."

Another incident was probably not helpful to her academic career. Emily's public- spirited cousin Anne Withington telephoned one day to say she was sitting with a leader in a strike of street car workers, trying to think up a suitable slogan. "I laughingly suggested *Hands Across the Track* and others no more felicitous. Notes of my suggestions among other papers were thoughtlessly handed over to a reporter who was to cover the strike, with the consequence that according to the Sunday papers I was taking part in a strikers' street parade with a party of my Wellesley students, a parade of which I had not even heard. But a college is like Caesar's wife and it is well not to be in the papers except as desired by the college publicity office."

A less dangerous aspect of her social concern was connected with problems of slum environment, poverty, and crime. Even before she began her college teaching Emily had organized private courses in Boston dealing with such questions. In Wellesley she gave a regular undergraduate course on this subject, presenting the sort of problems later dealt with by professional schools of social work. The conception of social work as a profession was still to develop. "I am pretty confident that I had never heard of any attempt to deal with this material as academic material and that

I had no model." True to her desire to give her students a chance to check their impressions derived from books by direct contact with reality, she took small groups of students to institutions for paupers and for the feebleminded, to reform schools and prisons. The college received letters from irate parents protesting against having their daughters taken to investigate "brothels."

As she soon came to realize that her course was giving a one-sided and unduly black and unreal impression of the social situation, she supplemented it with another course emphasizing the forces at work building up a community. She took the North End of Boston as a subject for social study. She had learned something of that "rather isolated foreign quarter" during her apprenticeship work under Charles Birtwell after her return from Paris. The students were eager and conscientious. Each student handed in a final paper describing the section from personal observation, together with a "social map" showing centers of social signifi-cance—schools, hospitals, saloons, churches, and settlement houses. Some students wrote fairly solid monographs on specific immigrant groups in their own home towns. Others drew up some of the first attempted family budgets for certain types of earners.

Another practical subject which she was early in annexing to the curriculum was immigration which she shaped into a college course, and which grew to be her special field. Other courses dealt with statistics and the theory of consumption. She was interested in the new studies in the psychology of labor and the studies of fatigue and incentive.

In 1900 the trustees of Wellesley had come to feel that the college was behind the times in having no course in sociology. They asked Emily Balch to undertake it. Considerably against her judgment she consented. "I think I felt that if I did not know what a course in sociology should cover, neither did anyone else. I was only rather confident that Professor Albion Small [with whom she had studied in Chicago] had not the right idea. It was an ordeal. At any rate, I was much interested and read widely in new fields, and I hope my students too gained something from this very odd class."

In her twenty years of teaching social subjects and of helping her students to understand their social responsibility and express it effectively in action, she felt she was doing social service as truly as though she were in the field, "if with less sacrifice," she added. During this time she became increasingly convinced of the need of great social change, "a view," she said in 1945, "then less generally accepted than now."

Emily Balch was in a certain sense not a good teacher. She herself knew that she was absentminded and unsystematic. With a multiplicity of civic duties, with her college courses covering too wide and too various a field, and with the necessity of constantly having to prepare new courses, she often overlooked some of the mechanical details of teaching—roll call, class assignments, periodic reviews. "How well one remembers," wrote her Indiana undergraduate, "Professor Balch dashing into the classroom at the last minute, loaded down with all sorts of papers, pamphlets, reports, even heavy reference books. Often she would forget to return our examination papers, and the required reading in the reference books would also slip her mind." Sometimes she might seem to forget her class altogether. The class would sit the required number of minutes after the beginning bell and then be informed that "our teacher was delivering a lecture in Boston or New York or attending a conference of civic leaders in Chicago." She was, however, a new type of college teacher. With her involvement in philanthropy, labor movements, and social reform, she was actually a part of what she was trying to teach. It was like taking a course in poetry not with a professor of English literature but with an Auden, a Frost, or a C. Day Lewis.

In one of her more candid and less self-deprecatory fragments she says of her teaching, "It had the advantage of considerable originality, of a certain first-hand quality, and of a never wearying and genuine interest in the subject-matter and a certain enthusiasm, if that is the right word. And that these qualities were contagious is clear, I think, by the considerable number of students who were kindled to continue work in economic or social-economic fields." In her frequent absences from college to serve on state or municipal commissions or in arbitration duties, she was a precursor of the contemporary college and university professor who is always being called away to Washington or elsewhere to give expert information or advice, and who is as much applauded for his prolonged leaves of absence to assist in the "national defense," as Emily Balch was to be censured in World War I for taking a year's leave of absence without pay to assist in the preservation of peace.

It was during her Wellesley professorship that on the invitation of William English Walling—Emily Balch together with Mary Kenney O'Sullivan, Mary Morton Kehew, Helena S. Dudley, Philip Davis (of the North End Settlement of Boston), and others—founded in 1903 the Women's Trade Union League. Emily Balch was for a time president. The object of the Women's Trade Union League was to assist in the organization of women wage earners into trade unions, to help them secure healthful and efficient conditions of work, and to obtain a just return for such work. Membership in the League was open to all workers, men as well as women, and to persons sympathetically interested in the aim of organized labor. These latter were known as "allies." The early presidents of the League, Mary Morton Kehew and Emily Greene Balch, were drawn from the ranks of the "allies."* Later women from the trade unions were chosen. Through the Women's Trade Union League, Emily Balch had further contacts with unusual personalities like Julia O'Connor who was one of the first officers of the Women's Trade Union League drawn from the ranks of labor and who later became president of the International Telephone Operators' Union, and with needleworkers of the South Cove and North End, all of whom, she said, "were an education to me and helped to educate my students." Emily gave credit to "the far-sighted generosity of Wellesley College" (was the generosity here her own?) that she was able while teaching to widen and test her thinking by carrying on voluntary public work in different fields. "But the most important work for the Women's Trade Union League," wrote Emily, "was not done by me, but by others, notably Mrs. Mary Morton Kehew and Mabel Gillespie."

Mary Morton Kehew was perhaps the most remarkable of that remarkable group of what Emily called "the Boston aristocracy

---

* It is interesting to note that it was from middle-class initiative like that of the Women's Trade Union League and of the Consumers' League (founded in 1899 of which Emily Balch was an early member) and not from trade unions that the first demands came for the abolition of child labor, of home manufacture in tenements, of excessive hours of work for women, and for the establishment of minimum wage laws and social insurance.

of goodness and public spirit." Mrs. Kehew, meeting the young social worker Emily Balch in the early nineties, thought Emily was "usable" ("I had some ideas too," said Emily), and was anxious for her to continue in her public civic work after she began teaching at Wellesley. Even in her old age Emily was to refer to Mrs. Kehew as "the greatest social statesman that it has been my privilege to know." Today, the names of Jane Addams, Florence Kelley, Julia Lathrop, Grace Abbott, Frances Perkins, and Lillian Wald are still revered as shaping American liberalism and educating a whole generation in social responsibility. Yet the name of Mary Morton Kehew is practically unknown except in the flourishing Women's Educational and Industrial Union on Boston's wide and busy Boylston Street just across from the Public Gardens, Mrs. Kehew's great monument. Of this she was the moving spirit from 1892 till her death in 1918. Emily thought that perhaps the fact that she died at a time when America was preoccupied in helping reconstruct a shattered world deflected attention from her unique life work, so that the important chapter of social history that her work constituted was never written.

Mrs. Kehew was a woman of wealth and culture. No doubt Boston forgave much in her trailblazing career because she was a Morton of Plymouth and a Kimball of Boston. Emily Balch had already heard of Mrs. Kehew as an unusual and powerful personality when she first met her in connection with the founding of Denison House in 1892. Always sensitively observant, Emily saw how generously Mrs. Kehew gave not only of her cooperation but of herself. She attended to all the laborious details of choosing a suitable neighborhood and finding a usable house for the settlement. No day was too hot, no stairs too steep, no cellar too dark and slimy to deter her. During the first experimental year at Denison House when Emily Balch was headworker, Mrs. Kehew was in close touch with those making up the household, particularly with the housekeeper, Mrs. Hartwell, and her little girl, who was ill with "consumption." Mrs. Kehew would find time to write a funny little letter to send with a doll to the sick child. Such acts sank deeply into Emily's consciousness and were hoarded for the future. This solicitude about details and these instances of intimate personal kindnesses Emily thought the more striking in view of the amplitude and powerful sweep of Mrs. Kehew's mind, "busied with wide effects to be achieved in the far future— a future for which it was never too soon to build."

"Mrs. Kehew was a leader and an initiator," wrote Emily Balch. It was Mrs. Kehew who, with her sister Hannah Kimball, brought the young Mary Kenney* from Chicago to Boston to see what could be done to help to organize women in factories. Emily contributed her scholarship and knowledge to the projects planned by Mrs. Kehew. She worked with Mrs. Kehew on the Industrial Protective Committee which became the Massachusetts Factory Inspection Commission, on which Emily was asked to serve, and on the Massachusetts Minimum Wage Commission established in 1913, of which Emily Balch was chairman and which drafted the first minimum wage law in the country.** The need for legislative action to protect workers became more pressing, but there were no industrial data on which to base reform measures. Mrs. Kehew established the research department at the Union to train women to secure the facts. This department led to the creation of the Massachusetts Department of Labor and Industry. As an experiment in education it served as a model for courses in universities and colleges. She initiated the Appointment Bureau for vocational direction, which paved the way for other bureaus of occupation.***

---

* See Chapter 3, p. 83.

** A young Boston lawyer, Caroline J. Cook, drafted the first minimum wage act which became part of Massachusetts law.

*** Education was the pivot on which her reforms turned. She pioneered in workers' education—the trade school for girls, evening classes for adult women, the school of salesmanship—were all cradled in the Women's Industrial and Educational Union. She founded the New England Kitchen, which developed into the school lunch, an idea which spread throughout the United States to the smallest rural districts. The social reforms she initiated for the Commonwealth of Massachusetts spread from coast to coast.

As if all this were not enough, she founded agencies for infant welfare, including day nurseries. Though not a college graduate herself, she helped in the establishment and growth of Simmons College; she turned her energies toward serving the blind, a lifetime of work in itself. She developed the Massachusetts Association for Promoting the Interest of the Blind in 1903. Three years later the state took it over. She promoted a Loan and Aid Association for the Blind, the founding of Woolson House, a settlement for the blind, and an establishment of a magazine for the sightless, *The Outlook for the Blind.*

Emily Balch said of her that she was so witty that she could infuse the dullest committee meeting with life, and so resourceful that she could make a deficit in a treasurer's report sound hopeful.

Mary Morton Kehew, therefore, can be acclaimed as the archetype of the volunteer professional woman of her time and as the forerunner of the professional career woman of the twentieth century.

In all these correlated reforms Mrs. Kehew was "essentially the statesman" wrote Emily Balch. "She looked over the social situation and considered it. She saw where there was a thing to be done and what old or new organization might effect it; where there was a need of change and what long-range alteration of existing conditions might be brought step by step, and the first step she then and there initiated. And this step was followed by others as planned."

Many of the traits which were to make Emily Balch influential in the peace movement and which she passed on to two generations of her colleagues there, she herself derived, by the contagion of respect and admiration, from Mary Morton Kehew. No one, least of all a person as delicately responsive as Emily Balch, could work with a woman like Mrs. Kehew without catching something of the quality of her spirit and her methods: her sense of dedication, her unconventionality, her courage and vigor in attempting untried programs, her refusal to be discouraged, her clarifying sense of humor, her abiding faith in her fellow workers, her willingness to plod along side by side with them to accomplish what she had in mind, and not the least, her sound business sense and feminine attention to detail.

On a torn scrap of paper among Emily Balch's notes is a fragment on Mary Morton Kehew: "She believed *literally* in democracy and a fair deal for every one. Like Marcus Aurelius, she showed how even in a palace, life may be lived well. She was not seeking credit, but *results,* and if the credit went elsewhere so much the better."

In 1904-1905 Emily Balch became entitled to a professorial sabbatical year of leave. She decided to use this for a comprehensive study of Slavic immigration to the United States, the nature of which was then little known or understood. The next year she asked for a further leave of absence without pay, to finish her investigations. It was not, however, till 1910 that her magnum opus, *Our Slavic Fellow Citizens,* was published.

Her early and persisting concern for better relations between people, her consequent interest in "disadvantaged" groups, led her before World War I to special studies in immigration problems and in aspects of colonialism and imperialism. After the Treaty of Versailles it pushed her to considering the tragic situation of displaced persons the world over. In the 1930's she devoted herself to the problem of refugees in the United States.

The kind of study of Slavic immigration Emily Balch planned had not been undertaken systematically for any group of immigrants before. It was to be based upon firsthand inquiry both in Europe and in America. She spent the greater part of the year 1905 in Austria-Hungary studying emigration. She felt the immigrant could not be understood without observing him in the conditions which shaped him, and which he had shaped, in his own old village and among his own people, without studying the culture of which he was a living part, but which he was for the most part powerless to transport with him to his new home. She set out to learn from what districts the immigrants came, when and how the migration had begun, the types of people that came, why they came, how they succeeded, how the home district was affected by the drawing off of workers, by the money sent home, and by the immigrants returning with or without savings. Generally they returned with savings, but pretty well worn out by American work, its unaccustomed speed and tension, and, too often, its accidents. Each group was dealt with separately—Bohemians (later called Czechs), Slovaks, Moravians (often called Griners in America), Ruthenians (Ukrainians today), and all the rest. At that time relatively few Great Russians emigrated to America, and Jews, not being Slavs, came into her study only incidentally.

For the second part of her book, she planned a study of Slavs in the United States after their migration. In carrying this out it was not practicable to make separate studies of different linguistic groups. They were too intermingled in their new environment. Therefore she sketched a chronological history of the sporadic early arrivals and learned what she could about the varied environments and types of occupation in which they were most numerously represented. For more than a year she visited Slavic colonies in the United States from New York to Colorado, from Michigan to Galveston, Texas.

•

The summer of 1904 she boarded in mining villages in Pennsylvania. The autumn of that year she spent as the member of the family of a Bohemian, or Czech, workingman—living in one of the old-style tenements in the Bohemian quarter of New York's upper East Side. This was no settlement house experience; it was something far more intimate. The bedrooms of the flat depended for light and air on a narrow shaft ending in a well into which garbage was dumped. Her object was to learn the Bohemian, or Czech, language, which she decided would be the most useful of the many Slavic languages for her purposes. "I did not succeed in mastering the difficult tongue, but I learned enough of it to have some use of it, and also as a key to Polish, Russians, Croatian, and so on."

She sometimes lived in settlement houses: Hull-House in Chicago; Hiram House in Cleveland; Woods Run House in Allegheny, now part of Pittsburgh. Often she stayed in drab commercial hotels in some industrial center if making a longer visit. In Texas she studied the Polish settlement of 1850. She spent a month in a Colorado mining camp near the New Mexico border. Here she had varied experiences. She boarded at a place full of working people. She observed in the churches the picturesque piety of the Mexican women in their black mantillas. She walked about a good deal in the rain and encountered the alarming phenomenon of the arroyos suddenly filled with rushing water capable of engulfing a vehicle. She came within range of a fighting horse and was not afraid. And here she had her first and only proposal of marriage. Without women the mining community was a lonely one. One of the miners—not a Slav—took her for a long walk, and when they sat down to admire the view, he slipped an arm around her waist and "proposed." When she quietly told him of the profession she was engaged in and mentioned her salary, there was no further talk of marriage.

She also spent some time with the Polish farmers of the Connecticut River Valley and with the Bohemians in Nebraska and Wisconsin, hearing stories of the early pioneer days. In such industrial centers as Pittsburgh, Bridgeport, and Yonkers, New York, she was much impressed by the social leadership of the priests.

Early in January, 1905, Emily Balch set out on the Austro-Hungarian part of her travels, accompanied by a young resident of

Mary Simkhovitch's Greenwich House, the twenty-three-year-old, Effie (Euphemia) Murray Abrams. In her book Emily was to acknowledge her obligations to Effie, "my unselfish traveling comrade." "A perfect treasure," Emily wrote to Annie, "who about doubles my available time and more than doubles my pleasure."*

Their journeyings led them through parts of Europe which were on the whole little known to the Baedeker traveler, and where the old European peasant life still lingered. "And the study of the Slavic world is full of fascination," wrote Emily. They were present at a Slovak wedding which combined elements of marriage by capture and purchase. In a Ruthenian village a ring dance on the green—the young men in long white tunics belted with bright woven bands, the girls in embroidered jackets—took them back to the Middle Ages. From Trencsén, in Slovakia, Emily wrote to Annie, "Every crag has its castle, and every castle its more or less tragic legends." On the plain of central Hungary they saw the superb herds of cream-colored, wide-horned cattle, and there, where its vast expanses shimmered in the hot sun, they saw the illusory groves and pools, a mirage which the Hungarians said was the work of the fairy Délibáb. The native costumes were a continual delight to Emily, and she brought home a fine collection of Slavic embroidered textiles. "What a taste these people have. The daring colors they combine to good effect," she wrote to her three sisters in Jamaica Plain.

Nothing rare or beautiful missed her eyes—a shepherd girl by the roadside, at her lonely work where it would seem that no one was likely to see her, decked out in a plastron of coins covering the front of her bodice; spring showers drawing a bright wet veil between herself and the hillsides; in an interval of sunshine a shepherd boy playing on double pan pipes by a brook; the slender needles of minarets in the town of Mostar; in Bukovina a sulphur sunset over a field of stubble; and, wherever she went, always she could name the wild flowers of woods and meadows, ancestors of those she knew and loved in New England.

Emily Balch's book, *Our Slavic Fellow Citizens*, interpreted

---

* Effie subsequently became the wife of Walter Ernest Clark, president of the University of Nevada, and the mother of Walter Van Tilburg Clark, the novelist.

with rare insight, sympathy, and humility, the much deprecated Slavic immigration. The book served to refute the prevailing assumptions that an undiluted old English stock was indispensable to the American experiment in democracy, that the United States could no longer assimilate the ever growing "alien hordes," especially not the "newer" immigration from Russia, Poland, Italy, and the Balkans, from Slav, Latin, and Asiatic "races," and that it was time for the traditional policy of free immigration to stop. In Emily Balch's own New England an association of ideas bolstered by pseudoscientific racist theories had been built up over the years, leading to a rationale for the restriction of immigration. This culminated in 1894 in the formation of a group which became the Immigration Restriction League of Boston. The group influenced not only New England but the nation at large. The League was able to enlist in its ranks such varied personalities as Henry Cabot Lodge, its main political sponsor; John Fiske, the historian and popularizer of evolutionary philosophy; Joseph Lee, the father of American playgrounds, one of Emily Balch's "Boston aristocracy of goodness and public spirit"; the Columbia sociologist Franklin H. Giddings, once Emily's mentor and guide at Bryn Mawr; John Farwell Moors, a philanthropic investment banker and longtime friend of the Balch family; Robert A. Woods, Emily's colleague in settlement house experiments and Boston's most distinguished social worker; A. Lawrence Lowell, president of Harvard (1909-33); John R. Commons, professor of economics at the University of Wisconsin; and David Starr Jordan, president of Stanford University, who later worked with Emily Balch in trying to keep America out of war in 1916-1917.

Representing the voices of the older New England tradition, a distinguished minority upheld the values of free immigration— Charles W. Eliot, president of Harvard (1869-1909); Thomas Wentworth Higginson, literary arbiter and editor; Alice Stone Blackwell, feminist; Charles Fletcher Dole, Emily's earliest spiritual inspiration; Josiah Royce, Harvard philosopher and cultural pluralist; William James, psychologist and philosopher of pragmatism; and Emily Greene Balch, who alone of all these had made immigration her special study. Unlike those who saw in continued immigration the "shipwreck of the American enterprise in democracy," she declared that "others with a still wider horizon and still more daring faith" saw in the enormous influx "a new advance" in creating a civilization to be, in which all kinds of Americans, new and old, "each freely irradiating each," would find unity by building "themselves and us alike into a greater and wiser culture"—a universal and inclusive America comprised of "Catholic and Jew, Italian and Pole, Slovak and Yankee and Chinaman."

She saw that the "newcomers" (she could always find and use the most persuasive term) drawn from layers of population where pressure was greatest, gained not only in comfort, but in freedom and self-respect. She had faith that these newcomers in America would bring "fresh vigorous blood to a rather sterile and inbred stock, and that they would add valuable varieties of inheritance to a rather puritanical, one-sided culture rich in middle-class commonplaces, but poor in the power of creating beauty except in the great field of literature."

Emily Balch's book, *Our Slavic Fellow Citizens,* also served to refute many of the restrictionist arguments and misconceptions— that it was steamship companies that were primarily responsible for stimulating immigration; that the peasant emigrants were drawn from the lowest social classes in their countries, "the scum" of Europe; that the national character of Slavs prevented political and cultural development. "There is no such person as a Slav any more than there is such a person as a Teuton or a Celt. . . . I feel a profound scepticism as to the value of generalizations in regard to the character of nations or races, more especially if it is assumed that such characters are inherited and unchangeable. Group types are perhaps quite as much products of social development and imitation, determined by historical causes economic and other, as they are the expression of innate qualities."

Instead of dwelling on the dangers in the declining vitality of the Anglo-Saxon stock, as her fellow Bostonians did, Emily Balch depicted the sufferings which emigration brought on the foreign born: the deep-seated antipathy or contempt of the native American for the unlike—"less than kin being regarded as naturally 'less than kind'"; the replacing of the good manners and customs of the homeland with inferior American substitutes; the disastrous gulf between the older and the younger generations; the loss when children reject their parents' language and thus give up the intel-

lectual advantage of being bilingual; and, worst of all, the isolation
of the immigrant and the economic pressures and low standards
incident to his belonging to an inferior industrial stratum.

"My people do not live *in* America. They live *underneath*
America. America goes on over their heads." These picturesque and
profoundly suggestive words, said Emily Balch, were uttered by
one of the wisest Slav leaders she met in America, a Ukrainian
Orthodox priest, Father Paul Tymkevich of Yonkers. Economically,
thought the priest, his people gained by coming here, "physically
and morally, no. . . . They have no habits. The first step in civilization is to acquire habits, and where can they acquire them? On
the streets? In the saloons?" The isolation was even harder for the
educated man than for the laborer. In talking to Father Tymkevich,
whom Emily called "a shepherd of immigrants," she sensed his
"almost intolerable loneliness," that of a sensitive, intelligent man
"separated from his own people by all that separates a scholar
from peasants, from Americans as an alien in a communi' v unused
to look for friends and associates among foreigners."

The Slavs, concluded Emily, are orphans in this country, cut
off from the life of their old country without coming into contact
with the true life of their new home. "To them, both parents are
dead, the fatherland that begot them and the foster-mother that
supports without cherishing them."

To give the immigrants the simple fundamentals of fair treatment, honest government, wholesome, decent living and working
conditions, was not possible, thought Emily. America could not fulfill these obligations even to her native citizens. "We can and must
do what in the end will be a better thing," Emily concluded. "We
must get our new neighbors to work with us for these things. . . .
We must learn to connect our ideals and theirs, we must learn to
work together with them for justice, for humane living conditions,
for beauty, and for true, not merely formal, liberty." This would
conduce to a higher unity in which "we may preserve every
difference to which men cling with affection, without feeling ourselves any the less fellow-citizens and comrades."

"For this work of two and a half years," wrote Emily Balch in
the ingenuous manner she could sometimes assume, "I think I
received seventeen dollars in royalties besides a generous number

of gift copies. I spent thousands of dollars preparing for it.* It was well worth it if only in the pleasure it gave me, and I hope it has been of service."

In 1914, just before the spring holidays, a great fire at Wellesley College burned down College Hall, destroying much of Emily Balch's scholarly material, the labor of years. She lost the notes for several courses, her valued collection of maps, and practically all of the records and observations of her Slavic researches.

Outstanding during her Austro-Hungarian year was her friendship with Thomas Masaryk, then professor of philosophy at Prague, and his delightful wife, the American Charlotte Garrigue, whom he had met at Leipzig when she was a music student there. "They were hospitable without limit. I was constantly their guest, always for dinner on Sundays, and at other odd times." Professor Masaryk was at the time fifty-five years old and already had behind him years of service to the cause of Czech independence. He was "a great man, a very good man, a man to love dearly. I wish I had space and memory for anecdotes." Once when Emily was walking with him in Prague, they saw a court carriage stop at a church. He waited till the notables came out. "I was a little surprised at his interest in waiting to see them, and he explained that his feeling against them was so strong, that it gave him a satisfaction to see them. It gave release to his hostility."

Two incidents in his life made a lasting impression on Emily Balch. An old Czech document which gave Czech nationalists great prestige was suspected of being a forgery. Masaryk had a careful investigation made of these early manuscripts and published the findings that they were spurious, although the discovery was disadvantageous to the cause he had so deeply at heart. He paid the cost for his courage and his loyalty to his scientific conscience. He was called a traitor bought by the Hapsburg

---

* Emily did have a curious backing from the Carnegie Institute, a subsidy of $300, not to be paid in advance or during the progress of the work, but on her return, and then only in case the work seemed valuable. The professor in charge wrote to her, "I have no desire to assume control of your work, much less to direct your movements, but it would clearly be better for me, as you imply [sic—she had not], to delay payment until I can judge more exactly than at present of the probable value of your work." This is a far cry from the more generous policies of the foundations today.

government to discredit the Czech nation, his expulsion from the university was demanded, and his promotion with its higher salary was withheld for thirteen years.

In 1899 he was involved in another cause célèbre concerning a Jew who had been condemned to death on a charge of ritual murder. Masaryk attacked the sentence, proved that the evidence was worthless, that racist* prejudice had dictated the verdict, and that popular superstition countenanced by dignitaries of the Church in Austria was responsible for the myth of ritual murder. Again Masaryk was denounced, this time as a traitor to Christianity, howled down by a mob and urged to suspend his work at the university.

While Emily was in Prague, a demonstration was held in favor of universal suffrage for men, tribunes for speakers being set up at the four corners of the great square in the center of Prague, for crowds which were to come from four different factory quarters. Masaryk's daughter Alice told Emily that she had asked her father how his being one of the speakers was likely to affect his professorship at the university. He smiled and replied, "Let us think of that afterwards." Ten years later Emily was to remember his fearlessness and the faith symbolized by his motto, "Truth prevails."

On December 31, 1906, after her return from her Slavic journey, Emily wrote in her journal, "Within the year I have decided to call myself a socialist and accepted appointment at Wellesley only on condition of the president knowing this. It will lead to some misunderstanding, of course, but I hope to some better understanding too."

She had long struggled with the question of her relation to Socialism. She herself thought she had unconsciously dramatized in her mind a future situation in which she would be sufficiently converted to a belief in Socialism to make it a duty to challenge a sort of martyrdom by accepting the name. As a student in Berlin she had been much in contact with Democratic Socialism among students, and State Socialism among the German professors. Although never a Marxist, she had been influenced by the Fabians in England, by Kingsley and the Christian Socialists, and by revi-

---

* A contributing factor to Czech anti-Semitism was the fact that for the most part Jews were pro-German.

sionist and reformist tendencies in the Socialist movement in America. "I never accepted Marx's theory of surplus value, which appeared to me as definitely and provably wrong as a wrongly added column of figures, neither did I ever accept his economic interpretation of history, though I was so deeply conscious of what we owe him for calling attention with whatever one-sided emphasis to the importance of this economic element in history. I never accepted the theory or practice of the class struggle, which I rejected both on scientific and on ethical grounds." But the existing competitive system seemed to her to be so bad that she hated to appear to acquiesce in it. A system in which production was shaped not with the purpose of making what was needed and making it beautiful and good of its kind, but with the purpose of making a profit, appeared to her a basic topsy-turvydom which had widespread vicious results. To make the fundamental relation of men in the whole economic field competitive and self seeking, instead of cooperative and for mutual benefit, appeared to her the negation of Christianity or any other ethical system.

Her final decision to accept the name of Socialist was precipitated by an incident when she was living in Prague. One unbearably bleak winter morning she saw a man fumbling with his bare fingers in an ash barrel to try to find something to eat. She had seen enough misery and actual starvation in Boston in 1893 when Denison House was new; she had come in contact with the worst kind of sweatshop home industries around the Rivington Street Settlement in New York City before the garment trades were unionized; she had had the sickening experience of being publicly prayed for by the poor outraged little delinquent boys in an institution that was a disgrace to her native city; she had lived in Allegeny when social-political corruption was rampant "with plenty of unpunished murder." But the bare fingers in the icy ashes were somehow final, and led her to call herself a Socialist.

Furthermore, during her prolonged stay in Prague when she was constantly the guest of the Masaryk family, she had been influenced by the ideas as well as the personality of Professor Thomas Masaryk, the future first president of the Czechoslovakian Republic. He had made critical studies of Marxism and of Marxist ideas in Germany, Austria, and Russia. In 1899 he had published *The Philosophical and Sociological Foundations of Marxism*. He was

never a Marxist or even a Socialist. It is not surprising if some of
her views resembled his: sympathy with the ethical claims of
Socialism, rejection of the materialist philosophy of history and of
class warfare, recognition that changes in methods of production
eventually result in changes of social structure. Like Masaryk, she
thought Marxism to be morally inadequate and economically one
sided.

After World War I she ceased to call herself a Socialist, not
because she had moved more to the right in her social politics,
but for other reasons. The word seemed to her to have come more
definitely to connote the Marxian doctrine, if not actual party
membership; the war had made her more sceptical of governments
as such and much more afraid of trusting them with great new
powers; and lastly, she felt a growing distaste for tags and labels
"which while often necessary and sometimes useful are terribly
obliterative of vital shades of difference and in general suit only
simple situations."

At the end of 1906 her Slavic adventures over, returning
home to an unbroken family circle, Emily resumed her interrupted journal which she had kept from 1889 to 1904. "This
last year has been to me personally a happy one—not that
there was not much loneliness and malaise and discontent with
what I was accomplishing in my journeyings. . . . I must try in my
little world of will and thought and love to do better, for I have
not done well.—I would like to learn self-discipline and good
sense and all irradiating enthusiasm, the enthusiasm that makes
one do the little dull things well and that kills shirking dead. It
really isn't easy—for me it is very hard."

In 1909 the new year opened with a shocking disaster—the
Messina earthquake. On January 3, Emily was writing in her
journal: "The accounts are horrible, almost beyond imagination.
It lacks the horror of human malice of the Russian pogroms: on
the other hand it is, as far as we can understand, quite senseless,
not related to any progress or rational human sequence—but we
cannot understand, and it is only in magnitude of scale, not in
quality, that it differs from the tragedies of every day.—The Lisbon
earthquake of the 18th century made if I remember rightly sceptics
of believers. It takes a very strong and elastic web of faith to hold

under such a strain, one which does not involve any expectation of interpreting happenings in terms of human purposes."

The next long passage in this last consecutive journal Emily was to keep, reveals both her devotion and her common sense. In November, 1910, the newspapers all over the world blazoned an event in headlines that even many children were to remember all their lives, the death of Tolstoi in a railway stationmaster's house a few days after his final decision to renounce the world still further by leaving his home. Tolstoi moved his age as Gandhi was to move the succeeding one. It was Gandhi who was later to stir Emily Balch to place him first in her calender of saints and heroes. However, thousands of Emily's contemporaries were to turn to the Russian, in the words of Jane Addams, "not as to a seer—his message is much too confused and contradictory for that—but as to a man who has had the ability to lift his life to the level of his conscience, to translate his theories into action." [3]

Jane Addams herself, in 1896, had visited Tolstoi at Yasnaya Polyana, hoping to find in his solution a clue to the tangled problems of the city poverty she was encountering, and to see whether Tolstoi's "sermon of the deed" was bringing him peace. The conversation during the day and at dinner, where she ate the European meal presided over by the Countess while Tolstoi ate only the porridge and black bread of the peasant, stirred within her misgivings as to whether Tolstoi was not "more logical than life warrants." [4] Could the wrongs of life be reduced to the terms of unrequited labor?* She left Yasnaya Polyana in a heightened tumult of feelings which in the end she resolved for herself, not by descending to the level of poverty, but by making of Hull-House in the slum district of Chicago a center for beauty, for education, for the arts and the amenities, for the widest range of human activities, as well as a "cathedral of compassion."

Emily Balch spent an evening discussing St. Francis and Tolstoi with Vida Scudder, who had always been inclined to change the silver spoon she had been born with for one of tin, with Mary McDowell of the Stockyards settlement, in Chicago, and Mrs.

---

* On the subject of nonresistance which arose, she was disappointed in Tolstoi's position. It seemed to her that he made too great a distinction between the use of physical force and of that moral force which can override another's differences and scruples with equal ruthlessness.

Robert Woods. "For the first time in a long season," wrote Emily in her journal, "I felt the fire of the renunciation of men like these burning in my spirit. For the moment it seemed to me that everything but the literal acceptance of absolute personal poverty was compromise, was refusal. But I see again that for us in this age this is not true. Miss Addams is right. . . . If this is not the literal example for us today it is not that we are called to do less, love less, or to less completely make our whole life and all its circumstances instruments of our love. . . . Incapable of the hard simple literal renunciation, we are yet faced with the call to keep as resolute and fervent, as simple and direct in a voluntarily continued tangle and wealth of distractions. There is, I well know it, no saint-hood for me—not on any conceivably approachable plane of my being, not for eons of spirit, but it is up to me now and tonight, tomorrow morning and every morning, and all day and every day to keep on trying to see how I can be of use, how I can live nearer to God, nearer to other people, not in a puritanical self-discipline but trying honestly and hard to learn, to curb, and to spur, to feel after the light, to do all I can as well as I can for the best purpose I can see. This is not an easy job."

In 1907 Emily Balch was asked to write a review of H. G. Wells's book *The Future in America* for *the Wellesley Magazine.* She called it "What's Hecuba to me or I to Hecuba? or Thoughts on the Text of Mr. Wells' Impressions of Wellesley College." [5] In this article she developed some of her theories of education. Fundamental in her own college teaching and in her public civic work was the idea, also stressed by Wells, that progress is not something automatically assured (a point of view often held before 1914), but depends on the good sense and good will brought to bear on the problem of ordering human life—in other words, on the exercise of intelligence and decision. H. G. Wells's hero in the confused drama of human life was "intelligence, intelligence inspired by constructive passion."

Emily thought that H. G. Wells's visit to Wellesley represented not faultfinding but his characteristic interrogative attitude. "We who make up the present Wellesley and do the work of our little lives through her," she wrote, "are we not 'in a mighty doubting' too? How far is 'intelligence inspired by constructive passion' kindled and trained among us? How far does the College help prepare our young apostles to heretic England?* How 'far capable of a long plan' are we, of dealing with 'ends that are not obvious, that are intricate and complex and not to be won by booms and cataclysms of effort?' What is our Vision?"

These ultimate questions concerning ends Emily was always raising in her own mind and teaching also. But when it came to what she called the lesser questions of subject and method, of what part in the training "that we desire for the generation of our successors" does all that we call culture, and especially does a study of the past supply, she parted company with H. G. Wells or suspected that his judgment of America suffered from the shortness of his stay. She agreed with him as to the personal dangers of being overloaded with information and "culture," of the danger of the mood in which only the remote in time or space is beautiful or interesting, though she confessed that when a scholar pointed out the curious resemblance between the forms of mortgages of the Assyrians and the ancient Chinese, it struck her as far more interesting to investigate than, say, mortgages in Massachusetts. When the house is on fire, when something is pressing to be done, is no time for looking up quotations. "What's Hecuba to me or I to Hecuba?" is the cry not only of Hamlet, but of many a spirit who grudges seeing thought and emotion needed for immediate use consumed in unrealities and in classic and foregone discussions. Unlike some of her fellow Boston Brahmins, she decried the danger of intellectual snobbery, of salvation for the educated only. Emily Balch was not one to declare that uneducated people cannot enjoy Shelley. "Why not?" she asked. "The native quality that responds or does not respond to a given kind of spiritual harmony or beauty appears irresponsibly here and there. We ought to recognize this from the fact that the makers themselves have so often sprung direct from soil and toil. The spirit bloweth where it listeth."

Not in Boston only was it easy to identify education with one's own special brand, where "to be ignorant of the particular kind

---

* This concerns the story of Saint Filipo Neri at Rome, who, in the days of the Elizabethan persecutions, "set himself opposite the doors of the Papal College of Rome, that he might look into the faces of the English students destined to go forth to triumph or to martyrdom for the faith, in far-off heretic England."

of thing I know is unpardonable, but to be ignorant of the things I do not chance to be informed about is by no means strange," she said. "Not Greek and Latin, not reading and writing, not cleanliness and a whole coat are criteria of education. When one sees people like the Slovaks of Hungary or the Servians of Montenegro, men in the preliterate stage but themselves poets, artists and bearers of an ancient tradition, one realizes anew what different forms culture can take. When one catches the erudite man off his own ground, one realizes that there are many kinds and depths of ignorance."

But when all the dangers on this side are taken into consideration, there is quite as much risk of shipwreck from too little ballast as from too much. And in the America of that time Emily thought the former trouble was much the commoner. In 1907 she was decrying the anti-intellectualism that was to become more rampant during her old age in mid-century. "There is a snobbery of ignorance, too often met with, which despises learning and discounts experience and training, to which chance amateur attack and expert scientific skill are equally respectable, unless indeed the former be preferred."

She upheld the value of a living sense of history in furnishing background and guidance for the problems of the present. There were those to whom the past was so unreal that they lacked all sense of continuity and structural growth, all perspective. They were as ready to try again the routes that have been proved to lead nowhere as those that have been charted to great ends. History had no lessons for them, for it did not exist in their consciousness.

Emily Balch always valued everything that drew men closer together, everything that made for communication. The past, to her, supplied the present with a sort of auxiliary language. "At best, with every resource, we are poorly enough equipped to communicate to one another our unanalysable sensations and states of mind, our infinite and inexpressible mental reachings. When an allusion, a phrase dies, then a symbol is lost, a coin goes out of circulation. Hecuba is thus, among other things, a character in this language common to everyone who has received a share of the old inheritance of the centuries."

The past presented a moral challenge as well as the future, she thought, and one in some ways more moving, to those who have once really understood that they and their fellows have been bought with a great price by those that went before. "We are mean-spirited enough if after we have once seen that we have been charity scholars, not only in college, where no students pays a full share of the expense, but in life at large, we do not respond with an effort to do our best to hand on and if possible to add to the inheritance."

But in the main, Emily concluded, whether education is real or not, whether the students are feeding mentally for themselves, depends not on the pabulum offered but on the quality of their own purpose. "This demand of purpose may be awakened at the most unexpected moment, by what appears to be a chance touch. The college atmosphere that calls it into life, the vital personality in fellow-students or in teachers that proves contagious 'does the trick.' . . . As the character of her purpose so will the character of her accomplishment be. If conscious that she is not an unrelated atom but a living part of a living whole, her study of science, her study of art, will have broad issues. Her lifetime will be seen by her to be cast in the most interesting of epochs, to open up the most absorbing opportunities, and her education will prepare her to play her little part for 'all there is in it.'"

Had 1914 not burst on the world, Emily Balch would doubtless have taught on at Wellesley, and in due course retired in the thirties, laden with academic honors and honorary degrees. As it was, the shock of that fateful year, through a series of circumstances, led her to embark on a new, a third career, that brought her indeed no honorary degrees, but gave her instead the Nobel Prize for Peace in 1946. This was the career of a patient, indefatigable, fearless, modest, yet original and inspired worker for peace. In it she applied her scholarship, with inventiveness and flexibility of mind, to develop qualities of "constructive statemanship, in the understanding and solution of the complicated concrete poblems of organizing the affairs of a dynamically peaceful world."* She was to have no political office or public connections. She was to work as a private citizen of the world. Yet she was to work, as human beings must work, through an institution. She

---

* John Dewey, Appraisal of Emily Greene Balch, Leaflet, 1946 (Swarthmore College Peace Collection).

found that institution at the International Congress of Women that met at the Hague in April, 1915, under the presidency of Jane Addams, which became the Women's International League for Peace and Freedom. Through this latter organization, of which she was one of the founders, she worked for the rest of her long life, and the story of that career becomes a central thread as well as a mainspring in the story of the Women's International League.

CHAPTER FIVE

First Steps Against War

In April, 1915, when the guns of the First World War had been thundering over the Western front for nine months, a group of forty-two American women sailed for Holland over mine-strewn waters. Aboard the Dutch ship *Noordam* was not a delegation of ill-informed idealists, but a group of some of the most responsible and influential women in America. It included Jane Addams, internationally known, universally beloved, Emily Balch, Grace Abbott, Dr. Alice Hamilton, Professor Sophonisba Breckenridge, Madeleine Z. Doty, and many others who had long made their mark in the professions, in the fields of social work and of labor, in the educational and peace movements.

Their mission was unique and dramatic. It attracted a good deal of attention in the American and European press. The group were on their way to an international congress of women to be held at The Hague. They had been called, in the middle of the agony of war, to meet with other women from neutral and belligerent countries, to protest against the war, to stop the slaughter if possible, and to take counsel together on ways of preventing future wars. To this congress they had been invited by a small but distinguished group of European women, Dutch, English, German and Belgian.

It is hard for us to realize today how much courage it required for those women to enter the war zones. Women were still on the whole a sheltered and protected sex. They were not yet directly subject to the dangers of war as they were to be in World War II. They were not exposed to wholesale bombing. Women journalists, such as they were, were not permitted to expose themselves to the firing lines. Women were not only sheltered and protected, they were also a disqualified sex. Many of the professional schools—law, medicine, architecture—were closed to them. In the one profession in which they were numerous, teaching, they did not receive equal pay with men. In the United States and in most European countries they did not even have the vote.

Not only women but nearly all Americans (and this was to include President Woodrow Wilson himself) were on the whole ignorant of European power politics. They were provincial and, except for a body of immigrants, little interested in European and Asiatic affairs. With her training abroad and her knowledge of languages, Emily Balch was a notable exception to this.

Although they did not know it, the lives of several of the women on board the *Noordam* were to be completely changed by the trip. Jane Addams was to lose her tremendous national prestige, to regain it only in the course of time. Emily Balch was to forfeit her professorship and her means of livelihood. Both were to be drawn into a new career, into international political work. They were to devote their fine minds not only to planning for international reconstruction after the war, but to reorganizing international society and to working out ways of eliminating specific and remediable evils in the international and social order. Both were to become leaders in educating large numbers of Americans, notably women, to this point of view. And finally, to crown their pioneering though unspectacular labors, each was to receive the accolade of the Nobel Peace Prize. This international honor had previously been granted to only one other woman. In 1905 it was given to the Austrian, Baroness Bertha Von Suttner, author of the novel *Lay Down Your Arms (Die Waffen Nieder)*.

To understand what impelled these American women to press forward on this difficult and uncertain venture one must go back to the first days of World War I, to August, 1914. At this point, in the manner of the inimitable Izaak Walton in his *Lives* it should not be unfitting to "make a stop, and, that the reader may the better judge of what follows, give him a character of the times and temper of the people."

It is almost impossible to convey to a younger generation the reaction to war experienced by sensitive men and women in America and Europe at the outbreak of European hostilities in 1914. The impact of the blow was staggering. "Most normal people," wrote Jane Addams some years later in 1922, "had not yet acknowledged the necessity and propriety of war. . . . They went about day after day with an oppressive sense of the horrible disaster which had befallen the world and woke up many times during the night as from a hideous nightmare." [1] The nightmare was made a reality to Jane Addams by an unexpected sight from her peaceful summer cottage on Mt. Desert Island in Maine. One beautiful August morning there loomed up in the waters of Frenchman's Bay, a German ocean liner. The captain of the ship, on hearing at sea of the German declaration of war, had turned back towards the shore for fear that his cargo of gold bullion might be captured. "The huge boat in her incongruous setting," said Jane Addams, "was the first fantastic impression of that strange summer when we were so incredibly required to adjust our minds to a changed world. . . . It is impossible now to reproduce that basic sense of desolation, of suicide, of anachronism, which that first news of the war brought to thousands of men and women who had come to consider war as a throwback in the scientific sense." [2]

Jane Addams records the astonishment in United States newspapers, cartoons, and editorials that such an archaic institution as war should be revived in modern Europe. She describes the universal approval of the press when a procession of women in New York City, in protest against the daily slaughter, marched down Fifth Avenue, led by Fanny Garrison Villard, the daughter of the abolitionist and nonresistant William Lloyd Garrison, and by Lillian Wald, founder of the Henry Street Settlement.

Emily Balch also recalls her shock of incredulity in 1914: "My formative years were passed in the long Victorian peace and war seemed as obsolete as chain armor." To Emily Balch, as a social worker and practical reformer, as well as a professor of economics, the war was felt first as an extraneous interruption of social progress: "When the World War broke out in 1914 my reaction to it was largely a sense of tragic interruption of what seemed to me the real business of our times—the realization of a more satisfactory economic order. To that problem I had given myself unreservedly from my undergraduate days—first as a student and then as a teacher (though always as student) and also as sharing in efforts to change conditions in the desired direction, as occasion might offer.

"Now all the world was at war, one hardly knew for what—for reasons of ambition, prestige, mutual fear, of frontiers and colonies. None of the war aims seemed very relevant to progress, in any important sense." [3]

In England, a belligerent country, there was also at first equal surprise, and shock and inability to realize the unrealizable. Goldsworthy Lowes Dickinson, the charming, the beloved Cambridge don who represented the European humanist tradition at its best, felt that all he had cared and worked for, the enthronement of reason in human affairs, had vanished and a "grim obscene power" had taken its place. His novelist-biographer, E. M. Forster, describes his state of mind: "Dickinson's feelings when the war broke out are best conveyed by an analogy: they resembled the feelings which arise when a promise has been broken by a person whom one loves. One knows all the time that the promise will not be kept, perhaps cannot be kept, yet the shock is none the less mortal. Though all his observations had convinced him that men do not live by reason, he hoped that they would be converted in the hour of trial. . . . But that modern Europe, including his own country, should fall into the Devil's trap—that he never believed, however much he may have maintained its possibility in argument. The shock broke something in him which was never mended." [4]

Passion broke through the traditional veneer of calmness of the British upper classes. Bertrand Russell wished he had died. Kate Courtney, the wife of Lord Courtney of Penwith who was a strong opponent of the war, records in her diary on September 2, 1914: "This morning George Trevelyan—young George, but he looked quite old and worn—called. Personally he has nothing to fear, but anything more tragic than his face and manner I never saw. Everything he cares for has gone down. . . .

"After some talk, I said: 'Don't you wish you could sleep through until the war is over?' G. T. said, passionately, in a tone I shall never forget: 'I wish I could die,' and he covered his face with his hands and sobbed." [5]

In the United States, the first concerted arraignment of war and the first public appeal for possible future action came from the social workers, less than a month after the declaration of war in Europe. In this Emily Balch played a part. Jane Addams, Lillian D. Wald, and Paul U. Kellogg, editor of *The Survey*, a widely read national magazine for social workers, invited a small group of leaders and thinkers "who deal with the social fabric" to a series of meetings at Lillian Wald's Henry Street Settlement in New York. Emily Balch, Florence Kelley, John Haynes Holmes, George Kirchwey, Julian Mack, and Rabbi Stephen S. Wise took part in the round table discussions.

The results were put together in a rather long unwieldy statement, "Towards the Peace That Shall Last," which received considerable circulation at the time. Emily Balch had tried her hand at drafting a statement. In October, from Wellesley, she wrote Paul Kellogg urging him to make it "an absolutely simple, restrained, brief, hard hitting statement. It is not easy. If one must have a model I think Tolstoi is the perfect one—simple as a child's primer and pellucid as St. Mark."

Out of this informal, groping committee grew the American Union Against Militarism, from which sprang the American Civil Liberties Union, still flourishing today. Several of the signatories participated in the League of Free Nations Association, which in turn gave rise to the Foreign Policy Association. The Foreign Policy Association in the years to follow was to be a most powerful force in educating the American mind in foreign affairs and thus lessening American provincialism. This committee of Paul Kellogg's showed how the smallest of minorities, if moved by deep and selfless interests, may have far reaching influence in shaping segments of public opinion.

Most of the group, including Emily Balch, had worked among immigrants and held somewhat the same philosophy as Jane Addams. Jane Addams was in 1914 the best known, perhaps the best loved and most influential woman in America. Her name was synonymous with the Hull-House Settlement at Chicago and known all over the world. She had written *Newer Ideals of Peace*

(1907) and *A New Conscience and an Ancient Evil* (1911). In 1910 appeared her widely read *Twenty Years at Hull-House.*

In the streets that bordered the Hull-House Settlement were emigrants from all the countries of Europe—Austrians, Croats, Greeks, Bulgarians, Poles, Russians, Germans, Irish, Italians. They had left old-world enmities behind and were able to live side by side in reasonable harmony. Jane Addams could see that democratic development in this country cut under and across barriers of race and class, and that the leadership of the United States in uniting the multiple and diverse strands composing American life might be used as a pattern for a future international association, or as she called it, "a wider life of co-ordinated political activity." [6]

To Jane Addams, as to Emily Balch and other social thinkers, war, seeking its end through coercion, meant the reversal of the friendly and cooperating relationships of all the migrant races to whom she was a neighbor at Hull-House. These relationships they hoped would gradually extend to include the whole human family. If war prevailed, "all social efforts would be cast into an earlier and coarser mold." Also, Jane Addams feared the spirit of fighting would burn away that "finely tempered sense of justice" which she believed should form the keystone of political and social activity. This view is of particular interest, as pacifists were later charged with being indifferent to the claims of justice.

Emily Balch for a long time had been interested in the peace movement, as expressed in the Hague Congresses and the growing provision for arbitration. She had taken these up with her students as practical social problems, "but I had not come to the conviction, which later I gradually but inevitably reached, that there is no half-way house and that resort to war can and must come to an end.

"At first the war seemed almost incredible. Returning from isolation in the country, I was surprised to find that people generally, like myself, were condemning Germany. (I had thought that it was the other way 'round.) I was reading Tolstoi but could not (and cannot) [this was written in 1933] accept the use of physical force as in itself the criterion of right and wrong, though in deep sympathy with his position as a whole." [7]

As the war progressed she came to feel that the most effective

work for a better social and economic system was first to get rid
of the overhanging threat of war, and that until this was out of
the way no permanent or trustworthy progress could be made in
human relations. Later she came to realize more and more how
much the two sets of problems were but different aspects of the
supreme social task.

The first large-scale American movement to urge a new road to
peace was the Woman's Peace Party, formed in Washington in
January, 1915. Emily Balch, engaged in her teaching at Wellesley,
was naturally attracted to this movement. As the organization grew
and flourished she became active in the Boston and Wellesley
branch, and a year later, during a sabbatical leave from Wellesley
College, became closely affiliated with the more radical New York
City branch. Through these affiliations she became more and more
involved in the crusade for peace, and through them was drawn
into active participation in the Hague Congress of Women.

The Woman's Peace Party attracted widespread attention
because the two women who called the initial convention were
figures nationally and internationally known and respected, Mrs.
Carrie Chapman Catt, the leader of the American suffrage movement, and Jane Addams, the great social pioneer. The Peace Party
also attracted immediate attention because it was rather a novel
thing, a separate woman's movement for peace. The impulse for
the formation of the Woman's Peace Party was not American,
however, but came from abroad, from two European suffragists,
Rosika Schwimmer and Emmeline Pethick-Lawrence. This gave it
an international character from the beginning and linked it to a
large extent with the ideology of the woman suffrage movement.

Rosika Schwimmer, Madame Schwimmer as she came to be
called, was a Hungarian suffragist and journalist—dynamic, imaginative, emotional. She came to this country on September 6, 1915,
to present to President Wilson a petition endorsed by women's
groups of the International Woman Suffrage Association, urging
collective mediation with armistice. She also hoped to enlist the
support of American women in a possible world-wide women's
pacifist movement. In October an equally dramatic and equally
eloquent personality, the English Mrs. Emmeline Pethick-Lawrence (later Lady Pethick-Lawrence), good-looking, vivacious,
courageous, formerly a leader in the British militant suffrage move-

ment, had come to the United States to inaugurate a new suffrage campaign. "It seemed to me," she said in her memoirs,* "to offer an opportunity for enlisting the support of the suffrage movement in the neutral country of America for the idea of world peace secured by negotiation, and therefore just to all." In her talks and printed articles she stressed both feminism and pacifism. She also familiarized American audiences with the platform of the British Union of Democratic Control. This was an organization of pacifistic liberals and Socialists founded at the very outbreak of the war. Its aim was to secure popular control of foreign policy and work out the basis of a lasting peace.**

The new organization, the Woman's Peace Party, launched in Washington, D.C., at a mass meeting of 3,000 women in the Grand Ball Room of the New Willard Hotel, elected Jane Addams national chairman. *The Independent Magazine* of January 25, 1915, edited by Hamilton Holt, in a prominently boxed notice, declared, "They issued a manifesto, unsurpassed, we think, in power and moral fervor by anything that has been issued here or abroad since the Great War began. They adopted a platform, radical, sound, statesman-like, constructive. Though not a line about the conference appeared the next morning in five of the six leading New York newspapers, which found space to devote sixty-three of their valuable columns to the man-killing in Europe and the alleged reasons why the United States should increase her army and navy, we think the conference so important, that we publish in full the final document issued by it, and we urge every one of our woman readers to join the Party."

---

* Emmeline Pethick-Lawrence, *My Part in a Changing World* (London, Victor Gollancz, 1938), p. 308.

** It was initiated by a Parliamentary group, J. Ramsay MacDonald, Charles Trevelyan, Arthur Ponsonby, and by leading editors and authors such as Norman Angell and E. D. Morel. To it rallied men and women like Arthur Henderson, Bertrand Russell, Helena Swanwick, H. N. Brailsford (author of the widely read *The War of Steel and Gold*), Mr. and Mrs. Philip Snowden, and Chrystal Macmillan. The historian of the Union, Helena Swanwick, wrote: "To many people it was a rallying point, the one light in a terrifying darkness, and it become increasingly the only body to which people learned to look for an objective study of international relations amid the clamant din of war propaganda."[8] The most important restatements of U.D.C. points were those made by President Wilson in his Fourteen Points speech of January 8, 1918; his Mt. Vernon Address of July 4, 1918; and his Fourth Liberty Loan Speech in September 27, 1918.

The platform so highly praised was accompanied by a "ringing preamble" written by Mrs. Anna Garlin Spencer, which declared that war is "the sum of all villanies" and "the denial of the sovereignty of reason and justice." It declared further, and this sounds stranger to modern earns: "As women, we feel a peculiar moral passion of revolt against both the cruelty and the waste of war. As women, we are especially the custodians of the life of the ages. We will not longer consent to its reckless destruction." The justification for a separate woman's peace movement therefore was based on woman's peculiar grounds of protest against war, and also on her peculiar social and political disabilities in deciding on questions of war and peace. "We demand that women be given a share in deciding between war and peace in all the courts of high debate—within the home, the school, the church, the industrial order, and the state."

The historian of the Woman's Peace Party, Marie Louise Degen, declared that if it were not the first woman's peace society in the United States, it was at least the first in America, and one of the first in the world, to command wide-spread attention. "It was destined," she wrote, "in the course of the momentous events with which its dramatic history became interwined to exert rather considerable influence upon many Americans, men as well as women, to receive the commendation of President Wilson and other statesmen for its plan of international reconstruction and ultimately, rechristened as the Women's International League for Peace and Freedom, to figure powerfully among public pressures shaping the present foreign policy of the United States" (written in 1939).[9]

Of the program for constructive peace Jane Addams wrote seven years later, "Of course all the world has since become familiar with these 'Points,' but at the time of their adoption they were newer and somewhat startling." [10] Most of the proposals, in fact, though they seemed "startling," had been embodied in the peace programs of various contemporary groups: The Union for Democratic Control in England; The Dutch Anti-Oorlog Raad (Anti-War Council); The International Peace Bureau, The National Executive Committee of the United States Socialist Party, and others. They were to be incorporated among the objectives of the Congress of Women at the Hague in April, 1915; of the Central

Organization for a Durable Peace, with its "Minimum Program" antedating the pronouncements of the Women's Congress at The Hague by three weeks; and of the Henry Ford Peace Expedition in December, 1915.

The proposals merit attention because they foreshadowed the international programs which President Wilson was to advance. The peace societies therefore may be said to have paved the way for Wilson's international program. The planks the women adopted ran:

1. The immediate calling of a convention of neutral nations in the interest of early peace.

2. A concert of nations to supersede the balance of power.

3. A court, or courts, for the settlement of all disputes between nations.

4. Limitation of armaments and the nationalization of their manufacture.

5. Democratic control of foreign policies.

6. No territory to be transferred without the will of the people.

7. Neutralization of the seas and international control of strategic waterways, such as the Dardenelles, Panama, Suez, the Straits of Gibraltar.

8. No war indemnities to be assessed except when international law has been violated.

9. Removal of economic causes of war by national and international action.

10. An international police force to replace rival armies and navies.

11. Extension of franchise to women as a principle of self-government.

When the call came to hold an international congress of women at The Hague, Emily Balch obtained from President Pendleton of Wellesley leave of absence to attend the Congress. It was natural that Jane Addams, as the head of the American Woman's Peace Party and as one of the first citizens of a great neutral country, should have been invited by the European conveners to serve as chairman. Many of the officers and leading women of the new organization accompanied Jane Addams, paying their own expenses and trusting to the usefulness of the venture.

The honor of initiating The Hague International Congress of Women belonged to Dr. Aletta Jacobs of Amsterdam, a pioneer

woman doctor, a woman of courage and faith, and president of
the Dutch National Society for Woman Suffrage.* From this Congress resulted the international women's pacifist movement of
which Rosika Schwimmer had dreamed.

It came about in this way. The biennial meeting of the International Woman Suffrage Association, which was to have been
held in Berlin in June, 1915, was called off on account of the war.
Carrie Chapmen Catt was the International President at the time.
Many of the suffrage leaders who were internationalists were
deeply disappointed. Dr. Aletta Jacobs felt strongly that in time
of war and hatred, women should meet to show that they, at least,
could retain their solidarity and maintain their mutual friendship.
Holland was a neutral country, accessible to women of all nations.
The Hague was the citadel of peace. Dr. Jacobs was supported
in this by the Scottish woman lawyer, Chrystal Macmillan, a
secretary of the International Woman Suffrage Association. Therefore, a small committee of women—British, German, Belgian and
Dutch—was summoned at short notice in February to plan the
Congress at Amsterdam. The committee drew up a preliminary
program, issued a call to women of various nations, including the
Woman's Peace Party of America, and invited Jane Addams to
preside over the Congress.

Many European women welcomed this first attempt to renew
international ties and to consult on questions of war and peace.
But fierce criticisms also came, even from some of the women's
organizations. It would be impossible to hold the Congress in time
of war. No one would attend. The nationalities would quarrel
among themselves. The promoters of the Congress were probably
being financed by a belligerent. The announcement that Jane
Addams had accepted the chairmanship, however gave courage
to the initiators. Jane Addams and Fannie Fern Andrews (of the
American School Peace League) were asked to be the two American members of the Executive Committee. They undertook to
bring a delegation from the United States, not only from the

---

* Born in 1854, she was one of the first women medical students in the
Netherlands, beginning her studies at the University of Groningen in 1871.
After a year in London hospitals she began the practice of medicine in
Amsterdam in 1879. She became an ardent feminist, and accompanied Carrie
Chapman Catt, then president of the Women's International Suffrage Alliance,
on a trip around the world in 1911.

Woman's Peace Party, but from other interested organizations as well.

The suffrage women, therefore, were able to put through what the powerful Socialist International had failed to do. In the supreme hour of crisis, the closely welded Socialist "workers" and many of the great Socialist leaders of Europe (and later of America) had capitulated to nationalism. Men who had professed a closer tie with their fellow workers in other countries than with the possessing classes in their own, and who were solemnly pledged against "all capitalist wars," went out to slaughter their "comrades" in the enemy camp.*

"And now," says Izaak Walton, ending fourteen closely printed pages, "after this long digression, made for the information of my reader concerning what follows, I bring him back to venerable Mr. Hooker, where we left him in the Temple"—and to Emily Balch where we left her on the *Noordam*.

So it was almost like an edict in destiny that Emily Balch found herself one of the forty-two delegates sailing from Hoboken on Tuesday, April 13, on the Holland-American liner *Noordam*. The steamer flew a fragile homemade banner, white with blue letters, spelling out the word "Peace." Besides Professor Emily Balch, representing the Wellesley branch of the Woman's Peace Party and the Women's Trade Union League of Boston, and Jane Addams of Hull-House, "our incomparable leader," as Lillian Wald called her, there were Grace Abbott, director of the Immigrants' Protective League; Mrs. Fannie Fern Andrews, of the American School Peace League; Professor Sophonisba P. Breckenridge of the University of Chicago and dean of the Chicago School of Civics and Philanthropy; Dr. Alice Hamilton, Special Investigator of Dangerous Trades for the United States Department of Labor;

---

* Several attempts to convoke international Socialist action in favor of peace failed, including a generous effort of the United States Socialists in September, 1914, to finance an international conference in Washington, D.C., "for discussion of ways and means to most speedily and effectively stop the war."

A year later in September, 1915, a small international socialist conference of thirty-one delegates met secretly in the little village of Zimmerwald, near Berne, Switzerland. A second, larger conference was held in April, 1916, in Kienthal, a little village near Berne. Interestingly enough, the women Socialists were able to transcend national animosities. The International Congress of Socialist Women met in Berne, March 26, 27, 28, 1915, and sent greetings to the forthcoming Hague Congress.

Madeleine Z. Doty, representing the Woman's Lawyers' Association; Mrs. Lucy Biddle Lewis, a trustee of Swarthmore College, delegate from a group of Philadelphia Friends; and Mrs. Alice Thatcher Post, wife of Louis F. Post, Assistant Secretary of Labor. Also on board were Louis P. Lochner, secretary of the [American] National Peace Federation and the Chicago Peace Society, who acted as secretary for the delegates and handled the literature; and Mr. and Mrs. Pethick-Lawrence, the latter being an English delegate.

In spite of the undoubted distinction of so many of the delegates, they encountered bitter criticism which the newspapers were not hesitant about publicizing. The most vehement assailant was ex-President Theodore Roosevelt, who characterized the movement as "silly and base" and described the women as champions of peace "without regard to righteousness" and as "influenced by physical cowardice." He advised the women to "hold a meeting specifically to denounce the invasion of Belgium by Germany and to demand that in the interests of peace the United States do what it can to put a stop to those wrongs. . . ." [11]

The replies of the women were also publicized. The New York *Times* printed the objections of Mrs. Amos Pinchot, head of the New York City branch of the Woman's Peace Party, to Roosevelt's militarist doctrines. She did not agree with his premise that any effort to examine the causes of war with a view to diminishing them in the future by rational methods was both "foolish and noxious." Mrs. Fanny Garrison Villard, another leader of the Woman's Peace Party, observed "that the charge of base motives was a strange one to apply to a movement which seeks to conserve human life, and the accusation of cowardice a curious one to level against Jane Addams and the other women who have devoted their lives to the work of improving social conditions for working people."

Jane Addams, on the eve of sailing, reflected her usual serenity of spirit when she said: "We do not think we can settle the war. We do not think that by raising our hands we can make the armies cease slaughter. We do think it is valuable to state a new point of view. We do think it is fitting that women should meet and take counsel to see what may be done." [12]

Emily Balch, like Jane Addams was inclined to be deprecatory.

She thought before sailing that it seemed doubtful how valuable the meetings could be made. "I felt, however," she wrote a month later, "that even a shadow of a chance to serve the cause of peace could not today be refused. Never have I been so thankful for any decision. As I look at it now, the undertaking repaid all that it cost a hundred-fold.

"In this world upheaval the links that bind peoples have been strained and snapped on every side. Of all the international gatherings that help to draw the nations together, since the fatal days of July, 1914, practically none have been convened. Science, medicine, reform, labor, religion—not one of these causes has been able as yet to gather its followers from across the dividing frontiers." [13]

For Emily Balch and the other women delegates, the *Noordam* voyage was not the usual restful interlude of the peacetime tourist. As the delegates were almost the only passengers on board they were able to use the salon for daily conferences and lectures. "Sunny weather and a boat steadied by a heavy load of grain," wrote Emily Balch, "made it possible for the forty-two American delegates to The Hague Congress to meet and study and deliberate during the voyage. The secretary of the Chicago Peace Society [Louis P. Lochner] who had come with us, gave a brief course of lectures on peace questions, and after these were over we set about the consideration of the preliminary programme submitted to us by the committee at The Hague who were arranging the Congress. Some days we met morning, afternoon and evening and we added largely to the contents of the programme as sent to us. We recommended the so-called 'Wisconsin Plan' for continuous mediation without armistice. This plan, as formulated by one of our delegates, Julia Grace Wales, an instructor in the English department at the University of Wisconsin, had been officially endorsed by the Wisconsin Legislature, and recommended for the consideration of the Congress of the United States.

"We had just succeeded in working out our proposals by the time we sighted land, and it was well we had done so, for, though we were on the *Noordam* for five days longer, we were hardly placid enough to work to advantage." [14]

The *Noordam* was first stopped on Thursday evening about ten o'clock by an English boat coming alongside and training a little machine gun on the ship. "Think of Jane Addams," exclaimed Mrs.

Louis Post, "with a machine gun trained on her." [15] The English boat had come to take off two German stowaways. "If the proceedings had been staged for dramatic purpose," wrote Emily Balch, "it could not have been more effective. One prisoner, with a rope about him to prevent his escaping or falling overboard, shouted *Hoch der Kaiser, Deutschland über Alles* before he stepped upon the swaying ladder over the ship's side; both prisoners in the boat below us, with hands held up above their heads, were searched in front of that ever-pointing little cannon, then the soldiers carried blankets and cups of hot coffee to them in the hold. All this, lighted by the ship's lanterns, was just below us as we hung over the ship's side. Every now and then out of the darkness a new vessel drew up to us. At one time five were alongside."

"At last we were allowed to proceed, but not for long," said Emily Balch. The next morning, in the English Channel, directly off the cliffs of Dover, they were stopped by an English cutter and held motionless again for four days almost like prisoners of war. "We chafed and fretted," wrote Emily, "and telegraphed and brought to bear all the influence that we could command, but there we stuck, not allowed to land, not allowed to have any one come aboard, and for all one day, Sunday, with no chance even to send or receive messages. When telegrams were possible they were severely censored, and no indication of our whereabouts was allowed. 'All in the Downs our fleet was moored,' the old song says, and so it was and so was the *Noordam*. Around us were vessels not only of the English fleet, but of every sort, Norwegian, Greek, Spanish, and plain 'United States,' all with immense flags painted on their sides. Dispatch boats, torpedo boats, and torpedo destroyers rushed past, sometimes five in a string; a silver-glistening dirigible, probably scouting for submarines, was visible all one lovely afternoon. Once we saw firing, probably the shooting of a stray mine. Inshore gleamed the white and green of the chalk cliffs, and a cosy old windmill twirled its leisurely arms." [16]

The English cutter made repeated visits to bring fresh provisions. Coast guard ships and private boats brought English newspapers informing the delegates that all traffic, including mail, between England and Holland was suspended and publishing rumors of activity of the German fleet in the North Sea. The delegates also found bitter and scurrilous attacks on the Woman's Congress. The delegates were called "Pro-Hun Peacettes," and, as Jane Addams reported, "the enterprise was loaded with ridicule of the sort with which we later became only too familiar." [17]

The opinion gained ground that the whole stoppage of traffic with Holland was to prevent the holding of The Hague meeting. This seemed to Emily "a preposterous overvaluation of this little effort to many of us but the Pethick-Lawrences held this view. Gradually as one saw other vessels to and from Holland arrive it began to look as though after all the holding up of our ship might be to this end." Jane Addams sent a telegram off on Saturday to American Ambassador Page in London saying in effect that forty-two delegates on board the *Noordam* would be very grateful if their departure could be hastened. A second telegram to Ambassador Page asked that the delegates be transferred to the first boat going to Holland. Emily wrote in the journal she kept on the *Noordam* voyage, "By what right even in war time can they refuse neutrals passage to another neutral country? Our desire to see the seas neutralized increases as is readily intelligible as it comes home to us what it means for a single irresponsible power however well-intentioned to exert its own will unchallenged over all shipping.

"We are a very heterogeneous group of mostly highly individualized women used to being leaders and playing a conspicuous role, 'rebels' by temperament in many cases—we find ourselves being nerved to face a certain amount of danger, suddenly caught and stopped in an invisible net of a power we do not understand and in a situation to which we have not the key. No one, certainly not the men either, know what it is sensible to attempt or to leave undone. As a consequence there is naturally some nervous tension, a lack of cohesion, a tendency to criticize and to suspect the authorities and pull apart. This is not bad and I think we are trying to prevent such a tendency gaining on us. Miss Addams shines, so respectful of everyone's views, so eager to understand and sympathize, so patient of anarchy and even ego, yet always there, strong, wise and in the lead. No 'managing,' no keeping dark and bringing things subtly to pass, just a radiating wisdom and power of judgment and action without red tape when the moment for that comes without ever usurping or overriding or giving grounds for criticism." [18]

On Monday afternoon a boat came alongside with an answer from Ambassador Page saying he could do nothing as all traffic between Great Britain with Holland was stopped—that not even diplomats could cross. About twenty minutes after this another boat came with the news that they were released. By Tuesday afternoon they landed in Rotterdam in time for the first session of the Congress scheduled that evening at The Hague, half an hour away.

While the British government was providing drama and suspense for the American delegates, it was subjecting its own nationals to complete frustration. One hundred and eighty English women had accepted the invitation to The Hague. On April 16 the Permit Office announced to the British committee of women that "His Majesty's Government is of the opinion that at the present moment there is much inconvenience in holding a large meeting of a political character so close to the seat of war." [19] Therefore they would refuse and cancel all permits. Catherine Marshall and Mrs. Hill at once brought pressure to bear on the Home Office, and Lady Courtney of Penwith who was friendly to the whole undertaking went on April 17 to see Lord Haldane. He said frankly the Congress could do no good and might do harm, but he agreed to talk to McKenna, the British Secretary of State for Home Affairs. The latter consented to allow twenty-four members to be selected by himself to go. Then came the Admiralty order closing the North Sea for naval reasons. On being assured however that a Zeeland boat was to leave Tilbury dock at 7 a.m. on April 20, the chosen delegates hastened to Tilbury. And at Tilbury they remained, waiting for ship, airplane or even submarine, till the Congress was over. Fortunately two very able British women, Kathleen Courtney, not to be confused with Kate Courtney (Lady Courtney), and Chrystal Macmillan, both of whom were on the important Resolutions Committee and had reached The Hague earlier, made together with Emmeline Pethick-Lawrence, who had crossed on the *Noordam* with the Americans, a small but very brilliant delegation.

Emily Balch kept a diary of the voyage on the *Noordam*.

Passages from it not only furnish illuminating vignettes of her fellow delegates, but they also convey the seriousness with which these women approached the task their consciences would not let them evade. And the diary makes clear the essential sanity and sobriety with which Emily Balch and most of her fellows judged the limitations which circumstance was bound to set to their efforts.

"The boat is very pleasant, the service especially so. How can Dutch people so perfectly look their part. There is one tiny little cabin boy directly off a Christmas card, rosy cheeks and all.

"I have a great stateroom all to myself. Miss Molloy [Annie E. Molloy of the Telephone Operators' Union and the Central Labor Union of Boston] is in the room just opposite and I am glad for I would like to look after her a little especially as she represents a faction of the union opposed to those in the Women's Trade Union League.

"I came on board with a headache, tired and curiously depressed, but all that is going off. I had various telegrams and letters awaiting me on board, and a box of wonderful flowers from the Planning Board and some exquisite hepaticas, looking as though just picked, sent by one of my students.

"*Tuesday, April 13.* The Chicago group includes, with Miss Addams, Grace Abbott, most cordial and tonic and fine, Miss Breckenridge with her peculiar personal charm, and lovely Dr. Alice Hamilton, the specialist on industrial diseases and an integral member of the Hull-House group.

"From Boston came Mrs. Glendower Evans, eager and self-deprecatory Miss Molloy, a little trim figure sent by the Electrical Workers' Union, herself a telephone operator. The whole experience is new to her and she has a happy dignity neither ashamed to be pleased and interested, not over naive. Leonora O'Reilly from New York is another working woman representative, an old-time acquaintance of mine in trade union circles.

"We were pleased for its significance at a cable from Queen Wilhelmina, 'too gladly would be of service.' [Later, we fear this was a fake message. Too bad.]

"*Wednesday, April 14.* This evening Mrs. Pethick-Lawrence spoke, a friendly rather blousy lady in an ultra gown of the following materials swathed about her—brilliant green silk with large rose pattern in two shades of orange, black fur round part of neck and hanging in a tail behind her shoulders, crimson silk tight about the lower part, with a black and silver Egyptian scarf (adorned at the ends with large buttons with some sort of a rosette behind them) fastened very tight, across the breast diagonally, a lot of tarnished gold lace with crimson silk under it. I studied this as she talked—she told a series of stories about working girls, and slum children with the friendly unconscious patronage that hurts us in an English person of this type. It was genuine enjoyment of human nature, friendly and meant to be democratic but really disloyal and disrespectful, to our feeling. Miss O'Reilly's face was a study. I tried to counteract a little with a story of a shirtwaist worker who came out to Wellesley College to tell some of our students about a strike. 'At first I thought it was no use trying to tell them anything. I could see they did not know a thing. They offered help but could not go in the evening without a chaperone. What are the inmates here allowed to do?' I think Miss O'Reilly enjoyed my effort to turn the tables."

"*Thursday, April 15.* I am pecking away at a Dutch story for language interest, also with Dr. Hamilton at a Dutch translation of Miss [Julia Grace] Wales' pamphlet on arbitration. I have finished Anatole France's *Monsieur Bergeret à Paris* and began Suttner's *Die Waffen Nieder* which I have never read. I have also read Kant's fine essay on Eternal Peace.

"*Saturday, April 17.* Mr. Lochner's last lecture on the case against war created so much interest that we arranged for a discussion in the evening on the question whether war is ever justified. Mrs. Pethick-Lawrence spoke on the Yes side and Miss Addams explained Tolstoi on nonresistance, or moral substitution as she likes to call it. . . . It was agreed that it is no disadvantage if we do not agree on these theoretical points.

"*Sunday morning, April 18.* Miss Wales presented her plan of mediation without armistice and money was raised to pay for copies for distribution in German, French, and Dutch.

"It is a heavenly lovely day, sea blue as flowers and sky blue and high and soft with great 'cloud galleons' on the horizon. I have been out on the bow, talking with Dr. Alice Hamilton about her work in the study of industrial disease for the U. S. Bureau of Labor. She speaks of the great changes during the last five years; formerly most employers were crassly ignorant, now it is rare to

find one who is so and the employer is not now to be met who
says he is going to run his business his own way and so forth.

"*Monday, April 19.* We began having conferences on the program for The Hague meeting sent to us from Holland. We soon
organized with me as secretary and different members of the
delegation presiding. Some days we have met three times, morning, afternoon and evening, and as I had my minutes to keep in
order and was on various subcommittees to thrash out the wording
of disputed resolutions I have been too busy to do much else;
today especially I was busy all the time from breakfast up to five
o'clock and had not even discovered that the day was misty and a
little wet. Great letters are fixed on the balustrade on each side
of the upper deck spelling NOORDAM and in the evening these
are illuminated. We may see land tomorrow morning. We talk
interestedly at table of submarines and mines and the Captain
seems not to mind giving us all the facts. No one seems at all
nervous, nor to object to talking about such things.

"These days together have been invaluable, they have welded
us together and have revealed to a great degree our strong and
weak points. I think one thing that is disarming is that though we
are proposing to put forward all sorts of Utopian plans we do not
ourselves greatly misconceive the situation. We do not suppose
that we have power or knowledge or importance. We just mean to
do what we can and hope to stir little waves of thought and
feeling that may multiply and expand as every living thing can do
and so add our little momentum to the great whole that is rolling
up against war and advancing reason and good feeling between
nations. It does take faith but faith we have got and we do care.
We know we are ridiculous but even being ridiculous is useful
sometimes and so too are *enfants terribles* that say out what needs
to be said but what it is not discreet or 'the thing' to say and which
important people will not say in consequence."

CHAPTER SIX

The Hague Congress of Women, 1915

The Congress opened on April 28, 1915, in the largest hall in The Hague, the Direntuin, an incongruous, pseudo-Moorish structure in the Zoological Gardens. There were present 1,136 voting members, the largest number of whom were, of course, Dutch women. To many of the sessions the public were admitted as auditors, the attendance often reaching 2000. In the evenings a series of open meetings was held.

It was a novel conclave that confronted Emily Balch. "For the first time in the world women came together as women to give expression to their opposition to war and to consider ways of preventing it in the future."* Women from the enemy countries were meeting each other face to face while their husbands, sons, and brothers were fighting each other in the trenches. They had braved ridicule and every sort of difficulty to attend the Congress. Many came against the opposition of their governments, incurring the hostility of the press, the scorn of their families, the ostracism of their friends.

In spite of all the obstacles to meeting in time of war, twelve countries were represented, neutral and belligerent: Austria, Bel-

---

* From unpublished mss. by Gertrude C. Bussey, "History of the Women's International League for Peace and Freedom," Chapter I, p. 1 (Swarthmore College Peace Collection).

gium, Canada, Denmark, Germany, Great Britain, Hungary, Italy, the Netherlands, Norway, Sweden and the United States. Jane Addams in her presidential address on the last evening of the Congress expressed her admiration for these women who had come from home "at a moment when the national consciousness is so welling up from each hearth . . . that the individual loses not only all concern for his personal welfare, but for his convictions as well, and gladly merges all he has into his country's existence.

"It is a high and precious moment in human experience; war is too great a price to pay for it, but is it worth almost anything else.

"I therefore venture to call the journey of these women, many of them heart sick and sorrowful, to this Congress, little short of an act of heroism. Even to appear to differ from those she loves in the hour of their affliction has ever been the supreme test of a woman's conscience." [1]

Jane Addams also paid tribute to the women coming from neutral countries, especially those from Norway and Denmark, who had the vote and therefore bore a measure of political responsibility. They were sensitive to the delicate political conditions which could easily compromise a neutral people and plunge them into the same pit in which other nations were struggling. "At a Congress such as this an exaggerated word may easily be spoken, or reported as spoken, which would make a difficult situation still more difficult. But these women have bravely taken that risk and made the moral venture." [2]

In the course of this Congress Emily Balch was to play a constructive though unobtrusive part. At its end she was chosen as one of the six envoys to go directly from the Congress to see the chief statesmen of various neutral and belligerent governments in Europe, and to President Wilson in the United States, to urge upon them a concrete plan for attaining an early peace. With Jane Addams and Dr. Alice Hamilton she was later in 1915 to write the story of the Congress, *Women at The Hague,** and with Rosa Manus of Amsterdam and Chrystal Macmillan she was to edit the detailed proceedings*** of the Congress in three languages.

---

* Jane Addams, Emily G. Balch, Alice Hamilton, *Women at The Hague* (New York, Macmillan 1915).
** *Report of the International Congress of Women*, The Hague, 1915.

Outside the Direntuin, Emily found Holland gorgeous with the spring blossoming of lilacs, tulips, narcissus, and jonquils. Within the hall she encountered restrained emotions, painful attention, and quiet determination not incompatible with a realistic sense of the possible. The eyes of the women were fixed on a goal, and in the spring of 1915, even with Armageddon let loose, that goal did not seem unattainable to a hopeful realism.

The first evening Emily Balch heard Dr. Aletta Jacobs, president of the convening committee, welcome the members and voice the mood of the occasion. Three things Dr. Jacobs said may sound strange to us today: that it was too late in the day for war, that woman suffrage would prevent future wars, and that she was hopeful that this Congress would prove the dawn of a better world. The fourth conviction she expressed seemed stranger and more dangerous in her time than in ours—that the interests of humanity transcend the interests of country.

"With mourning in our hearts," she said, "we stand united here. We grieve for the many brave young men who have lost their lives in barbaric fratricide before even attaining their full manhood; . . . we will not endure in this twentieth-century civilization that governments shall longer tolerate brute force as the only method of solving their international disputes . . . .

"There are persons who believe it would have been better if we had postponed this international meeting and had waited till the war was over. Those who hold this opinion have forgotten to take into consideration that an international congress of women held after the war would bear a totally different character. The discussion on 'how to prevent war in the future' would be rendered more difficult if the Congress included both the conquering and conquered nations. . . . Far from being premature in holding our meeting at this stage, we might rather be reproached for having delayed so long before sending forth our cry of protest to the world. . . .

"We consider that the introduction of woman suffrage in all countries is one of the most powerful means to prevent war in the future. . . . But to accomplish this we need political power. . . . The governments of the world, based on the insight of the [male] half of humanity, have failed to find a right solution of how to settle international disputes. . . . Only when women are in the parliament of all nations, only when women have a political voice and vote, will they have the power effectively to demand that international disputes shall be solved as they ought to be, by a court of arbitration and conciliation. . . . May this congress be the dawn of a better world, a world in which each realizes that its is good to serve one's own country, but that above the interests of one's country, stand the interests of humanity, by serving which a still higher duty is fulfilled." [3]

The Congress was by any standards an unusual gathering in the caliber of its members. Many of the delegates were nationally known leaders in their countries, accustomed to action. Germany sent a splendid group of twenty-eight women, among whom the most impressive were Dr. Anita Augspurg and Lida Gustava Heymann, both pioneers in the German woman suffrage movement. There were also Dr. Helene Stöcker, pioneer in the German movement for "the protection of mothers and sexual reform," and Elisabeth Rotten of Berlin, of the League for the Care of Prisoners. A great disappointment was the absence of Freda Perlen of Stuttgart, who was refused a permit to leave Germany. She had been very active in the preliminary organizing committee in February. With Theodora Wilson of Keswick, England, who was prevented from coming by the British authorities, Freda Perlen had been responsible for the original controversial resolution entitled "To urge a Truce." There were nine delegates from Hungary, including the forceful Rosika Schimmer, who proved to be one of the leading and most colorful spirits of the Congress, and Vilma Glücklich, President of the Hungarian Feminist Alliance. From the Austrian Woman Suffrage Union came Leopoldine Kulka, "with quiet blue eyes and patient face," and Olga Misar. Italy sent only one delegate, Rosa Genoni of Milan, lecturer and writer. She did not claim to represent widespread feeling among her country women. Twelve delegates came from Norway, twelve from Sweden, and six from Denmark. Holland naturally sent the largest delegation of all neutral nations—about 1,000 voting members. The next largest group were Emily's fellow Americans, about forty-seven in all. Some—Lola Maverick Lloyd, Florence Holbrook, and others—had gone earlier than the party on the *Noordam.*

There was no delegate from France and none from Russia.° The Conseil National des Femmes Françaises and L'Union pour le Suffrage de Femmes sent a touching protest, sincere but pathetic in view of the future, declining a share in the Congress for French women: "In order that future generations may reap the fruit of this magnificent display of self-sacrifice and death, French women will bear the conflict as long as necessary." [4]

Five women managed to come from devastated Belgium. Eugenie Hamer and Marguerite Sarten and three companions had somehow obtained from the German authorities permission to attend. They went by automobile to Esschen, where they were searched; from there they walked two hours to Rosendahl across the Dutch border, and from there they traveled to The Hague by train. It was, therefore, a dramatic moment when they entered the great hall on the second day of the Congress. When a German woman, Dr. Anita Augspurg, whose country had overrun Belgium, rose to welcome them to a seat on the platform, they were given an ovation.[5]

Though 180 British women, including many of high distinction, were prevented from coming, the three who accidentally were able to be present were among the outstanding personalities— Chrystal Macmillan, Kathleen D. Courtney, and Emmeline Pethick-Lawrence.°°

Emily Balch described the temper of the gathering. "What stands out most strongly among all my impressions of those thrilling and strained days at The Hague is the sense of wonder at the beautiful spirit of the brave, self-controlled women who dared ridicule and every sort of difficulty to express a passionate human sympathy, not inconsistent with patriotism, but transcending it." [6]

Towering above the others, according to all accounts, was Jane Addams, the chairman. "Again and again, when she rose to speak and when she closed," reported Mrs. Elizabeth Glendower Evans

---

° No branch or section was ever formed in Russia. Sympathy for the Congress was expressed by Dr. Shiskina Javein, president of the Russian Society for Women's Rights. She subsequently entertained Emily Balch in her home when Emily was sent by the Congress as an envoy to Petrograd.

°° Among those prevented from coming were Helena Swanwick, Margaret Bondfield, Maude Royden, Emily Leaf, Mary Sheepshanks, Catharine Marshall, and Margaret Ashton.

of Boston, who was later to be prominent in the Sacco-Vanzetti case, "the audience would stand and applaud—until one pitied her for this challenge to her gentle modesty." [7] She "led without dominating," said Emily Balch, summarizing the general impression and praising the "extraordinary parliamentary skill" with which Jane Addams "led and clarified and interpreted the polyglot congress of women. I have never seen an exhibition of clear headedness, nervous poise and moral quality that approached this achievement."

The police who had filled the galleries at the first sessions gradually withdrew as it became evident that there was to be no disturbance. "A very curious thing," wrote Emily Balch, "has been the attitude of the majority of the press representatives who were present. Most of them apparently had been sent to get an amusing story of an international peace gathering of women—'base and silly' enough to try to meet in war time—breaking up in a quarrel. Day by day they went away with faces long with disappointment. 'Nothing doing today, but something worth while may happen tomorrow.' In England the Congress was reported to be in the interest of Germany; in Germany the delegates were threatened with social boycott for attending a pro-British meeting; and in many countries the meetings were reported to have been practically unattended or to have closed in a row. Nothing could be further from the truth than all these stories. . . . Difficult as it is to conduct business with so mixed and differing a constituency, with different languages, different rules of parliamentary procedure, and divergent views, Miss Addams and the other officials carried on orderly and effective sessions, marked by the most active will for unity that I have ever felt in an assemblage." [8]

According to the rules of order, two subjects were to be avoided: discussion of relative national responsibility for the war and the methods of conducting it.

Membership in the Congress implied adherence to two fundamental planks: first, international disputes should be settled by pacific means; secondly, the vote should be extended to women. This made for a very substantial unity of opinion, though it laid the Congress open to criticism as being a suffrage meeting as well as a peace meeting. Certainly many of the Americans, including Emily Balch, felt that the suffrage element was overstressed, though "after all," as she said, "it was the question of peace that, out and out, dominated the discussions and focussed our purpose and interest."

"The sessions," continued Emily Balch, "were heavily fraught with emotion, it could not be otherwise, but the emotion found little expression in words. When it did, it was on a high and noble plane. . . .

"There was not one clash or even danger of clash over national differences; on every hand was the same moving consciousness of the development of a new spirit which is growing in the midst of the war as the roots of the wheat grow under the drifts and tempests of winter.

"Because there were no clashes along national lines, it must not be thought, however, that the Congress was stagnantly placid. People cared too much for the subject under debate for that to be possible. There were most vigorous differences of opinion over details, and some energetic misunderstandings, for which the necessity of translating each speech into two other languages supplied many openings. . . .

"One's every faculty was on the stretch hour after hour, and we wondered afterwards why we felt so exhausted." [9]

The linguistic skill of many of the speakers was notable. "The first though not the only delegate to speak in all three of the official languages [French, German and English] was our own Emily Balch," wrote Mrs. Alice Thatcher Post, who kept a private diary of the proceedings. Julia Grace Wales, a Canadian delegate, described the impression Emily Balch made on the members: "She was outstanding both for the distinguished quality of her work as an officer and on important committees and for her delightful personality. No one knowing Miss Balch could fail to be impressed by her charm, keen intellect, never-failing sense of humor, wit and skill in debate, fine Christian spirit, imagination, expert knowledge in the fields of both politics and economics. . . . Her work was democratic, open, unspectacular work, constructive, solid, and sound. Her addresses were illuminating and inspiring, and her brilliant but kindly wit made for harmony, and was disarming to prejudice." [10]

The Congress drafted a series of proposals or resolutions which attempted to offer a basis for a just peace. "They were marked," said Emily Balch, "by insight and foresight." [11] On her return home, Jane Addams presented these Hague propositions to President Wilson. Many of them were later embodied in his famous Fourteen Points. "He was very much interested in them," said Jane Addams, "and when I saw him three months later, he drew out the papers I had given him. They seemed to have been much handled and read. 'You see I have studied these resolutions,' he said. 'I consider them the best formulation which up to the moment has been put out by anybody.'"[*]

Emily Balch wrote that the political thinking of the women was reflected in what they said of the hoped-for peace settlement: "Since the mass of the people in each of the countries now at war believe themselves to be fighting, not as aggressors but in self-defence and for their national existence, there can be no irreconcilable differences between them, and their common ideals afford a basis upon which a magnanimous and honorable peace might be established. The Congress therefore urges the Governments of the world to put an end to this bloodshed, and to begin peace negotiations. It demands that the peace which follows shall be permanent, and therefore based on principles of justice." [12]

As conditions of a permanent peace they listed the following:

1. No territory should be transferred without the consent of the men and women in it. The right of conquest should not be recognized.

2. Autonomy and a democratic parliament should not be refused to any people.

3. The governments of all nations should agree to refer future international disputes to arbitration or conciliation and to bring social, moral, and economic pressure[**] to bear upon any country which resorts to arms.

4. Foreign policies should be subject to democratic control.

5. Women should be granted equal political rights with men.

With the League of Nations still four years away, the Congress urged that the organization of the society of nations should include

---

[*] *Report of the International Congress of Women,* Zurich, 1919, p. 196.
[**] "This," wrote Emily Balch in April, 1938, "was novel and revolutionary doctrine in 1915. It was before Wilson's formulation of his Fourteen Points; four years earlier than the Covenant of the League of Nations. It was before the word 'sanctions' or the word 'aggressor' or the phrase 'collective security' had come into popular vogue."

a permanent international court for justifiable disputes and a permanent international conference. The latter was especially urged
by the American delegates to deal with matters of international
cooperation among the states and to formulate and enforce principles of justice, equity, and good will—not only in the interests of
great powers but of subject communities, weaker countries, and
primitive peoples.

As these planks were also on the platform of the Woman's
Peace Party, Emily Balch and the *Noordam* delegates were especially vigorous in supporting them as conditions of settlement. To
Emily Balch, both on the *Noordam* and at the Congress, was often
given the task of reconciling contending viewpoints and finding
solutions satisfactory to all. She was given the chairmanship of
difficult committees or subcommittees. Her judicial ability to see
both sides of a question and propose a new or third way was to
develop, as she became more involved in international political
activity, into a statesmanship that could deal with all facets of a
politically intricate question and then work out a unifying formula.

Further resolutions called for general disarmament to be
realized through international agreement, nationalization of manufacture of arms, control of arms traffic, liberty of commerce, free
seas and trade routes open on equal terms to all, foreign investments to be made at the risk of the investor (first suggested by
Sophonisba Breckenridge), secret treaties to be void, future treaties
to require legislative ratification, women to share all civil and
political rights and responsibilities on the same terms as men.

Two other resolutions concerned the education of children
towards the ideal of constructive peace and the participation of
representatives of the people, including women, in the conference
of the powers to be held after the war.*

Looking to its own future the Congress perpetuated itself by
forming an International Committee of Women for Permanent
Peace, to meet at the same time and the same place as the official
peace conference at the end of the war. Until then, the work was
to be carried on by a committee of five women in each country.
Emily Balch was named a member of the United States Committee. Jane Addams was made president of this new body and

---

* *Report of the International Congress of Women,* The Hague, 1915, pp.
35 ff.

Dr. Aletta Jacobs and Rosika Schwimmer were vice-presidents. Four years later, at the second Congress at Zürich, the name was changed to The Women's International League for Peace and Freedom.

The most novel and courageous proposal of all, the most ingenious and most unprecedented in traditional international thought and action, concerned the action to be taken for immediate peace. This was a plan for "continuous mediation without armistice." This was a substitute for an earlier resolution on the preliminary program calling for an immediate truce. Over this there was a good deal of controversy before the opening of the Congress. Many would not have thought it worth while attending the Congress if they had not hoped to pass such a resolution. On the other hand many women refused to attend the Congress or even to express sympathy with it, because they did not wish to ask for peace if there were any doubts as to the justice of that peace. These difficulties were met by putting into one resolution the demand for an end to the bloodshed and for establishing peace based on principles of justice.

The resolution on mediation adopted by the Congress embodied the specific proposal of the Canadian delegate Julia Grace Wales of the University of Wisconsin. It had been worked out on the *Noordam* by the American delegates. The Americans had asked to move the resolution for setting up machinery for continuous mediation *without waiting for the belligerents to stop fighting.* The *Noordam* delegation also raised money to print English, French, and Dutch copies of Julia Grace Wales' pamphlet, "Continuous Mediation without Armistice," for distribution among all Congress members.*

When the time came to present the resolution, it was Rosika Schwimmer who proposed it and Julia Grace Wales who seconded it. The resolution was adopted. Since this resolution led to the boldest action for peace to be taken by the Congress, the sending of women envoys, among whom was to be Emily Balch, to the belligerent and neutral governments, and since it also led, strangely

---

* Notes on *Noordam* discussions by Emily G. Balch, Secretary (Swarthmore College Peace Collection); Private Diary of *Noordam* Voyage and Hague Congress by Mrs. Louis F. Post (files of M. Randall). See also Chapter 5, p. 145.

enough, to the entirely separate venture of Henry Ford's Peace Ship, it is worth examining the origins of the idea.

The idea of a continuous conference of neutrals offering mediation had been advocated by Rosika Schwimmer at the very outset of the war. With her fellow suffragist, Mrs. Carrie Chapman Catt, she called on President Wilson on September 18, 1914 with an appeal from women in European suffrage organizations entreating the President "to combine the neutral nations under your own wise leadership in an insistent demand to all belligerent powers to call an immediate armistice until mediation has been given a fair opportunity to find a just settlement of international differences. Let the demand be repeated again and again until it is heeded." She campaigned widely on the subject in twenty-two states and issued a manifesto or broadsheet: "To All Men, Women and Organizations who want to stop the International Massacre at the earliest possible moment." Rosika Schwimmer later wrote to Emily Balch of this manifesto saying that it was "started the day of the outbreak of the war and circulated all over the world."*

Julia Grace Wales, a Canadian who was an instructor in the University of Wisconsin, had conceived a somewhat similar idea independently. Her plan, carefully worked out, revised many times, and put into print, was rather widely circulated and commended itself to many responsible people in America and Europe, and became known as the "Canadian Plan" and the "Wisconsin Plan."

Julia Grace Wales began to formulate the idea which she called "Continuous Mediation without Armistice" soon after the war broke out in August, and all during the autumn of 1914.** Her plan

---

* From mss. (13 pp.) in handwriting of Emily Balch, a transcript of information sent to her in July, 1938, by Rosika Schwimmer concerning Rosika Schwimmer's relations to the early history of the W.I.L.P.F. (Swarthmore College Peace Collection). The broadsheet (undated) was reprinted in the October 1, 1914, issue of *Jus Suffragii*, the organ of the International Women Suffrage Association. See also *The Outlook*, Vol. 109, March 24, 1915, pp. 676, 677 *re* Rosika Schwimmer's urging mediation with armistice, "being confident that this armistice would be the first step toward permanent peace."
** During the Christmas holidays Julia Grace Wales wrote an article, "the result of four months' intense thought and feeling," she later said. She had correspondence with Goldsworthy Lowes Dickinson of England and had discussed the pros and cons with university colleagues. The article she wrote was called to the attention of President Wilson on January 13, 1915, and to the attention of Secretary of State William Jennings Bryan, Jane Addams,

provided for an international commission of experts to sit as long as the war continued. They were to have a scientific function rather than a diplomatic function (i.e., they would be without power to commit their governments). The Commission was to explore the issues involved, in order to make proposals to the belligerents in a spirit of constructive internationalism. If the first effort failed, it was to revise the original propositions or offer new ones, coming back again and again if necessary until at last some practical basis for actual peace negotiations might be found.

Some of those who were working for some type of mediation through a neutral conference, like Rosika Schwimmer, hoped it would press for an early armistice. The essence of Julia Wales' idea was that *public standing proposals should be presented* to all the fighting governments *simultaneously* without waiting either for an armistice, for permission to mediate, or for the warring powers to be consciously ready for mediation. "Although the initiative could best come from a neutral government or governments," wrote Julia Grace Wales, "the plan was in its tendency not morally neutral but international, designed to bring out a clear definition of issues, and hence tending to an ethical international line up."

"Miss Wales," wrote Kathleen Courtney in an interesting comment in her introduction to an English edition of the Wales pamphlet, printed shortly after the Hague Congress, "does not, of course claim to have originated a new idea; it was indeed pointed out at the [Hague] Congress that 'continuous mediation without Armistice' is the most modern method of settling war, and that it replaces the ancient idea of a truce with its semi-religious associa-

---

David Starr Jordan, Louis Lochner, Senator La Follette, Jenkyn Lloyd Jones, and others.

The Wisconsin Peace Society in February, 1915, printed the article anonymously, lest her Canadian citizenship be prejudicial in the minds of neutrals. One thousand copies were distributed to the National Peace Conference which met in Chicago in February, 1915, the plan presented and the pamphlet read. The pamphlet was entitled: *Mediation without Armistice: The Wisconsin Plan.*

On April 1, 1915, a resolution was passed by the Wisconsin legislature commending the Wisconsin Plan to President Wilson. Later editions of the pamphlet were printed in England, Holland, and the United States. One was published in Sweden in 1916 by Henry Ford's Conference of Neutrals. Letter from Julia Grace Wales to M. M. Randall, September 14, 1950 (in the Swarthmore College Peace Collection).

tions, and that the first Balkan War was, in fact, settled by this method on the initiative of Sir Edward Grey. We believe, however, that the idea has not elsewhere been so fully worked out in an easily accessible form, nor has it before been put forward as a means of settling this war." [13] When Jane Addams was in London after the Congress, the foreign office told her that throughout the whole of the first Balkan War, mediation through the ambassadors of various nations had been offered on the initiative of Sir Edward Grey, and that it was to be expected that some other nation might suggest it in regard to the present war.

The Hague Congress decided to do more than merely place its decisions on record. The most important step was to urge the plan for continuous neutral mediation upon neutral governments for action, and to find out whether the belligerent nations would welcome or oppose such a conference. The energetic and persistent Rosika Schwimmer especially desired to use resolutions not merely as "paper expressions of pious wishes" but as tools to start action. Accordingly she introduced a new resolution—that the Congress of Women select some of its delegates as envoys to carry the resolutions in person to the heads of belligerent and neutral governments and to the President of the United States.

This was the most warmly debated proposal of the entire Congress. Many of the women thought it impractical. Emily Balch and Jane Addams both had grave doubts, though they were both to participate in the missions. Kathleen Courtney strongly opposed it and said that with the exception of Mme. Schwimmer every one who spoke in favor of it came from a neutral country. "I will speak in a calm manner," runs her talk in the *Proceedings* of the Congress, "and I don't appeal to your heart but to your head. Just one moment try to keep your heart out of the matter and keep your head on the question, and then you will see that this . . . is not likely to help to end the war. . . . I don't want to take steps which look well on paper but which are not practicable." [14]

Rosika Schwimmer asked for a word as a matter of personal privilege, as no one was allowed to speak more than once on a motion. She closed the debate by a passionate one-minute speech. The motion was carried with applause.

Jane Addams underlined the human achievement of the Congress in the words with which she brought it to a close: "This is the first International Congress of women met in the cause of peace in the necessity brought about by the greatest war the world has ever seen. We have been able to preserve good will and good fellowship, we have considered in perfect harmony and straight-forwardness the most difficult propositions and we part better friends than we met.

"It seems to me most significant that women have been able to do this at this moment and that they have done it, in my opinion, extremely well." [15]

Thirty-one years later, in 1946 in New York City, Emily Balch was addressing a group of members of the Women's International League in a Union Theological Seminary apartment overlooking the beautiful quadrangle dressed in its spring green. She was seventy-nine years old; she had just lived through a second World War deadlier than the first. She spoke of the women at the Hague and of their efforts. Reaction to the world situation in 1946, she said, could be twofold. It could be passive or it could be active like that of the pioneer women at The Hague; it could be resigna-tion or it could be opposite. And she quoted from memory the lines of Emily Dickinson:

> I took my power in my hand
> And went against the world;
> 'Twas not so much as David had,
> But I was twice as bold.
>
> I aimed my pebble, but myself
> Was all the one that fell.
> Was it Goliath was too large,
> Or only I too small?

CHAPTER SEVEN

The Delegation to the War Capitals

The pursuit of Emily Balch's career now leads to a bit of history almost completely overlooked in history textbooks and in accounts of the war—the action for peace undertaken by the envoys sent by the Hague Congress to explore with the governments of Europe the possibilities of neutral mediation. In this mission Emily Balch took an active part. It is significant of the respect she had won, that though her labors for the Congress had been so quiet, so unspectacular, she was selected as one of the emissaries. "For one brief accidental episode of my life," she later wrote, "I consorted with men in the seats of power. We talked with Prime Ministers and Foreign Ministers in Saint Petersburg and Copenhagen and Christiania and Stockholm and The Hague and London, and King Haakon chatted with us familiarly. In England Bernard Shaw and his wife invited us to tea and Lowes Dickinson dripped rain from his drenched coat and depression from his burdened spirit, standing on the hearth rug. In Washington I had an interview with Woodrow Wilson whom I had just missed the privilege of having as a teacher in Bryn Mawr." [1]

The delegation to the war capitals consisted of Jane Addams, the president of the Congress; Dr. Aletta Jacobs of Holland, the vice-president; and Rosa Genoni of Italy. They were accompa-

nied by two unofficial envoys, Dr. Alice Hamilton in her role as
"confidante in white linen" to Miss Addams, and Frau van Wulfften
Palthe of The Hague. Rosa Genoni had to return to Italy when
her country entered the war.

The second delegation, of which Emily Balch was chosen as a
member, was assigned to the neutral Scandinavian countries and
to Russia. "It comprised," wrote Emily Balch, "Chrystal Macmillan,
one of the [three] very able British delegates at the Congress:
Rosika Schwimmer, politically a Hungarian, but to whom nothing
human is alien; Madame Ramondt-Hirschmann, one of the most
active of the hospitable and capable Dutch women who prepared
the way for the Congress; and myself, coming from the United
States." [2] Julia Grace Wales, the author of the pamphlet *Neutral
Mediation without Armistice*, accompanied this delegation to the
Scandinavian countries, nominally as its secretary.

"Surely," wrote Catherine Marshall in June, 1915, "never since
Mary Fisher, the Quakeress, set out on her mission to preach
Christianity to the Grand Turk was such an adventure undertaken
by women. Those who were privileged to hear Miss Addams'
report[*] of their experiences felt as though they were listening to
some tale of medieval romance." [3]

Certainly the Second World War produced no episode so striking to the imagination and so unprecedented as these journeys
made by a handful of women seeking peace, not in the name of
governments, but as unofficial spokesmen for millions of deeply
sorrowing men, women, and children. At a time when the foreign
offices of the great belligerents were barred to each other and
attention was fixed chiefly on the war offices, these women went
from capital to capital conferring with the civil governments.

Both Jane Addams and Emily Balch, among others at the Congress, had been dubious as to the wisdom of the scheme. Jane
Addams felt that the Congress had ended very happily in good
will and understanding, and that it was perhaps unfortunate to
venture further in acrimonious debate. Emily Balch wrote in June,
1915, "Personally I may confess that at the Congress, I was among
the sceptics, that I did not believe the mission advocated by Frau
Schwimmer was wise, and that I agreed to go out of loyalty to a
collective decision. I am wholly a convert to the plan." [4]

---

[*] In London, in May 1915, after her interviews.

The women, according to Emily Balch, were neither impulsive nor very optimistic; they shrank from sensationalism. "We meant to leave no stone unturned but I doubt if any of us was ever hopeful of success." [5]

In all, the delegations visited fourteen countries in a little more than five weeks. When these unaccustomed representatives knocked at the "doors of the Chancelleries of Europe there was not one but opened," wrote Emily Balch. "They were received gravely, kindly, perhaps gladly, by twenty-one ministers, the presidents of two republics, a king, and the Pope. All, apparently, recognized without argument that an expression of the public opinion of a large body of women had every claim to consideration in questions of war and peace." [6]

The envoys were received by the following belligerents:

Prime Minister Asquith and Foreign Secretary Sir Edward Grey, in London.

Chancellor von Bethmann-Hollweg and Foreign Secretary von Jagow, in Berlin.

Prime Minister Stürgkh and Foreign Minister Burián, in Vienna.

Prime Minister Tisza, in Budapest.

Prime Minister Salandra and Foreign Minister Sonnino, in Rome.

Prime Minister Viviani and Foreign Minister Delcassé, in Paris.

Foreign Minister d'Avignon of Belgium, in Le Havre.

Foreign Minister Sazonov, in Petrograd.

and by the following representatives of neutral governments:

Prime Minister Cort van der Linden and Foreign Minister Loudon, in The Hague.

Prime Minister Zahle and Foreign Minister Scavenius, in Copenhagen.

King Haakon, Prime Minister Knudsen, Foreign Minister Ihlen, and Messrs. Loevland, Aarstad, Castberg, and Jahren, the four presidents of the Storthing (Parliament), in Christiania, Norway.

Foreign Minister Wallenberg, in Stockholm.

President Motta and Foreign Minister Hoffman, in Berne.

Pope Benedict XV and the Cardinal Secretary of State Gasparri, at the Vatican.

President Wilson and Secretary of State Lansing in Washington.

While in Rome, the delegation went unofficially (without a

mandate from the Congress), to the Vatican and had an audience with Pope Benedict XV and the Cardinal Secretary of State.*

The envoys laid before the statesmen the resolutions of the Congress with special emphasis upon the resolution urging the summoning of a neutral conference for continuous mediation. "As women," declared Jane Addams, "it was possible for us, from belligerent and neutral nations alike, to carry forward an interchange of questions and answers between capitals which were barred to each other. Everywhere, save from one official in France, we heard the same opinion expressed by these men of the governments responsible for the promotion of the war; each one said that his country would be ready to stop the war immediately if some honorable method of securing peace were provided; each one disclaimed responsibility for the continuance of the war; each one predicted European bankruptcy if the war were prolonged, and

---

* Although the interviews of the women with the rulers were prominently reported in the *New York Times* and other leading newspapers in America and Europe, the facts set forth in this book come from firsthand sources written almost immediately after the event.

1. Jane Addams, Emily Greene Balch, and Alice Hamilton, *Women at The Hague* (New York, The Macmillan Company, 1915); a collection revised into less colloquial form from articles printed in *The Survey* in the summer and fall of 1915.

2. A "strictly private and confidential" memorandum of August 2, 1915, by Chrystal Macmillan and Rosika Schwimmer, and a slightly amended memorandum of August 13, 1915, by Aletta Jacobs, Chrystal Macmillan, and Rosika Schwimmer (Swarthmore College Peace Collection). These were compiled from the notes and reports of the delegates. They give the dates of the interviews and the words of the statesmen.

3. K. D. Courtney (Lady Courtney), *Extracts from a Diary during the War* (privately printed in England in December, 1917). This contains notes of a report, probably confidential, given by Jane Addams in London to a select committee of British women on her return from the interviews.

4. A typescript, edited and arranged by Jane Addams herself, of a confidential talk she gave at the Colony Club in New York City on July 8, 1915, three days after her return from Europe (Swarthmore College Peace Collection).

5. "Manifesto issued by Envoys of the International Congress of Women at The Hague to the Governments of Europe and the President of the United States (October 15, 1915)." Printed in *Women at The Hague*, as Appendix IV; and in *Report* of the International Congress of Women (Zürich, 1919), pp. 469 ff. Signed by Aletta Jacobs (Holland), Chrystal Macmillan (Great Britain), Rosika Schwimmer (Austro-Hungary), Emily G. Balch (United States), Jane Addams (United States).

each one grew pale and distressed as he spoke of the loss of his gallant young country-men; two of them with ill-concealed emotion referred to the loss of their own sons. We heard much the same words spoken in Downing Street as those spoken in Wilhelmstrasse, in Vienna as in Petrograd, in Budapest as in Le Havre, where the Belgians had their temporary government." [7]

The women began the first lap of their mission on May 7, 1915, by interviewing the Dutch Prime Minister Cort van der Linden at The Hague. He received Emily Balch and some of the northern delegation for the second time two months later when they returned from the Scandinavian countries.

Then began the more dramatic part of the mission, the visits to the belligerent countries. Though Emily Balch did not go with this delegation, its findings were a fundamental part of the project she was to press during the next few months. Jane Addams and her group arrived in London at a very inopportune time—two days after the sinking of the *Lusitania*. So profound was the bitterness and hatred inspired by this "crowning outrage of German piracy upon helpless women and children," [8] that the English Parliament decided to intern German subjects living in London.

Through the reluctant offices of American Ambassador Page, who had nicknamed the Women's Congress "The Palace of Doves," [9] they secured an interview with Sir Edward Grey. Jane Addams was also received alone by Asquith.* Emily Balch wrote her brother Frank from Amsterdam on May 16, 1915: "Miss Addams has just returned from England where the whole delegation were received by Sir Edward Grey—and she was received alone by Asquith. Unfortunately not all that was said can be given out, but it was extraordinarily interesting. The situation is really much like a strike where neither party can admit that it is ready to let go. Women being outsiders have a peculiar *locus standi* which is proving to have considerable strategic value. . . .

"An interesting thing the representative of the English government said was that the belligerents could not do anything, the neutral nations must act. *This must not get into print.*" One of the encouraging things the women heard was from Sir Edward Grey. In response to a remark that the neutrals thought they should

---

* No record of this interview is available.

wait till the right moment came before taking mediatory action, he "indicated his astonishment by asking when did they think that the right moment would come."*

The envoys reached Berlin while the German citizens were still rejoicing over the victory their tiny submarine had achieved over the *Lusitania*, the "great auxiliary cruiser of the British navy." [10] Apparently most Germans accepted the sinking of the *Lusitania* without question. She was carrying ammunition, she was armed, the passengers had been warned and had no more reason to complain than if they had deliberately entered a city that was besieged. Germany was fighting in self-defense—they were sure of that. The invasion of Belgium was a military necessity. The American sale of munitions to the Allies was bitterly resented.

The American Ambassador in Berlin, James W. Gerard, reluctantly arranged the interviews. "Early summer," he wrote in his memoirs, *My Four Years in Germany*, "brought also a number of cranks to Berlin. Miss Addams and her fellow-suffragists, after holding a convention in Holland, moved on to Berlin. I succeeded in getting both the Chancellor [von Bethmann-Hollweg] and von Jagow to consent to receive them, a meeting to which they looked forward with unconcealed perturbation." [11]

The first visit was with Foreign Secretary von Jagow on May 21. He said "it was the right of women to do this sort of thing, he was surprised they had not done it sooner."** Herr von Jagow "said he thought it very desirable that peace should come soon but thought that the first step should be taken by the neutrals because it could not be taken by them [the belligerents]. When asked if he thought the United States should take the first steps to invite the neutrals, he asked whether the United States was neutral. He said that the neutral countries should form a conference such as the delegation proposed as soon as possible."***

Jane Addams saw Dr. Bethmann-Hollweg alone in the Chancellery on the Wilhelmstrasse overlooking a great shady garden in the heart of Berlin. She reported: "Von Bethmann-Hollweg was cordial. He was glad some one had begun to talk negotiations. French critics said why didn't Germany do thus and so, while

---

* Confidential Memorandum.
** Courtney Diary, pp. 42, 43.
*** Confidential Memorandum.

they themselves did nothing, unless it was to call the Germans Huns and barbarians.

"He said he had never heard a German say he wanted to crush England. I said I had never heard an Englishman say he wanted to crush Germany, but that they wanted to crush German militarism. He said that was a distinction but not a difference. The army in Germany is part of the government, and he went on to talk in that half mystical way they do—so difficult for us to understand. It is as if their feeling for the army was that of a church for its procession. It is a part of it."*

The delegation reached Vienna on the evening of Whitsunday. Italy had just declared war. There was a scarcity of wheat in Austria. The Viennese, many of them, looked starved. The horses were so thin that one could count their ribs. Everywhere were convalescent soldiers hobbling along the streets or wheeled in chairs.

The first man to be interviewed was Prime Minister Stürgkh, "a large, grizzled formidable man." This was to be a highlight of their mission, long to be remembered by the women. "We told him our little story," relates Jane Addams, "and he said nothing. I never have a great deal of self-confidence—I am never so dead sure I am doing the right thing, and I said to him:

"'It perhaps seems to you very foolish that women should go about in this way; but after all, the world itself is so strange in this war situation that our mission may be no more strange nor foolish than the rest.'

"He banged his fist on the table. 'Foolish?' he said. 'Not at all. These are the first sensible words that have been uttered in this room for ten months.'

---

* Jane Addams' Typescript. Courtney Diary: "Bethmann-Hollweg spoke more freely [than Jagow] and took things more seriously—had lost a son. Said 'No nation at war could begin. Neutrals were playing too feeble a part. Belligerents would not accept offer, but neutrals should begin and make propositions and go on making them.' He pressed Miss Addams to go to Belgium. Would give her every facility to see what good legislation they had introduced there. He said English constantly say 'Crush Germany.' Never hear Germans say 'Crush England.' Miss A. said it was German militarism. B. H. said that was an integral part of their life. English could understand no other type of government but their own—had no accommodation. He struck Miss A. as a good man, desiring some way out—representing civil opinion vs. military which perhaps was too strong for him," pp. 43, 44.

"He continued: 'That door opens from time to time, and people come in to say, "Mr. Minister, we must have more ammunition, we must have more money or we cannot go on with this war." At last the door opens and two people walk in and say, "Mr. Minister, why not substitute negotiations for fighting?" They are the sensible ones.'"*

Of the interview on May 27 with Count Burián, Minister of Foreign Affairs for Austria-Hungary, the women stated: "Graf Burián, the Foreign Minister, said he thought that a conference as proposed should be brought together as soon as possible. He did not think that America should begin because America did not know enough about European interests. He thought that America should send a representative to such a Conference but that it ought to be someone who understood European interests. Mr. Wilson's way of offering mediation was impossible because it was only offered, if the belligerents wanted it. Both parties were obliged to say no. He did not consider that the right way to offer mediation. He thought that definite propositions should be made to both parties. The neutrals can come again with proposals, if the first are not accepted."**

Because the Hungarians did not consider themselves Austrians, and because their Prime Minister Tisza had such high prestige, the two American women decided to go to Budapest while the two Dutch delegates went to attend a peace meeting in Berne. The suffrage society in Budapest was eager to hear Miss Addams and arranged an interview with Count Tisza and secured a letter of introduction to the Vatican.

Dr. Hamilton accompanied Jane Addams to see Count Tisza and was much impressed by her first experience of an "official palace, with many antechambers and lackeys." Tisza himself "looks curiously like pictures of General Grant, only that he is very tall and broad-shouldered. Like many Hungarians, he is a Presbyterian. He impresses one as a rather somber, stern man with great resolution, but not as the fire-eater, the fierce war-lord, which the

---

* *Women at the Hague,* pp. 96, 97.
** Confidential Memorandum. Kate Courtney also recorded Jane Addams as saying: "Von Burián received them, and was favorable to the idea of continuous mediation, but doubted U.S.A. leading. They did not understand Germany. Must send somebody who did. Holland afraid."

Austrians had described to us; certainly to us he said nothing of
the glories or gains of war, only of its senseless horrors." [12]

Of this interview Jane Addams said: "Count Tisza, of Hungary,
expressed the feeling that the Hungarians were getting nothing
out of the situation. Let Germany settle with the Belgians. He
would welcome negotiations."*

Leaving Budapest, the two American women, Jane Addams and
Dr. Hamilton, joined Dr. Jacobs at Berne and saw President Motta
and Foreign Minister Hoffman of Switzerland. "The Swiss officials,"
said Jane Addams, "were rather timid. They spoke of the immense
cost of keeping armies up on all their borders and the necessity of
keeping on friendly terms with all their neighbors."**

Rome was the next objective. On their way they stopped at
Milan and were brought face to face, wrote Dr. Hamilton, with
"Italy in war paint, for the streets were decked with flags of the
five allies and placarded with posters reading 'Vogliamo Salandra'—
It would never be difficult in Milan to stir up old animosity against
the Austrians, but among the devices used to extend this to the
Germans we saw conspicuously displayed in the shop windows
large photographs of a Belgian child with one hand cut off. . . .
It was evident [to Dr. Hamilton's professional eye] that the little
hand had been carefully amputated, but such trifling evidence was
of course not considered."***

Rome was in the greenness of spring, soldiers in fresh uniforms,
flags flying everywhere. No cripples as yet, no blinded men, no
widows, orphans, or starving refugees. Prime Minister Salandra and
Foreign Minister Sonnino, who had just led Italy into war, received
the delegates. It was hardly a favorable moment to urge peace.

Lady Courtney recorded the fruitlessness of their mission:

---

* Jane Addams' Typescript. Kate Courtney's diary states: "At Budapest, Count
Tisza very friendly. P.M., warrior, reasonable, Calvinist in religion. Grieved
over shock to religion. Hungarians did not dislike Russia. Fought her, but
Slavs understood them. Germans and Austrians did not. Austria-Hungary
would not be unreasonable about terms."
** Jane Addams' Typescript. Kate Courtney's diary added: "Berne. Saw
President Motta—open—Switzerland could not move, but when neutral coun-
tries combine would come in. Foreign Minister heard but said nothing.
Polite and cold, and they were soon out of his room."
*** Alice Hamilton, *Women at The Hague*, pp. 44, 45.

"Then to Italy. A War Ministry who had just 'downed' Giolitti.' Struck her (J.A.) as boyish and pleased with their new toy. Sonnino spoke lightly. Salandra (P.M.) more serious. 'Too early to talk about peace—some time.' Miss A. felt it was only a formal carrying out of their mission."

A much greater encouragement awaited them at the Vatican. They first saw the new Papal Secretary of State, Cardinal Gasparri. Jane Addams quoted Cardinal Gasparri as saying: "The Vatican was not supposed to want to go into anything that failed. That was not so, at least in this case. They would go into this undertaking. We discussed the possibility of a group which would not attempt to conclude the war but would conceivably create some basis in which we could go ahead. The Vatican was eager to go into such an undertaking and thought the President [of the United States] should be the leader. 'Why, certainly, it was the women's part to hold the conference.' "*

She also described the audience with Pope Benedict XV. "We had an interesting half hour with the Pope, who spoke of the war being a throwback for the church, after its teaching through all the ages. He thought the President of the United States ought to lead. If asked to send a representation to a conference of neutrals he would appoint, he said, a neutral and a secular. We took it that he meant that he would accommodate himself—would not stand on ecclesiastical grounds."**

The most discouraging experience was in France—understandably. France had been invaded. Part of her country was in the hands of the conqueror. No French woman had come to the Congress at The Hague. A group of leading women had sent a protest against the holding of such a congress. Of the women they met, every one had at least one near relative at the front or already killed. They saw Foreign Minister Théophile Delcassé and on June

---

* Jane Addams' Typescript.
** Jane Addams' Typescript. Courtney Diary: "Saw Cardinal Gasparri. Pope's Secretary of State. Spoke with great freedom and sweetness. He would go in to help even with slight chance of success. The Pope she saw unofficially for half an hour. He struck her as younger and less impressive than she expected. Keen, ready, alert, talked like a good man and an able one. 'Difficult position.' If President Wilson led the way, would follow. Would appoint a Catholic neutral a secular. (?)"

14 interviewed Prime Minister René Viviani. "M. Viviani said that
France would 'not resent' the formation of a neutral conference
for the offering of continuous mediation such as we propose."*
But more revealing of French feeling than Viviani's grudging
remark, was Lady Courtney's brief record of Jane Addams' story:
"France next; very discouraging. Government vs. women. Delcassé
frankly jingo. 'No negotiations, even the best. Destroy Germany so
that she would not come up for 100 years.' Everything heavily
censored. Viviani more reasonable, but still no negotiation, but
moved his position after their talk. They were always followed by
police in France."**

Though not present at the interview with Viviani, Emily Balch
had nevertheless heard the confidential reports of the first mission.
She recalled their saying that Viviani had listened to the women
more patiently than had Delcassé, and "even declared that he had
drunk in pacifism with his mother's milk."***

The last visit was to the Belgian Minister of Foreign Affairs,
M. d'Avignon, on June 16. "Poor little Belgium," wrote Alice Hamilton, "has had to accept the hospitality of France, and her government is housed in hotels and villas on the seashore near Le Havre.
The Belgium minister for foreign affairs was a sad, gentle person,
who took the mission of the delegation very seriously and spoke
with real feeling of Belgium's longing for peace, although, as he
said, she was in the hands of her allies and must leave such things
to them." [13] M. d'Avignon said "that Belgium would rather have
the enemy leave their country as the result of negotiations than
have the armies fighting over it a second time."****

At Le Havre the French police objected to their mission, even
though the French ministers had received them, and they found it
best to go back to Paris without staying for the night at Le Havre.

With this visit the Jane Addams' delegation concluded its man-
date from The Hague Congress until the resolutions and their
European reception could be presented to President Wilson. Jane
Addams had a week in England before sailing home from Liver-

* Confidential Memorandum.
** Courtney Diary, pp. 45 ff.
*** Letter of Emily Balch to Marie L. Degen (undated).
**** Confidential Memorandum.

pool. In response to her request to see Sir Edward Grey, she received from him a handwritten letter on his personal notepaper:*

> Falloden, Lesbury
> Northumberland
> June 20, 1915

(Private)

Dear Miss Addams,

I have received your letter and I should personally be most interested to hear the impressions gained by you of the views of Statesmen in other belligerent countries.

I think it is also important that these should be known to the British government; but this latter object can best be effected by your seeing one of the ministers or some responsible person in London.

I am by the urgent advice of an oculist having treatment and complete rest for my eyes and am not to return to work in London till next month. By this means it is hoped to save my eyesight which, from long standing trouble and inability to give it rest and treatment before, had been in danger. Meanwhile my work has, since the change of government, been handed over temporarily to my colleagues. I am therefore sending your letter to the Foreign Office and asking them to communicate with you.

From all I have heard of President Wilson, I have a very great respect for him, and I had reason to believe before I left London that he would be very fully informed of my own personal views about the war and the future peace.

> Yours sincerely,
>
> E. Grey

During this time in England, Jane Addams, largely through the energy of the influential Lady Courtney, author of the *War Diary*, conferred with British statesmen and figures in public life—Lord Robert Crewe, Lord Robert Cecil, David Lloyd-George, the Archbishop of Canterbury, the Bishop of Winchester. She was also warmly received by many unofficial people.

The last overcrowded week of Jane Addams in England was recorded by Lady Courtney: "During this stay [in London] she (J.A.) privately saw a good many people. L. [Leonard**] went

---

* E. Grey to Jane Addams, June 20, 1915 (Swarthmore College Peace Collection).
** Lord Courtney of Penwith.

to the F.O. and she saw Lord Crewe in Sir E. Grey's absence, and I arranged with Lady Selbourne for her to ask her to lunch, and Lord Robert Cecil to meet her. Also Lloyd George, who was full of his munitions, and went for the complete crushing defeat of Germany. The official element here were not encouraging any more than in France. She lunched with Lord Morley, but either was tired there, or overborne with Lady Lyttleton's vivacious militarism, and dined with Lord Loreborn. The last day of her stay it occurred to me she ought to see the Archbishop of Canterbury, so off I boldly went to Lambeth, but was a bit disconcerted when the Chaplain came down and said the Archbishop was ill and in bed. Still, I was moved to persist, and found he was getting up soon, but 'had important interviews and must go to Lords.' However, I told the young man a little about Miss A's journey through Europe, and he went off to his chief, and promptly came down to say the latter would certainly see Miss A. It was most important. So she went in the afternoon, and the Bishop of Winchester was present also. Miss A. told L. in Lords, and Sir K. Digby also; he had been much interested and impressed, and Miss A. said the two bishops have asked her more questions than anybody else, about the Pope especially.

"And now [July 7] I hear she is back in America. May she help to inspire the President, and above all press on him the idea of 'continuous mediation' by neutrals—without armistice and without being asked by the belligerents."*

In summing up the conclusions which the delegates drew from their experiences in war capitals, Jane Addams declared that the first thing which struck the women was that the same causes and the same reasons for the war were heard and assigned everywhere. All the warring nations solemnly assured them, in different tongues but in almost identical phrases, that they were fighting in self-defense.

Another striking thing, repeated by all the foreign offices, again in very similar phrases, was that a nation at war cannot ask for negotiations or even express a willingness to receive negotiations, for fear the enemy will construe it as a sign of weakness.

But in all of the foreign offices except in France they heard that if neutral powers commanding the respect of the foreign

---

* Courtney Diary, p. 46 ff.

offices to whom their proposals would be presented, should present tentative propositions, over and over again if necessary, something might be found upon which negotiations might begin. None of the warring nations except France would fail to be glad and ready to receive such a service. "That came to us unequivocally," said Jane Addams.

In each country they found two segments of public opinion, one finding expression in the military party, which believed that the matter could be settled only upon a military basis; the other, a civil party that deprecated the growing power of the military in censorship of the press, in depredations on civil life and civil government, and longed more and more for some other form of approach to the terrible conflict.

"Our mission was simple," concluded Jane Addams, "and foolish it may be, but it was not impossible. Perhaps the ministers talked freely to us because we were so absolutely unofficial. . . . Responsible people in all the warring powers said that if the right medium could be found, there would be no difficulty in submitting the case.

"We do not wish to overestimate a very slight achievement nor take too seriously the kindness with which the delegations were received, but we do wish to record ourselves as being quite sure that at least a few citizens in these various countries, some of them officials in high places, were grateful for the effort we made." [14]

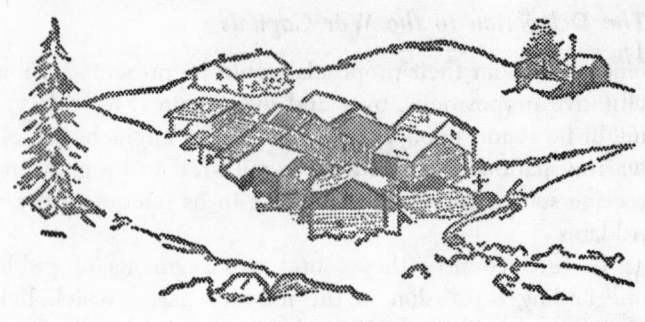

CHAPTER EIGHT

The Delegation to the Northern Capitals

Meantime Emily Balch, and the second delegation consisting of Chrystal Macmillan, Cor Ramondt-Hirschmann, and Rosika Schwimmer who headed it, were making the rounds of the northern capitals. Julia Grace Wales and Lola Maverick Lloyd accompanied them unofficially.

From Amsterdam on, the party could not travel together. The route to Copenhagen was through Germany. Under war conditions it took two days, with an overnight stop at Hamburg. But British Chrystal Macmillan and Canadian Julia Grace Wales were not permitted to cross into enemy territory. To find a boat was not easy. They finally found a little packet unfit for passenger use. It had no cabin but the captain's and there was no woman on board. The captain told them that if they struck a mine or were torpedoed they would sink without any chance of rescue. "The other three of us went by train," wrote Emily "through fields with thriving crops and few men-folks, over heaths where prisoners of war were at work converting the moors into ploughland, past station-platforms where fathers and wives were bidding sad goodbyes to their soldier boys, and where girls with the red cross on their arms were serving refreshments to passing troops."[1]

In Copenhagen they were given interviews with Prime Minister

Zahle and Minister of Foreign Affairs de Scavenius. Emily Balch wrote to Louis Lochner from Christiania [Oslo] on June 1: "Now, what we are asking the Scandinavian governments is, 'Would you three with Switzerland and Holland send out an invitation to a neutral conference if you knew that the U. S. would be glad to respond?' This on the supposition that the present state of public opinion in Germany excludes the U. S. as the first mover. (I am not at all sure that this is true.) Of course people say, 'Wilson has already offered mediation.' Is it not important that Wilson should make it clear that he has not taken a position such that it would be a discourtesy to the U. S. if some other neutral nation or nations acted?" [2]

Emily Balch also wrote Louis Lochner that Mme. Schwimmer had had a talk in Copenhagen with the German ambassador there, and had reported back to Miss Balch that he had spoken very frankly and was "quite international minded. He thought that President Wilson of the U.S.A. had behaved very badly. Ammunition? No. It was *etwas unerhört* that a great neutral country like the U. S. had not come forward in such a war."

In Christiania they had a full program. Their first interview was with King Haakon VII, who kept them so long that they began to fear that, in their ignorance of ceremonial, they had missed the signal which ends a royal reception. From the King they went directly to Foreign Minister Ihlen and later to Prime Minister Knudsen. They were also given an honor which the women, being unofficial persons, prized highly, a reception in the Parliament House. It is hard for us today to realize that it could thrill the women to observe on the walls a portrait of Anna Rogstad, the first woman to sit in the Norwegian parliament. At a meeting at the Nobel Institute they had an opportunity to discuss peace programs with Christian Lange, secretary of the Interparliamentary Union, who was to receive the Nobel Peace Award in 1921.

In Stockholm the delegates had what they considered the most hopeful of all their interviews, with Foreign Minister Wallenberg. He was not only foreign minister, but also an influential banker. Of all the statesmen he appeared to the women the most enthusiastic for the plan of neutral mediation.

Among the distinguished Swedes who showed their sympathy and interest, was Selma Langerlöf, who, at the beginning of the war had said, "The political mission that is waiting for women upon their entrance into political life is to make the idea of the holiness of life accepted." [3] In 1918 she was to write a pacifist novel *The Outcast*.

The next assignment carried the delegation to a belligerent country, Russia. At this point a change had to be made. Rosika Schwimmer, technically an enemy, could not go to Russia. Her place was taken by Baroness Ellen Palmstierna, a distinguished Swedish woman.

On the evening of June 7, the group started for Russia. "The usual route from Stockholm to Petrograd is across the narrow seas to Abo in Finland," wrote Emily Balch. "This passage is now closed to travellers, which means that one must make a railroad journey of three days and three nights round the head of the Gulf of Bothnia. We had been told that this journey would be very hard travelling, but we did not find it so, although we were glad to reach the Hotel Astoria a little before midnight on June 10. We stayed here [Petrograd] an unexpectedly long time,—a fortnight, in fact,—and this gave us an opportunity to see much of this fine and interesting capital, filled today with Red Cross 'lazarets' and with wounded; a clean, orderly, and friendly city, as we observed it." [4]

Their object was an interview with Sazanov, Minister of Foreign Affairs. Then as now, any interview within the borders of Russia with a history-making personality was a memorable experience. Sazonov, in the interview of June 16, repeated in part what the British statesmen had already told Jane Addams and were to tell Emily Balch in London.

"In Petrograd," wrote Emily Balch, "Dr. Shiskina-Javein, the President of the Russian League for Equal Rights for Women, was most hospitable, and insisted on carrying all four of us to her house. . . . It was, of course, not possible to hold meetings, nor was it easy to meet many people, 'everyone' being already in the country. We had several interesting private talks with M. Miliukov, the leader of the Cadet Party, who had known Miss Addams in America." [5]

On their return to Stockholm, the warmest welcome awaited them, reflecting the peace sentiment in Sweden. In Stockholm alone five meetings took place. The demonstration Emily Balch attended gathered about 2,000 people, beside an overflow of some

1,200, while 800 could not get in at all. This, in spite of the fact that it was a season when people were scattered and meetings thought to be impracticable. All the meetings affirmed the main resolutions of The Hague Congress and called for mediation.

Foreign Minister Wallenberg received the women a second time. The hopes they pinned on this statesman are recorded in Emily Balch's letter* to Jane Addams which she wrote when she reached Amsterdam.

> American Hotel
> Amsterdam
> July 3, 1915

Dear Miss Addams:

In Copenhagen we found most markedly that fear of being committed to anything that had been shown by the Danish women at The Hague. We were received most formally by the prime minister, Mr. Zahle, and the minister of foreign affairs, Mr. Scavenius. We were told that only two of us were expected to speak and they would reply by handing to us a ready written response. . . . This of course was in the most general terms.°°

Net result—we were officially recognized and our arguments may have created some sympathy with our ideas.

In Christiania the atmosphere was lighter. Norway is in a much easier position with no belligerent neighbor, no Schleswig-Holstein difficulty and a safe situation as regards contraband traffic.

---

* This letter is also the only general account available to date of the experiences of the second delegation in Denmark, Norway, Sweden, Russia and Holland. The papers of Rosika Schwimmer, who died in 1948, have not so far been made accessible.

°° Statement made to E. Balch, C. Macmillan, C. Ramondt-Hirschmann and R. Schwimmer by Prime Minister Zahle and Foreign Minister Scavenius in Copenhagen on Friday, May 28th, 1915: "The wish expressed by the Congress as to the discontinuance of the present dreadful war—a wish which, I feel sure, is most warmly entertained amongst the women of all countries— will meet with universal sympathy in this country. As far as the Danish Government is concerned the Government will—as declared in August last year by the Minister for Foreign Affairs in reply to an address from the Danish Peace Union—gladly render their co-operation when possibilities might offer themselves for endeavours on the part of neutral States aiming at the restoration of peace. I shall have the honour to give His Majesty the King information of your address and also report to His Majesty what has been pronounced here." Archives, W.I.L.P.F. International Headquarters, Geneva.

We were received in private audience by the king who talked much of the time and most informally for almost two hours. He seemed genuinely interested in our ideas especially in our plan of continuous mediation. After this we had a formal interview with the minister of foreign affairs, Mr. Ihlen. It looked as if we should not be able to see Mr. Knudsen, the prime minister, a well known pacifist, as his wife is very ill; nevertheless he made an opportunity and invited us to come and speak with him. He was very much in sympathy I think. He asked many questions and promised that the cabinet would consider our plan. . . .

In Stockholm we had only one official interview but that was worth all the others put together. The Swedish minister of foreign affairs is a powerful personality, an able man. The case appears to be that he desires to have the conference when peace comes to be made, held in Stockholm and that he would be glad to play a role in all this. We therefore played on this string.

What follows is very private and probably should not be confided to any one but the president [Woodrow Wilson].

We brought Mr. Wallenberg to more and more concrete positions. He finally said that he would be willing to take the initiative in regard to a neutral conference if he had sufficient evidence that it would be "not unacceptable" to the belligerents. We pressed the question of what would be sufficient evidence and got him to say that if a lady for instance brought a little billet from the two chief representatives on both sides that would be enough.

In Petrograd we were advised to strike for M. Sazonov, the minister of foreign affairs, as the man of most power. The British Ambassador was very helpful and after about a week we got our interview. We wasted a second week waiting to learn whether or not the Czar would also receive us. M. Sazonov very kindly made the request for us but it was a peculiarly difficult moment and our request was not granted.*

---

* Emily Greene Balch, Report of the Envoys' Interview with Sazonov, Petrograd, written July 3, 1915, Archives, W.I.L.P.F. International Headquarters, Geneva: "We asked if we might see the Czar and present our resolutions to him as the promoter of international peace. On our first suggesting it Sazonov said nothing but on our making the request quite definitely to ask it for us he said he would do so but it would be very difficult. The Grand Duke Constantine had just died the night before (?) or that morning (?) (this was the first we had heard of this news). That this would make it difficult

The interview with Sazonov was deeply interesting. He talked with us quite freely for the greater part of an hour. He did not talk as an extremist but affected an entirely moderate tone about the war. Of course he said that the Germans caused it and blamed them for their way of conducting it. He spoke slurringly of the way the U. S. took Germany's behavior to her at which I fired up, but there was none of the sort of talk that we had been hearing from English and American reporters of the necessity for destroying Germany. He spoke of the inexhaustible numbers of the Russians and of their historical expansion but he said that Russia has now reached her natural bounds and would "roll over" no further territory. As regards the Dardanelles Russia wants only free passage assured her.*

We pressed the point of continuous mediation by a neutral conference. He said he had read our resolutions and understood our idea. When we asked him if he would consider the calling of such a conference an unfriendly act he smiled and said of course not how could he? He himself used the phrase "not unacceptable." Mrs. Ramondt asked if in order to be sure that we got his meaning correctly we might write down what he had said. He was quite willing provided we included his remark that he did not think that it would lead to any results at the present time. So we wrote all this down and he was so kind as to read it through and to state that it was correct. He asked us not to make it public.**

Returning to Stockholm we again saw Wallenberg and told

---

for the Czar to have time as he was going to the front again after the funeral. He spoke of the Czar being out of the city as though this precluded our seeing him. Miss Macmillan replied we would be perfectly willing to go outside St. Petersburg to see him. I think he did not *look* amused at this. He said that if we saw the Czar we should find him most charming. He spoke in praise of the dead Grand Duke, so charming a man, so gifted, a poet, one of the most beloved of the whole family." The delegation received word that an interview with the Czar was not possible.

* Sazonov was disingenuous. He had already concluded agreements with Great Britain in March, 1915, and with France in April, 1915, providing for Russian annexation of several Turkish provinces, including Constantinople and the Straits.

** On the same day this letter to Jane Addams was written, July 3, 1915, Emily Balch wrote out an informal report never revised for publication, giving a much fuller account of the envoys' interview with Sazonov. Since the details of this visit are of great human interest, the larger part of this report is appended to this chapter.

him all this. He said now that he had said he would be willing to act if we brought evidence that the belligerents asked him to but on our stating our remembrance of it as given above I think he tacitly admitted our version. He seemed to think the attested transcript of a conversation such as we had brought adequate but he claimed that the clause as to not expecting any results as making it valueless. He asked us to come back and tell him if we had anything further to report. All this sounds more negative than the first interview but I think he was taking the whole thing even more seriously.

In Christiania Miss Macmillan saw Ihlen again and in Copenhagen Mrs. Ramondt and I were received quite privately and with a request not to put it in the newspapers by Mr. Edouard Brandes, the minister of finance. He was cynical or at least very skeptical but he said he did not doubt that Denmark would join a neutral conference if Sweden and Norway did so. Doubtless Norway would say the same.

Here in Holland Mr. Cort van Linden seems to be in quite an oncoming mood. Dr. Jacobs and Madame Schwimmer have seen him and he asked to be informed if we had any further news so we are to report our experiences to him on Wednesday. I think Dr. Jacobs is very anxious to have Holland be the country to do this great thing so much so that that unconsciously makes her oppose our idea of going again to Berlin and London to try to get something like what we got from Sazonov. Our present plan is to try to do this unless Holland is so promising that it does not seem worth while. [Signed] Emily Balch.[6]

In Amsterdam the two delegations met and exchanged reports. One conclusion the women drew was that the neutrals seemed to be afraid that the immediate calling of a neutral conference might be considered inopportune or unfriendly by the belligerents. The delegates, therefore, decided to revisit at least one of the important belligerents on each side to bring assurance, if possible, to the neutrals.

Rosika Schwimmer and Cor Ramondt-Hirschmann went to Berlin to interview von Jagow. Emily Balch and Chrystal Macmillan journeyed to London where they were received by Lord Crewe, acting Foreign Secretary in the absence of Sir Edward Grey, and later Emily Balch was received by Edward Grey himself. The women explained in each case that it would strengthen the hands of the neutral governments towards the calling of a neutral conference, if they were convinced that such action on their part would not be taken as unfriendly by the belligerents.

A written statement in two versions from von Jagow on July 15, and a letter from the London Foreign Office to Miss Macmillan were obtained and interpreted by the delegates as the necessary reassurance and as evidence that neutral action would not be resented:

> Herr von Jagow sagt Deutschland würde nichts Unfreundliches darin finden, wenn eine Conferenz von Neutralen einberufen würde, glaubt aber man soll sich nicht zu viele Illusionen davon machen.*

After he had read the above version, Herr von Jagow said that it did not express his meaning, and he changed it to the "more encouraging" form, as follows:

> Herr von Jagow sagt Deutschland würde nichts Unfreundliches darin finden, wenn eine Conferenz von Neutralen einberufen würde, fragt sich aber ob es practische Folgen haben würde.**

As a further indication of von Jagow's not unfavorable attitude, another statement of his which he made to Rosika Schwimmer and Cor Ramondt-Hirschmann was mentioned. "In response to a remark of our delegation, that, if the side in the strongest position were to ask for peace, the weaker side would resent mediation because it would be thought that the stronger wanted to dictate terms; while were the weaker side to ask for peace, it would be considered as a confession of defeat. Acknowledging the truth of this, Herr von Jagow said: 'But at this moment neither side is strong enough to dictate terms and neither side is so weakened that it has to sue for peace.' "***

---

* "Herr von Jagow says that Germany would find nothing unfriendly in the calling of a conference of neutrals but thinks we should not form too many illusions about it."
** "Herr von Jagow says that Germany would find nothing unfriendly in the calling of a conference of neutrals but asks whether it would have practical consequences."
*** Confidential memorandum.

The letter from Sir Eric Drummond to Chrystal Macmillan reads as follows: *

Foreign Office
July 22, 1915

Dear Miss Macmillan,

Lord Crewe has asked me to reply to your letter of yesterday on the subject of the private interview which you and Miss Balch had with him on July 14.

In the record of the conversation which Lord Crewe has made it is stated that you proposed the immediate formation of a League of Neutrals and that this League was to be brought into existence at once if possible, not so much with the hope of formulating any definite proposals at this stage as with the idea of preparing the ground, and inducing a state of mind which, on the one hand, would enable the neutral countries to come forward promptly with such proposals and, on the other, would familiarize the belligerents with the prospect of their introduction.

You then asked what the attitude of the British Government would be towards such a proposition.

Lord Crewe replied that it would be impossible for the Government to invite the formation of such a body because it would be thought equivalent to an indirect proposal for terms of peace.

You then asked whether it might be said that the Government accepted the idea of the immediate cooperation of the neutral countries in instituting a Committee to examine the subject.

Lord Crewe answered that he did not like the word "accept" to which a meaning would probably be attached going beyond anything to which his Colleagues and he could agree, but you could say that the Government would not place any obstacles in the way of the formation of such a body or make any protest against its existence if it should come into being.

I trust that this will give you the information which you desire.

Yours very truly,
Eric Drummond

Emily found her fortnight in London in some ways the most absorbing of all. She made the acquaintance of many of the leading British internationalists, men and women with whom she was

* Confidential Memorandum.

destined to cooperate in countless ways in the next decades. This was her first real introduction into these European circles of intellectuals, and the beginning of that continually widening range of contacts that were to play so large a part in her work and in her life.

Aside from her interviews with Lord Crewe, and with Sir Edward Grey, she met many interesting people: Margaret Bond-field; Emily Hobhouse, who had become famous for her humanitarianism during the Boer War and had sent a courageous "Letter of Christmas Greeting" to the women of Austria and Germany in December, 1914; Catherine Marshall of the clan of the "Lakes" Marshalls; Kate Courtney (Lady Courtney); and other women of the British Committee. She also met various members of the Union of Democratic Control: H. N. Brailsford, author of the widely read *The War of Steel and Gold;* John A. Hobson; Vernon Lee (Violet Page); Ramsay MacDonald, M.P.; Arthur Ponsonby, M.P.; and Bertrand Russell.

Everybody was anxious to meet her as she had so recently come out of Russia: Roden Buxton, authority on the Balkans; Mr. and Mrs. Stanton Coit, of the London Ethical Society; Lord Courtney of Penwith; Felix Moscheles, artist and pacifist; Sylvia Pankurst; S. K. Ratcliffe; Ethel Sidgwick, the novelist; and Graham Wallas, political theorist.

Most vividly of all she remembered Goldsworthy Lowes Dickinson, and a visit at the home of Bernard Shaw, then at the height of his fame, and Mrs. Shaw.

"All were eager to hear of our undertaking and, with one or two marked exceptions, all were in their own way more or less distinctly pacifist in their outlook. I was conscious that they were far from being average samples of English feeling; yet, even so, what a testimony to the genuineness of English liberty of thought and the breadth of English humanism were their keen and generous views." [7]

At the end Emily Balch was able to say of the missions to the governments, "I may say that what was planned as a comparatively formal presentation of the resolutions of our Congress developed into something more than this. Never again 'must women dare to believe that they are without responsibility because they are without power. Public opinion is power; strong and reasonable feeling is power; determination which is a twin sister of faith or vision is power." [8]

Appendix to Chapter 8

Emily Green Balch, *Report of the Envoys' Interview with Sazonov*, at Petrograd on June 16, 1915 (written at Amsterdam, July 3, 1915); Archives, W.I.L.P.F. International Headquarters, Geneva.

We were shown into an anteroom done up in cambric covers for the summer and entertained there for a few minutes by Prince Wolkonsky, who had written the letter to us in which Sazonov told us he could not receive us, not being now *en ville*.

We were soon ushered into Sazonov's own bureau, where he placed us with the light full in our faces and behind him. He was a small elderly white-haired man, courteous and reserved in substance more than in manner.

Somehow or other we were tumbled suddenly *in medias res* and could not follow at all the order planned. Sazonov said war could not be brought to an end till it was fought out. He referred to the possibility of its lasting a year more. He spoke of Russia's love of peace and that it was Germany who had brought on the war.

Miss Macmillan spoke of the dangers of the continuance of the war, that if it went on it might destroy the white race.

In reply he began to speak of the 160 millions of Russians, of the small proportion of the losses, of the good health of the army, of the power of multiplication of the people. He explained the growth of Russia in geographical terms, spoke of her people, rolling on and continually covering new territory. Then he seemed to feel we might get an impression from this that Russia was a menace and hastened to explain that Russia has now reached its natural frontiers, which it had not previously. He also specifically said that of course on the West it was now in contact with a people too vigorous and self-conscious and numerous (not his exact words) to make it suitable that Russia should roll over them.

M. Sazonov also spoke of the Dardanelles that Russia only wanted to be sure of free passage.

One of us said we did not suppose any of the belligerents dreamed of wiping out Germany. He said in reply that she needed a heavy lesson.

We spoke of Belgium not wanting the Germans driven out by force.

Apropos of delaying the end of war Miss Balch spoke of being in a car under which one man was crushed and of how long a half hour's delay seemed then. I thought he perceptibly winced and then hardened again when she drew the moral of what suffering every moment's prolongation of the war means.

He spoke at some length, I think about Poland; I am pretty sure he talked of the necessity of reuniting Poland and giving her independence under Russia or something to this effect.

I think I spoke of the danger to future peace of Europe if Italy were allowed to acquire Slavic territory on the Adriatic.

Beginning with complimentary reference to Russia's part in initiating international peace conference we seemed to have struck an acceptable view. Before Miss Macmillan could bring it out, he spoke of Russia's having sought to bring about a conference when the outbreak of the war was imminent, and having exchanged letters as to this with Sir Edward Grey.

In connection with the question of the neutral nations he mentioned the U. S. and spoke in a challenging tone of what she permitted from Germany without retaliation. Miss Balch fired up at this and said she was proud of the way her country was proving its real belief in peace.

The question of the use of poisonous gas was brought up by him. Miss Balch spoke of how much would be gained in moral prestige and in approval of neutral powers if Russia (or allies) would take the position that they would not condescend to such methods.

We began on the mediation plan and he shut off details, saying he had read our resolutions and was informed as to our ideas. We told in a general way about the interviews at the different capitals, particularly London and Berlin. He seemed little interested about Germany, though he did ask whom we saw there. He asked if we had been in France. Spain was mentioned as one of the neutrals.

We spoke of a conference of neutrals to offer continuous mediation and asked him if he would consider this an unfriendly act. He said it would not be such. He also used the phrase "not unacceptable." Mrs. Ramondt asked if she might write this down and get him to approve what had written. He seemed a shade taken aback, but agreed v demur, on condition that we give it entire, i.e., that we included his statement that in his opinion it would not lead to any results. Mrs. Ramondt then wrote down the above, saying "it" would not be regarded, etc. She wrote in pencil. I begged that it might be more fully worded, as "it" was not explained. Miss Macmillan then wrote it out in ink and with a full phrase as to conference of neutral powers offering continuous mediation, and at my request allowed substituting for the "not unfriendly" "not unacceptable." I also asked that instead of only reading it to Sazonov as had been done it be shown to him. All this he sanctioned and read Miss Macmillan's statement as she had it and said it was all right. After our return home we all signed a statement to this effect on the same paper.

CHAPTER NINE

Envoys in the United States—Woodrow Wilson

The last and most difficult part of the mission remained—to lay the garnered information before President Wilson and persuade him to head or join the neutrals in a mediating conference. They failed. Wilson preferred to work alone or through Colonel House—secretly, not openly. The historian Merle Curti said in 1936, "It now appears that had Wilson moved in this direction on one or two occasions in 1915 and early in 1916, he might have brought the war to an end under circumstances that would have furthered a more durable peace than the one finally made at Versailles. When at length he did what Jane Addams (and Bryan) had long urged him to do, it was too late." [1]

From August, 1915, till the end of November the offices of President Wilson, Colonel House, his confidential advisor, and Robert Lansing, Secretary of State, were besieged by the envoys of The Hague Congress as well as by other pacifist delegations using their findings. Jane Addams herself made several visits to President Wilson and Colonel House, with both of whom she was on terms of personal friendship. On August 6, Jane Addams visited Secretary of State Robert Lansing in company with other advocates of negotiating peace, Lillian D. Wald and Oswald Garrison

Villard, journalist, both leaders of the American Union Against Militarism.* They presented to Mr. Lansing a memorial urging "immediate initiative of a peace movement, led by the United States as the natural leader of the neutral nations." An unofficial committee having the President's sanction should make and revise propositions, "coming back again and again, if necessary, until a basis may be reached upon which actual negotiations looking towards peace could begin." [2]

According to Ray Stannard Baker, the biographer of Wilson, Secretary Lansing declined to make any comment upon the memorial, merely forwarding it to the President. Wilson returned it next day with a note saying: "Have [you] . . . any opinion about this proposal that you would be willing to express to me? I ask because I know these good people are not going to let the matter rest until they bring it to a head in one way or another. I must, I suppose, be prepared to say either Yay or Nay." [3]

"Lansing," writes Ray Stannard Baker, "in his reply disagreed with the premises of the argument: 'I do not believe that it is true that the civil leaders of the belligerents would at the present time look with favor on action by the neutral nations; and, even if they did, the military branches of the belligerent governments dominate the situation, and they favor a continuance of the war.'

"'The Central Powers,' he said, 'would demand territorial and financial compensation on the basis of their military success; while the Allies would hold out in the confidence of ultimately turning the tide.' He concluded: 'Holding these views I would strongly favor discouraging any neutral movement toward peace at the present time, because I believe it would fail and because, if it did fail, we would lose our influence for the future.'

"Wilson responded on August 19th: 'I entirely agree.'" [4]

Ray Stannard Baker commented: "This reason, which House

---

* Letter from Oswald Garrison Villard to Emily Balch, August 10, 1915, after this interview with Mr. Lansing: "My interview with Mr. Lansing resulted about as I had expected. He was not at all impressed with our arguments and did not feel that the foreign governments were ready to consider mediation. He also thought that Miss Addams had been more or less imposed upon. However, he volunteered to lay our proposal before Mr. Wilson though without holding out any hope that Mr. Wilson would act at this time. . . . I feel that our committee had better be considering now what it would do in the event of the President's refusal to act in any way at all." (From Villard Papers, By permission of the Harvard College Library.)

and Lansing continually advanced—that we must keep our influence strong *by never moving toward mediation until success was guaranteed**—was throughout the basic cause for Wilson's hesitation in acting publicly for peace.

"The President, in short, considered that this direct and persistent approach [of the pacifist memorial] was not the best method of reaching the ends which he himself desired quite as much as did the memorialists who signed the petition.

"Colonel House, devoted to secret negotiation, had also douched the efforts of the pacifists with the coldest of cold water. After Jane Addams had returned from Europe in July, House wrote the President scornfully:

> Manchester, Mass.
> July 17, 1915
>
> Dear Governor:
> Jane Addams comes on Monday—
> She has accumulated a wonderful lot of misinformation in Europe. She saw von Jagow, Grey, and many others, and, for one reason or another they were not quite candid with her, so she has a totally wrong impression.
>
> Affectionately yours,
>
> E. M. House" [5]

Ray Stannard Baker wonders whether Grey and other British statesmen had been "quite candid" with House. Only three weeks after the above letter was written, on August 4, 1915, Colonel House wrote to Ambassador Page, "virtually admitting," says Baker, "that the British had been playing a game with him since the previous autumn by putting off American activity in behalf of peace."

> Manchester, Mass.
> August 4, 1915
>
> Dear Page,
> His [Wilson's] judgment and mine was that last autumn was the time to discuss peace parleys and we both foresaw present possibilities. War is a great gamble at best, and there was too much at stake in this one to take chances. I believe if we could have started peace parleys in November, we could have forced the evacuation of

---

* Italics mine.

both France and Belgium and finally forced a peace which would eliminate militarism both on land and sea. *The wishes of the Allies were heeded with the result that the war has now fastened itself upon the vitals of Europe, and what the end may be is beyond the knowledge of man.* * [6]

Lord Bryce was of the same opinion as House. On November 26, 1915, he wrote to Colonel House that there was not the slightest change in British sentiment regarding the duty and necessity of prosecuting the war with the utmost vigor and listening to no suggestions for negotiations with the German government. He had heard that Jane Addams, "who ought to have known better after her journey around Europe, and other women had been trying to engineer a movement for mediation. They might have spared themselves the trouble." [7]

On the other hand, leaders of the warring countries were not altogether opposed to peace ventures and not unfavorably inclined to the efforts of the women. This appears in a letter from Sir Edward Grey to Colonel House on August 26. He expresses belief that efforts of "several neutrals" to promote peace in the European war could not be resented, but that such mediation must be through the United States.

London
August 26, 1915

Dear Colonel House:

. . . Several neutrals have pressed me about a Conference of neutral states to be formed so that it may be ready to undertake mediation whenever it is opportune. I have said that no one could resent any efforts of neutrals which were impartial and independent to promote peace, but I did not think a Conference of neutrals would be of much use unless the U.S. was in it.

If the end of this war is arrived at through mediation, I believe it must be through that of the United States. All our efforts are of course concentrated on saving ourselves and our Allies by securing victory in the war. But it is in my mind continually that the awful sufferings of this war will, to a great extent, have been in vain unless at the end of it nations are set and determined together that future generations shall not fall into such a catastrophe again. . . .

And though a great number of people in the United States and

* Italics mine.

everywhere may be indifferent, absorbed in things of the moment and in material interests, you have a great body of reflecting public opinion so disposed that it can give a great impulse and guidance to this idea. Therefore I look forward to the help of your country under the guidance of the President and impelled by this section of public opinion in those larger conditions of peace, which looking to the future, interest neutrals as much as belligerents. . . .[8]

Yours sincerely,

E. Grey

On August 18, Emily Balch had almost an hour's discussion with President Wilson, the nature of which she disclosed in a letter written to Jane Addams on August 19:

Dedham [Mass.]
August 19, 1915

Dear Miss Addams:

. . . Wilson was very nice and talked with me about an hour. He said definitely that he would not wait to be asked to mediate, if he saw any opportunity to be of use he would take it. This was a comfort as I had feared that he really meant to stand aside.

This is what stands out most positively to my mind from the interview. Most of it went in my report of course.

Speaking of a conference of neutral governments I said that you now felt differently towards this plan, that your mind turned toward an unofficial body. He said that he had heard so and that when you and Miss Wald were with him Miss Wald had wanted you to develop this point but that you had preferred to give merely your report. (I cannot report even approximately accurately, but it was something like this:) With regard to an unofficial body he spoke of some of those who would be the natural persons to be on such a body being perhaps not quite well fitted to serve successfully. The out and out pacifist, seeking a solution in terms of right, could not understand sympathetically and deal with those who came at the problem from the point of view of military advantage. (This is very roughly approximate to his sense.) I asked him whether he would be willing to name those he alluded to. He replied by instancing President Eliot: he had the greatest admiration personally for President Eliot but he could not accept anything as "amoral."

I told him about Dr. [Aletta] Jacob's coming. He said he could not see a foreigner. "What, not a neutral? Colonel House had seemed to think there would be no difficulty." He had had unfortunate experiences, newspapers misrepresented any such interviews, it was not as if he could see any one privately. She could tell everything to one of us who could tell it to him. (So he implied this sort of interview would be given, at least I think he definitely implied telling not writing.) I asked if it would be easier if the interview were nominally with one of us and if nominally Dr. Jacobs just came along. He finally did say that he had not given a final answer and that he would consider it further.

I wonder if it would have been better if my interview had been postponed. I feel such a babe in judgment in all these things. . . . I left memoranda with Wilson as you suggested and he seemed to like to have them. I did not include any written statement of the Wallenberg statement. . . . When he was saying how reporters always gave things wrong I took the opportunity to slip in remarks about the "dope" embroglio* saying how absolutely within the bounds of your information, and how guarded your statement had been. He seemed very sympathetic and comprehending.

He told me what he would like me to say to the reporters about my interview with him, "not that that would prevent their saying what they liked."

I had begun the interview by asking how many minutes I had and he set no limit. At last he obviously closed the interview. Do you know whether this implies I had stayed too long? I had many qualms after the interview as to my manners, and my management of the golden moments but that way madness lies so I won't worry.[9] Signed: Emily Balch.

On August 25, Dr. Aletta Jacobs arrived in the United States

---

* Jane Addams, in a speech at Carnegie Hall in New York City, a week after her return from Europe, had made an incidental statement to the effect that young men at the front had stimulants administered to make them willing to perform the bloody work of bayonet charges. She said this to indicate the revolt against war taking place in the midst of war itself. But it was interpreted as impugning the courage of the soldiers. A storm of journalistic anger all over the country and a barrage of abusive letters for months to come was the result.

with an "important message" from her government. Holland would be willing to call a conference if it could be assured of American participation. "Our Government wants to know," she wrote in English to Jane Addams on August 26, "before it takes any step in that direction, if perhaps Pres. Wilson likes to take the lead and if not, is willing to join the Europ. neutrals in sending representatives of the U.S. to such a conference. Our Premier Cort v. D. Linden believes that such a question should be asked and answered in the same unofficial way we get the other statements." [10]

Shortly after she landed, Dr. Jacobs and Emily Balch had an interview with Secretary Lansing. "The talk with Secretary Lansing was a disheartening experience," wrote Emily Balch to Oswald Garrison Villard.* "I hate to think of his representing our country. What he said to us was on an unspeakably lower moral level** than what was said by any of the European statesmen with whom we talked. Of course words are not everything, but to openly take an absolutely amoral and cynical attitude and defend it seems to me to unfit him for any large or constructive action in international affairs, however shrewd and capable he may be as an international lawyer."***

---

* Letter to Oswald Garrison Villard, September 28, 1915 (Villard Papers, by permission of the Harvard College Library.)
** See Chapter 16, p. 382, footnote.
*** Typed memorandum by Emily G. Balch, August 31, 1915, of interview of Dr. Aletta Jacobs and Emily Balch with Secretary Lansing (Villard Papers, by permission of the Harvard College Library). It reads: "He said this was not the time to make peace, when the Germans were so victorious. Germany wanted to make peace, but England and France did not. He spoke of the financial pressure in Germany.

"He said continuous mediation was impossible; that a conference of neutral nations for such a purpose was impracticable. He said that a mediator could merely offer to mediate and then withdraw. He was scandalized at the idea of proposing terms. This was meddling in other people's affairs. The United States would never do anything like that. Miss Balch proposed the term conciliation instead of mediation in regard to the conference plan, and this mollified him somewhat.

"Mr. Lansing spoke favorably of a conference of neutrals to define and claim neutral rights. He seemed somewhat interested when Miss Balch explained why she dreaded a conference which should crystallize rights of neutrals as opposed to those of belligerents, create a new clash of interests and deprive a conference of neutrals of the character of disinterested mediators."

A few days later, Dr. Jacobs and Emily Balch visited Colonel House. Colonel House records in his diary: "September 1, 1915, Dr. Jacobs and Miss Emily Balch came in the afternoon by appointment. Dr. Jacobs is the Dutch lady who called the Women's Peace Conference at The Hague in May over which Jane Addams presided. They had just been to Washington and the President, in a letter which they showed me, referred them to Lansing and to me. Their interview with Lansing was thoroughly unsatisfactory from their viewpoint. They claimed he was pro-Ally and very unsympathetic with their suggestion that the U.S. should call together all neutral countries in order to make peace overtures. I tried to show them how utterly impracticable their plan was, while evidencing the deepest sympathy with their general purpose. I am to have an interview with Dr. Jacobs later in New York. . . ."[11]

Emily Balch had paved the way for Dr. Aletta Jacobs' visit with President Wilson on September 15. The President, wrote Aletta Jacobs to Jane Addams, was very "kind" and "gentleman-like." His answers were very "diplomatique." "The United States," Dr. Jacobs wrote, "were now in such great difficulties with the belligerents that a definite answer in one way or the other was impossible. The Pres. was very thankful for the informations I brought, but about his attitude towards peace he could not say a word. Every day that attitude could be changed, according to the circumstances, and even a quite unofficial statement in one way or another could bind him in a certain degree. He wants to remain free to act in the best way as he sees the things himself."[12]

Meantime, during early September also, the Woman's Peace Party was devoting itself to warmly supporting Jane Addams, Emily Balch, and Dr. Jacobs in furthering the conference of neutrals. Emily Balch felt strongly that the next two months might be crucial ones psychologically, and that it was important to get the conception of a neutral conference for mediation working in the minds of the American people.* Her article "The Time for

---

* She confessed, however, in a letter to Paul Kellogg, September 24, 1915, that "the chances of Wilson calling a Conference look to me frankly equivalent to nil, but if the European neutrals or one of them would write the United States to join we ought to be able to put on pressure to insure acceptance."

Making Peace" appeared in an October issue of *The Survey*. "If, in the wisdom that comes after the event, we see that the United States was dilatory when it might have helped to open the way to end bloodshed and to make a fair and lasting settlement, we shall have cause for deep self-reproach. . . . With a given balance of relative strength as between the two sides, an equilibrium may be reached in more than one way, as there are equations which admit of more than one solution. . . . A mediating group, without throwing any weight into the scale of one or the other side, can help to find the equilibrium on the higher rather than the lower level. . . . Each side is ready to concede more and to demand less than appears on the surface or than it is ready to advertise." In all these initiatives the women were aided by the Chicago Peace Society and by the activity of Dr. David Starr Jordan, president of Stanford University and head of the American Peace Society, who also used the data the women had gathered. On November 12, Dr. Jordan and Louis Lochner, secretary of the Chicago Peace Society were received by Wilson. Dr. Jordan had been commissioned by the Fifth International Peace Congress meeting in San Francisco (October 10-13) to request the President to initiate a neutral conference.*

Colonel House records further interviews in his diary—on November 21 with Miss Addams, Miss Wald and Madame Schwimmer; on November 22 with Frau Selenka of Munich, who had

---

* Lochner described the interview: President Jordan "laid before the President data in support of his assertion that the European neutrals were ready and anxious to participate in a mediatory conference. The President, who assured us that he had revolved the proposal in his mind dozens of times, voiced two main objections: 1. That America might, in a neutral conference, be outvoted by other neutral governments which in some cases were out of sympathy with their own peoples, and therefore were not truly representative; and 2. That one side (the Allies) might object to mediation as a partisan measure.

"In the course of the discussion which followed, however, we felt that we were meeting the objections to his satisfaction. Indeed, we felt so confident of having scored our point that we were encouraged to say to him at the close of the interview, 'Then may we take the message with us that you will act?'

"The President's rather informal manner suddenly changed. He was the cautious statesman now. 'No, that is for me to say when the right moment, in my judgment, arrives,' he replied."[13]

been a delegate at The Hague Congress; and also on November 22 with Henry Ford.°

"November 21, 1915: Misses Jane Addams, Lillian Wald and von [sic.] Schwimmer of Vienna [sic.] called by appointment this afternoon. It was the same old story of trying to get the President to appoint a peace commission jointly with other neutral nations, to sit at The Hague [sic] and to continue making peace proposals until accepted. I explained that the President could not do this officially. They then wanted to know whether he would object to an unofficial commission doing it, and I thought he would not. As usual, I got them into a controversy between themselves, which delights me since it takes the pressure off my self.

"November 22, 1915: Henry Ford, the automobile manufacturer, called by appointment. He also came in the role of a pacifist. He brought with him David Starr Jordan's Secretary [Louis Lochner], a young man who did most of the talking, despite the fact that I indicated very clearly that I wished to talk to Mr. Ford. Ford's views regarding peace were so crude and unimportant that I endeavored to lead him into a more fruitful field; but just as I got him to discussing his great industrial plant at Detroit and the plans for the uplift of his workers, the young man would break in and turn the tide of conversation into another channel. Ford, I should judge, is a mechanical genius . . . who may become a prey to all sorts of faddists who desire his money." . . .°° [14]

° It will be seen that access to the President and high ranking officials by private citizens was not difficult at that time. The pressures on President Wilson from various interests were tremendous. Certainly he gave generous attention to the advocates of continuous neutral mediation, though he received more advice against such a course. An instance is recounted by Herbert Hoover in *The Ordeal of Woodrow Wilson*, 1958. After reporting to Wilson on a technicality concerning the Commission for Relief in Belgium and Northern France in May, 1915, Hoover said that the President "detained me for some time, discussing the war and the possibilities of American intervention to make peace. I advised him that the emotional situation of the belligerents, if nothing else, made such an effort hopeless at this time."

°° In Louis Lochner's account of the interview with Colonel House, he says, "Colonel House listened courteously and attentively, agreed with us that the plan for neutral mediation was meritorious, and was even moved to say, 'I agree with you that something of that sort ought to be done. . . .' I had the temerity to say, 'Then why don't you see to it that it is done?' Whereupon the Colonel floundered, taken somewhat by surprise, 'You see I am not the Government.' This elicited a parting shot from Mr. Ford, 'But you are pretty close to it.' "[15]

By November 21, then, the women pacifists had been told definitely by Colonel House that the President could not "do this officially."

Jane Addams had gathered that there were two reasons for President Wilson's reluctance. Before leaving for Europe in April she had understood from the sympathetic Mr. Bryan, who was then Secretary of State, that the United States could not call a neutral conference and ignore South American countries. To include them would make the conference large and unwieldy. Secondly, the Central Powers at the moment had the technical military advantage.

"We thought," said Jane Addams, "that we had adequately replied to both of these objections, but because of them or for other reasons President Wilson would not consider the proposition."* 16

---

* An interesting reflection on the various pressures to which President Wilson was subjected came from a deputation of three Socialists who visited President Wilson on January 25, 1916, to urge the same plan of neutral mediation upon him: Morris Hillquit, the brilliant Socialist leader; James H. Maurer, president of the Pennsylvania Federation of Labor; and Meyer London, the Socialist member of Congress.

"Our interview with Woodrow Wilson proved exceedingly interesting," wrote Morris Hillquit in *Loose Leaves From a Busy Life* (1934). "The President received us in the White House. He looked pre-occupied and tired, and at first seemed inclined to give us a short and perfunctory hearing; but as we proceeded with our argument he became interested and animated and our interview developed into a serious and confidential conversation. Mr. Wilson, after some general discussion of the international situation and the terms of our peace program, informed us that he had had a similar plan under consideration, but that he hesitated to put it to the test because he felt uncertain about its reception by the other neutral nations.

" 'The fact is,' he asserted, 'that the United States is the only important country that may be said to be neutral and disinterested. Practically all other neutral countries are in one way or another tied up with some belligerent power and dependent on it.'

"He hinted at the possibility of a direct offer of mediation by the government of the United States and assured us that he would continue to study the question with deep and serious interest.

"Throughout the interview I acted as a spokesman for our committee; but as we got up, ready to take our leave, James Maurer, looking at the President with steady and appraising eyes, delivered himself with slow and pondering tones of the following sentiment: 'Your promises sound good, Mr. President, but the trouble with you is that you are surrounded by capitalist and militarist interests who want the war to continue; and I fear you will succumb to their influence.'

"The Pennsylvania-Dutch bluntness of my diplomatic colleague evoked an amused smile on the pale and intellectual face of Woodrow Wilson.

What the "other reasons" unknown to the women were which determined the attitude of Wilson and House did not become known until much later. Colonel House had worked out a plan of mediation of his own. From October, 1915, to February, 1916, he and Wilson were developing this "positive policy" through secret negotiations with Sir Edward Grey. The negotiations finally led to the House-Grey Memorandum of February 22, 1916. At the very time when Jane Addams, Emily Balch, and the other Hague delegates were pressing for neutral mediation, President Wilson, through Colonel House, was carrying on delicate negotiations with England offering American intervention to end the war. Colonel House states his plan in his own words: "I outlined very briefly [to the President, October, 1915] a plan which occurred to me and which seems of much value. I thought we had lost our opportunity to break with Germany, and it looked as if she had a better chance than ever of winning, and if she did win our turn would come next. . . . Therefore we should do something decisive now—something that would either end the war in a way to abolish militarism or that would bring us in with the Allies to help them do it. My suggestion is to ask the Allies, unofficially, to let me know whether or not it would be agreeable to them to have us demand that hostilities cease.

"If the Allies understood our purpose, we could be as severe in our language concerning them as we were with the Central Powers. The Allies, after some hesitation, could accept our offer or demand and, if the Central Powers accepted, we would then have accomplished a master-stroke of diplomacy. If the Central Powers refused to acquiesce, we could then push our insistence to a point where diplomatic relations would first be broken off, and later the whole force of our government—and perhaps the force of every neutral—might be brought against them." [17]

The President concurred with this plan, hoping it might lead to genuine mediation. But Sir Edward Grey employed delaying

---

" 'If the truth be known,' he said, 'I am more often accused of being influenced by radical and pacifist elements than by capitalist or militarist interests.' This ended our interview. I have often thought of it, wondering whether subsequent events did not bear out the apprehension of James Maurer rather than the reassurance of Woodrow Wilson." But perhaps Morris Hillquit was not entirely right.

tactics. After much pressure on Grey, he finally drafted the Memorandum embodying the proposals of Wilson and House in February. But Grey made no effort to put the offer of mediation-intervention into effect, in spite of frequent suggestions from House that the "opportune moment" had arrived. By June, 1916, Wilson realized that the "positive policy" had failed.

In the meantime, the women were realizing that as far as a governmental conference of neutrals was concerned, they were at an impasse unless tremendous pressure of public opinion could be brought to bear on the President. The newspapers were closed to any serious advocacy of proposals by pacifists. But Rosika Schwimmer, whose will-to-peace ran down as waters and her passionate concern as a mighty stream in the arid landscape of diplomacy, had a new idea. She persuaded Mrs. Henry Ford to give $10,000 to the Women's Peace Party to mobilize public opinion among United States women to send telegrams to President Wilson from all over the country urging neutral mediation at once. Twelve thousand telegrams poured in at the White House for three days. The telegrams were to be sent on November 26, the day on which President Wilson had agreed to see Madame Schwimmer and Mrs. Philip Snowden of England. Mrs. Snowden in her book *A Political Pilgrim in Europe* (1921) recorded the interview of half an hour or more as she remembered it: "Frau Schwimmer and myself were received by the President with the dignity of a *grand seigneur* joined to the simplicity of a plain American citizen. . . . During our conversation with him his hatred of war was clear. His desire to maintain the peace in America and restore it, if possible, to Europe, was unequivocal. He expressed very warmly his sympathy with the idea of a neutral conference. But the thought of practical difficulties oppressed him. Would China and the South American Republics be invited to such a conference? What should be the basis of representation? Would such an effort be looked upon with favor by the fighting Powers? Could anything be done except through the ordinary diplomatic channels? He welcomed Lord Courtney's brave speech in the House of Commons and hoped it might be symptomatic. He looked for signs of growing peace sentiment amongst the belligerents but found none. I agreed with him on this last point and remained silent." [18]

The women were now convinced that President Wilson would

act only in his own good time. They were, therefore, obliged to turn to their alternative plan, a conference initiated and conducted as a private enterprise. They hoped to raise a sum of money large enough to defray all expenses. "At this time," wrote Jane Addams, "an unexpected development gave the conference of neutrals only too much publicity and produced a season of great hilarity for the newspaper men of two continents." [19] The eloquent Rosika Schwimmer, presumably on the strength of the evidence the women envoys had gathered, and the persuasive pacifist Louis Lochner, had secured an interview in Detroit with the automobile magnate Henry Ford and induced him to finance an unofficial conference. "I'm going to back the work of the International Committee of Women," Lochner reports Ford as saying.

What happened next proved to be one of the most sensational episodes in the history of World War I—the voyage of the famous Ford Peace Ship in December, 1915. The story of the voyage itself centers on Rosika Schwimmer and on Henry Ford. It concerns Jane Addams only indirectly. She had intended to sail, but was prevented by illness from doing so. Emily Balch did not sail on the Peace Ship though she was often wrongly reported to have done so. But she did take part in the essential project of the whole enterprise, designed to implement the proposals of The Hague Congress. She served for several months as a member of the unofficial neutral Conference for Continuous Mediation set up and financed by Henry Ford at Stockholm in January, 1916. The episode of the Peace Ship was Ford's way of "backing the proposals of The Hague Congress." Its dramatic impact and its consequences demand some brief record here.

On November 21, Henry Ford, accompanied by Louis Lochner, came to New York City to confer with such leading pacifists as Oswald Garrison Villard, George W. Kirchwey, Paul U. Kellogg, as well as Jane Addams and Rosika Schwimmer. The same evening Henry Ford announced that he had chartered the Scandinavian liner, *Oscar II*, to transport the delegates. Miss Addams at once became alarmed, insisting that it would be easy enough for the members of the conference to travel to Stockholm or The Hague by other steamship lines, paying their own expenses.

Events moved rapidly. The main object of the enterprise was

immediately lost sight of. The day when Mr. Ford's slogan, "Get the boys out of the trenches by Christmas," was spread all over the front pages of all the newspapers, as Jane Addams explained later, "I spent large sums of money telephoning to the secretary [Louis Lochner] in New York begging him to keep the enterprise in hand, which I reminded him was the conference of neutrals. Having so recently travelled in Europe under war time regulations I knew that such propaganda would be considered treasonable and put the enterprise in a very dangerous position." [20]

Mr. Ford began to issue a flood of indiscriminate invitations to senators, representatives, state governors, journalists, and student delegates from colleges and universities* Miss Addams remonstrated, pointing out that the latter could hardly be of direct value to the conference itself. "The offer of a crusading journey to Europe with all expenses paid could but attract many fanatical and impecunious reformers," [21] wrote Jane Addams.

The press was highly critical; the more unscrupulous newspapers pounced on the enterprise, transforming its essential idea into grotesque buffoonery. "The conference itself was seldom mentioned," wrote Jane Addams, "but the journey and the ship were made all important and mysterious people with whom Madame Schwimmer was said to be in communication, were constantly featured. . . . With many notable exceptions," concluded Jane Addams sadly and gently, "a group of very eccentric people had attached themselves to the enterprise, so that there was every chance for a fiasco."[22] Nevertheless Jane Addams, her national public prestige still high, her dignity and poise unassailable, felt herself committed to the enterprise. "I was fifty-five years old in 1915; I had already 'learned from life' to use Dante's great phrase, that moral results are often obtained through the most unexpected agencies." [23]

What might have happened had Jane Addams' steadying presence been aboard, is problematic, for when the ship sailed she

---

* The advocates of this policy pointed out that this inclusiveness was in accord with a "democratic, people's effort to stop the war." Jane Addams, on the other hand, though always sympathetic with youth in its revolt against war, agreed with the original idea of Julia Grace Wales and The Hague Congress that mediation efforts should be by a commission of experts.

was lying ill in a Chicago hospital.* On a bitter cold winter day, December 4, 1915, the famous Peace Ship was launched "to the undying shame of American journalism upon one vast wave of ridicule." [24] Difficulties developed on the voyage. The peace pilgrims were torn by cleavages. According to many accounts, Madame Schwimmer's tactics and her much publicized "mysterious black bag," presumably containing the confidential responses of the statesmen, caused dissensions. In Christiania Mr. Ford, who had come down with a cold, secretly abandoned the party the day before Christmas under unexplained circumstances. Rosika Schwimmer resigned in the spring of 1916 from the Neutral Conference which was established in Stockholm on January 26, 1916.**

Years afterwards in a charming autobiography, *Three Score*, the Vermont pacifist Sarah Cleghorn, whom Robert Frost called "saintly and a poet," summed up the episode with economy: "Mr. Ford's peace ship, that effort to save the lives of young men which aroused mirth among some people."[25]

What did the women envoys themselves think of the outcome of their mission? In the middle of October three of the European delegates who were in the United States, Aletta Jacobs, Chrystal Macmillan, and Rosika Schwimmer, joined Jane Addams and Emily Balch in issuing a public statement or manifesto.*** "This document is long since forgotten," wrote Jane Addams in 1922, "lost in the stirring events which followed, although at the time it received a good deal of favorable comment, in the press of the neutral countries on both sides of the Atlantic, perhaps because it was difficult openly to oppose its modest recommendations." [26] The signers explained that their visits to the war capitals convinced them "that the belligerent Governments would not be opposed to a conference of neutral nations; that while the belligerents have rejected offers

* She was suffering from severe hemorrhage from the kidney. This information is from Dr. Alice Hamilton who attended Jane Addams. Several contemporary accounts stated that she "pleaded illness" to avoid sailing.
** Why Rosika Schwimmer withdrew from the Stockholm Conference (March 8, 1916) is not quite clear. In a speech of December 4, 1937 (Archives, Swarthmore College Peace Collection) she said that "serious destructive work against its success was made, that American and Dutch pseudo-pacifists combined with the forces around Mr. Ford to break up the neutral conference. . . . Rumors were spread, small-town tactics employed and I was made the center of all the trouble."
*** *Women at The Hague*—Appendix IV, Manifesto.

of mediation by single neutral nations, and while no belligerent could ask for mediation, the creation of a continuous conference of neutral nations might provide the machinery which would lead to peace." The envoys believed that of the five European neutral nations visited, three were ready to join in such a conference, and that two [Holland and Sweden] were deliberating the calling of such a conference. "Of the intention of the United States we have as yet no evidence." They cited as assurance that the belligerents would not resent neutral initiative for peace, the declarations from high officials quoted in previous chapters. In October, 1915, no names could of course, be attached to these confidential statements. They believed that the plan of continuous neutral mediation "is today being seriously discussed alike in the cabinets of the belligerent and neutral countries of Europe and in the press of both."

The last part of the Manifesto ended on a rather gentle note more effective than a stirring appeal to action: "We are but the conveyers of evidence which is a challenge to action by the neutral governments. . . . We in turn bear evidence of a rising desire and intention of vast companies of people in the neutral countries to turn a barren disinterestedness into an active good will. In Sweden, for example, more than four hundred meetings were held in one day in different parts of the country, calling on the government to act.

"The excruciating burden of responsibility for the hopeless continuance of this war no longer rests on the will of the belligerent nations alone. It rests also on the will of those neutral governments and people who have been spared its shock but cannot, if they would, absolve themselves from their full share of responsibility for the continuance of war."

Jane Addams, Emily Balch, and the other women did not drop the agitation for neutral mediation. In January, 1916, although she was still far from well, Jane Addams pursued the idea * at the first

---

* Speaking of Wilson and a conference of neutrals Jane Addams said, "We found, however, that the administration here, doubtless for the very best of reasons, felt that the time had not yet come for action, a decision concerning which we never for a moment felt critical as the government has much more information than we have. . . . No one expects such a conference to end the war. The war must be ended by the accredited representatives of the governments; but a conference of neutrals may make it impossible that the war should end by the secret diplomacy with which it began."

annual meeting of the Woman's Peace Party in Washington, as
also did Emily Balch. Two days later, on January 11, 1916, Jane
Addams again advocated it at a hearing before the House of Representatives Committee on Foreign Affairs on a resolution urging
the plan.* Emily Balch worked actively for neutral mediation
as a member of the Stockholm conference from April till July, 1916.
On August 9, 1916, about a year after her first visit to President
Wilson, she had another interview with him and laid before him
the plans and conclusions worked out at Stockholm. On August 30,
1916, she was again at the White House with Dr. Jordan and others
of the American Neutral Conference Committee. She was to advocate the idea vigorously again and again in the 1930's and 1940's.

Looking back from the perspective of twenty-five years of
disillusioning experience, at least two of the envoys in the missions
stated that had it not encountered President Wilson's firm reluctance, the plan for neutral mediation might have borne fruit. In
1938 in *A Venture in Internationalism* Emily Balch wrote: "In spite
of real interest in the plan in some responsible quarters, it was
wrecked by President Wilson's refusing to take it up. He doubtless
felt that he could act better alone when the time came, but when
it came he was no longer a neutral but completely involved in the
power politics of the Allies." Four years earlier she had said, "His

---

* At the hearing, in response to a query that perhaps the women's mission
in Europe was not taken seriously, Jane Addams replied, "I know people
have said that. I cannot understand why they do. They say two things: first,
that we were received very lightly, and second, that we were received politely
because we were ladies, and bowed in and out, and pleasant things were
said to us on that account. Von Bethmann-Hollweg, the Imperial Chancellor
of Germany, had lost his son a few weeks before, in the trenches. He was a
solemn, sad, overwhelmed man, and to say that he received us lightly, or
merely in a polite way is perfectly absurd. If people only knew how the
men in those countries feel. This war is no light matter, and the men who
are responsible for the government are not handing out compliments to
anybody. They are not doing anything lightly; they are doing everything in
the shadow of death and destruction. They indict the war and say, 'Thank
goodness somebody has come who does not ask for more war or more money.
Go back and see what you can do.' The Pope, for instance, in Rome said
that he did not see why women had kept quiet so long. He said, 'For heaven's
sake, why do not women express themselves; it is woman's business to oppose
war.' I do not mean that is the Pope's exact language; he does not use such
informal language, but that is practically what he said, and that is what
was said in substance everywhere we went."[27]

procedure by no means fulfilled the same purpose as the plan of 'continuous mediation', nor did it come early enough."

Dr. Alice Hamilton, in her autobiographical *Exploring the Dangerous Trades,* wrote in 1943: "It [continuous mediation] still seems to me the wisest and most practical scheme put forward by any group during the World War and I believe had President Wilson (or Colonel House) been willing to try it, success might have followed instead of failure, and the war been brought to a close by a compromise peace without our having entered it."*[28]

---

* How romantic and mistaken were the women in their view of the possibilities of peace in 1915-1916?

Emily Balch had said the women were neither impulsive nor very optimistic; she doubted whether any of them were ever hopeful of success. (Rosika Schwimmer surely was an exception to this.) Did this statement illustrate Emily Balch's sometimes curious tendency for interposing a veil, a haze, between the facts and her hopes, desires, and fears? Jane Addams had declared that she did not wish "to overestimate a very slight achievement nor take too seriously the kindness with which the delegates were received, but we do wish to record ourselves as being quite sure that at least a few citizens in these various countries, some of them officials in high places, were grateful for the effort we made." Was Jane Addams spreading a characteristic screen of self-deprecation over her actions?

Arthur S. Link, the eminent Wilsonian scholar, has written: "European statesmen told the ladies that they all favored peace, both because they did in principle and because they knew this was what their listeners wanted to hear. They told Colonel House the same thing. They could not risk alienating neutral opinion by giving the impression that they wanted to prolong the war." Now that historians are in a position to see behind the facade, owing to the availability of many European archives, Professor Link thinks it may safely be concluded that each side wanted peace, but peace on its own terms, and this tended to be true the longer the war proceeded and the investment in it grew. "During a good part of 1916 the Germans would have been willing to go to the peace table (so long as only belligerents were there) both because they doubted their ability to win in a long war, and because they held all the military advantages. The Allies could not accept a peace bid at this time because the Germans held all the trumps, and they tended to view serious proposals of peace as being unfriendly. Wilson tried to break this impasse, and tried with mounting determination and almost desperation, in 1916-1917, first through the agency of the House-Grey Memorandum and then through independent mediation. . . . Wilson might well have succeeded in late 1916 and early 1917 had not a number of things happened . . . which convinced the Germans that they had to fight to the finish. . . . Wilson was working night and day, and (as we can now see) along the only lines that promised any success." Letter, Arthur S. Link to M. Randall, April 20, 1963.

Jane Addams and Emily Balch, however, to the end contended, "Nothing could be worse than the fear that one had given up too soon and had left one effort unexpended which might have saved the world."

As active participants, Emily Balch and Alice Hamilton may be suspected of undue partiality. But certainly a responsible historian like Merle Curti, already quoted, shared their general judgment and a political journalist like Oswald Garrison Villard continued to think that it would have done no harm to try at least to inquire openly whether there was not some satisfactory basis of settlement, "after which, if necessary, the slaughter can go on as before." Walter Millis added his voice in the *Road to War*. "On May 16, 1916 Tumulty sent a memorandum to President Wilson: 'It seems to me that the time is now at hand for you to act in the matter of Peace,' suggesting mediation by the United States. One may regret that this idea had not been more cordially received when Jane Addams had been agitating it a year and a half [sic] before, or when Henry Ford had brought it to the White House in November." [29]

The proposal for continuous mediation by a conference of neutrals led by the United States, on which, during the summer and autumn of 1915, the women had set their hopes, came to nothing. It failed because President Wilson was convinced that he and House had a more intelligent and a more realistic policy of American mediation of their own. Wilson's attitude is made clear in a speech he later made to the American Federation of Labor: "My heart is with them [the pacifists], but my mind has a contempt for them. I want peace, but I know how to get it, and they do not."* But Wilson's plan of mediation failed also. And when he took the proposal up again seriously in December, 1916, in a desperate effort to stave off America's involvement in the war, it was too late. Were the women and their supporters, in the summer and fall of 1915, really too early?

---

* Wilson, "Address to the American Federation of Labor Convention," at Buffalo, New York, November 12, 1917. But Professor Link added that groups such as "those with which Miss Balch, Miss Addams, and others were associated in this country were most important because they did articulate the best thinking of liberals all over the western world about the reconstruction of a new world order and, even more importantly, because these groups and their ideas not only had a profound influence on Wilson, but he also thought that he was speaking for them, and that they represented the great silent masses of mankind." Letter, Arthur S. Link to M. Randall, April, 27, 1963.

"Then he showed four lights when he wished them to set full sail and follow in his wake." Magellan

CHAPTER TEN

Stemming the Tide at Home

"In the spring of 1916," wrote Emily Balch in her recollections, "I was again given leave of absence to go to Stockholm to join the International Committee on Mediation set up by Henry Ford as a sequel to the voyage of the famous Peace Ship. This was an instructive experience and I still regard it as a terrible pity that [in March, 1917] Mr. Ford abruptly ended his experiment. I had a great respect for the Secretary of the Conference, Louis Lochner."

When Emily Balch returned in July, 1916, from the Neutral Conference for Continuous Mediation, she believed that the conference was playing "a modest part"[1] in bringing about an early peace. She called it "the sober offspring of that highly experimental peace ship. Here in the United States the ridicule which was heaped upon that picturesque and much misrepresented demonstration of American knight-errantry, the Ford Peace ship, still clings. . . . Many things were said of it that were not true, but among the most untrue was the charge that it had no defined plan or purpose, and that it proved fruitless. Its purpose was *to call into being a neutral conference, and this it did.*"[2]

The Neutral Conference was not what the women at The

Hague had at first desired—a governmental body. It was unofficial, but in many ways it was representative. At the time Emily Balch served on it, there were twelve delegates, two from each of the six chief neutral countries. The first phase of the conference, before Emily Balch arrived, was mainly occupied with formulating an appeal to the neutrals asking for the calling of an official conference, and an appeal to the belligerents proposing specific peace terms.

The two American delegates were the Reverend Charles Aked of San Francisco, chosen by the peace ship group, and Emily Balch, chosen as an alternate to Jane Addams, who was too ill to go. Louis Lochner was made General Secretary.* Emily Balch's main interest in the neutral conference was to do her part towards helping people in one belligerent country know what enlightened groups in their own and other belligerent countries were suggesting in the interests of peace. The work of the anti-annexation movement in Germany, a group that insisted that Germany must hold no territory conquered as a result of the war, should be known and discussed in England, and the proposals of such associations as the *Union of Democratic Control* in England should be accessible to Germans. These groups found it difficult to publish their proposals even in their own countries owing to the censorship of the press. The neutral conference, in translating and republishing these programs, could reestablish international communication and bring about open democratic discussion. Emily Balch was to gather together various proposals for peace terms into a book, *Approaches to the Great Settlement* (1918).

Emily herself served on the Mediation Committee. For the important Committee on Constructive Peace she wrote two studies. One was a "Plan for a Rehabilitation Fund Contributed by Neutral Countries as a Substitute for War Indemnities." The pamphlet suggests that in order to hasten peace, all neutral countries contribute to a restoration or indemnity fund to take effect when the

---

* Louis Lochner was well known among American college students as one of the founders of the "Cosmopolitan Clubs," an early attempt to bring together in American universities students of different races and nationalities. In 1939 he received the Pulitzer Prize for distinguished services as a foreign correspondent.

belligerents have agreed to an armistice. Such a plan for an international fund to take the place of reparations paid only by the defeated party might have eliminated much of the bitterness that followed in the years after 1918. The other pamphlet was a proposal for international administration of colonies, which anticipated the later mandate system of the League of Nations.

As Emily Balch sat with the other members of the central committee around the big green table in a room of Stockholm's Grand Hotel, just across the water from the palace and the Parliament House, she was thrown into intimate contact with another group of earnest internationalists, representatives of Scandinavian and Dutch opinion. Her acquaintance, destined to grow so large, with spokesmen for varying strands of European thought on peace was expanding rapidly. Some of her fellow members were striking personalities, she said: "Carl Lindhagen, burgermaster of Stockholm, a leading radical member of the parliament, a middle-of-the-road idealist, very useful as a leaven and a stimulus, the Danish Dr. Klausen, a solid genial Socialist, Dr. Wigforss (Swedish), a young university man, full of initiative and fire. Outstanding was Dr. B. de Jong van Beek en Donk of Holland, the moving spirit of the Dutch 'Anti-Orlog Raad' and of the international 'Central Organization for a Durable Peace.' . . .

"The Conference set itself to get in touch as far as possible with the belligerents, endeavoring to find the least common multiple of their conflicting purposes. The difficulties are enormous and often it has been like fighting a fog, yet the wonder is not that so little but so much recognition should be given to a purely unofficial group. . . .

"The feeling toward the United States is interesting. With enormous prestige and illimitable resources she is widely felt to have failed the cause of international order by her inaction and preference for playing a lone hand. If she does not yet take a bolder and more constructive policy she will lose a miraculous opportunity to serve belligerents, neutrals and her own cause. . . .

"American public opinion receives much less of this clarifying leadership in international affairs than does European opinion, and both cause and result are to be traced to our provincialism. . . .

"In helping to clarify and unify the opinion that will finally bring peace, the Conference is, incidentally, also making history, if only on the 'little drops of water' principle."* [3]

Emily Balch returned to the United States in July, 1916, to find a preparedness movement in full swing and a steady pull toward war. The period of 1916-1917, fortunately for Emily, brought her the freedom of a year's sabbatical leave from Wellesley College. She went to New York City, ostensibly to do some graduate work at Columbia University. She took classes with Professor Franz Boas, the anthropologist, "for whom as a teacher and man, I had a very deep respect."

As things turned out, she spent three hectic and eventful years in New York City. She aligned herself with various peace groups which were springing up. With the impetus to action given her by The Hague Congress, and the ever-stirring pricks of her own New England conscience, she could not sit back and merely await events. She became a member of the American Union against Militarism, headed by Lillian D. Wald, which, as Emily said, "did brilliant work towards stemming the rising tide of military feeling in the United States."

Emily also worked actively for the New York Branch of the Woman's Peace Party, led by the "brilliant and beautiful Crystal Eastman," sister of Max Eastman. Emily's coworkers were a diversified group: Margaret Lane, Pauline K. Angell, Mrs. Fanny Garrison Villard and the youthful Freda Kirchwey, who was later to succeed Oswald Garrison Villard as publisher of *The Nation*. Some of her younger associates were so-called radicals and Bohemians from Greenwich Village. In their circle, bobbed hair, the retention of maiden names after marriage, and unconventional

---

* In November, 1959, there was strangely enough a delightful allusion to the "neutral mediation" of 1915 at the dedication of the controversial Guggenheim Museum in New York City, designed by the stormy petrel of architecture, Frank Lloyd Wright. In the dedication speech Robert Moses, another stormy petrel, said that Frank Lloyd Wright "always reminded me of his distinguished uncle, Dr. Jenkin Lloyd Jones of Chicago, who accompanied Dr. Aked on the famous Ford Peace Ship. I met Uncle Jenk at the pier when the ship returned and asked him what he had accomplished. Uncle Jenk stroked his white whiskers reflectively and replied, 'We made a deep impression in the neutral countries.'

"And that, my friends, is just what his nephew did all his life. He may not have conquered all his enemies, but he surely made deep inroads in the neutral countries."

marriage customs were considered part of advanced thought. In this world the reformer from Boston— aged fifty, "spinster" as she called herself, thin, spare, precise of speech—moved with unruffled and lively interest.

Here she also met a trio of dedicated women who were to become the spearhead of that group of peace workers who stood for absolute and uncompromising pacifism: Tracy Mygatt, her face like a tranquil Victorian portrait, dark hair parted in the middle and combed smoothly down the sides; Frances Witherspoon, implacably gentle, of a conservative family from the deep South, her father having been Congressman from Mississippi; and Jessie Wallace Hughan, a founder of the War Resister's League, as tenacious and blunt as her Scottish forebears, a high school teacher of English. All three had decided literary ability.

This group of the Woman's Peace Party was to publish all through 1917 an original and forthright little four-page organ called *Four Lights,* with the subtitle *An Adventure in Internationalism.* It proclaimed its pioneering nature in an arresting masthead representing a galleon in full sail with four lights shining from four windows in the stern. The caption, from Antonio Pigafeta's *First Voyage Around the World, an account of Magellan,* read: "Then he showed four lights when he wished them to set full sail and follow in his wake."* Two issues were later barred from the mail by the Post Office Department in accordance with a section of the Espionage Act of June 15, 1917, which declared nonmailable any publications "advocating treason, insurrection, or forcible resistance to any law of the United States." In July, an agent from the Department of Justice descended upon the office to ferret out pro-Germans among the editors and contributors.

"Working with such organizations," said Emily Balch, "meant headlong collision with prevailing public opinion in favor of formally joining the hard pressed Allies, with the press in particular, and above all with governmental policy and President Woodrow Wilson.

"This still seems to me to have been right. That war seemed to me to have been essentially a struggle for power between the

---

* In 1940 the United States Section of the W.I.L.P.F. through Ellen Brinton revived both the name, *Four Lights,* and the masthead for its monthly organ. Many of Emily Balch's articles appeared in it.

empires of Britain and Germany. Though there was much to dislike in the policies of both, Britain was more democratic and less aggressively militarist. I thought with abhorrence and dread of a Europe dominated by Prussian ideas and educated for war and trained by drill sergeants and only too likely to turn to widespread aggressive imperialism.

"Nevertheless it seemed to me that war was not the remedy. Of course no man can say what would have been the course of history had the United States stayed out nor what sort of world would have resulted had Germany won a substantial victory."

As the situation developed, Emily Balch became especially identified, as well as compromised, with what she called "a younger and more adventurous group"—the American Neutral Conference Committee—which was doing what it could to prevent the United States from entering the war. It was a changing group which altered its name and sponsors from time to time, as the situation tightened and as members of the executive committee resigned.

"The moving spirits," wrote Emily Balch in her recollections, "were two clever and active and devoted pacifist girls, Rebecca Shelley and Lella Faye Secor. Mr. Villard, editor of *The Nation,* and his mother, Mrs. Henry Villard, who was an active peace-worker of the consistently non-resistant type, following in the footsteps of her father, William Lloyd Garrison, were helping to support this group. Mr. Villard told me that if I would come on and work with this committee, he would continue his support, otherwise not. He wanted a balance wheel of some one older and more sober than the young staff. He recognized their originality and devotion but felt that they needed a steadying partner. I accepted although it was a delicate proposition and it entirely wrecked my position with Wellesley."

Of these young, vibrant groups staffed by Lella Faye Secor and Rebecca Shelley, the American Neutral Conference was the first in the field. Emily Balch had her desk in the office. The letterheads of these varying organizations, with the names of their chairmen, executive committee, and lists of sponsors bring to memory a certain strand of American liberal conviction. The names were all well known at the time: Hamilton Holt, editor of *The Independent;* Professor George W. Kirchwey, of the Columbia University Law School; Jane Addams, of course; Zona Gale, novelist;

Charlotte Perkins Gilman, feminist; the Reverend Washington Gladden, editor of the *Outlook;* Paul U. Kellogg, editor of *The Survey;* George Foster Peabody, banker and philanthropist; Ben B. Lindsey, a Denver judge noted for his innovations in the treatment of juvenile offenders; Rabbi Stephen S. Wise of the Free Synagogue of New York; Thomas Mott Osborne, prison reformer.

After the German Ambassador Von Bernstorff was handed his passports on February 3, 1917, and war appeared inevitable, the American Neutral Conference Committee became the Emergency Peace Federation "to defend American ideals of liberty and democracy in wartime, and to work for an early and enduring peace."

"Overnight it burgeoned into a great anti-war mass movement," said Rebecca Shelley. "Miss Balch was the balance wheel, though at times she must have felt herself on a 'rolycoaster,' shaken in all directions." [4]

Funds were few and they had little important backing. "Courage was about the only thing we had," as Lella Faye Secor wrote, "and so with that we bought a page [advertisement] in the *New York Times*," appealing for support and money. Emily Balch recalls that when the office opened the next day, the mail bags were full of letters with contributions. Hundreds of people came in person, blocking the office, and lining up in the hall. "The people," said Emily Balch, "were largely poor women from the East side who knew what war meant. They all came with dollar bills in their hands. There were so many and we were so crowded in every way that the dollar bills were temporarily held in waste-baskets, our own and borrowed ones. In an unlucky moment, one was carried into the hall with the bills in their envelopes. It was quickly salvaged but it made a good story at our expense." Lella Faye Secor records, "Dawn was breaking the next morning before we finished counting the money that had poured in that day. We had $35,000. That was the spectacular beginning of an organization which in a few days' time grew to amazing proportions. . . . I seldom slept more than four hours a night. Once or twice I didn't leave the office at all—just worked through a 36 hour shift. . . . I have never lived through such a vivid and buoyant emotional experience. The work was exacting and exhausting, yet one never felt tired." [5]

When the war came and the conscription act was adopted,

there was need to turn from negative protests against entering the war to constructive proposals for an early peace. The Emergency Peace Federation became the core of the People's Council of America on May, 31, 1917. Emily Balch's championship of this organization was to cost her dear. The name was the idea of the youthful and impulsive Rebecca Shelley, who became, as Morris Hillquit called her, the "Maid of Orleans of the movement." It was inspired by the recent Russian revolution. This label tended to associate it in people's minds with revolutionary activities, and from the beginning it ran afoul of American public opinion. As sober an historian as Merle Curti, calls it a "liberal organization." Like other pacifist groups, it opposed conscription and suppression of civil liberties, favored a league of nations and a just and democratic peace based on no punitive indemnities and no forcible annexations. But it went further—it denounced war profiteering, urged adequate wages for labor, and demanded vigilance in maintaining the civil and political rights of the workers. It not only clashed with prevalent public opinion but invited persecution by expressing sympathy with the ideals of economic and social justice which the new Russia was then championing. It believed that some of the roots of war lay in an unjust social order. A year and a half earlier, at the first annual meeting of the Woman's Peace Party in January, 1916, Marian Tilden Burritt, a grandniece of the famous American pacifist Elihu Burritt, the "learned blacksmith," had pointed out that "the word 'pacifist' meant peace-maker and that the making of peace involved nothing less than the reconstruction of society." [6] Of course this was tantamount to treason.

Certainly the organizers and supporters of the People's Council, Emily Balch, Judah L. Magnes, Morris Hillquit, Algernon Lee, Bishop Paul Jones, John Haynes Holmes, and Roger Baldwin did not belong to that class of American educated people, castigated by Randolph Bourne, who were shaken out of their slumbers by the horrors in Belgium and the tragedy of the oppressed nationalities of Europe, but who had never felt responsibility for labor wars and oppressed and excluded masses at home.

Emily Balch with her clear, calm dispassionate vision voiced her reservations about the People's Council in a private letter to Jane Addams in June, 1917. She confessed to wishing for "a fresh perspective after my rather feverish winter ending in the raising

of this Djinn or Frankenstein of a People's Council. . . . I want to
see the spirit of it more constructive. Protest is such a sterile spirit.
The war people command more sacrificial ardor, at least the best
of the idealists do. Boston—old Puritan Boston—is in a white glow
of it. I can imagine how I look to them."* On the other hand, a
month later, she quickly came to a public defense of the People's
Council after a series of riotous demonstrations against it. She
wrote to the New York *Tribune*: "The attitude of the People's
Council is, as I believe, dictated by the highest patriotism as well
as by regard for men and women in all countries as well as in our
own. It is because we hold the American traditions of liberty and
the American achievements in democracy as incomparably precious
and as a most sacred deposit, that we are ready to meet mis-
representation and difficulty when war-time psychology makes such
service to the country doubly necessary and doubly costly.

"It is because we regard the sacrifices of the boys who bear the
brunt of the war and the sacrifices of the mothers who let them
go as of a literally infinite preciousness that we are determined to
do all that in us lies that none of that sacrifice shall be wasted.
We hope to see in the councils of the nations and among the
plain people everywhere, . . . a convinced and openly announced
will to make peace so soon as those ranged against us are ready to
renounce all thought of annexation, all thought of indemnities, and
ready to agree to disarmament all round, and the formation of a
society of nations which shall carry on the common business of
the world and thereby ensure 'that this thing shall never happen
again,'

" 'If this be treason make the most of it.' But it is patently not

---

* How Emily Balch looked to her brother Francis in Boston, appears in a
letter he wrote to her June 27, 1917: "Of course I don't know at all what
you are doing. I live in uneasy suspense. I have been told your name has
appeared much in the New York press but I have not seen it here."

Her sister, Mrs. Alice Stone, of Jamaica Plain wrote to "Dearest Emily. . . .
I have felt so bitterly part of the time about your activities that I just didn't
dare write. . . . I have known all the time that you acted from the highest
principle. It only seemed to me that you assume all the world is as good as
yourself and that you are easily deceived. . . . You live in a world of pacifists,
I in the reverse so I suppose we both get testimony which upholds our
views. . . . I would like you to know that while I do not agree with your
propaganda, I do thoroughly admire you for your courage and devotion"
(April 20, 1917).

treason but an honest effort toward realizing the aims set more than once before the nation by its chosen leader and chief servant, President Wilson." [7]

A characteristic touch in the above letter was her reluctance to employ the word "enemy." She used instead the expression "those ranged against us." This implies a whole philosophy underlying the faith of a pacifist.

Many of the organizations Emily Balch worked with were housed at Fifth Avenue and Twelfth Street, in the Ginn Publishers Building, which became a rallying point for lively dissenting groups. In this neighborhood, in lofts and cheap offices up several flights of wooden steps, with a distinctly proletarian atmosphere, some militant pacifist youth groups had their meeting places. Among these groups were the Young Democracy and the Collegiate Anti-Militarism League. Here Frances Witherspoon with her friend Tracy Mygatt founded the Bureau of Legal Advice offering to conscientious objectors the first service of the kind in the country. Here many young people had their apprenticeship in working for peace—men and women college students, theological students, young Quakers, conscientious objectors to war, and young ministers, of whom some of the most radical were Episcopalians. Among them were Devere Allen and his wife; Cedric Long, too soon to die; Donald Winston; Ray Newton; George Hallett; Lella Faye Secor; as well as Tracy Mygatt, Frances Witherspoon, Harry W. L. Dana, and others. Lella Faye Secor (later Mrs. Philip Florenz of Birmingham, England), was one of the outstanding figures among this younger group. A vivid figure with her flaming red hair, she possessed maturity, poise, and a warm voice. As a young journalist, two years earlier she had been a member of the Ford Peace Expedition. A young fellow pilgrim who later became a distinguished publisher, B. W. Huebsch, years afterwards remembered her as she appeared on the *Oscar II*, at a turbulent evening meeting, her sober black dress offsetting her glorious hair, rising in all her youthful dignity to defend Rosika Schwimmer.

To these young people "Professor Balch" was not only a rock of stability but a link with the senior world of pacifists. The mere fact that a person of such undoubted distinction was espousing the same unpopular cause gave them courage and assurance. Emily Balch's close coworkers, Paul Kellogg and Oswald Garrison Villard, were well aware that in consorting with these young idealists who had plenty of sail and not always so much keel, she gave the appearance of flirting with irresponsible elements and was ruining her academic prestige. Emily Balch, with her eyes open, however, was willing to take the risk.

Tremendous energy was consumed in organizing mass meetings at huge Madison Square Garden and at Cooper Union in New York City. They were addressed by William Jennings Bryan, Wilson's first Secretary of State, an ardent "evangelical pacifist" and negotiator of the "cooling-off" agreements; Rabbi Judah L. Magnes, young, eloquent, of compelling charm, later Chancellor of the Hebrew University in Jerusalem; Morris Hillquit, internationally known Socialist leader, magnetic, persuasive, logical, to whom being in a minority was no new experience; James H. Maurer, veteran Socialist and trade-union leader. Parts of such audiences were motivated by Socialist distrust of "Wall Street," and dislike of the "capitalist system." A sprinkling were pro-Germans, and Irish who were antiwar because they hated England.

"Working for peace has its stormy moments," wrote Emily Balch. "We took a delegation to Washington, where disgusted soldier boys painted our office door yellow and drummed their heels on the corrugated-iron roof of the hall where we were trying to hear our speakers.

"The hottest experiences were not in New York. Louis Lochner and Max Eastman had gone West to organize meetings for us. In Minneapolis the lobby of their hotel was invaded by a threatening mob of men with ropes who wanted to 'get them.' Max Eastman in speaking of this in public said, 'My knees shook under me, but Louis Lochner was perfectly cool and undisturbed.'

"A meeting [of the People's Council] was held in Chicago under painful and dramatic circumstances. We became the center of a political tussle.* The meeting was forbidden by the Governor of the state and permitted by Mayor Bill Thompson of Chicago. [William Hale Thompson]. We met [September, 1917] in a Jewish Social Hall which was available up to a certain hour, at which time it was then engaged for a Jewish wedding. It was essential to us to vote for a constitution at this meeting, so we could work. The

---

* See Chapter 11, p. 249.

Governor ordered troops to disperse the meeting. We debated the Constitution with one eye on the clock and the sound of marching men in our ears. We just finished before we had to give up and leave the hall."

Morris Hillquit in describing this meeting added: "We had to work fast. For the first time in my experience I witnessed a meeting of radicals ready to cut out discussion and eager to settle down to practical work. . . . The contingent of troops was within an hour from Chicago. The wedding was in full progress when the troops arrived and surrounded the hall, spreading alarm and consternation among the guileless wedding guests." [8] This meeting, originally planned for Minneapolis, Minnesota, had been shifted to Fargo, North Dakota, then to Hudson, Wisconsin, then to Milwaukee, Wisconsin and finally to Chicago because each time "patriotic" elements stepped in to veto "un-American" meetings.

"Another very stormy occasion," wrote Emily Balch in her recollections, "was in Palm Garden in New York. Albert Rhys Williams, recently returned from Russia, was to address the meeting. Mr. Villard was chairman. His mother, in all the dignity of her age and personality, was on the platform. Some unfriendly person had tipped off returned soldiers, then in their thousands in barracks outside New York. Before long a howling mob of these men was outside the building. They were only prevented by police from entering. Mr. Williams, with characteristic courage, wanted an invitation sent out to the soldiers to send a deputation into the hall to present their case and talk things over. The police vetoed this as too dangerous. In the end, the soldiers got tired and drifted away. The only sufferer was a lady returning from the theater who happened to wear a red blouse and was more or less manhandled by the crowd."

But this is anticipating. The early summer of 1916 had brought added complications. United States relations with Mexico had become very strained. The preparedness movement in the United States was further stimulated by those who had oil investments in Mexico and by munition manufacturers. The American Union against Militarism fought intervention in Mexico and in one case, the Carrizal incident, was to some extent instrumental in averting a crisis. Through the quick action of Lillian Wald, Amos Pinchot, Oswald Garrison Villard and others, a paid advertisement in the

Emily Greene Balch
"If all the good people were clever
And all clever people were good,
The world would be nicer than ever
We thought that it possibly could."

Francis V. Balch
"It was his nature to act the part of a peace-maker."

Annie, Emily, and Elizabeth Balch
"A close-knit sisterly trio."

Ellen N. Balch
*"Quick-tempered — deeply loving, a
fascinating personality."*

Jane Addams
"*So utterly real and first-hand; so subtle, so simple and direct.*"

New York dailies, often an effective device, printed a letter from an American army officer which threw an entirely different light on a fracas south of the border, in which Mexicans were accused of having treacherously attacked a famous American regiment of colored troops without any provocation.

The presidential campaign in the autumn of 1916, with its slogan "He kept us out of war," brought many wishful peace votes for Woodrow Wilson. Jane Addams threw her influential support to Wilson both for his policy of neutrality and for his advocacy of a League of Nations.

In January, February and March, 1917, involvement of the United States in the European war became more and more probable. The pacifists worked all the harder as the temperature of the war spirit rose to fever pitch. Colonel Theodore Roosevelt, the most militant of the Nobel Peace Laureates, had long ago entered the war by himself. The pulpits with few exceptions resounded with war sermons. The zeal of the clergy outran that of President Wilson. He exclaimed, "I think our ministers are going crazy." [9]

Great financial and industrial interests that had formerly been hostile to the President, offered to place all their resources at his disposal. Even Henry Ford was only reflecting the general change in public opinion when in February he withdrew his monthly support of the Neutral Conference in Stockholm, effective March 1, 1917, and offered his factory and his resources to the government for making munitions in the event of war.

Prominent peace workers renounced their pacifism. Mrs. Carrie Chapman Catt, a founder of the Woman's Peace Party, offered the services of the suffragists in case the United States went to war. Rabbi Wise became the Ichabod of the pacifist cause. He had worked valiantly in the American Union against Militarism, and from the influential pulpit of the Free Synagogue he had raised a powerful and effective voice against "the armament gamble." Paul Kellogg in a letter to Jane Addams on February 9, 1917, describes the impact of Wise's dramatic change of heart upon his colleagues: "I have just come from a meeting of the American Union which morally and spiritually was the most gripping experience I have ever been through. As Miss Balch has just said over the 'phone, it was a struggle for a man's soul.

"Rabbi Wise came to the meeting with a determination to

preach to the Free Synagogue Sunday on the choice between war and Prussianism, casting his lot with war as the only way to throttle the greater evil as he saw it. There was Amos Pinchot, who urged that war and force would not throttle it; it reached to the soul, and that as individuals we must fight for the triumph of ideas over force. There was L. Hollingsworth Wood, the Quaker, who pleaded in the name of his co-religionists who are on the rack for their conscience' sake in England, that he stand out against the spread of Prussianism to the New World which would come from our entrance into the war. There was Villard who felt he was breaking with and renegade to the Garrisonian ideals of a life time; and Miss Balch, who appreciated his courage in coming to us and breaking with us if need be, if that was his conviction, but who protested that for America to go into the war would put the German people in bondage to the Junkers for all time and lay the seeds of a German, Russian, Japanese alliance that would be a threat to western civilization and democracy for a century to come. . . . There was Miss Wald and Crystal Eastman and Henry Mussey and I.

"Rabbi Wise said when he left that he would say this much; that we had shaken him, that he must think it through again; he had been wrestling with it for a week; he would perhaps take longer." [10] The defection of Rabbi Wise, Emily Balch later recalled, was one of the "shocks" in her life.

Jane Addams wrote sadly, "The long established peace societies and their orthodox organs quickly fell into line expounding the doctrine that the world's greatest war was to make an end to all wars. It was hard for some of us to understand upon what experience this pathetic belief in the regenerative results of war could be founded; but the world had become filled with fine phrases, and this one, which afforded comfort to many a young soldier, was taken up and endlessly repeated with an entire absence of the critical spirit." [11]

Perhaps most disconcerting of all was the almost 100 percent unanimity with which the American intellectuals accepted the challenge of the flung gauntlet and enlisted in the fight. In England Goldsworthy Lowes Dickinson had sickened in disillusionment with the universities and historians. Those who should have been leaders, as he thought, were like the rest, and "moved by passion, by fear, by the need to be in the swim, had followed the crowd down a steep place." [12] As for America, Randolph Bourne, in a widely read essay, "War and the Intellectuals" (June, 1917), decried the universal acceptance by American intellectuals of "the use of war technique in the war crisis in which America found herself. Socialists, college professors, publicists, new-republicans, practitioners of literature, have vied with each other in . . . the riveting of the war-mind on a hundred million more of the world's people." [13]

The American academic mind, which in 1914 had recoiled in horror at the famous manifesto of ninety-three German professors in defense of their war, had left behind in the passage of two years a "proud" neutrality, created reasons for following the preparedness advocates of big business, and finally joined, and according to Randolph Bourne, even led, the enthusiastic participation in a war. Laying aside hesitations, ironies, consciences, considerations, says Randolph Bourne, they plunged "into the blessed relief of action and with thankfulness, they lay down and floated with the current." [14]

But the opponents of war redoubled their efforts even as their ranks dwindled. Emily Balch, never a mere floater, struggled upstream with the vanguard.

On January 31, 1917, the Germans announced that they would carry on unrestricted submarine warfare. Immediately the American Union against Militarism telegraphed President Wilson that the United States should "refuse to allow herself to be dragooned into war at the very end by acts of desperation committed by any of the belligerents." [15] The telegram, which also appeared as an advertisement in the press, was signed by Lillian Wald, Emily Balch, Crystal Eastman, Mary K. Simkhovitch, O. G. Villard, Henry W. L. Dana, Carlton J. H. Hayes, George Foster Peabody, John Haynes Holmes, and others.

Three days later, on February 3, 1917, Wilson announced that diplomatic relations between the United States and Germany were at an end. It was at this point as previously described that the more uncompromising of the peace forces merged for joint action as the Emergency Peace Federation in which Emily Balch was a prominent leader. They hoped at the eleventh hour to precipitate action for peace, and they urged every possible expedient other than war.

On February 26, the day after Wilson learned of the Zimmermann note,* he went before Congress and asked for power to arm American merchant ships. Bryan, in last minute desperate efforts, used his silver tongue to urge his countrymen and Congress to use the machinery he had evolved for keeping out of the holocaust. La Follette and a group of Senators whom Wilson called "willful men" defeated the resolution for the arming of merchantmen by a filibuster.

Two days later the Emergency Peace Federation appointed a committee to wait upon the President with suggestions for possible alternatives to war: Jane Addams; Emily Balch; Professor William I. Hull of Swarthmore College, a former student of President Wilson; and two labor people, one of whom was James H. Maurer, president of the Pennsylvania Federation of Labor.

Professor Hull urged adjudication of injured American shipping according to historic American precedent; the two labor men still expressed a hope for a popular referendum if it should come to war, and Jane Addams and Emily Balch once more pressed for a conference of neutrals. The reactions of the President were described by Jane Addams:

"The President's mood was stern and far from the scholar's detachment as he told us of the recent disclosures of German machinations in Mexico and announced the impossibility of any form of adjudication. He still spoke to us, however, as to fellow pacifists to whom he was forced to confess that war had become inevitable. He used one phrase which I had heard Colonel House use so recently that it still stuck firmly in my memory. The phrase was to the effect that, as head of a nation participating in the war, the President of the United States would have a seat at the Peace Table, but that if he remained the representative of a neutral country he could at best only 'call through a crack in the door.' " [16]

---

* A wireless message of January 16, 1917 (intercepted by the British and sent to President Wilson on Feb. 25, 1917), from the German Foreign Secretary Arthur Zimmermann to the German Minister in Mexico, proposing a Mexican-German alliance in the event of the United States entering the war on the Allied side, and offering as a reward Mexico's "lost territory" in Texas, Arizona, and New Mexico.

Jane Addams, Emily Balch, and the rest were bitterly disappointed. They could not agree that Wilson's foreign policy which they "so extravagantly admired" could have a chance only if he were to take his place at the Peace Table as a belligerent. When peace finally came, there was no umpire of stature left to take a seat for only *victors* were permitted to attend. "The President," said Jane Addams, "had to drive a bargain for his League of Nations, he could not insist upon it as the inevitable basis for negotiations between two sides, the foundation of a 'peace between equals.'" [17]

By the middle of March the American people had become convinced that war, if not actually desirable, was unavoidable. On March 9, President Wilson ordered the arming of American merchant ships. Defense committees were organized all over the country. Representatives of American labor pledged support in case of war, for "ideals of liberty and justice." Some leading Socialists joined them—not Morris Hillquit, not Eugene Debs.

When, on March 15, the amazing news burst upon the world that the Russian autocracy had fallen,* the idea that the war was now really a "fight for democracy" against absolutism received powerful support. The pacifists, however, interpreted this great event not only as a turning to democracy but also as evidence of the revulsion of the war-weary Russian peasants and soldiers from fighting.

The submarine sinkings, the Zimmermann note, the arming of the American merchant vessels, the opposition of the "willful men," and the daily incitement by newspapers, inflamed public opinion more and more towards war. The newspapers blazoned the headlines "Country in Militant Mood."

If the pacifists were out of step with the rest of their countrymen, it was, as Thoreau said, because they heard a different drummer. The final efforts for peace were made by those few who did not recant, who did not compromise. On March 31, Emily Balch's group published an advertisement in the New York *Times*— "WAR IS NOT NECESSARY." It proposed several substitutes.

On Sunday, April 1, 1917, the last Sunday of the peace, the pacifist forces were gathering together in New York City for one

---

* The United States was the first nation to recognize the new government and welcome it, March 22, 1917.

last desperate effort, a mass descent upon Washington the next
day. That morning one of the few ministers of the Gospel who
refused to be engulfed by the tidal wave was preaching a final
passionate declaration of his faith in the Unitarian Church of the
Messiah in New York City. The Reverend John Haynes Holmes, in
his crisp, pungent tones, was saying: "If war is right, then Christianity is wrong, false, a lie. The God revealed by Jesus, and by
every great spiritual leader of the race, is no God of Battles. . . .
No order of president or governor, no law of state or nation, will
persuade me or force me to this business of killing. . . . Other
pulpits may preach recruiting sermons; mine will not. Other parish
houses may be turned into drill halls and rifle ranges; ours will
not. Other clergymen may pray to God for victory for our arms; I
will not. In this church, if nowhere else, the Germans will still be
included in the family of God's children." [18]

About fifty women, led by Emily Balch, Frances Witherspoon,
Tracy Mygatt, and including Elizabeth Glendower Evans of Bos-
ton, Mary McDowell of the Stockyards Settlement of Chicago, and
Dr. Alice Hamilton, entrained for Washington as delegates of the
Emergency Peace Federation. Jane Addams, David Starr Jordan,
and Louis Lochner went separately to Washington. Colonel House,
also hurrying to Washington that night, might have seen at the
Pennsylvania Railroad Station representatives of the Woman's
Peace Party and The Hague Congress ("les forces de demain?" [19])
waiting for the train. Some one was distributing to the waiting
delegates The Hague peace flower—white tulips, a frail and futile
symbol.

In Washington, the pacifists were prevented by the police from
holding a peace parade. But they did demonstrate before the
Capitol. With the encouragement of such Senators as La Follette,
Norris, Stone, Vardaman, and other strong opponents of the war,
they spent hours wearily pacing the long stone corridors of the
Senate and House office buildings, interviewing man after man,
trying to win over the doubtful and make an impression on the
bellicose legislators. Representative Claude Kitchin of North Carolina, majority leader of the House, came into the corridor to speak
encouraging words to them.

One incident received much publicity to the detriment of the pacifists. Some Massachusetts peace lobbyists were interviewing Senator Henry Cabot Lodge of Massachusetts in the corridor. According to the newspaper stories the next day, and according to Senator Lodge's own account, one of the pacifists, the athletic Alexander Bannwart, a graduate of Princeton, called the Senator "a damned liar" and struck him. The sixty-seven year old Senator struck back and a fracas ensued. Bannwart was taken off by the Capitol police. Two years later the Boston *Evening Transcript* printed a correction by Senator Lodge of his earlier statement. It had not been "strictly accurate." Senator Lodge now declared he became angry at some of the expressions used, and had in fact struck Bannwart first, and was then struck by Bannwart.

The same evening a mob of 500 Baltimoreans invaded Washington and tried to break up a mass meeting of the Emergency Peace Federation at Convention Hall.

That night, April 2, in a soft spring rain, President Wilson drove to the Capitol to deliver his war message. The avenues were lined with cheering crowds. A troop of United States Cavalry escorted the President to protect him from the "embattled pacifists." At 8:30 that evening, before a brilliant assemblage—Congress the Supreme Court, the cabinet, the diplomatic corps—the President began his fateful message. The beautiful phrases were to be quoted time and time again by pacifists and war supporters alike:

"The German submarine warfare against commerce is a war against mankind. . . . Armed neutrality it now appears, is impracticable. . . . There is one choice we cannot make . . . we will not choose the path of submission. . . . With a profound sense of the solemn and even tragical character of the step I am taking. . . . Our object. . . . is to vindicate principles of peace and justice . . . against selfish and autocratic power. . . . We have no quarrel with the German people. We have no feeling towards them but one of sympathy and friendship. We are glad . . . to fight thus for the ultimate peace of the world and for the liberation of its peoples, the German peoples included: for the rights of nations great and small and the privilege of men everywhere to choose their way of life and of obedience. The world must be made safe for democracy. . . . It is a fearful thing to lead this great peaceful people into war, into the most terrible and disastrous of all wars. . . . But the right is more precious than peace. . . . The day has come when America is privileged to spend her blood. . . . God helping her, she can do no other."

Perhaps it does not belong to this story to say that later that evening, in the Cabinet Room, according to the memory of the President's secretary, Joseph P. Tumulty, the cheers from the crowds as Wilson drove to the Capitol returned to his ears. "My message today was a message of death for our young men. How strange it seems to applaud that." [20] And a little later the President broke down and wept.

The same side, the side he did not show to Jane Addams, to Lillian Wald, to Emily Balch, and the other men and women pacifists, the side he did not show even to Colonel House, he turned to Frank Cobb, editor of the New York *World*, who later reported that he had spent the early hours of the dawn of April 2 with Wilson in his White House study. "The President looked as if he hadn't slept," said Cobb, "and he said he hadn't." He said he had never been so uncertain about anything in his life as about the decision to go before Congress to ask a declaration of war. For nights he had been lying awake going over the whole situation. "Do you know what that means?" he said to Cobb,* "a declaration of war would mean that Germany would be beaten and so badly beaten that there would be a dictated peace, a victorious peace. It means an attempt to reconstruct a peace time civilization with war standards, and at the end of the war there will be no bystanders with sufficient power to influence the terms. There won't be any peace standards left to work with. There will be only war standards. . . .

"Once lead this people into war, and they'll forget there ever was such a thing as tolerance. To fight you must be brutal and ruthless, and the spirit of ruthless brutality will enter into the very fibre of our national life, infecting Congress, the courts, the policeman on the beat, the man in the street. If there is any alternative, for God's sake, let's take it." [21]

---

* This conversation of Woodrow Wilson with Cobb was reported by Cobb to Maxwell Anderson and Laurence Stallings. See John L. Heaton, *Cobb of "The World,"* (1924). Confirmed by Laurence Stallings in letters of Feb. 23, 1961 and March 15, 1961, to M. Randall. "The account, which I annotated, is correct. Cobb talked of his visit to Wilson often."

The next four days were strange and curious. The long debate on the war resolution began in the Senate on Tuesday. The great speech in opposition was made by Senator La Follette who spoke for three solid hours. On Wednesday, April 4, after eleven o'clock at night, the vote was reached. The Senate adopted the war resolution by a veto of 82 to 6.

The six senators who stood against the tide and staked their reputations and their careers, were Asle J. Gronna of North Dakota, Robert M. La Follette of Wisconsin, Harry Lane of Oregon, George W. Norris of Nebraska, William J. Stone of Missouri, and James K. Vardaman of Mississippi.

One last step remained, the vote in the House of Representatives. On Thursday morning, April 5, the House took up the discussion. All day long, from morning to evening, the oratory rolled on. In the gallery the pacifists, Emily Balch, Mary McDowell, Frances Witherspoon, and Tracy Mygatt, were listening. Representative Claude Kitchin announced that he would vote against the war resolution. "I know I shall be . . . denounced from one end of the country to the other. The whole yelping pack of defamers and revilers in the nation will at once be set upon my heels." [22] Congressman Fred A. Britten, Republican from Illinois, injected a disturbing note: he declared he could name probably seventy-five percent of the Congress secretly opposed to the war resolution. "There is something in the air, gentlemen, . . . that seems to be picking us up bodily and literally forcing us to vote for this declaration of war when away down deep in our hearts we are just as opposed to it as are our people back home." [23]

As the hours wore on towards midnight, the pacifists began to sense a distinct feeling of uneasiness among the legislators. Tracy Mygatt thought the Roman Catholic Congressmen, especially, were becoming deeply disturbed. Some one said, "This is the day of the Betrayal." Another one cried, "Get a Bible and read it."

At a quarter to three in the morning the roll call came. The pacifists, as Frances Witherspoon remembers, about twenty of them, including Emily Balch, "crept up into the gallery and stood well back against the wall in the shadows so as not to have our presence noted. Hardly breathing and whispering to one another we heard the vote cast, heard Jeanette Rankin of Montana [the only and the first woman member of Congress] say, 'I love my country but I cannot vote for war.'"[24] A few minutes after three o'clock in the morning the result was announced—373 for war, 50 against. It was Good Friday, April 6, 1917. Not only to good Episcopalians like Tracy Mygatt and Frances Witherspoon, Christ had been betrayed again.

In the *Congressional Record* of April 5, 1917, Representative Isaac R. Sherwood of Ohio inserted a letter "by that student of the humanities at Wellesley College, Emily G. Balch."[25]

"The situation here in Washington for the last four days has been extraordinarily interesting. Members of the peace delegation have been talking with their representatives in Congress and their reports which I have been helping to tabulate are illuminating. The fact that stands out is that so many Congressmen are ready to vote against their own judgment, against their conscience, and against what they have reason to believe to be the will of their constituents.

"I take up the first pile on my desk—that of a New York Congressman. He is reputed to have said substantially as follows: 'The people of my district are seven to one against war. But I shall vote for it. They will soon forget about it, but the men who voted in the Senate against war will go down in history in obloquy.'

"A Minnesota delegate reported that several Congressmen told him that they knew their constituents were opposed to war; that they themselves knew no reason why the country should enter the war, but 'somehow they felt that patriotism demanded that they should vote for war.'

"A North Carolina Congressman is reported as saying 'he would really rather be dead than vote for war,' but that he proposes to do it.

"An Arkansas man will vote for war but does not like it . . . I next take up the report on two Ohio Congressmen. One is against war but calls opposition hopeless. The other is against war but will not commit himself as to how he will vote. . . .

"Many Congressmen are in the most acute distress of mind. They are white with drawn faces. Some shed tears. They are on the rack, drawn one way by one set of considerations and in the contrary direction by another.

"It is impossible to know how many would vote against war if they voted on their convictions or if they intended to represent the will of the majority in their home districts.

"One Congressman claimed that a secret vote would result in a majority of two thirds for peace. Representative Britten, of Illinois, has claimed on the floor of the House that 75 percent of the Representatives want to vote against war.

"The early days of April, 1917, may appear in history as more fateful than the early days of August, 1914. A war urged by the President on a reluctant Congress upon the grounds of the most disinterested idealism, will apparently be 'wished upon' the country against its will by the votes of men who fear the press more than they fear their consciences.

"So nearly 1900 years after the death on the cross this is to be the celebration of Good Friday.

Emily G. Balch"

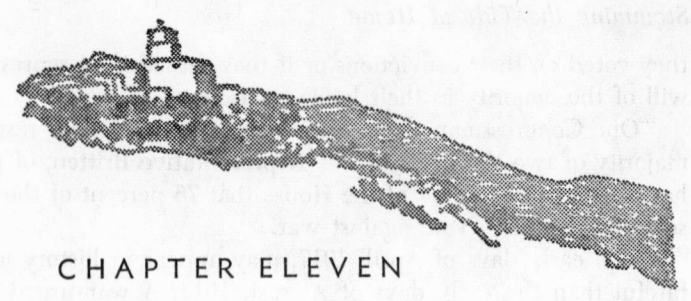

CHAPTER ELEVEN

Pacifists in Wartime—the End of a Career

Emily Balch and the peace workers had to bow to the inevitable. But without any pause they began the next chapter of their history. Their ranks had dwindled still further. David Starr Jordan declared: "Our country is now at war and the only way out is forward."[1] William Jennings Bryan offered his services to Wilson as a common soldier. The American Peace Society, the League to Enforce Peace, the Church Peace Union, the American School Peace League, the Carnegie Endowment for International Peace, all of whom were against war in general, were in all sincerity making an exception in favor of "this war," urging lovers of peace everywhere to "assist in every possible way in the effective prosecution of the war."

Only a handful of ministers refused to abandon their pacifist faith. John Haynes Holmes, Jenkin Lloyd Jones, Rabbi Judah L. Magnes, "one of the very few divines who took the spirit and teachings of Christ seriously,"[2] as Morris Hillquit said, Norman Thomas, John Herman Randall, Sr., all men of breadth and vision, were able to keep their churches, though their trustees were often pained and their congregations dwindled. Harry Emerson Fosdick was not to deliver his famous sermon "Apology to the Unknown Soldier" till later. A. J. Muste, then aged thirty-two, who was to become the most outstanding advocate of religious pacifism in the United States, left his church in Newton Center, Massachusetts, because his position as a pacifist minister had become psychologi-

236

cally untenable among parents of soldiers in the congregation.
During two difficult years, he said later, he had been sustained by
the sympathetic support and intellectual prestige of "three brilliant
women at neighboring Wellesley," Mary Calkins, Vida Scudder,
and Emily Balch.

After the war, many ministers and many Christians never
regained the same faith in the churches that they had had before.
They felt that the greatest crisis in history had found the churches
unready, without counsel, without policy, merely reechoing the
passions of the crowd. Emily Balch thought that perhaps those who
lived "on the outskirts of faith" were the disillusioned ones. "They
confused," she said, "as it is so easy to do, the failure of fallible
men and women with the failure of that in which they professed
to believe." [3]

Emily's own calling, the academic profession, was quick to bow
to tribal gods. As the church took no nonsense from the saint, the
University made short shrift with intellectual dissenters and non-
conformists. Emily Balch was very soon to have occasion to remember the testing time of her academic friend of 1905, Professor
Thomas Masaryk of Prague. Nicholas Murray Butler, president of
Columbia University and head of the Carnegie Endowment for
International Peace, declared in a Commencement Day address
to the Alumni on June 6, 1917: "This is the University's last and
only word of warning to any among us, if such there be, who are
not with whole heart and mind and strength committed to fight
with us to make the world safe for democracy." [4] This meant, in
plain words, that academic freedom was suspended at Columbia
University for the duration of the war.

At about the same time, in different vein, the Woman's Peace
Party of which Emily was one of the guiding spirits, was issuing a
statement: "Let those of opposed opinions be loyal to the highest
that they know, and let each understand that the other may be
equally patriotic. Our special part in the agitation and propaganda
of this hour of trial is the cultivation of even-handed justice, largeness of vision and breadth of sympathy, which may even now,
while the battle rages, weave threads of a better social fabric yet
to be." [5]

And yet Nicholas Murray Butler was an ardent internationalist
and a sincere advocate of peace. Like many other American

scholars who had studied in German universities in their youth, he was grieved to the core by the excesses of German *Shrecklichkeit* and by the betrayal of the European civilization he had known. For many years, and all during World War II, one of the most moving events in the Columbia University calendar was the annual reception to the foreign students from many lands, at which President Butler always appeared in person, and spoke, simply, and unmistakably from the heart, for a world of law and understanding between all nations.

Earlier in the spring, before war was declared, on March 5, 1917, the Columbia Trustees had succumbed to the coercive spirit of mass hysteria. It was the first private governing board to institute a general program of investigation to find out "whether doctrines which are subversive of, or tend to the violation or disregard of, the Constitution or the laws of the United States, or of the State of New York, or which tend to encourage a spirit of disloyalty to the government of the United States, or the principles upon which it is founded, are taught and disseminated by officers of the University." [6] This move did not pass unprotested by some of the faculty, themselves not pacifists. But it was plain that the sword of Damocles was hanging over the head of Emily Balch of Wellesley, too.

Forty years later, in 1957, from the perspective of two world wars, the Trustees of Columbia University candidly admitted the truth of the statement: "At Columbia University [in 1917], an overzealous board of trustees, a dictatorial president, and a distinguished but personally offensive professor [J. McKeen Cattell] were the figures in a loyalty case that shook the academic world."[*] Two other teachers at Columbia were dismissed.[**]

---

[*] *The Development of Academic Freedom in the United States* by Richard Hofstadter and Walter P. Metzger, New York, Columbia University Press, 1955.

[**] The three officers dismissed from Columbia University were Professor James McKeen Cattell, a leading psychologist but a reputedly difficult person; Henry Wadsworth Longfellow Dana, a grandson of the poet, an assistant professor of comparative literature, who had worked with Emily Balch in the People's Council (also in the Collegiate Anti-Militarism League and later in the Young Democracy); and Dr. Leon Fraser, instructor in Politics who later became director of the Bank for International Settlements and president of the National City Bank.

Cattell was dismissed for writing to Congressmen on Columbia University

A year later, in 1918, Emily Balch, too, was to figure in a "loyalty case." But owing to her quiet, controversy-hating nature, it did not rock the academic world, though it shook her smaller world of Wellesley to its depths.

The pressure for conformity in support of the war was felt on hundreds of other campuses. State institutions, being subject to political control, were particularly vulnerable to the whipped-up popular demand to tolerate no "subversives." Only the strongest university administrations, like that of Lowell at Harvard, were courageous enough to support the lonely dissenter. Even without public pressures, there would have been few dissenters on college faculties. American professors were overwhelmingly enlisted in Wilson's crusade for a "war to end war."

While the loyalty craze was running its course, peace advocates like Jane Addams and Emily Balch and peace organizations, except those that came out for war, were ridiculed, taunted, abused. They were called "pro-Germans," "traitors," "cravens, cowards, poltroons." The "little group of willful men" in the Senate were called "the eleven Iscariots." La Follette's two young sons, one of whom was to become a state governor, the other a United States Senator, saw their father hanged in effigy. David Starr Jordan had been threatened by a Baltimore mob chanting "We'll hang Dave Jordan to a sour apple tree." German music—Mozart, Schubert, Beethoven—was largely banned from concert programs; the Austrian born violinist Fritz Kreisler and the famous German conductor, Dr. Karl Muck, were boycotted. School teachers were made to meet after school to paste in school music books blank sheets of paper covering "The Watch on the Rhine" and "The Lorelei"; German cooks who had served years in the households of American families were suspected of being spies; and half in sport, half in hysteria, German measles and sauerkraut became Liberty Measles and Liberty Cabbage.

Jane Addams, who as head of the Woman's Peace Party was opposing the conscription bill, compulsory military training as a

---

letterheads urging them to vote against a bill, then pending, to send American draftees abroad. Harry Dana was condemned for having encouraged students to agitate against the conscription bill while it, too, was pending. Fraser, in 1916, made critical remarks about the voluntary military training camp at Plattsburgh, New York. He was discharged the following year.

permanent policy, and the passing of the drastic espionage bill, was vilified and reviled as no other American except Senator La Follette. "Let Miss Addams and her peace-loving associates . . . emigrate to their dear Germany . . . and convert the gentle barbarians of Louvain, of Rheims, of the Lusitania."

"The force of the majority was so overwhelming," wrote Jane Addams, "that it seemed not only impossible to hold one's own against it, but at moments absolutely unnatural, and one secretly yearned to participate in the 'folly of all mankind.'"[7]

A newspaper attack on Emily Balch and her "ilk" in the New York *Evening Sun* of May 31, 1917, shows the sort of thing that had to be faced even by as soft-spoken, as courteous, and undogmatic a person as Emily Balch.

To-Night's Pacifist Meeting.*

Pacifist meetings in Cleveland, Chicago and elsewhere have been marked by rioting and great disorder, in spite of the useless denial of this fact by Professor Emily Greene Balch of Wellesley College, who is a member of the "Committee" which is now arranging for such a meeting in Madison Square Garden this Thursday night. Professor Balch possesses her share of the calm effrontery which marks her kind. The country is at war, conscription is about to begin, and all good citizens are urged not to give aid or comfort to the enemy. Thereupon pacifists deliberately hold meetings to protest against war; they might just as well hold meetings to protest against epidemic disease or sudden death.

Professor Balch remarked to a reporter casually that she "expects no trouble" at Thursday's meeting. "The peace mass meeting in Washington the very night President Wilson asked Congress for a war declaration was orderly," said she, slipping easily over the obvious fact that a peace meeting at such a moment was intrinsically and in its essence a disorderly meeting. "The Bryan peace meeting, when the submarine issue was most acute, was orderly," The fact that at that time the country was still under the anaesthetization of "neutrality" makes no difference to the pacifist. The pacifist dislikes war equally whether the country is actually at war or not. It is a theory, not a condition, which inspires these rhetoricians.

At the present time, on the eve of the national registration day, such pacifist meetings are inherently disorderly, and their backers

---

* Editorial from New York *Evening Sun*, May 31, 1917.

stand in no questionable position—they are doing the work of sedition
and treachery to the law of the land and the country whose citizenship they abuse. It would be a most salutary procedure to place a
considerable number of the anti-draft offenders in jail as by law
provided. The whole country would benefit by a little tonic action
of this kind.

The People's Council was singled out for persecution by not
too responsible newspapers and by lawless mobs. Its leaders were
harassed and its meetings broken up, as has been described. Pacifism was bad enough, but when linked to what was thought to be a
subversive type of social radicalism, it was anathema.

According to Randolph Bourne, it was association with the
People's Council that condemned Harry Dana as being "disloyal"
and inflicted "the gravest damage upon the good name and influence of Columbia University." [8] It was probably her role as a
founder and advisor of this organization that, as Emily Balch later
expressed it, "overstrained the well known liberality of Wellesley
College," and terminated her teaching career.

Perhaps the most difficult thing all the pacifists had to contend
with was not the reviling, not the opprobrium, not the persecution, but the sense of extreme loneliness. To oppose their fellow
creatures went counter to their ingrained community-mindedness.
Jane Addams gave classic expression to this feeling of spiritual
isolation in moving, yet restrained passages in *Peace and Bread in
Time of War,* the volume Emily Balch liked best of all Jane
Addams' books.

"The misunderstanding encountered by the pacifist," said Jane
Addams, "with his precious cause in the keeping of those who
control the sources of publicity," brought her, "very near to self-
pity, perhaps the lowest pit into which human nature can sink."
The pacifist in war time "finds it possible to travel from the mire
of self-pity straight to the barren hills of self-righteousness and to
hate himself equally in both places." As Jane Addams and her
comrades, after the entry of the United States into the war, became
more and more set apart from the rest of the community, she could
reflect, "We never ceased to miss the unquestioning comradeship
experienced by our fellow citizens during the war, nor to feel
curiously outside the enchantment given to any human emotion

when it is shared by millions of others. . . . In the hours of doubt and self-distrust, the question again and again arises, has the individual or any small group, the right to stand out against millions of his fellow country men? . . . Even if one were right a thousand times over in conviction, was he not absolutely wrong in abstaining from this communion with his fellows? . . ."

"We could not however lose the conviction that . . . moral changes in human affairs may (also) begin with a differing group or individual."

None realized more clearly than Jane Addams or Emily Balch, with her academic reputation at stake, that they were surrendering all possibility of future influence, that they were committing professional suicide. They were also afraid of fanaticism, of preferring a consistency of theory rather than a pragmatic recognition of the actual situation. "We slowly became aware that our affirmation was regarded as pure dogma. We were thrust into the position of the doctrinaire. . . . On the other hand there were many times when we stubbornly asked ourselves, what after all has maintained the human race on this old globe despite all the tragic failings of mankind, if not faith in new possibilities and courage to advocate them?"

It was only after much inner struggle that Jane Addams and her fellow pacifists came to the conclusion that "the ability to hold out against mass suggestion, to honestly differ from the convictions and enthusiasm of one's best friends did in moments of crisis come to depend upon the categorical belief *that a man's primary allegiance is to his vision of the truth and that he is under obligation to affirm it.*"*9

Looking back some fifteen years later on the bitter choices of those days of war, Emily Balch recalls, too, the spiritual ordeal of the conscientious pacifist in wartime. She, too, makes central the sense of loneliness and isolation. In her confession there is perhaps a little more of intellectual doubt and searching of mind. Trained as a social scientist to seek a truth on which informed and intelligent men might agree, she could not rest in dogmatic assurance when the conclusions of her best thinking differed so radically from those of men she respected and looked up to. It was only the ties

---

* Italics mine.

of human companionship, the fellowship of those who thought and deeply felt as she did, that could support her resolution.

"It is needless to say that to me, as to everyone else, the war years brought pain, although it happened that I had no poignant personal anxiety nor bereavement, nor personal hardship or danger. It is a hard thing to stand against the surge of war-feeling, against the endlessly reiterated suggestion of every printed word, of the carefully edited news, of posters, parades, songs, speeches, sermons. In spite of a consciousness at times as clear as Luther's *Ich kann nicht anders,* at other times one staggered. To the question, 'What if Germany wins and militarizes the world?' I had no answer ready. Bitterest of all was the sense that if America kept out of the war it would be largely, perhaps mainly, not for noble reasons, but from greed for profits. Conscience was uneasy, as well it might be. Where is the line dividing inner integrity from fanatical self-will?

"I do not know whether what held me should be called a religious faith, or an irresistible set of the inner self, or fanaticism. My support in my belief that one must not resort to war for any purpose, came largely from friends whom I revered and who felt as I did. Conscientious objectors, too, whose sufferings for their convictions in England and here were known to us (those on the continent we could not then know of) shamed me and encouraged me. So did the courage of men like Bertrand Russell and Romain Rolland." [10]

All through the difficult months of the war, Jane Addams with her indisputable power of attracting and her gift of expression, remained the "incomparable leader" and one of the chief spokesmen for the peace seekers. Jane Addams really came to know Emily Balch well on the *Noordam* and at The Hague Congress and to admire and love her personally. In the next twenty years she was to lean on her intellectually for her careful scholarship, her wide knowledge of political and international affairs, and her judicial temper of mind. Between these two women, and extending to the other women who did not change their credo when the war broke out, was formed a comradeship unique, strong and lasting, as only a fellowship can be, composed of individuals who differed from the mass in time of danger—Lucia Ames Mead, Lillian Wald, Anna Garlin Spencer, the Quakers Hannah Clothier Hull and Lucy

Biddle Lewis, as well as Alice Hamilton, Florence Kelley, Alice Thatcher Post, Sarah Cleghorn, and others.

A few weeks after the declaration of war, the members of the Woman's Peace Party meeting "under the shadow of the war which we hoped our country might not be called upon to enter," reaffirmed their credo that the "internationalism to which the Woman's Peace Party is pledged came to fulfil the highest national life and not to destroy it," [11] and pledged themselves to promote mutual comprehension between persons of varying points of view. At a first meeting of the Board in October, 1917, held in a beautiful country house near Philadelphia to escape publicity, the women stated: "We have avoided all criticism of our Goverment as to the declaration of war, and all activities that could be considered as obstructive in respect to the conduct of the war, and this not as a counsel of prudence, but as a matter of principle." In recommending to their members the attitude to take towards the detractors and revilers of the pacifists, the Board counselled: "We gladly note all the incitements to noble and unselfish action of which these troubled times bear fruit. Any suspicion or resentment manifested toward any 'pacifist' group meets with no 'reprisals' from us. . . . We throw back no verbal brick-bats; *on the contrary, we set ourselves to sympathetic understanding of those from whom we differ, and to grateful recognition of their contributions to that common fund of ethical idealism and of wise mastery of political problems upon which the reconstruction of the world depends."*[12]

As to their program in war time, the women were advised to work for a league of nations to substitute law for war. They were constantly accused of wishing to isolate the United States and to keep it out of world politics. "We were, of course," said Jane Addams, "urging a policy exactly the reverse, that this country should lead the nations of the world into a wider life of co-ordinated political activity." [13]

As immediate objectives, the women were to oppose the Espionage Act, conscription, and military training of school children, and to support President Wilson in opposing compulsory military training as a permanent policy. Finally, the women were urged to

---

* Italics mine.

uphold respect for minorities and guarantees for the rights of minority opinion. "It often happens that the minority of today is the majority of tomorrow. Let us who are outvoted be neither abashed nor discouraged." [14] This meant working to uphold the right of conscientious objectors to war and trying to obtain for them consideration similar to that which prevailed in England. Jane Addams with a committee called upon Secretary of War Baker, who cryptically assured them, "There will be no conscientious objector problem in the United States." [15] Emily Balch lost no opportunity, however small, however hopeless, to urge the cause of the conscientious objectors, neglected for the most part by peace advocates who were not pacifists.* Her letter to Bishop Cooke of August, 1917, pleading for understanding of the conscientious objectors' position, shows her ability to sympathize with an opponent, her gift of disarming, not alienating. It also indicates the loneliness and self-searchings of the pacifist as well as of the conscientious objector. Bishop Cooke had criticized conscientious objectors for refusing to bear their share of the cost of preserving our heritage of free institutions, won and maintained by war. It was the same argument as that attributed to a Roman Emperor concerning young Christians thrown into the arena for refusing the military oath: "These pitiful wretches enjoy the peace and splendor of Rome but will not move a finger to protect or to extend either."

Emily replied to the bishop by an analogy. The conscientious objector refuses to assist a community of people who insist on putting out burning oil by pouring water upon it, and he is as public spirited in his refusal as they in their method of fighting the flames.

"In practice," Emily's letter went on, "the conscientious objector may be doing a harder thing than the men who submit to the pressure of public opinion and go to war. He bears the almost intolerable burden of separation from the movement of his own time. He stands lonely against the overwhelming rush of his fellow countrymen to war. He makes himself a by-word and a hissing. He faces not only disgrace but torture (for imprisonment in many

---

* For a definition of pacifist see Chapter 15, p. 343 (footnote) and page 352 ff.

American prisons is today literal bodily torture) and the possibility
of death as a mutineer.

"He does this to serve, as he believes, first his own country and
then all men everywhere. He is seeking so far as in him lies to
open the road to the Kingdom, to the day when literally the meek
shall inherit the earth, and he testifies to his conviction that war
puts back liberty, destroys democracy, shames Christianity.

"If he has any humility or (what is closely allied to that grace)
any sense of humor, he is alive to the danger of priggishness that
lies in his isolation, in his claim to deeper moral insight than his
elders and betters and those who have given and are giving their
lives in war. In his moments of depression and self-searching he is
likely to fear, even to morbidity, lest unworthy elements are entering into his own sacrifice that he would like to keep so clean.

"His is not an easy path. Let us at least be fair enough to
recognize that he believes that he is serving not himself but us." [16]

The greatest penalty Emily Balch was to pay for her convictions was the loss of her professorship at Wellesley after "twenty
years of happy teaching." She was the head of the Department of
Economics and Sociology. In characteristic generosity and ironic
understatement, she wrote of the action in these words in her
recollections, in 1933: "When in the spring of 1917, as my Sabbatical year was drawing to a close, the United States entered the
war, I felt that my return to Wellesley the next year would be
embarrassing to the college and to me, and that it would be better
for my students for classes to continue as they were for another
year. I therefore asked for, and received, a year's leave of absence
without pay. At the end of this year my existing appointment
expired, and *much as I grieved that the well-known liberality of
Wellesley College should have been over-strained by me,** I could
not be surprised, when, after much discussion and much friendly
advocacy of my reappointment, the trustees decided against it.

"This left me at fifty-two with my professional life cut short
and no particular prospects." [17]

On March 31, 1918, she was writing in her journal: "It is to
be decided whether the Trustees will reappoint me, my 'loyalty'

---

* Italics mine

being in question. I am making a statement to President Pendleton for her use as she sees fit. I want to do what is right both with reference to my own best service such as it is and to the general cause of freedom and especially 'academic freedom.'

"After a long period of indecision I had decided to return to Wellesley after two years of absence and Miss Pendleton expressed a cordial desire to have me return and all seemed settled. But the accidental fact that my five years appointment runs out this year so that it is a question of a fresh appointment, not of a mere continuance, brings the matter before the Trustees for action and what action is highly uncertain.

"But all personal fates seem small matters and I will try to find something serviceable to do if I can, anyway."

The statement to President Pendleton, written from Morningside Heights, New York City, April 3, 1918, runs as follows:

"I should like to state to you, as well as I am able, my fundamental position in these tragic and heroic days through which our country and all the world is passing.

"In the first place I am entirely in sympathy with the purposes of our country in the war as expressed for us by the President. I rejoice in his international leadership and am thankful that such a leader has been raised up to us. I feel moreover that we can never adequately appreciate the heroism and self-sacrifice that are being poured out so unstintedly in the war day by day. I could desire nothing more than also to give myself wholly in trying to bring about a better world.

"In such a time when love of country is conscious as never before, and when patriotism has such special claims upon us all, it is a very painful thing to be obliged to forego, in any degree, full inner cooperation with the methods by which the ends for which we all are working are being sought. Nevertheless I believe so deeply that the way of war is not the way of Christianity, I find it so impossible to reconcile war with the truth of Jesus' teachings, that even now I am obliged to give up the happiness of full and unquestioning cooperation where the choice is mine to make.

"On the other hand any effort to obstruct the war, to work against enlistment or anything of the sort, would seem to me not only inexpedient and silly, as well as unlawful, but also morally wrong. It is, I suppose, hardly necessary to add that Junkerism and militarism and all their manifestations, from faithlessness and fraud to atrocities and annexations, are abhorrent to me.

"In all such activities as food conservation and relief reconstruction work of all kinds I can of course take part gladly to the limit of my ability.

"I fully realize that wiser as well as infinitely more spiritual disciples of Christ believe that they are following him in taking part in the war according to their respective functions. This does not excuse me however from doing what seems to me right as I see it. I may have a larger vision some day, then I can follow the new leading. Meanwhile one of the hardest things about holding the position that I do is that it is so hard to keep it clear of Pharisaism.

"Now as to the practical side of all this. It means that I have no temptation to dampen patriotism even in forms that I could not personally adopt nor to carry on any propaganda for my own peculiar views in connection, direct or indirect, with my teaching. It means that at Wellesley or elsewhere I desire to do all that in me lies toward making the world safe for democracy by whatever phrase we may choose to express our national purpose at its purest, to work for honest and vigorous thinking, self-control and above all for service."

Feeling that the above statement did not go fully into some aspects of her problems, Emily Balch added a supplementary letter. The last paragraph of this letter states succinctly the principle of the freedom of association, which has ever since enjoyed so varied a career in the face of the political passions of our century.

"I want to say something about my affiliation with various peace organizations—that is, organizations devoted to the cause of ultimate peace and justice in an organized world such as this country is striving for. Of several of these I am an official in one way or another, but in the one that has been especially criticized, the People's Council, I do not now hold any office.

"The newspapers have spread much misunderstanding of the purposes and character of this organization. It has never been a 'stop the war' party nor followed an anti-government policy. The federal Department of Justice, which keeps, I believe, in close touch with the doings of all peace organizations, has never, so far as I know, had any criticism to make of its activities.

"The bitterness of the newspaper attacks upon the People's Council are especially due to two things so far as I can understand.

(1) The constituent meeting unfortunately came at a time of great tension when the first draft was about to be called and it fell a victim to a local political fight between a conservative governor and a radical mayor. This situation repeated itself in all three states (Minnesota, Wisconsin and Illinois) where the attempt was made to hold the meeting. My understanding of the situation in Minnesota is that the governor was the spokesman of the mining interests and that while the meeting in Minneapolis was prevented by him ostensibly on political grounds the real ground was far more an unwillingness to have industrial matters discussed. Minnesota having led the way no other political governor could afford to appear less patriotic than the governor of Minnesota. Perhaps even more detrimental to the People's Council than the fact that it was opposed by three governors was the fact that it was befriended by Mayor Thompson of Chicago.

"(2) The other great cause of misunderstanding and opposition to the People's Council was, I think, the phrase about 'opposing conscription' which stood in its first platform, or rather in the draft for a platform voted at a preliminary meeting. This was while the draft act was under discussion and opposition to its policy entirely permissible. There never was any idea of opposing the draft after it had become law.

"The foreign policies of the People's Council are practically those of President Wilson so far as I understand either.

"In this question of membership in one or another organization there is involved a question that far transcends any personal or particular application. I care because it appears to me to be very dangerous in a democracy for citizens—day laborers or professors or anyone else—to feel that they are controlled in their decision as to joining or not joining a (legal) political organization by considerations as to retaining their opportunity to work."

Three weeks later, President Pendleton sent Emily Balch an extract from the minutes of the meeting of the trustees on April 23, stating their decision: "While recognizing the sincerity of the views expressed by Miss Balch and her essential nobility of spirit, the

Trustees decided to postpone further consideration of her reappointment." The question of an eventual reappointment was left open, but she was deprived of her position for the coming year.

As soon as this inconclusive decision was announced, Vida Scudder wrote to Emily:

Wellesley, April 25, 1918

My dearest Emily:

You know I think how wholly I am thinking and feeling in your life these days. I cannot believe the incredible has happened, and I do not for a moment consider the issue closed, as I am sure Miss Pendleton does not. But to lose you for even another year is a sore loss to the college. And an unlovely light falls on the Board of Trustees, so far as their intelligence goes. . . .

I find my mind dwelling much on your father. You will never know how much my brief glimpse of him has meant in my life; how clear my impression of his gentleness, clear vision, utter courage. I am sure he would be very proud of his daughter.[18]

V.D.S.

A younger colleague in Emily's own department, Anna Youngman, wrote: "I do feel as if I should like to give up college teaching forever. . . . Miss Pendleton seemed very much broken up."

Mary Whiton Calkins, professor of philosophy, wrote Emily the day of the Trustees' meeting, April 23: "I agree with you in believing it wise and right to concur in Miss Pendleton's plan of *postponing* the decision and for your reason—in order to save the trustees and thus the college, from an action so subversive of a spirit of freedom and tolerance.

"But I asked Miss Pendleton definitely to state to the trustees (at my request) my position: that I concur entirely with your views, pacifist and (probably) social-economic, and that I belong to most of the pacific organizations of which you are a member. I also definitely told Miss Pendleton that I should offer my resignation in case the trustees later vote unfavorably on her recommendation. . . .

"Finally, is it not wonderful for us to have the whole-hearted support of a woman like Ellen Pendleton?" [19]

A few days later Miss Calkins wrote to Emily: "I understand that your department has turned off, at white heat of indignation, an appreciation that should make your dear heart glow." [20] This unanimous statement, addressed to the Board of Trustees of Wellesley College and dated April 29, 1918, by the members of Emily's own Department of Economics, emphasized the serious loss the department would suffer if deprived of the services of Professor Emily Greene Balch. During her two years' leave of absence the department had nevertheless been conducted under her guidance, and their general plan of work had been submitted to her for approval, advice, and assistance. They had counted on her return the next year, and her absence would be a serious handicap.

"It will, indeed, be impossible to find anyone so well equipped as she to offer certain courses which were to have been announced for the coming academic year.

"A long period devoted to special investigations, together with extensive travel at home and abroad, has enabled Professor Balch to develop a course in Immigration that any student would consider it a rare privilege to be able to elect. It is safe to say that there is no present-day economist who has made more scholarly or more valuable practical contributions to the solution of the problems of immigration. The course in the Economics of Consumption has been conducted by Professor Balch with intent to emphasize the function of women in directing household expenditure. It is perhaps unnecessary to call attention to the peculiar value of such a study at the present time. Unfortunately, it will be impossible to offer an adequate substitute for the projected course, as the material for discussion must be obtained from most diverse sources and is difficult to assemble into a coherent whole. A course in the Principles of Sociology was also to have been offered for the first time in many years, and Professor Balch has devoted a large portion of this past winter to direct preparation for this work.

"But Professor Balch brings to her work much more than the expert knowledge necessary for the efficient handling of particular courses. Her personal qualities lend distinction to the department and to the institution with which she is associated. She is a teacher who has always been able to present her subject dispassionately, unmarred by any spirit of propagandism. She is a scholar whose impartiality of judgment has not been shaken by the strength of her personal convictions. She is an original and far-sighted thinker

who is possessed of that fine imaginative power which enables her
to see the problems of the present in relation to the needs of the
future. For that reason, her work has an enduring quality, appreciated by her students and by all those who have worked with her
and under her kindly direction. We feel that a person of her keen
mind, broad outlook, and inspiring personality is indispensable
not only to the Department of Economics but to the whole College. Her permanent withdrawal would mean an irreparable loss."

The storm of indignation and the tenor of the faculty protests
when it became known that Emily Balch was not coming back to
Wellesley, show that her "failure of reappointment" had not been
precipitated in her case by a brash, tactless, and pugnacious personality. Neither had she ever been accused of indoctrinating her
students with her pacifist or other heterodox views. She had always
consciously striven for objectivity in her teaching.

The faculty asked for a meeting in chapel to thrash out the
whole question. The trustees sent as their representative the distinguished George Herbert Palmer, professor of philosophy and
husband of Alice Freeman Palmer, the first president of Wellesley.
To the end of their days, and in the salubrious climate of Wellesley
many of them lived to be over ninety, the women professors
remembered that meeting as one of the most dramatic, unforgettable episodes in their lives. Professor Palmer, they recounted, was
very astute. He said almost nothing, but listened carefully. The
high point was reached when Adelaide Locke, professor of Biblical
History, who had been sitting in the front row, rose to her tall
length, looking every inch a prophet, and shaking a long forefinger
at George Herbert Palmer declared: "If the trustees persist in a
policy like this, they will fill Wellesley College with a faculty of
nonentities." [21]

Vida Scudder wrote again to Emily, May 11, 1918: "You
couldn't expect the people who know your value to the college not
to express themselves at this juncture. . . . I think the time might
easily come when you would have to consent to some publicity for
the sake of what you represent. Oh, and you represent so much!
A splendid young Congregational minister has been spending the
afternoon with me, a friend of Norman Thomas, exactly in your
position, and I felt what you, with all your mental power and
maturity, would mean in the fellowship of all these perplexed

people." Then she added, regretting her inability to follow her nearest friends Emily Balch, Helena Dudley and others in their pacifism, a position which she reversed after the war, "I am very wistful because I am not with you, but I can't help it. I don't dare take the stand which would discredit in the human race the impulse to defend the weak. I suppose I have said this to you before, but you see I feel very much on the defensive, and rather bewildered to be for once on the majority side; really a little disgraced. . . .

"The real issue is of course freedom. But it is a proper preliminary for your colleagues and your department to express to the trustees their sense of your value." [22]

The matter was not conclusively settled till the spring of 1919. As late as April 2, 1919, just before Emily sailed for Europe for the Second Congress of Women, Katharine Lee Bates was writing to her: "I hope with all my heart that if the battle is won with the trustees, you will not negative it all by refusing to return. . . . As far as the cause of academic freedom goes, it will never be generally understood and believed that you were asked to come back if you don't come back.

"And surely these hundreds upon hundreds of eager girls—truly eager about the problems of reconstruction—about to enter, with the vote, on a more potential womanhood than ours has been, need the wisest and most liberal teaching obtainable. It is Katharine's [Coman] department and yours. Don't you feel a certain responsibility for the work? There will be difficulties at first, perhaps, but with your own bright, loving presence in our midst, they will soon vanish.

"Please think hard, if the offer comes, before you say no." [23]

It was while Emily Balch was attending the Women's Congress in Switzerland that President Pendleton sent her a cable and a diplomatic letter (May 8, 1919) announcing the final decision of the trustees not to reappoint her. "The whole question was very thoroughly discussed at the Trustee's meeting, and I think I can say that every opportunity was given to present all phases of the subject. You will be interested to know that the vote was a very close one, although I have not said this to others. With the exception of possibly three members, who, I think, probably were unconsciously influenced by their conservatism, I think it is fair to say that the decision was not based on grounds which were contrary to the policy of academic freedom.* Many warm expressions of admiration of the work which you have done, and especially of your publications, were made.

"Although you will not be actively connected with the college, I do not need to assure you that you will always have many warm friends who will be interested in seeing you at Wellesley as often as possible." [24]

It is a measure of the persistence of wartime emotions and of the continuing pressure for social conformity that the trustees voted to terminate the services of Emily Balch six months after the war was over. Their reason was doubtless, as J. H. Randall, Jr. pointed out in his brochure *Emily Greene Balch of New England, Citizen of the World,* "because of her activities for peace and her outspoken pacifist position—all the more unpalatable in the light of her progressive economic views."

The word "finis," however, had not yet been written. In the summer issue of the *Wellesley Alumnae Magazine,* July, 1919, appeared a tribute to Emily Greene Balch signed by fourteen members of the faculty and staff:

"The term of service in Wellesley College of Emily Greene Balch has ended, after twenty-one years, as Instructor and Professor of Economics.

"Those of her colleagues whose names are given below, of various opinions and habits of mind, take this occasion to express their esteem for Miss Balch as economist, teacher and woman.

"During these years through her published work she has achieved an international reputation for careful, exact and original scholarship.

"Many students have gone out trained by her in honest, critical methods, inspired by her to continue their studies in the field of economics, and effectively prepared to take a sane and wholesome part in the guidance of public opinion.

---

* "It was the narrowest of majorities in the trustees' meeting. All the alumnae trustees, including the president, were strongly for you, and Dr. Horr of Newton Center Theological Seminary, I was told, made a magnificent plea, on the ground of your standing and value as an economist, but the hard-headed business men just succeeded in carrying the vote." Letter of Katharine Lee Bates to Emily Balch, September 1, 1919.

"Even when differing from her in opinion or action, we have respected her essential fairmindedness, her courageous and conscientious regard for truth. We feel we have had in our midst a person of rare distinction and nobility.

"We desire, therefore, to express our belief that Wellesley College has incurred a grave loss."*

The names of Katharine Lee Bates and other strong supporters of Emily Balch were missing from the signers. A number of Emily's friends on the faculty, including Katharine Lee Bates, wanted to press the trustees still further. "We had a very earnest June faculty meeting," wrote Katharine Lee Bates on September 1, 1919, "and those of us who loved you dearly but didn't want this statement printed at this time, urged the alternative of further effort, perhaps in union with the Alumnae, to induce the trustees to change their decision. . . . The faculty has a committee (of which I'm chairman) to consider what may yet be done. . . .

> With constant love and honor,
> Katharine Lee Bates" [25]

Thirty years later, when the history of Wellesley College came to be written, the delicate episode was handled as follows:

"There was another member of the Wellesley faculty whose primary concern was peace, and who became, at the outbreak of the first World War, a crusading pacifist. Though it appeared to some people that the decision to terminate her appointment as head of Wellesley's Economics Department was because of her conspicuous pacifist activities both before and after the United States' entry into the first World War, there was also the contributing factor of her prolonged absences from College on her various peace missions. Her energy was given to a cause. However the Trustees viewed that cause, there was still the fact, to paraphrase Miss Bates, that she was employed to teach Economics, not pacifism. Even so, it was by a narrow margin of two votes that Emily Balch failed in reappointment to her post. Every alumna

---

* The fourteen signers were: Alice Van Vechten Brown, Mary Whiton Calkins, Elizabeth K. Kendall, Eliza H. Kendrick, Vida D. Scudder, Adelaide I. Locke, Marian E. Hubbard, Eleanor A. McC. Gamble, Julia Swift Orvis, Agnes F. Perkins, Josephine H. Batchelder, Anna Youngman, Donald S. Tucker, Katharine P. Raymond, M.D.

and administration member of the Board voted to retain her. A
tribute to her as "economist, teacher and woman," signed by fourteen members of the faculty and administration, was published in
the Wellesley Magazine in 1919. . . .

"President Pendleton invited her in 1935 to give the Armistice
Day address to the College. . . . Again, some measure of restitution was offered for what may have been an unjust decision when
Wellesley's seventh President [Mildred McAfee Horton] added her
voice to those who were hoping to secure the Nobel Peace Prize
for Emily Balch. She became the third woman and the second
American woman to receive this high honor. She was seventy-nine
years old in 1946 when it was awarded for her lifetime of work
for the cause which meant everything to her and to which she
had given most of these years."[*26]

In later years, whenever she was questioned about this "failure
of reappointment," Emily Balch would say gravely, "I wasn't dismissed, you know." None the less, as Vida Scudder, Katharine Lee
Bates, Mary Whiton Calkins, and other colleagues acknowledged,
it was a clear case of violation of academic freedom. And, of
course, it would be so judged by the now accepted standards of
the American Association of University Professors. Such episodes
had much to do with the fact that during World War II almost no
faculty members in American colleges were disciplined for pacifist
activities.

Professor Charles Beard of Columbia University, who in 1917
had resigned in protest against the dismissals of Cattell and Dana,
gave Emily the impression that she had not done her part in "the
common cause" and was afraid she "had made things too easy for
the trustees." But Emily Balch had not been unmindful that "the
occurrence," as she called it, should be made to serve and not
hinder the cause of "reasonable academic freedom." "It is the
grievous part of it to me," she wrote Katharine Lee Bates from
Geneva in February, 1920, when talk of reinviting her to Wellesley

---

* According to Agnes Perkins, the above section of the history was submitted
to Emily Balch for her approval before publication. She was content to let
it pass. But when the passages were read aloud to her after publication she
lifted her eyebrows at the mention that "however the Trustees viewed that
cause, there was still the fact, to paraphrase Miss Bates, that she was
employed to teach economics, not pacifism," and murmured, "How absurd."

Mary Kingsbury (Simkhovitch)

*"To her beauty was added the
charm of her delicious warm voice."*

Emily Balch at Bryn Mawr
"It was not an apple but a book that did the mischief."

Dr. Aletta Jacobs of the Netherlands
"Apotheosis of the Victorian upper middle class at its best."

Lida Gustava Heymann and Dr. Anita Augspurg of Germany
"In all the winds of fortune, they kept their colors flying."

Clara Ragaz, Switzerland
"So lovely to look at, combining such personal gentleness and modesty with such heroic devotion."

was in the air, "that I have strained the toleration of our Trustees to the breaking point and broken in upon our good Wellesley tradition. But what is breakable in such matters is perhaps well broken, so that the unbreakable living conviction may replace tradition. At any rate you know that I did not act wantonly nor lightly nor without many different kinds of cost, experienced at the time as well as foreseen for the future, in these last difficult years."

In short, Emily Balch refused to make a cause célèbre out of the affair, though the fighting liberal, Oswald Garrison Villard, and other impetuous supporters of freedom, urged her to. "The creature in me does hate controversies," as she had written years before in her journal, of the Marlboro strike report. No word of censure or recrimination ever passed her lips. She admitted, however, that it had been a "shock," though not an unexpected one. Her income was suddenly cut off. Her forgiving and conciliatory spirit accounted for the friendly relations she was to have with Wellesley College in the future. In 1925 she made her permanent home in the town of Wellesley. For Emily Balch, the episode was a closed one, never to be referred to voluntarily.

> I aimed my pebble, but myself
> Was all the one that fell.

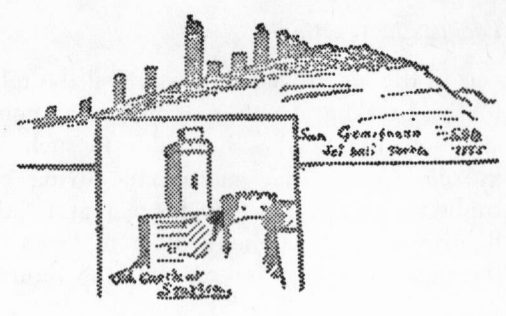

CHAPTER TWELVE

Women and the Peacemaking, 1919

It was May, 1919, six months after the signing of the Armistice. From 1914 to 1918 the war-numbed peoples of Europe had looked forward to the end of the slaughter, none more so than the women of the International Committee for Permanent Peace. Many of them had endured a threefold anguish: they had lost some of their closest of kin; they had lost them in a war they had opposed; and they had appeared to betray their native country in the interests of a larger humanity. Something like eleven million men had lost their lives in the war. Still there was no peace, and the Allied blockade was continuing to starve the men, women, and children of Germany, Austria, Hungary, and Russia.

The women who had faced Goliath at The Hague Congress in 1915 were now, four years later, meeting again, in Zürich in friendly Switzerland, conscious again of their collective responsibility, looking, if possible, for a common solution and a common deliverance. Their compassion had not been deadened by the blunting process of war.

During those four years Emily Balch had acquired considerable prestige in America as an outstanding advocate of peace. She had published, together with Jane Addams and Alice Hamilton, *Women at The Hague* (1915), an account of The Hague Congress and its

results. She had written "A Double Alignment," "The War in Its
Relation to Democracy and World Order," and many other articles.
Of these, "A Time to Make Peace"* was regarded by many as one
of the most statesmanlike utterances on the settlement of the
European war that had appeared in any periodical, American or
foreign. The spring of 1916 found her in Stockholm as an American
delegate to the commission of international lawyers, experts, and
peace workers.

In New York, during these years, besides her more dramatic
work with the emergency peace organizations, Emily had engaged
in quieter but no less assiduous types of peace work. Under the
aegis of the Woman's Peace Party in the autumn of 1916 she had
carried on, with Norman Angell, a course of eleven lectures on
"Current Developments in World Politics." These lectures gave her
listeners, "as I afterwards learned, their first conception of a pacifist
internationalist approach to current happenings." After the United
States entered the war, she continued lecturing, holding discussion
classes on the Russian Revolution.

In cooperation with the American Union against Militarism,
Emily Balch published in March, 1918, *Approaches to the Great
Settlement,*** with a fourteen page introduction by Norman Angell.
It was an objective account of various peace proposals, parties,
issues, and methods. It included texts of documents issued by
Socialist and labor groups since these were not as familiar to the
public as the state papers and official pronouncements. She also
devoted some fifty pages to the peace programs of unofficial peace
bodies.*** With its collection of such historical documents as were

---

* *The Survey,* October 2, 1915.
** *Approaches to the Great Settlement.* Introduction by Norman Angell, New
York, B. W. Huebsch, 1918.
*** These included the "minimum program" (April, 1915) of the Central
Organization for a Durable Peace; the proposals from the Neutral Conference
for Continuous Mediation, Stockholm, Easter, 1916; the program of the Amer-
ican section of the International Committee of Women for Permanent Peace,
1915-1918; The League of Nations Society (British); The League to Enforce
Peace (June, 1915); the peace program of the Union for Democratic Control
(England); proposals for a desirable peace settlement by David Starr Jordan
(summer, 1917); and the proposal for a peace conference by President
Charles W. Eliot of Harvard (August, 1917).
It is interesting to see how some of these programs foreshadowed the
proposals later formulated in Wilson's Fourteen Points.

then avaliable, its contemporary portraits, and its cartoons, Italian, Dutch, American, it is still of interest and value. The concluding item, recorded on March 31, 1918, in her last consecutive journal concerned this book: "My book *Approaches to the Great Settlement* on which I began work the first of August and the first draft of which was finished on October first, is now at last out—has been out about a week. It was a lot of work and I am not at all proud of the method or lack of it in the way it was done but I hope it will be useful a little and that I shan't be found to have made any egregious blunders. It is so easy to, that I feel as if the book were a sort of powder mine. It looks very nice and I think the illustrations add decidedly. I am glad I urged having them."

About this time she also became a member of the Council of the Fellowship of Reconciliation, one of the first religious pacifist bodies.

At the end of 1918, when her existing appointment at Wellesley College expired, she was left adrift at fifty-two without a professional income. "It was naturally with great appreciation" she wrote "that I accepted from Oswald Garrison Villard an invitation to join the staff of the *Nation*. I worked for the most part in the most modest capacities [too modest, as Freda Kirchwey, then a very youthful member of the staff, afterwards recalled], but I remember one day when Mr. Villard came in and telling me that Austria-Hungary had collapsed, asked me if I could write a leading article on the subject before the paper went to press in two hours' time. From studies which I had made on the spot for my book, *Our Slavic Fellow Citizens*, I knew well the component parts of that conglomerate empire. I was especially interested in the effect of the change on the nationalities, but I was blind, as were the responsible statesmen who framed the peace settlement, to the fact that, monstrous as the Hapsburg empire might appear politically, it was a functioning economic organism, and that to tear it apart without further concern was to create chaos and entail the hideous suffering of the post war years, especially in Vienna."

The *Nation* was at that time occupied with getting out an international relations supplement. To this, the editor, Oswald Garrison Villard, said she made most valuable contributions. "I found her intuition extraordinary, her judgment remarkable in its accuracy, and her scholarly attainments surprising at all times." [1]

For Emily Balch, the Zürich Women's Congress of 1919 was to effect a complete turning point in her career. Most of the women gathered together in the Glockenhaus found the Congress one of the most moving experiences of their lives. At the very moment when the fate of Europe was being decided at Paris by the Big Four—Clemenceau (the Tiger), President Wilson, Orlando, and Lloyd George—160 women from sixteen countries were meeting with the gloomiest of fears and misgivings in their hearts, during a week of unbroken splendor of spring sunshine, with flowering apple trees in the valleys, the gleaming lake of Zürich beside them, and snow-capped mountains beyond.

When the women from The Hague Congress had disbanded in 1915, they had agreed to hold a second woman's congress at the end of the war, at the same time and in the same place as the official peace conference. They did not know that they would have to wait four dreadful years to keep this novel international promise. They had assumed, like the rest of the world, that the conference of diplomats would meet in a neutral country with both sides of the conflict represented.

When Paris was chosen as the place of the peace conference, the plans of the women fell through, for of course the German, Austrian, and Hungarian women delegates could not go to France. So after much cabling and changing of plans, the Women's Congress was convened at Zürich on May 12-17, the very week during which the delegates of the chief defeated powers were called to listen to the terms imposed upon them, including the extorted confession of their responsibility for the war, and during which the Treaty of Versailles was made public by the Allies. "Miss Addams," Emily Balch was to write a few days after the sessions ended, "came to the Congress direct from her various interviews in Paris, with the first still scarce copies of the peace terms, just then announced, in her hands, and the voice of this little united group of women is the first impartial judgment to be passed upon them." Other international groups also held their congresses at the same time, but probably none had planned their meetings so far in advance. The women were only too well aware of the fact that the official peace conference would be composed of diplomats bound by traditional conventions and attitudes. "Because in every country such men are seldom representative of modern social thought," said Jane Addams, "and the least responsive to changing ideas, it was considered supremely important . . . that other groups should convene in order to urge the importance of certain interests which have hitherto been inarticulate in international affairs." [2]

How shocking and incredible the terms of peace and policy of reparations turned out to be caused even a brilliant British economist, John Maynard Keynes, neither a woman nor a pacifist, to exclaim that they were "abhorrent and detestable" and that "never in the lifetime of men now living has the universal element in the soul of man burnt so dimly." [3]

On April 9, 1919, the group of American delegates had set sail for Le Havre on their old friend, the *Noordam:* Jane Addams, Emily Balch, Mrs. Florence Kelley, Mrs. Lucia Ames Mead, Dr. Alice Hamilton, Lillian Wald, the Hon. Jeanette Rankin, whose vote in the war roll-call, "I love my country but I cannot vote for war," had been heard round the world, Mrs. Louis Post, Mrs. John Jay White, Mrs. Lucy Biddle Lewis, Madeleine Z. Doty, and others.

"Our delegation," wrote Dr. Alice Hamilton, in a letter to Jane Addams' closest friend, Mary Rozet Smith of Chicago, "is much better than the last time but really there are only three who count, Jane Addams, Mrs. Kelley and Emily Balch. I like her [Emily Balch] ever so much and she certainly knows a lot and her disposition is fit for the Kingdom of Heaven. . . . Jeanette Rankin is clever and attractive and people are all immensely interested in her." [4]

There was a two weeks' delay in France for the American delegates during which they met with their French colleagues and had interviews with various officials of the Peace Conference. The French delegates, headed by the brilliant Gabrielle Duchêne, had been refused their passports to Zürich by a government unsympathetic to pacifist congresses, but they cooperated from Paris and "were magnificent in their generous fidelity" said Emily Balch. Mrs. Helena Swanwick, one of the commanding personalities in the British peace group, and earlier in the suffrage movement, was left behind when the British delegation sailed, as she was unable to get a French visa. The Congress was nearly over before she was allowed to travel to Switzerland. Mrs. Ayrton Gould of the International Committee of Women for Permanent Peace had been kept away from Zürich by the British government for her part in holding a huge "Lift the Hunger Blockade" meeting in Trafalgar Square, attended by 20,000 people. She and Miss Rhoyds, later Mrs. George Innes, one of the future International chairmen of the W.I.L.P.F., had performed amazing feats of organization in procuring in England one million rubber nipples to be sent to German mothers too starved to nurse their babies. The infants, for lack of these nipples, were unable to take the milk that was being sent to Germany. This compassion and moderation on the part of so many British people who had suffered much more than the Americans, astonished the delegate Dr. Alice Hamilton. Such moderation "was simply unimaginable in our country," she said, remembering an incident of the previous autumn. On November 15, 1918, four days after the Armistice was signed, two cables had arrived in the United States from German women. One was addressed to the wife of the President, Mrs. Woodrow Wilson, signed by Alice Salomon and Gertrude Baer. The other to Jane Addams, was signed by Anita Augspurg. The cables protested against the hunger blockade and the seizure of 3,000 milch cows in Germany. Jane Addams never received her cable personally and learned of it only through the newspapers. A wave of patriotic rage swept over the country and Jane Addams received angry and scurrilous letters. "Except for the time of the 'bayonet charge' episode," said Alice Hamilton, "I never saw anything so full of hate and bitterness as the letters she then received, all of them from people of the educated well-to-do class." [5]

Emily Balch herself did not remain unscathed after the war. On January 24, 1919, the "Stevenson List," drawn up by Archibald Stevenson of the Military Intelligence Bureau, was presented to the United States Senate Judiciary Committee. It contained a "Who's Who in Pacifism" with the names of sixty-two men and women connected with "pro-German pacifist movements prior to entry of the United States into the war."[*] The alphabetical list was headed by Jane Addams and included Emily Greene Balch, Sophonisba P. Breckenridge, Lillian D. Wald, as well as Charles A. Beard, the Reverend John Haynes Holmes, Jessie Wallace

---

[*] New York *Times*, Jan. 25, 1919; Philadelphia *Public Ledger*. Jan. 25, 1919.

Hughan, Judah L. Magnes, Tracy Mygatt, Vida Scudder, and others.

Emily Balch was designated as: "Economist, Studied with Professors Schmoller and Wagner; formerly professor political economy, Wellesley College; American Neutral Conference Committee; People's Council of America; Liberty Defense Union; Women's Peace Party of New York City; Emergency Peace Federation; American Union against Militarism; Collegiate Anti-Militarism League; Women's International League; Intercollegiate Socialist Society."

The advocates of peace, like the criminal, had defied the accepted standards of society. Jane Addams, whose experience with lawbreakers and malefactors around Hull-House as well as with other forms of human suffering, was reflected in the perpetual sadness of her eyes, said, "We also shared a certain daily experience with the criminal, for the surveillance of secret service men and the effort of military intelligence to 'get something on us' was not psychologically unlike the shadowing by detectives and the readiness of the police to arrest him." [6]

For the pacifist women, both American and European, the sense of separation from their fellows "was broken into at neutral Switzerland for a blessed fortnight." An American journalist reporting the Zürich Congress said "The will toward peace and international neighborliness, so often trampled under since the war, became alive again in that hall. The air was the old free air and the spirit lifted and expressed itself." [7]

Florence Kelley, who had not been at The Hague Congress, wrote to Mary Rozet Smith: "As you doubtless know, my going was an act of faith, not of conviction. When anyone asked me why I was going, I said, 'To black J.A.'s boots and lug her suitcases.' . . . But next time I would go on my knees. It was unbelievably wonderful. There were twenty-five English women sitting with the Germans in front, and the Irish at one side, alike engrossed in the common effort. . . . The English leaders amazed every one by emphasizing at every opportunity that they were all Socialists. This included Mrs. Pethick-Lawrence, Chrystal Macmillan, Mrs. Snowden (of course) and all the lesser lights. Hitherto, I have found it hard to like English women, but this time I found myself their humble admirer. . . . Never have I seen so generous a spirit in any group of human beings. Even Dr. Jacobs was amicable from the word 'Go!'

"The public meetings were in the aula of the University of Zürich where I was a student thirty-five years ago. The audiences were tremendous. Jane Addams was at her very best." [8]

For the first time Emily Balch and the other American women had the experience of meeting the "alien enemy" face to face. "Those who came to Zürich from the countries which had been spared the worst ravages of the war," wrote Emily Balch, "were aghast at the evidence of bodily suffering from famine and cold in the faces of their friends, and realized how little even this suggested of the desolation and disruption caused by the war." [9] Jane Addams describes her feelings on meeting in a Zürich street an Austrian delegate, Leopoldina Kulka, whom she remembered as a beautiful and blooming woman at The Hague. The Austrian was so shrunken and marked by hunger and privation that she was almost unrecognizable—in fact she died a few months later. "Her face and artist's hands were covered with rough red blotches due to the long use of soap substitutes, giving her a cruelly scalded appearance."

"What were we all about," said Jane Addams, "that such things were allowed to happen in a so-called civilized world? Certainly all extraneous differences fell from us as we stood together in the spring sunshine and spoke of the coming Congress, which, feeble as it was, yet gave a demonstration that a few women were to be found in each country who could not brook that such a state of things should go unchallenged." [10] At an evening meeting this dying woman recounted that many Austrian women had resented not so much the starvation itself as the fact that day after day they had been obliged to keep their minds steadily on the subject of procuring food to the exclusion of all other pursuits—intellectual, spiritual, and pleasurable—that make life worth living. People changed into selfish, sordid, almost inhuman beings who cared nothing about anybody but themselves and their children. Never again would she expect idealism or even intelligence from the abjectly poor. From all this sordidness she found release in meeting once more with her old comrades in a cause greater and beyond all thoughts of self.

"Food is a subject that has never left my mind for a day since

I came here," wrote Dr. Hamilton to Mary Rozet Smith. "All the time we were in Paris, we were hearing discussions of the deliberate use of starvation as a method, for apparently that is the new method of warfare, and it is very inexpensive and requires no courage and no sacrifice. You have no idea of the ghastliness of their policies. They are in force this very minute in any country where the 'Reds' are in power, as well as still largely in force in Germany, Austria and Hungary. Here in Zürich we are meeting the victims of it and I am perfectly certain of one thing and that is that no matter whether *war* is ever justified or not, nothing in the world can justify a food blockade. It is cowardly, it is hideously cruel and it is utterly unjust for it strikes hardest the people least responsible for the quarrel that started it. If you could see Frau Kulka from Vienna, Frau Knischewsky from Wiesbaden, Frau Pogony from Budapest—it brings a lump to my throat to look at them. They are emaciated, but it is the tragedy in their eyes that is the worst. . . .

"There were some intensely interesting times—when the women from Bavaria, Austria, Würtemberg, Prussia described the revolutions that they had themselves lived through. Another was when one of the German women [Lida Gustava Heymann] told of the protests that they had sent to the Government against the invasion of Belgium, the annexation of Belgium, the deportations, the Brest-Litovsk Treaty and the offensive of 1918. Naturally they were silenced. No paper could publish their protests, their mail was held up, telephone service denied them and they could hold no meetings, even in private, and they had domiciliary visits of the police over and over again. But we were all so thankful that they *did* protest."

With such experiences in mind and a knowledge born of actual sufferings, the Zürich Congress, on a motion urged by the Englishwoman Emmeline Pethick-Lawrence, passed a strong resolution with no dissenting vote, on famine and the blockade. They asked for the lifting of the blockade, for inter-allied machinery to provide relief, and if necessary, for the food rationing of people in every country so that the starving might be fed. The women in the blockaded countries did not enter into this part of the discussions, thus initiating a tradition in the future Women's International

League against any advocacy of the special interests of a speaker's own country.

The resolution was telegraphed in full to Paris and the women received a sympathetic reply from President Wilson: "Your message appeals both to my head and my heart, and I hope most sincerely that ways may be found, though the present outlook is extremely unpromising, because of infinite practical difficulties. Woodrow Wilson." [12]

Jane Addams describes the public reception of this telegram as one of the most striking moments of the Congress, revealing once more the reverence with which at the time all Europe regarded the President of the United States. "As I stood in the old fashioned high pulpit [in St. Peter's Church] to announce the fact that a telegram had been received from President Wilson, there fell a hush, a sense of tension on the great audience that is difficult to describe. It was as if out of the confusion and misery of Europe, one authoritative voice was about to be heard. Although the telegram but expressed sympathy with our famine resolution, and regret that the Paris conference could not act upon its suggestions, there arose from the audience a sigh of religious resignation, as if a good man were doing his best and in the end might succeed." [13]

As the Woman's Congress was in actual session the very week the Treaty of Versailles was published, it issued the first public declaration against the treaty by any body in the world, again with no dissenting vote. It was also the first international body to discuss the treaty and condemn many of its terms. Again the strongest denunciation came from the British delegates. The German women were silent. Mrs. Ethel Snowden of England proposed the resolution. It was seconded by Jeanette Rankin of the United States. In her memoirs, *A Political Pilgrim in Europe*, Mrs. Snowden tells how more than one of the delegates, including Emily Balch, had spent the best part of the preceding day and the whole of a summer night, digesting the elaborate clauses and fine details of the Treaty.

Unfortified by hindsight, the women spoke out in unequivocal terms and issued the following protest:

"This International Congress of Women expresses its deep regret that the terms of peace proposed at Versailles should so seriously violate the principles upon which alone a just and lasting peace can be secured, and which the democracies of the world had come to accept.

"By guaranteeing the fruits of the secret treaties to the conquerors, the terms of peace tacitly sanction secret diplomacy, deny the principles of self-determination, recognize the rights of the victors to the spoils of war, and create all over Europe discords and animosities, which can only lead to future wars.

"By the demand for the disarmament of one set of belligerents only, the principle of justice is violated and the rule of force is continued.

"By the financial and economic proposals a hundred million people of this generation in the heart of Europe are condemned to poverty, disease and despair, which must result in the spread of hatred and anarchy within each nation.

"With a deep sense of responsibility this Congress strongly urges the Allied and Associated Governments to accept such amendments of the Terms as shall bring the Peace into harmony with those principles first enumerated by President Wilson, upon the faithful carrying out of which the honor of the Allied peoples depends." [14]

By a unanimous vote of the Congress, this resolution was telegraphed to Paris. Later a delegation of four women was elected to accompany Jane Addams to Paris and together with Gabrielle Duchêne present the resolutions in person. The delegates chosen were Charlotte Despard, Rosa Genoni, Chrystal Macmillan, and Clara Ragaz. The diplomats were unmoved. The press of the Allied countries was bitterly hostile.

The first evening Jane Addams had said, "We wish to keep humble and sincere and say only those things which we believe and which our long experience in warfare has verified. Bear with us as we blunder along through those situations which are not clear even to the minds of instructed men. Believe us, we are striving only to find that which shall be of value to us, to our fellow countrymen when we return, and possibly of value to the men who may in the near future be rewriting some of the treaties which are just being presented to the world." [15]

Slowly public opinion veered to the women's point of view, and it was not long before the minds of "instructed men" were to uphold the women. A year later, in 1920, Maynard Keynes' book *The Economic Consequences of the Peace** was published. Two years later a British ex-sailor who had been badly wounded during the war said at an Armistice Day meeting in London, "For every man who a year ago knew and said that the Peace Treaty was immoral in conception and would be disastrous, there are thousands who say it now." [16]

Maynard Keynes had been official representative of the British Treasury at the Paris Peace Conference up to June 7, 1919, and deputy for the Chancellor of the Exchequer on the Supreme Economic Council. He resigned from these positions when it became evident that there was no hope for substantial modification in the draft terms of peace. "There are few episodes in history," he wrote, "which posterity will have less reason to condone,—a war ostensibly waged in defense of the sanctity of international engagements ending in a definite breach of one of the most sacred possible of such engagements on the part of the victorious champion of these ideals." And then he added, "Only after the most painful considerations have I written these words. *The almost complete absence of protest from the leading statesmen of England*** make one feel that one must have made some mistake. But I believe that I know all the facts, and I can discover no such mistake." [17]

However, in 1919, the women at Zürich had spoken out unequivocally and fearlessly.

A week after the Congress was over, as events began to fall into perspective for her, Emily wrote out some brief impressions. The unanimity that prevailed among the women was what loomed largest in her mind. "It is evident that there was expressed a way of looking at life and its values that is valid and holds its own as truly as the deductions of mathematics, universally, and unaffected by differences of place, politics or any sort of particularism. . . . It was not only that there was throughout a complete absence of disagreeable 'incidents,' there was no temptation to oppose the interests of one country to those of another: the most painful and difficult things could be discussed frankly because there was mutual trust and understanding. . . . Unanimity of purpose and feeling

---

* *The Economic Consequences of the Peace*, John Maynard Keynes, New York, Harcourt, Brace and Co., 1920.
** Italics mine.

did not imply uniformity of opinion. There was probably a left and right in every delegation. . . . The differences between the more radical and the more conservative delegates came out on two points. The first was the attitude of the Congress on the League of Nations." [18]

The Zürich Congress was the first international body to issue a constructive criticism of the Covenant of the League of Nations, a copy of which had been given Jane Addams in Paris on her way to Switzerland. The delegates, after a careful analysis made by three subcommittees representing three differing and strongly held points of view, agreed on a statement warmly welcoming the Covenant. But they deplored that in many respects it did not accord with the Fourteen Points, that it contained provisions that would stultify its growth, and omitted others essential to world peace. The statement specified essential provisions which had been omitted and set forth certain changes which it was desirable that the League of Nations should incorporate.

"The cleavage of opinion," Emily Balch commented in her impressions, "was the most pronounced within the ranks of the American delegation. Some shared the point of view of Lucia Ames Mead, who has given a life-time of unstinting service to the cause of international organization and who now sees in the League an incomplete and in many ways disappointing realization of her desires, yet immensely in advance over the anarchy of the past. On the other side were some who see in the faults of the present covenant such dangers as to make it worse than nothing. It looked like an *impasse* ahead yet it proved that there was agreement on the points of the League that are to be approved and on the changes that ought to be made in it. And can anything this side of Omniscience tell whether the Covenant as it now stands will do most good or harm? It recalls the story of a famous bishop's childhood, when he balked at the collect giving thanks 'for our creation, preservation and all the blessings of this life.' He told his mother that he wanted to wait and see how it turned out."*[19]

---

* It might surprise college students of today to learn that the young liberals and radicals of 1919 did not, on the whole, follow their mentor Emily Balch in supporting the League of Nations. They opposed the League of Nations because "It is only a league of governments, not of peoples; it is to be the means by which an iniquitous and war-breeding Peace Treaty is to be

The women at Zürich adopted the name Women's International League for Peace and Freedom. "*Freedom*" they made coordinate with peace for several reasons. "Only in freedom is permanent peace possible," one of the delegates said. Most of the members had long worked in social movements that aimed to free mankind not only from war, but from the restrictions of undemocratic governments, from discrimination against women, and from the tentacles of a competitive economic system. Those from the Continent were active as Social Democrats and as feminists. The British members were involved in the struggle for woman suffrage and many were close to the growing Labour Party. The Americans had lived through the progressive era, with all its eager activities for social betterment. Many, like Emily Balch herself, were strong trade unionists and even Socialists. But most of all, these women all shared the hopes so bright at the end of the war that now at last it was possible to liberate the energies of men from the confines of outgrown social institutions, loosened and weakened by the war and its aftermath.

"They felt the danger of confusing peace with stagnation," wrote Emily Balch in retrospect. "They believed that violence creates new wrongs in redressing old ones, but also they believed that a peace which rests on oppression maintained by force is an evil peace and cannot last, and that freedom must be won for all peoples by peaceful means.

"Because of what they had seen over four years they also believed that freedom, the basic condition of human personality and growth, could not be maintained *except under peace*. That, too, was in their minds in making 'peace and freedom' their objective.

"It may be that of those who voted for this new name, some

---

enforced; it excludes many nations, particularly Mexico, the former enemy countries, (Germany, Austria,) and Russia; it is not easily subject to drastic modifications; the secrecy, cynicism, intrigue, imperialism, and autocracy of the Versailles Treaty is thus to be made permanent; the Convenant is not built on the foundation of a new economic system and a new concept of governmental responsibility but rests on an order already crumbling." The writer, Devere Allen, adds judicially: "Somewhat arbitrary and not wholly dispassionate, this outline is by no means set forth as an infallible pronouncement." *Young Democracy,* Special College Number, Vol. I, Nos. 11, 12, October 1, 1919.

had also in mind the struggle that still lay before them, as women, to secure the right of suffrage and the full status of citizenship then not yet won in the United States. But this was not the chief consideration." [20]

The Women's International League for Peace and Freedom or, as it came to be known, the W.I.L., was to remain steadfast in its devotion to freedom in the face of the terrific assaults of the years between the wars. But unlike most other organizations, it was also to hold fast to the equal faith that men can and must find ways to win and maintain freedom without war.

This twin devotion to aims that for the vast majority since 1919, often seemed incompatible has given the Women's International League a remarkable feeling of solidarity and comradeship. The W.I.L. was not to become merely one more women's organization, distinguished only by its international scope. It was to evoke in its members the conviction that they belonged to a spiritual fellowship. Though the W.I.L. was to draw its members from diverse religious faiths or from those who professed none, its sense of spiritual kinship and cohesion resembled that of a genuinely religious brotherhood.

The dramatic origins of the League at The Hague in time of danger, its transcendence of national cleavages at Zürich in time of hatred, its isolation for a time as a heterodox group, the prophetic quality of its pronouncements, and the intellectual and moral caliber of its founders and leading personalities, helped give it the character of a companionship. Though the women could not help being aware that they were pioneers, they did not dream that they were assisting at the birth of traditions in their organization that were to be strong enough to weld the members together for the next half century.

All this made it natural that a woman like Jane Addams, whose intellectual position throughout the world in her generation was preeminent, should request to have inscribed over her grave these words: "Jane Addams of Hull-House and the Women's International League for Peace and Freedom." To her, both were genuine communities to which one could belong with all one's heart and without reservation. Few other organizations have been able to elicit such a deeply passionate sense of belonging.

This does not mean that the "beloved League" of Jane Addams

was always one continuing harmonious communion, or that what Emily Balch called "our gallant enterprise" did not at times in the next decade or two perilously skirt the rocks. There were, indeed, frequent divergences between strong, brilliant, decisive personalities, clashes of temperament and habits between national sections, misapprehensions due to differences in language and parliamentary procedure, painful and wasteful personal misunderstandings. But, Emily Balch emphasized in 1938, "If in quieter times these [differences] have sometimes made themselves felt, it is significant that they have never been able to prevail against the wish to understand one another and to continue to work together, so that the Women's International League for Peace and Freedom has never known a schism, nor the withdrawal of a group except where the heavy hand of political dictatorship has put an end to all possibility of work." [21]

This cooperation in diversity was in part due to the harmonizing genius of Jane Addams as a chairman, her power to assuage and reconcile, to discover and interpret underlying trends in a general situation that would draw from each member a "larger and finer" response. In part it resulted from the settled determination of the League to arrive at decisions, not by imposing the will of the majority, but by a genuine collective activity. "Therefore," urged Emily Balch in 1926 just before the Dublin Congress in an attempt to compose the differences of policy that were threatening to erupt, "we all try to discuss in such a way as not to gain votes, but to find the general will, as Rousseau used to say. We try both to create agreement and to bring clear expression to all the agreement there is latent among us. We must all the time be trying as much to agree with others as trying to get others to agree with us. This is as new in debate as peaceful settlement of disputes is new in international politics." [22]

This procedure somewhat resembles the Quaker technique of reaching conclusions, not by counting votes, not by evading the issues, but by patient efforts to elicit "the sense of the meeting." As Jane Addams expressed it at the last international congress she attended, at Prague in 1929: "We hope to maintain a cooperative rather than an argumentative attitude towards differences of views, to secure real freedom of expression of conflicting ideas and thus to obtain a self-determined adjustment.

"That harmony is a sham which is merely a glossing over of realities. We must state our issues clearly and compose them through what has come to be called creative discussion, the result of which is not compromise but a new solution born of good will and pooled intelligence." [23]

As one reads over the very interesting *Proceedings* of this postwar Congress, Emily Balch does not at first seem to have played any conspicuous or dominant role either as a speaker in the series of brilliant evening public meetings or as the mover of the more important resolutions and policies. This may partly be due to the fact that she edited the *Proceedings* of the Congress and may have minimized her own role. Except for one brief dramatic moment on the last day of the Congress, when she broke through the bounds of her New England self-restraint and self-discipline and stepped completely out of character, her work was unspectacular but fundamental. But she impressed the delegates at Zürich much as she had done at The Hague.

As a member of the Board of Officers and as one of the Executive Committee, she had spent six grueling days in Zürich before the opening of the Congress, working in her usual self-effacing way, in planning the agenda, deciding on resolutions to be presented, and using her expert knowledge of politics, economics, and languages in sorting, harmonizing, and translating the French, German, and English materials that had come in from different national groups. She was head of the subcommittee on educational and social questions. On the floor, she spoke to the resolution urging that consent replace coercion in government, closing her short comment by saying: "We have made but the merest beginnings in the highest of human arts, that of living and working together on the plane of consent and cooperation without coercion." [24] She presented the report of the committee on educational programs, and the resolution condemning control of thought and the misleading of public opinion by censorship of the press, government suppression of news, and government propaganda. At the banquet following the close of the Congress, her election to the Executive Committee of nine was announced.

Very characteristically it was Emily Balch who made the motion to send a telegram of greetings to Rosika Schwimmer, who was unable to leave Hungary: "We recognize in you one of the most passionate champions of the cause of peace and join you in wishes for the better time we are all working for."*

On the last day, the Congress adopted a simple constitution, and unanimously elected Jane Addams as international president. Emily Greene Balch, having become unexpectedly free, was chosen as international secretary-treasurer. The international office was to be located wherever the League of Nations was to establish its seat. So it came about that Emily Balch entered upon a new career and was to spend a good part of the next dozen years or so at Geneva.

Unlike the League of Nations, which at first excluded the defeated countries, the newly formed Women's International League rose above national differences by electing a German woman, Lida Gustava Heymann as international vice-president.** Its superiority to national cleavages was further shown in what was to many the most striking episode of the Congress. On the last morning, after the adoption of the program for future work, Jane Addams quietly announced that the French delegate from the devastated area of Carignan in the Ardennes, Jeanne Mélin, had managed to get through and had just arrived. The lovely sad-faced woman was welcomed to the platform with an ovation. Spontaneously the German, Lida Gustava Heymann, came forward, her gaunt figure tense, her eyes burning with passion, and welcomed her with a great bunch of roses she happened to have in her hands, saying, "A German woman gives her hand to a French woman, and says in the name of the German Delegation, that we hope we women can build a bridge from Germany to France and from

---

* Rosika Schwimmer became less and less satisfied with the League as time went on. In 1927 she withdrew, convinced that the pacifist aims of the League 'were weakened and obscured." Her temperament inevitably rendered her life dramatic and turbulent.
** "Whoever was not there cannot realize what these conferences meant to us in a time of heart-breaking sorrow and grief. For many of us they were the supreme moments of our life. . . . Let me give you some examples of our spiritual cooperation. At a time when the whole world stood against Germany, [1919] our members elected to the Board a German woman as Vice-President. In 1921, of ten members of the Board, two were German and one Austrian. What this meant will be clear to everyone who realizes that there are still today [1924] international organizations which do not admit Germans." Lida Gustava Heymann, *Survey of the Nine Years' History of the Women's International League for Peace and Freedom* (1924).

France to Germany, and that in the future we may be able to make good the wrong-doing of men."* The two women clasped hands on the platform.

Mlle. Mélin replied with a stirring speech, "eloquent as only a French speech can be," said Emmeline Pethick-Lawrence, which voiced the protest of women against the injustice of the statesmen at Versailles at that moment betraying the hopes of the people, and urged women everywhere to struggle for a new social order, joining international forces, "les forces de demain."

Emily Greene Balch concluded this dramatic episode by rising to her feet, thin and spare, raising her hand and solemnly pledging herself to do everything in her power to work towards the ending of war and the coming of permanent peace, inviting all present to join her. Not a woman remained seated.

"I have never," said Helena Swanwick, "witnessed or imagined so remarkable an affirmation. Such scenes can, of course, be staged, but only intense feeling can cause them to occur spontaneously as this did." 25

Resolutions do not as a rule make interesting reading, especially not resolutions passed nearly half a century ago. But in recording their protests the women were also laying down their program for the future. Besides the primary issue of universal disarmament many of the further resolutions became more and more pertinent as the years rolled by and their problems were to form a central concern for Emily Balch during the next thirty years. The resolutions were:

Race Equality

We believe no human being should be deprived of an education, prevented from earning a living, debarred from any legitimate pursuit in which he wishes to engage, or be subjected to any humiliation, on

---

* It was generally the most ardent suffragists like Lida Gustava Heymann, Rosika Schwimmer, and Dr. Aletta Jacobs who were "over-sanguine perhaps in their belief in the pacifist nature of women" as Gertrude Bussey said. Naturally many of the women at the Congress like Jane Addams, Emily Balch, Clara Ragaz thought it a debatable question whether the enfranchisement of women would in itself be a weapon for the prevention of future wars. Mary Ritter Beard, the economic historian, wife of Charles H. Beard, repeated again and again that history gives no support to the theory that woman is by nature a lover of peace in preference to war.

account of race or color. We recommend that members of this Congress should do everything in their power to abrogate laws and change customs which lead to discrimination against human beings on account of race or color.

The Jews

We hold that no restriction should be placed on the civil or political rights of the Jews because of their race.

Deportations

Mass deportations have become a world-wide phenomenon since 1914, and inflict suffering and death in many forms upon innocent people. The Women's International League for Peace and Freedom recommends that this subject should receive attention at the earliest possible moment. *The expulsion of thousands of innocent people cannot be treated as an internal affair of any of the nations concerned.**

Conscientious Objectors

We wish to record our deep sense of the heroism of those who have counted no sacrifice too great to serve the cause of peace. We recognize the devotion alike of those who believed that in offering their lives in war they were helping end war, and of those who with equal courage and, as we believe, with deeper insight, fought war by refusing to take part in it. It fortifies our courage and our faith in the achievement of permanent peace, to know that in so many countries thousands of young men have for that end counted it worth the cost to bear the loss of health, fortune and friends and to face imprisonment, obloquy and death.****

This resolution on conscientious objectors expressed a deep concern with the age-old problem of the relations of church and state, of conscience versus the law, a problem which most of the more conventional peace organizations did not handle and which most ordinary citizens often misunderstood.

"I not only feel profound respect and gratitude toward conscientious objectors," wrote Emily Balch in 1945, "but I believe they have done an enormous service to the cause of both peace

---

* Italics mine.
** *Report of the International Congress of Women,* Zürich, 1919.

and of freedom of conscience, and in protest against the state worship of the present day. . . . While many people fail to understand and certainly do not approve their position, I believe that it has been a very great service to a public too much affected by the conception that might makes right. It is interesting that at the Nuremberg war-guilt trials, the court refused to accept the principle that a man is absolved from responsibility for an act by the fact that it was ordered by his superiors or his government. This is a legal affirmation of a principle that conscientious objectors maintain in action."

Of great importance for the future work of the women in the decades to follow were the methods advocated by the delegates in facing the difficult problems of postwar social and economic reconstruction, "at a time when the habit of violence has been fostered by a world war." Many of the delegates represented countries such as Bavaria, Austria, and Hungary in which revolutions with or without bloodshed had already taken place. The members of the Congress, while recognizing the fundamentally just demand underlying most of these revolutionary movements, condemned the use of force in domestic crises as definitely as they stood against its use in international affairs.

"It is our special part in this revolutionary age," they said, *"to counsel against violence from any side."**

In the discussion of pacifism in revolutionary times, Emily detected a second difference of opinion between the right and left wing delegates. "Here," she wrote in her impressions "the difference was rather one of wording and tactics than of substance. All felt the possible imminence of social upheavals. It lies like a thundercloud over all Europe today. The Congress was filled with a sense of the tragic, the incalculable importance of people of every point of view coming to understand the insanity of endeavoring to solve social and economic problems by violence, whether violent suppression in the name of law and property or violent insurrection in the name of liberty." In a social war, she prophesied, pacifists would be ground to pieces between opposing factions. It was their business and the business of everyone not quite mad with passion and prejudice, to act before things came to that pass and

---

* Italics mine.

to help open "to the irresistible and cleansing and fructifying currents of social change peaceful channels, by means of a timely and generous renunciation of privilege. It may well prove that the measure of the will to do this is the measure of the capacity of our civilization to endure." [26]

During the debate, time was allowed for recounting firsthand experiences. The German women were in the midst of their unfinished revolution. Dr. Anita Augspurg and Lida Gustava Heymann of Munich, Yella Hertzka of Vienna, and Dr. Helene Stöcker of Berlin bore witness to pacifist efforts to keep their revolutions bloodless. When the bloody revolution came to Bavaria, the youthful Gertrude Baer, who had impressed the Congress by her eloquence, ability, and beauty, with two other young women from Bolshevist Munich had, with signal courage, managed to procure an automobile to cross the fighting lines and to urge a truce on the opposing forces. When their car was taken away, they proceeded on foot to plead with "red" and "white" headquarters to abstain from violence. They had half succeeded in their task when the swiftness of events made it impossible. Helena Swanwick years afterwards remembered the farewell words of Gertrude Baer at the end of the Congress: "Remember us. Goodbye. We go back into the night."

The Congress ended with a banquet at the Tonhalle, Zürich, arranged by the Swiss members. There shortly before midnight, Jane Addams adjourned the Congress in these words: "If some of us who are looking at the terms of the Peace Treaty and the prospects for the future are not very happy, we must remember that the people who made the Peace Treaty are also far from happy." Then she related what Herbert Hoover had told her in Paris just before the Zürich Congress when she was having dinner at his house one night. Of all the difficult things he had to do during the war and since the war, none was more difficult, he said, than to supervise the passing of trainloads of food through one starving country into another country that was also starving. At one dock, the men who had to unload a cargoful of food to go to an enemy country were hungry. Their wives and children were hungry. "We cannot do it," they said. So it was found necessary to appeal to their good will and use moral suasion. Then they did it. "When that great test was put upon them," said Jane

Addams, "to go hungry that their enemies might be fed, nothing but a moral appeal could meet the situation.

"We shall have to believe in spiritual power. We shall have to learn to use moral energy to put a new sort of force into the world and believe that it is a vital thing—the only thing, in this moment of sorrow and death and destruction, that will heal the world and bring it back into a normal condition.

"So we can say to one another that we have met, and discovered that even after a great and prolonged war women from the belligerent countries can come together, not in a pretended goodwill, not in mere outside sentimentalism, for there was nothing of that about this Congress, but in genuine friendship and understanding, because they have held themselves above the battle-line, and have tried to use this better force. If it can be done in small groups, it can be done on a larger scale." [27]

In this spirit the women faced their future tasks. It was a spirit which came to be known in the ranks of the W.I.L.P.F. as "the spirit of Jane Addams." It was shared, not in discipleship, but as a priceless possession by almost everyone who knew or worked with Jane Addams. To Helena Swanwick, one of the most intellectual of the great-hearted company of pioneers, it was "a spirit of pure beneficence, which created peace; a spirit of trust, which put courage into weak hearts; a spirit of courtesy, which made beautiful the relations between human beings." [28] To Emily Balch it was in addition, the spirit of intelligence facing the great social problems of humankind. It infused itself more deeply than any other factor into her life and thinking. With characteristic New England restraint she said: "It is to Jane Addams, too dearly loved for words, that as a pacifist I owe the most of all, and in every respect immeasurably much."

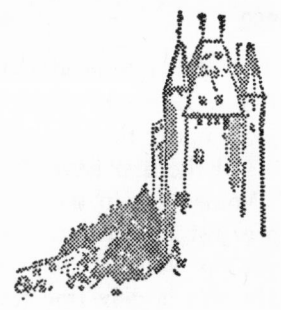

CHAPTER THIRTEEN

Geneva Years—Springtime of the League of Nations

It was while Emily Balch was at the Zürich Congress that she received the cable informing her of the final decision of Wellesley College not to renew her appointment. "This news," she wrote, "though not a surprise, was still something of a shock. I celebrated the occasion by smoking a cigarette with Mrs. Pethick-Lawrence and Madeleine Doty. At Wellesley, at that time, smoking was strictly taboo and I felt that for members of the faculty to smoke, certainly for them to smoke clandestinely at the college, was 'not the thing.' However," she characteristically added, "I found I did not like smoking and did not continue the habit."

Arrived at Geneva, Emily Balch's first care as secretary-treasurer was to find an office and organize the international work. Temporary quarters were soon found in light but noisy rooms in the Boulevard Georges Favon. Her salary was fixed at $200 a month, a sum which looked large to European eyes but not to American.

One of her early labors was the editorial work of preparing the proceedings of the Zürich Congress for publication in three languages, a task which, with her conscientious standards, took twelve months to complete. In the office Emily had two full time Swiss secretaries—one for French and one for German. A great deal of her time also went into the publication of a new organ, *Pax et Libertas*, which later was further developed by Madeleine Doty under the title of *Pax International*.

In the first issue, February, 1920, Emily wrote in an editorial, "Women are in the main outside of the politics of the past, and are just now entering in political life even when they have not yet the vote. If they are often inexperienced and ignorant they are also largely free from bad old political habits and traditions, and free to strike out a new political method, not dominated by party, in which social and moral values shall outweigh all others." She thought the new league should present and push through to success a determined and consistent political program. She hoped it would win convinced adherents as Christianity won believers in the early centuries. "It must have its missionaries," she said, and with Cassandra forebodings she added, "It may have its martyrs." [1]

One of the early numbers, in which Emily took great pride, was a special issue in folio format which dealt with the economic disorder of Europe after the war. This was prepared with the help of Henry Packwood Adams, a young English historian who had suffered severely through imprisonment as a conscientious objector. Emily Balch's responsibilities for the work in the headquarters were shared by Marguerite Gobat, daughter of Albert Gobat, the well-known Swiss pacifist and Nobel Peace Prize winner of 1902. "Marguerite Gobat was in many ways more fitted than I for the work," wrote Emily, "and I became conscious too late that in the flush of my new office I treated her too little as a partner and too much as an aide. She was the soul of generosity. I was constantly at her house and enjoyed many tramps with her and her friends and her little nephew, Pierre.

"We settled in Geneva some time before the League of Nations transferred their early office in London. The state of things as regarded the coming of The League of Nations to Geneva had its amusing side. Geneva gentlemen regarded internationalism as almost synonymous with Geneva and they looked on the coming of The League to their city as very much in the nature of things, and prepared to adopt it with open arms. Unfortunately, somehow or other their invitation to a proposed reception in The League's honor was neglected. The League of Nations was very official, very 'protocol' and the affair meant nothing to them. But their failure to reply to the Genevese gave a great deal of offense and resulted in a coolness which the good offices of Mr. Bertram Pickard of the Quaker Center in Geneva only later smoothed over."

"À propos of Genevese conceptions was an amusing incident. The British anti-slavery group had wanted to strengthen their work by the creation of an International Bureau *pour la Protection des Indigènes.* I was one of the original members and much interested in its work. I was surprised to find that a request for membership from some one in the neighboring city of Lausanne had much upset the Geneva group. As their feeling toward inclusion of anyone not a Genevan developed, I suggested that I sit in another room while this was discussed. This was gratefully accepted as a courteous and suitable gesture. It was voted not to accept a member from Lausanne on the ground that a Committee could *hardly* be *international* if it included people outside Geneva. So I naturally was a member no longer.

"During the three years I served in Geneva, I had the most interesting opportunity to see the development of the League of Nations in its earlier and more idealistic phase, before power politics had sensed its importance and sought to use it for its own purposes. In other respects these first postwar years were painful and disappointing—confused and disheartening to the last degree. Peace was a by-word. The reaction against war, which we had thought would make itself felt as soon as peace was made, did not do so at once, though it did come later.

"There was, however, great exhilaration in the sense of active and organized comradeship with women working for peace all over the world, in acting as a receiving and transmitting station of our round-the-world fellowship. I remember one day when I had letters from Iceland, South Africa and the Fiji Islands; and another when an American woman wrote me that when she was young she had devoted herself to abolishing slavery in the United States; that this won, she had worked for woman's suffrage, and that this now being won also, she was giving herself to the cause of peace—which is not yet won and which cannot be won so easily as the other two."

Before long a quaint old Geneva house in the rue du Vieux Collège was leased as an international headquarters and christened the Maison Internationale. It was perched high above an old city

wall, overgrown with creepers, on the steep side of the hill on
which stands the cathedral and much of the picturesque old town.
Here were the offices, a many-windowed library room for lectures,
conferences, and receptions. Here were bedrooms and a dining-
room for visiting members and friends from all quarters of the
globe—from Liberia and Persia, and China, from Spain and South
America, from Prague and Chicago. This helped to give the
W.I.L.P.F. a quite special cachet, a unique and much loved personality built up through the years. There was a little garden,
filled with roses in June, with a dripping fountain, where in summer the guests could eat together under the linden tree, meals
provided for many years by an inimitable cook, Maria [Cairus].

   "Here came Jane Addams," wrote Emily Balch, "who rear-
ranged all our furniture, presented us with a reading lamp for the
parlor, and filled the house with her lovely and tonic presence.
Here for a dozen years or so I spent much of my time, absorbed
by the peepshow that Geneva afforded of the events of that fateful
period during which there was complete failure to make any
intelligent or adequate effort to check the growing aggression that
began in Manchuria and swept on its triumphant way to Pearl
Harbor and beyond; during which the noble experiment of the
League of Nations failed, so far as its function of preserver of the
peace went, because the governments were not in earnest in using
it to that end; and during which consequently the peace was lost—
for a time." [2] In later years Emily Balch judged that the place of
the League of Nations in history might prove to be that of a
necessary forerunner, a pioneer experiment, instructive in both its
failures and its successes.

   Emily Balch began her work for peace through the International Geneva office, at the time when the young League of Nations
was just exploring its possibilities. To Emily, Geneva was not only
a lovely city on the shores of Lake Leman surrounded by beautiful
mountains—it was for her an idea—the idea of human cooperation
unlimited by national frontiers. She realized fully the limitations
of the League of Nations. But it did seem to her a promising
instrument for dealing with a multitude of practical international
problems. The majority of people were interested in the League
of Nations as a political organization of governments, as a league
to enforce peace. Emily Balch was mainly interested in its func-

tional aspect of achieving cooperative action between nations in social and economic affairs of universal concern, action to be carried out through the League Departments and Commissions, the International Labor Office, and other more or less independent services. Of prime importance to her were those agencies which dealt continuously with a variety of problems, with intellectual cooperation, transportation, education, currency, white slave traffic, control of opium and other narcotics, and much else. Cooperation through the League of Nations, she thought, had two fields: "the narrow but critically important field of 'peace and security' and the limitless field of constructive international activity, the whole complex of the world's business. . . . It is a crucial mistake to suppose that peace and security are mainly a matter of stopping violence and aggression instead of being essentially dependent on the positive cooperation, social and economic, by which any stable and fruitful condition of peace must be supported and nourished." [3]

This emphasis on directing international organization toward a variety of specific enterprises of constructive cooperation, Emily Balch shared with Jane Addams. It was an approach they worked out partly in independence and partly through reciprocal intellectual stimulation. Jane Addams expressed it at length in her book *Peace and Bread in Time of War*. It continued as a central theme in Emily Balch's later thinking and writing.[*]

Although the Zürich Congress had taken no official position for or against the League of Nations, (hoping that the Peace Commission which was still sitting in Paris, might modify the constitution of the League) complete latitude was given to Emily Balch

---

[*] Of this attitude John Dewey wrote in 1945 towards the end of World War II, "A generation ago men thought they could attain peace through an international organization of the traditional political kind, which relies more upon coercive force than upon constructive meeting of human needs. When I try to formulate what Miss Addams [and Miss Balch] said, I come out with a sense of the difference between two methods and attitudes. On the one hand we can trust to an international political organization of an over-all type to create the organs it requires. On the other, we can rely upon organs that have been formed to take care of human needs (including the need for change) to develop in the course of their own use an organization which can be depended upon, because it has become ingrained in practice. . . . It has been customary to give the name 'realistic' to the kind of organization that is based upon opposition to an enemy and that relies upon armed force to maintain itself. In contrast, the road indicated by Miss Addams is, I submit, infinitely more realistic." *Peace and Bread*, Introduction to 1945 Edition.

as international secretary (and to the national sections) for cooperation with the League of Nations as it existed.

"Geneva in that early spring time of the League of Nations was intensely interesting," wrote Emily Balch in fragments of autobiography. "Generally with one or more members of the W.I.L.P.F. and as its delegate and in connection with matters with which it was concerning itself, I went to interview one or another League of Nations committee, Assembly delegate or Secretariat official, all of whom were in general very approachable. I remember with special interest several interviews with Litvinoff. I was active in this way in such matters as drug control, the maintenance of Liberia as a member of the League, the admission of Albania, the internationalization of aviation, civil and military, and above all, disarmament.

"I found in Geneva a number of people who were most kind and helpful, among others, George D. Herron, Professor William Rappard, Inazo Nitobé of the League of Nations Secretariat, Iwao Ayusawa of the International Labor Office (a member of the Friends' Meeting in Geneva), Christian Lange, secretary of the Interparliamentary Union, K. Ziliacus, Dame Rachel Crowdy of the Social Section in the League of Nations. Helpful in a personal way was Madame Edouard Claparède, daughter of the Russian philosopher Spir, whose beautiful old 'Campagne' in Geneva with its noble avenue of ancient horse chestnuts, and its salon rich in old world pictures and souvenirs, was open to me."

Several months before the women were to hold their Third International Congress at Vienna, in 1921, Catherine Marshall of England had come to Geneva to help Emily Balch and Mlle. Gobat establish fruitful contacts with the League of Nations. The W.I.L.P.F. found itself in a highly favorable situation, not only for acquainting itself thoroughly with the activities and methods of the League of Nations, but also urging W.I.L.P.F. wishes upon League officials, both orally through deputations and informal talks, and through written memorials. It was especially gratifying when W.I.L.P.F. women came to Geneva to serve as delegates to the League of Nations Assembly from their respective countries—Henni Forchammer, technical advisor from Denmark; Anna Bugge-Wicksell, substitute from Sweden; Helena Swanwick, chairman of the British Section of the W.I.L.P.F., (sent from England by

Ramsay MacDonald in 1924 and again in 1929; Martha Larsen-Jahn, full delegate of Norway 1925-1927; and Madame Sofia Ciurlionis of Lithuania. Emily particularly valued the friendship of one official whose duty it was to keep in touch with other international organizations. This was Dr. Nitobé, Japanese by birth, American by education, Quaker by religion, and married to an American woman. With his genuinely international outlook he gave sympathetic and respectful consideration to the proposals of the women. The letters to Emily Balch on file in the Maison Internationale from such officials and other Geneva personalities show that her proposals recommended themselves as informed, judicious, and practical, and indicate the extreme respect in which she was held.

Catherine Marshall, who had at first dubiously regarded her Geneva mission as merely exploratory, in her first full report to the Vienna Congress declared that, contrary to her expectations a very great deal was being done and a great deal could be done in making an impact on the League of Nations. On such matters as inclusion on the agenda of the Assembly of questions which the W.I.L.P.F. hoped to see discussed and on more publicity regarding questions of procedure, the W.I.L.P.F. could exert an appreciable influence. "We do not want you to imagine," said Catherine Marshall, "that we ran the Assembly, but I would just remind you of a little sentence which we persuaded Miss Balch to leave in her report: ' "See the chariot go my way," said the fly sitting on its roof.' " [4]

No question was too small, no problem too great to be tackled by the women. The president of the Swiss confederation M. Motta, and M. Usteri, also of the Swiss delegation, received a deputation consisting of Madame Edouard Claparède, Catherine Marshall, and Emily Balch, in which they discussed: admitting the Central Powers to the League of Nations, the urgency of dealing with the economic situation of Europe, and the desirability of amending the covenant of the League of Nations, and especially urging the key amendment making the Covenant more easily amendable. Among other delegates whom they saw, some of them many times, were Lord Robert Cecil, acting as delegate for South Africa; G. N. Barnes and H. A. L. Fisher of Great Britain; Dr. Fridtjof Nansen and Dr. Christian Lange of Norway; Senator Lafontaine from

Belgium; Eliel Lofgren of Sweden, who played an important part in the Mandates Committee; and Doret of Haiti, "whose attitude was particularly gratifying to us," wrote Emily Balch in her report, "bringing to us as it did support from the colored population of a semi-tropical island to some of the most progressive parts of our program. Many of those to whom we talked undertook and carried out action proposed by us." [5]

For the one year of 1920 alone, the files of the Archives of the Maison Internationale reveal numerous letters and memoranda painstakingly prepared, carefully verified, tactfully worded, sent out by the Secretary-Treasurer Emily Balch. Various of these memorials were in turn sent out officially by the Secretariat of the League of Nations to all the governments represented or reprinted in its official publications. They pressed questions on immediate steps for the limitation of armaments by land, by sea, and in the air, for universality of the League of Nations, for democratic amendment of the Covenant of the League of Nations. They made recommendations on allocation of mandates, on the terms of the mandates, and the constitution and powers of the Permanent Mandates Commission. Other memorials dealt with the folly and horror of using hunger blockades as a means of international pressure; protection of women and children in mandated areas (white slave traffic) and of captive Armenian, Greek, Syrian, and other women and children deported from their homes in Asia Minor and still held in harems in Turkey and neighboring territory; an international commission to harmonize legislation concerning the legal status of persons adversely affected by laws regulating marriage with foreigners;* opposition to the military use or conscription of native populations in colonies or mandated territories; suggestions for exerting effective pressure to deal with the increase in violence and terror toward minority groups in Ireland and Korea, pogroms in Poland and other massacres in the Ukraine, use of torture (White Terror in Hungary) and worse than medieval cruelty in the chaos around the border of the former Russian Empire and in Turkey. "The matter covered by these memoranda does not give

---

* Cases of English women, who as widows of German citizens, though they had never left England and knew not a word of German, were threatened with deportation to Germany.

anything like a full idea of the points which we had opportunities to present *viva voce*." [6]

All this work, laborious, detailed, unremitting, represented consistent and repeated attempts to infuse into the bloodstream of public thinking changes making for constructive and cooperative solutions of actual problems. Towards the end of Emily Balch's life she was to say, "Certainly, my life like other little lives has not visibly affected the course of events but I do not believe that any good effort is wasted. The coral insect deposits its minute contributions far below the surface of the water, but it has done its part in building the coral island which ultimately sustains a group of living beings."

It was by a happy chance that the meeting place chosen for the first Assembly of the League of Nations, "a bare and puritanic hall, no decoration and display, no flowers, no flags of course," was just three minutes away from the Maison. This made it easy for "new friends" to come to the hospitable rooms that Emily Balch, through her drawing power had made into a "Center." Emily Balch discerned, as was to be expected, "plenty of cynical national self-seeking in the Assembly, plenty of intriguing, of wining and dining." But she also observed a considerable esprit de corps and a new group psychology—*a current of desire to consider the common interests*. Very conspicuous, representing the nonpolitical, purely humanitarian aspects of the League, was Fridtjof Nansen, nicknamed "the conscience of the League of Nations." He came to be one of Emily Balch's great admirations: "Nansen with his Viking eyes, which seem to be looking into vast uncharted spaces, was often to be seen standing, like a greyhound in leash, just below the platform on the alert to serve his cause." While Emily fully realized what the League failed to be, and what the first Assembly failed to do, she saw as a hard fact, that a League representing purposes opposed to men in power like Lloyd George and Briand, would not be allowed to function, would exist on paper merely. "The League, if it is to be a reality at all," she wrote in 1921 after the First Assembly, "must necessarily mirror the existing balance of power, but while it mirrors it, it modifies it. And modifies it for the better." [7]

"A striking occurrence," Emily Balch remembered, "was the

admission of Albania to the League of Nations under circumstances
in which we were directly interested. The question of the admission of Albania was before a sub-committee of which Mr. H. A. L.
Fisher was chairman. I had long been interested in Albanians. I
had made some study of Albanians in the United States, especially
in my own state of Massachusetts.

"I was the more interested when a group of Albanians led by
Father Fan Noli, well known not only as a priest but as an
Albanian leader, came to our Geneva office personally to ask us to
help them secure admission to the League of Nations. Our 'virtuous
lobbying' had to be 'within the four corners' of the accepted policy
of the W.I.L.P.F. In this case we had clear sailing as at the Zürich
Congress, just closed, it had been agreed that all nations desiring
to be members of the League of Nations should be received. We
told Father Noli we could not expect to exert any influence but
we would do what we could. Catherine Marshall had valuable
contacts with English political figures, especially with Lloyd
George, having a standing invitation at his breakfast table where
he received many people of many sorts. She accordingly secured
an appointment with Mr. Fisher.

"He could not thank us enough for our kindness in coming to
see him on this business, but told us that if we had a little more
experience and knowledge of realities, we could *hardly* suppose
it possible to admit a country with no government, no capital, no
boundaries (I give the substance of all this as I recall it). We
replied that these circumstances were certainly unfortunate but
that the *concert* of Europe stood for an independent Albania, that
in the present situation Albania was a war casualty and that her
rehabilitation was essential to the peace of Europe. The Serbs were
invading the country from the North, Italy from the Adriatic and
that it only wanted a Greek invasion from Epirus and the South
to create complete chaos or at least a horribly dangerous situation.
Mr. Fisher again thanked us and regretted that we did not understand the matter better.

"Within three days—I think it was—his committee reversed his
position and Albania was thereupon admitted.

"I am far from supposing that our representations had turned
the trick which I suppose was due to an unexpected decision on a

higher level but it was at least a pleasant coincidence and one which our Albanian friends interpreted in our favor."

This continuous concern with innumerable practical problems was by no means a dissipation of energy for Emily Balch. Rather it built up and strengthened the fundamental spiritual commitment from which it sprang. At this time a lifelong concern with the problems of a living religious faith flowed together with what had now become her central spiritual conviction. Her early traditional Puritan Unitarianism and her religion of peace had reached the fusing point. She found them both expressed in the Quaker community. It is characteristic that she preferred to join the unified English Society of Friends rather than the divided American Quakers. "Bertrand Pickard," she wrote, "was in charge of the Quaker Center in Geneva, where meeting was held every Sunday. A drawing toward the Society of Friends which I had felt for some years grew into a definite desire to become one of them. It was not alone their testimony against war, their creedless faith, nor their openness to suggestions for far-reaching social reform that attracted me, but the dynamic force of the active love through which their religion was expressing itself in multifarious ways, both during and after the war.

"However, I did not want to become a member of either of the two groups into which the Hicksite controversy had split American Quakers, an unhappy occurrence which seemed to me quite abhorrent to the ideals of Quakerism. I wanted to join in England where no division had occurred and I profited by the presence in Geneva of Edith Pye and Joan Fry to ask admission to the Society of Friends. I am deeply grateful to them for making my entrance possible, in spite of my vague and fumbling theological beliefs. I explained to them my own highly unorthodox position, Unitarian or even more radical. I said that I thought that the things that were central to Friends were central to me, that the inner light or communion with the spirit of God is a central reality. I suppose this is about what I said to them. In any case, I was accepted as a member of the London Yearly Meeting, February, 1921. I received much support and stimulus from the Geneva group of Quakers, which included, beside Bertram and Irene Pickard and the Nitobés, Iwao Ayusawa of the International

Labor Office and others connected with the League of Nations."

At about this time she wrote Jane Addams a letter explaining the motives and attitudes that lay behind this decision to join the fellowship of the Friends:

> Undated [written about February, 1921 from Geneva]
>
> Dear Miss Addams,
>
> I think you will be interested to know that I have applied for membership to the Society of Friends in London and have been admitted. It is something I have had in mind for years but I cannot recall whether I have talked of it with you. I am not in the fervor of conversion but it is a warming and helpful thing to me to be in fellowship with the little Friends' meeting that has been started. I am as frankly untrinitarian, as remote from orthodox Christian theology as ever and of course made this known. Of course going into anything means in a sense going *out* from what is *not* in (or that is the danger).
>
> What is central to the Friends is central to me—the wish to listen as it were, to understand and receive as much as we can and to try to live out as far as we can, all that one has of enlightenment—no creed, no pretending to know what we don't know—and with this a form of worship in which all, men and women, and insiders and outsiders, are free to be channels of expression as well as auditors.
>
> Yours with deep affection,
>
> E. G. B.[8]

The Third International Congress of the W.I.L.P.F. in 1921 was the only one for which Emily Balch was directly responsible. In 1921 one of the tragic regions of postwar dislocation was in the states which had been formed out of the old empire of Austria-Hungary, and in the Balkans. Vienna was, therefore, chosen as the seat of the Third Congress. During the difficult process of organizing the Congress in postwar Vienna denuded of the simplest necessities, including typewriters, and of course suffering from a terrible shortage of food,* Emily lived with Frau Yella Hertzka of Vienna, enjoying her "courageous and powerful support." Yella Hertzka was one of the most original and constructive minds in

---

* The Congress arranged for importation of special food supplies to offset any drain on the Viennese that the influx of Congress visitors might cause.

the W.I.L.P.F., and a whimsical, sparkling, generous personality. As her husband was director of an internationally known music publishing house, her home was the center of a Viennese musical circle. She was a pioneer in opening up a horticultural school for women, one of the first of its kind. At one time she had as pupils and guests thirteen Jewish survivors of pogroms in Eastern Europe.

The women who came to Vienna from thirty countries reflected of course the general European disillusionment and hopelessness. Nevertheless, as Jane Addams pointed out, these groups of women were united in one thing. They all alike had come to realize that "every crusade, every beginning of social change, must start from small numbers of people convinced of the righteousness of a cause." [9]

To arouse interest in the forthcoming Congress, Emily Balch had journeyed in April and May to southeastern Europe, visiting Prague, Agram (Zagreb today), Belgrade, Sofia, Bucharest, and Budapest. She saw at first hand the bitter prejudices left by the war. A promising gathering of women in Bucharest which began in a suave and friendly atmosphere was broken up when one of the women declared she would rather see her only child die than take her to a doctor in Vienna. After this demonstration of patriotism, no one else wished to appear less fervent and the temperature of the meeting fell to zero. However, as Jane Addams wrote in *Peace and Bread*, "Partly because the International Secretary, Miss Balch, had recently travelled in the Balkan states in the interests of the League, a large number of women came from the immediate territory. Miss Balch, years before when collecting material for her book entitled *Our Slavic Fellow-Citizens*, had made friends in Southeastern Europe and because they appreciated the unusual insight with which she had portrayed the situation then, they were ready to trust her again." [10]

At the Vienna Congress, Mrs. Henry Villard, daughter of the American abolitionist and nonresistant, William Lloyd Garrison, had come across the ocean with the express purpose of inducing the W.I.L.P.F. to require of its members a pledge of personal resistance to war under all circumstances. The Congress, after debate, voted not to require this—a decision supported by Jane Addams and Emily Balch, as well as by Quakers and others who had scruples about binding one's conscience by a pledge concerning future action. The adverse vote caused Mrs. Villard and a group of her absolute pacifist friends to decide not to join forces with the League. Mrs. Villard's proposal was different from Emily Balch's solemn pledge at the Zürich Congress to do all in her power in working against war and toward the coming permanent peace.

Throughout its history the W.I.L.P.F. continued to be open to peace-minded women of very different shades of opinion, from those who oppose war under all circumstances to those willing to work in any effective way to bring about a peaceful world. The trend towards absolute pacifism was stronger in some national sections than in others. In the United States a large and remarkable group of Pennsylvania Quaker pacifists impressed themselves deeply upon a great many of the members. Among these were Hannah Clothier Hull, Lucy Biddle Lewis, Emily Cooper Johnson, Mildred Scott Olmsted,* Grace Rhoads, Emily Parker Simon, Katharine Arnett, and many others. Emily Balch believed that the program of the W.I.L.P.F. was so inclusive that there was not only room for, but need of, different groups to emphasize different parts of it. "Some want to work for a League of Nations and some for suffrage and some for Tolystoyan pacifism," she wrote Anna Garlin Spencer, President of the United States section, in December, 1919, "and some for social justice and brotherhood. Surely this is all to the good." [11]

Emily Balch also believed that the peace movement as a whole should be inclusive and pluralistic in nature. Unlike many peace advocates who saw salvation only in their own particular brand of pacifism, she believed in a large number of organizations of quite different color, appealing to different sets of temperaments, using different dialects, but keeping in touch with one another, learning from one another, and cooperating on common aims or programs in the continuing fight for peace.

The Vienna Congress was followed by a very successful summer school at Salzburg. After the long blackout of any kind of impartial treatment of international affairs people, especially stu-

---

* Mildred Scott Olmsted, who had worked internationally with both Emily Balch and Jane Addams, was to serve as the administrative genius of the League in the United States for upwards of forty years.

dents,* began to clamor for less partisan information and discussion. The W.I.L.P.F. did pioneering work in this new method of education—international summer schools. The first W.I.L.P.F. summer school in 1920, in Buckinghamshire, England, was looked upon as an innovation. The Salzburg school in its beautiful setting was presided over by Jane Addams and brought together some 300 people from twenty-one countries, including China, Japan, Mexico, and India. The subject was "Education for Internationalism." Emily Balch's interpretation of the League of Nations as not merely a political but as a functional agency in important social and economic fields, "seemed to come" she said, with characteristic modesty and not immodest truth, "with fresh interest to Jane Addams and others." Both Jane Addams and Emily Balch through the years were to continue to emphasize that an international organization like the League of Nations would become real and precious to plain simple people as it came to deal for the general benefit, with concrete practical matters which touch every one.

At Salzburg the women had their first experience with the suspicion and misunderstanding roused by the name, Women's International League for Peace and Freedom. "International" had curious connotations in some minds. It called up echoes of the Third International connected with Russia. In the summer school in Austria, where anti-Semitism was rife, the women found that to many people "internationalism" meant friendship for the Jews and an attack on anti-Semitism.

Later, on her return to the United States, Emily Balch was to have the quaint experience of finding that the word "freedom" was suspect in the land of the free. "What do you mean by it?" people would ask. To some, it meant that the W.I.L.P.F. was advocating free love. To others it suggested only the struggle for woman suffrage. The word "peace" also sounded dangerous to many groups in the United States. It was identified with Bolshevism, and

---

* Many of the students at Salzburg made great sacrifices to attend, living in extreme simplicity, eating in a war kitchen, sleeping in a picturesque but uncomfortable old orphanage. Though they were marked by privation, they were so hungry intellectually that some would meet at seven in the morning for extra discussion, or organize an all-night tramp with one of the professors to talk things out.

reducing arms doubtless meant inviting attack on the United States by Bolshevists, and therefore bordered on treason.

In 1922 Emily Balch was asked to organize a summer school in Varese, Italy. Emily had found herself exhausted and at the end of her tether, and had in January gone home for awhile to recuperate and be cheered up by Bessie. She returned to Varese to complete arrangements. It was very cold; it was difficult to make businesslike arrangements and the summer school promised to be uncomfortable and expensive. The last minute preparations were unexpectedly interrupted by a sudden invasion of the town by Fascist bands. With great difficulty and expense, though followed with great success, the school was transferred to Lugano, Switzerland. Bertrand Russell and Romain Rolland were among the speakers. Emily remembered with gratitude that though Bertrand Russell was hesitating to pay fifteen dollars extra for a more comfortable railroad journey home, when she came to pay him his speaker's fee he was unwilling to take the money on account of the debt the W.I.L.P.F. had incurred by the change of locale due to the Facists.

In the autumn of 1922, Emily took a four months' leave of absence from her post as international secretary-treasurer to recover from the nervous fatigue and strain of continuous work and responsibility. "It does seem such bad management of one's life to work along not quite fit," she wrote to Annie, "never at one's best—as it were running a little way and then sitting down—and then running a little further." In December Emily sent in her resignation in order to clear the way for the appointment of a new secretary. She rather hoped to return to Geneva at the end of a year to resume her work, unless the Executive Committee "should prefer a younger woman and one technically a better secretary than I am," she wrote home to Annie. "It is work I love and where I may be useful and I realize it is going to be hard at my age to find any occupation at a salary—certainly any congenial one. Against it is the being so long away from home, being such a stranger to the children as they grow up and getting, as one does in a sense, dépaysé—I don't know any English word that just says it, the getting in some degree unadjusted to one's own country which is after all the *only* place where one lives fully and normally." [12]

Vilma Glücklich of the Hungarian section, and the successive secretaries—the American Madeleine Doty, 1925-1927, the British Mary Sheepshanks, 1927-1930, French Camille Drevet, 1930-1934—carried on brilliantly the traditions established by Emily Balch of making the Maison a friendly and stimulating International Center, of day-by-day immersion in political activity with a constant flow of correspondence from all over the world. To each of these secretaries in turn, Emily Balch gave counsel, encouragement, and strength as occasion required, and occasion often required it. "It is inevitable that a great part of office work is drudgery," she wrote Mary Sheepshanks, "and another great part is worry and responsibility and puzzle. I trust you will find the roses among the thorns at the helm." [13] To Madeleine Doty, who was editing *Pax International* as the regular organ of the W.I.L.P.F. in addition to her other duties, she wrote: "Just an added word of affection and sympathy. I suppose I know better than any one else what you are up against in Geneva. . . . Wait till spring comes and the mountains are hung high in the sky and the primroses are yellow splashes under orchard trees and the merles begin to sing. Winter may hold on even late but the sun wakes from its long autumn swoon and the everlasting gray veil overhead melts away." [14] And again, "I am very sorry about the Vienna Committee but it is a quite understandable clash of very different temperaments. Of course one wishes that the real spirit of all we stand for might have triumphed in each case over personal considerations—but how insidiously they always masque themselves as concern for general and impersonal principles." [15]

The winter of 1922-1923 Emily spent recuperating in Egypt as the guest of Helen Cheever. She took occasion while in Egypt to try to awaken interest in peace and internationalism among Cairo women—Copts and others. When she tried to persuade Egyptian women to attend the next International Congress, they asked what it would involve in time. "Three weeks altogether," said Emily Balch. "Three weeks!" they murmured, looking at one another, "three weeks away from home!" Moreover, they were absorbed in the struggle for national independence.

In the winter of 1923-1924, Emily Balch spent a semi-invalid four months in California, again the guest of Helen Cheever, working on a book dealing with the similarities and differences in the character of groups with ties based on different factors such as territory, race, language, religion, profession, function, and social class. She decided, however, that this must be either a solid work of erudition or a brief and brilliant sketch. Not feeling capable of producing either, she gave up the undertaking.

Helen Cheever was the friend who became disturbed when Emily, in losing her Wellesley position, lost with it any claim to a pension. She provided Emily with an annual sum that was supposed to represent the nonexistent pension. "I fear," wrote Emily, "that I accepted more than I should have on this basis. This continued until my generous friend realized that I was giving the money away for purposes she was not interested in." This vestigial trace of the system of patronage may grate harshly on modern sensibilities. Frances Hayward invited Emily to live with her and work on her book. Helen Cheever wanted Emily to live with her permanently. It was not an uncommon occurrence for unmarried women like Helen Cheever, who had no fixed career, or people like Frances Hayward, a gifted artist, to wish to share well-staffed homes and comfortable untaxed incomes with charming, talented, and less affluent friends. Jane Addams had her closest personal friend, the "Dearest" of her letters, Mary Rozet Smith of Chicago, a woman of rare charm in whose large and gracious home in Walton Place she could always take refuge; and in times of weariness and illness, she had the great-hearted and generous Louise de Koven Bowen to take her away on winter vacations to sunny climates.

From Cairo, in March 1923, Emily wrote to "Dearest Annie" à propos of Helen's wanting to "hitch up together permanently": "I don't really think it is a good plan. She utterly spoils me and at the same time while I love her deeply and enjoy a great deal with her she is the only person I know with whom I am really irritable and you know that a state of controlled irritation is not a gracious one even though infinitely better every way than *un*-controlled irritation. Much as I love her she brings out in me Aunt Mariana-ish characteristics that I honestly did not know were in my make-up. There things are too queer! It is also really wholesome for me to be out of the atmosphere of excessive and detailed solicitude about every thing concerning my health. Bessie may often tire me or hurt me but she is not 'on my nerves' and though

Frances [Hayward] with her carelessness and hectic moments are
of course on the negative side, they are like the weather—one
might not have chosen a windy morning but it is not annoying.
These things are hard to understand. Perhaps a psychoanalyst
would say that it is an obscure reaction against the sense of how
much I owe Helen, or of her giving me more love than I can
quite digest, or against her constant and unconscious tendency to
dominate in small matters. Do you suppose someday we shall see
all these inter-reactions clearly? I do think that even now there is
much in the workings of personality that we understand better
than previous generations and that we are learning to avoid many
of the old pitfalls. Don't you suppose the Bronté's might have
learned to let in the sun and wind and shake out the mould and
wrinkles, and do you suppose that if they had, the genius would
have evaporated too?" [16]

In 1924 Emily was mainly in Washington, living for a while at
the Friendship House Settlement and working first with Amy
Woods who was the national secretary, then with her successor,
the young Dorothy Detzer. Dorothy Detzer came to the League
with a background of relief service with the Quakers in Russia
and of work with Jane Addams in Hull-House. She was to become
a brilliant lobbyist on Capitol Hill and an incisive force in educating American women, through the W.I.L.P.F. leaders in their
states and through local communities, in the ways of effective
political action and in the necessity of accepting political compromise without abandoning convictions or principles. "In her selection" said Emily Balch, "I had played a very responsible part."

The year 1924 was eventful for the W.I.L.P.F. inasmuch as it
held its fourth Congress on American soil, bringing to Washington,
D.C., sixty-three foreign delegates. The women focused their
attention on different aspects of "A New International Order." A
composite program of immediate and ultimate aims, practical and
ideal, the *Cahier de la Paix,* was drawn up. Emily Balch contributed a cahier, *Economic Aspects of a New International Order,*
on international economics and the international relations of business and power politics. Into the organization of this Congress
Emily put much hard work, and she spent a good deal of time
after the Congress with Vilma Glücklich in Washington editing
the report of the Congress *Proceedings,* a voluminous polyglot

document which she felt had sufficient historical value to repay the time and trouble it entailed.

The American hosts of the Washington Congress were considerably embarrassed by a survival of war psychology shown in the hostility and opposition of certain newspapers. As a result, painful incidents attended a speaking tour of twenty-five of the European delegates in twenty cities, from Washington to Chicago. They were occasioned partly by misunderstanding of the purposes of the W.I.L.P.F. and the Congress but more largely by manufactured statements and "identical preposterous misinformation"* sent from one city to another.

"Internationalism was then suspect, as such," wrote Emily Balch in her pamphlet history of the W.I.L.P.F. "and military gentlemen, especially, were offended by statements made in the Congress in regard to chemical warfare." It was Emily Balch who had moved a resolution opposing chemical warfare and urging investigation of its special dangers, both for the sake of ending it and as a means of educating the masses as to the real character of war in general. Although Emily Balch knew that it was obviously more important to try to prevent war than to modify methods of fighting, she lost no opportunity, in the United States and later in Geneva, to decry the use of poison gas.**

In 1925 Emily moved about a good deal—in North Africa, the Middle East, and the Balkans—partly for health and pleasure, partly to make international contacts for the W.I.L.P.F. She spent six weeks in Algeria, Tunisia, Sahara, and Constantinople with

---

* "Striking items of this misinformation, furnished by a librarian employed in the Chemical Warfare Department of the War Department in Washington, were sent out in such a way as to appear to have the sanction of the government although the Secretary of War had definitely repudiated it." Jane Addams: Preface to *Report of the Fourth Congress of the W.I.L.P.F.*, Washington, 1924.

** "To permit it would enlist vast financial interests in each country on the preparation for war and so make it harder to prevent war. It would lead Governments to concentrate on a form of fighting which unlike others is never a means of self-defense but wholly a means of attack. It would mean the development of those weapons which are most easily used against massed populations of helpless people and which are more cruel to the weak than to the strong and in particular cruel to children just in proportion as they are smaller and more sensitive." E. G. Balch, *Pax International*, Vol. II, No. 5, March, 1927.

Frances Hayward, who, like Helen Cheever, liked nothing better than to have Emily Balch as a keenly observant, witty, imperturbable traveling companion. On arriving at their hotel, Emily would unpack the photo of her father, place it on the bureau top beside her pincushion, and at once the hotel room became a bit of home. For Emily these journeys to Algiers, Timgad, Biskra, Tunis, and Kaironan were like pages from *The Arabian Nights*, though she confessed in a letter to Annie that "being merely a tourist is not satisfying after one has travelled with an object." She recaptured the wonder of her first trip to Europe with Mr. Allen and Katie, "the unparalleled glamor of the land after days at sea," and the "supremely lovely masses" of the Sierra Nevadas of Spain. In the glare of the old slave market at Algiers, looking at the far-off snowy peaks of the Djurdjura mountains of the Atlas range, she wondered whether the Christian captives had drawn torment or solace from their beauty. In delicate lines, she made a sketch of the sand dunes of the desert with a small black beetle in the foreground, making a track of fine scratches, calling it "Cafard,* a beetle alone in the Sahara." Some of these scenes, later flashing upon her inward eye, became little poems in the slim volume of verses that was to be issued in 1941, *The Miracle of Living*. She never felt apologetic for time spent in pure enjoyment. "I hate to seem to put pleasure before W.I.L. business in any degree whatever," she wrote Mary Sheepshanks in 1928 à propos of the possibility of her missing a meeting of the executive committee, "but as you know we are human beings with social-personal considerations to take into account as well as our microscopic parts in immensely big issues."[17]

In April, May, and June of 1925, Emily was again traveling for the W.I.L.P.F. "with an object" and in Athens, Constantinople, Bucharest, Belgrade, Budapest, and Vienna she met and talked with groups of women, with journalists, with college students and faculties, and once more got further below the surface of events. Greece was in the throes of absorbing a million and a half refugees, and Turkey was in the high tide of nationalist feeling.

The year 1925 was marked by other events in the microcosm

---

*French: cafard = beetle; cafard = the blues.

of Emily Balch's private life. Auntie died in 1924 and Annie was recurrently ill. The fate of the roomy old house on Prince Street, Jamaica Plain—home of Annie, Emily, Bessie, and Maidie since 1879, and full of memories of their father and mother—hung in the balance. The family hoped not to sell. To the satisfaction of all, Francis Balch decided to take over the Prince Street house with his wife Polly and their three children, Katherine, Robert, and Vergnies. Marion was to make her home with them. "It is very hard," wrote Emily to Vilma Glücklich, "breaking up an old home where we have lived forty-six years. I realize that it is part of the process of life. And with all that is discouraging in the larger life of the world, of our times, one feels that too."[18]

The Quakers have a saying, "A way will open," and for Emily an unexpected and ideal way appeared. In January, 1925, Agnes Perkins, a former colleague of Emily's in the English Department at Wellesley College, and her friend Etta Herr (later joined by Mabel Cummings), were planning to build a house in the town of Wellesley. They offered to Emily a little two-story wing with four rooms and a separate entrance at the side. And so it was that 17 Roanoke Road, Wellesley, Massachusetts, at the end of little Birch Road, came to be synonymous with Emily Greene Balch. Here, as the brief December days closed in just before Christmas, 1925, Emily set up her household gods, lit her hearthfires, and welcomed her friends. She arranged her poetry books in an old family secretary, her share of the family silver and Annie's beautiful old green and white tea set in another, hung her father's large Blake scroll to cover the wall beside the eastern windows next to the antique walnut couch, saw that it was good and called it Domichek— Bohemian for The Little House. And here, in her green and pleasant Wellesley she lived and worked, departed and returned, in sickness and health, in war and peace, tending her tulips and valley lilies beside the little doorway, whacking the bushes in the "Thicket," a little plot of land she acquired behind the house, and making the stones fly as her Aunt Nannie used to do. When in the fall of 1948, the Norwegian Marie Lous-Mohr, the distinguished international president of the W.I.L.P.F., visited the United States, she marveled at Emily and Wellesley and the Domichek, and was to write, "when I think of those happy, beautiful autumn days, I see you in front of your house, taking the key out of the open letter-box outside of your door! I never had imagined Amerika was like that."

In 1925 some Haitian members of the W.I.L.P.F. requested the International Executive Committee to look into conditions in Haiti which had been occupied by the American Marines since 1915. Emily Balch was asked to take up the matter. The result was one of the most successful undertakings conducted by the League, the mission sent to Haiti in February, 1926. Emily Balch collected six people,* one of whom was "a brilliant young professor of economics in the University of Chicago," Paul Douglas, who later become a United States Senator. The object of the mission was not only to survey political, economic, and financial conditions, health and sanitation, education, public works, the judiciary, and the state of civil liberties, but also to undertake a piece of constructive statesmanship for a future American policy, working in cooperation with the people most concerned, the people of Haiti. Their findings were published in the book *Occupied Haiti* (1927), edited and largely written by Emily Balch.

Emily Balch set out from Wellesley one February morning when the snow was so deep that the car could not come to her house for the luggage. A warm welcome, however, was assured the group in Haiti, both by the nature of their errand and the fact that the mixed party of four women shared their sleeping quarters "in most friendly fashion." "These things" said Emily, "did not recommend us to the military. I also gave great offence by repeating without sufficient verification a story that reached me of discrimination in army clubs. I was officially called on the carpet by the commanding officer."

The mission spent three weeks on the island, chiefly in Port au Prince, but also in the north where they found themselves marooned by the unexpectedly early onset of the rainy season. The bridge that they had crossed in going out was under water and they had to be carried back over the stream on men's backs. "As my bearer was a lame man and stumbled over the loose stones of the river bottoms which rushing currents kept on the move—I was

* There were two women representing the United States section of the League, Emily Balch and Zonia Baber, a specialist in geography from the University of Chicago; two representative colored women; and two men.

a little disturbed when he shifted my weight to keep my feet out of water. When we reached the other side, the only transportation available was a chance truck which took us to Plaisance where the driver refused to attempt the slippery clay-ey newly-built road on the mountains. As the priest of the village had recently entertained a party of Americans who had behaved so outrageously that he refused to experiment with us, the foreman of the group that was building the road kindly took us into his house. I attempted to sleep that night on a slatted bench."

Nothing struck Emily Balch more than the complete hiatus between the viewpoints of the members of the American Occupation and those of the Haitians themselves. To the former the Occupation appeared a source of blessings to the little country because under it roads and bridges had been built (with Haitian tax-money), hospitals and rural clinics organized, and relief obtained from recurrent revolutions. To the Haitians of the articulate class, the Occupation seemed an unmixed curse because it had broken down self-government and left a whole generation to grow up without experience of political responsibility, because it tended to produce racial self-consciousness and an angry sense of hurt pride, frustration, and loss of self-respect. Emily Balch found a highly explosive situation of confused responsibilities, of governmental power divided between the United States military representatives and the other "Treaty officials," on the one hand, and the puppet Haitian government on the other.

What the Haitian needed more than roads, more than schools, more even than an elected legislature, Emily thought, was a title to his land. Until the land had been surveyed and legally valid titles to holdings secured, he was never safe from being forced out through chicanery and fraud.

"I am under no illusions," she said, "as to the state of things that will exist in Haiti after the United States withdraws. It will not be a paradise of uncorrupted children of Nature such as the eighteenth century dreamed of. But granting the likelihood of corruption as well as the ignorance and poverty that will be inevitable for a long time, yet men will have under their feet the solid ground of self-dependence and responsibility and the incentives that are felt under freedom and die apart from it."

When this unofficial W.I.L.P.F. mission returned to the United

States, Emily Balch was able to have an interview with President Calvin Coolidge and present the conclusions of the group. The first part contained plans for the ultimate status of Haiti, the second arrangements for a transition period. The occupation should be withdrawn and actual self-government restored.*

The American policy recommended by the official commission which President Hoover sent to Haiti and which was adopted by the President as the policy of his administration on March 28, 1930, four year later, long years no doubt for the Haitians, was very much along the lines recommended by the unofficial group of the Women's International League.

When the official Hoover commission was formed, Emily Balch submitted a memorandum embodying some of her observations. She pointed out concretely the difficulties the commission would have in getting behind the veil of appearances and understanding true Haitian feeling; the feeling of the opposition who were too mistrustful, too hostile, too fearful of reprisals to talk freely; the moderates of the Haitian intelligentsia who were timid and hated to be mixed up in politics but who were useful nevertheless as observers and councilors; the group most fitted to understand the situation in Haiti, the foreign business men, who did not want to incur the disfavor of the powers that be in Haiti, but being both inside and out, could explain a great deal; and finally the reactions of the inarticulate classes speaking a Creole patois.

"A thing that Americans tend to forget in dealing with these black men is that in their ideas and ways of thinking they are French and in some ways more French than the French. They have a fanatical love of liberty in a very touch-me-not sense and

---

* The mission suggested concrete interim measures. A small official commission appointed by the President should go to Haiti and work out transition programs in cooperation with the leaders of the Haitians. American officials should be replaced by suitable and trained Haitians, the American administration demilitarized, and the Marines withdrawn with the exception of a small body for possible emergencies. The mission recommended provisions for the holding of elections and for securing free and secret balloting. Court decisions should be respected by the United States officials and efforts made to end "preventive imprisonment" and secure the adoption of the principle of habeas corpus into Haitian law. In selecting the personnel to be sent to Haiti an effort should be made to send only such as will "refuse to draw the color line, they and their families, and who would be scrupulous in showing full official courtesy and respect to Haitians."

love the game of politics. Their attitude is worlds asunder from that of the United States Negroes. Haitians too often think of Americans as boors, brutal, ignorant and uncaring of literature and ideas, interested only in practical things. They feel that we have come and unthinkingly destroyed something which we did not understand. . . . In general one may say that each race interprets the other in terms of its poorest qualities and worst failures.

"What most injures the United States in Haitian opinion is the attempt to give a legal and constitutional color to what has been done not legally but by financial duress or by direct physical force. Our chicanery is maddening to them.

"It is going to take not only patience on our side but a willingness to have things done not in the American way, which we are always sure is best, but in their way, except as we can convince them that something else will serve them better."*

Emily Balch was much impressed by the culture and charm of the Haitians of the type illustrated by the Sylvain family. A young Dr. Normil Sylvain became a special friend, "a poet and scholar, as Haiti breeds them in surprising numbers considering how small and poor it is." He came of an old family whose members had given distinguished service to their country, one of his ancestors having signed the Act of Independence of Haiti in 1804. He was the leader of an interesting literary movement and was educated in France where his father had been Haitian Minister. He once told Emily Balch that the happiest moment of his life had been when his father lectured on Haitian literature to a great audience in the Sorbonne.

"We have the chance" concluded Emily Balch, "to do an epoch-making thing in establishing a new type of relationship between ourselves and our small neighbor. The colonizing and imperialist

* One outstanding incident for Emily Balch was an encounter with a group of resentful politicians who were carrying on a campaign for Haitian independence. Some of them were interesting men, but some of them were completely unscrupulous. One told Emily Balch that they were engaged in a conspiracy of wholesale poisoning of a rival political group. It was with great difficulty that she persuaded him to call off the coup, convincing him that it was as suicidal as it was wicked, for it would force the United States to intervene. He insisted that it was too late—plans had already been made and could not be recalled. According to Emily Balch, in the end he consented to put a stop to it.

countries have hitherto asserted that we must either leave 'backward peoples alone or else take control of them.' We have profited little by our evolving social experience if we cannot invent any way of being useful to a country like Haiti, in ways that Haitians themselves would approve and welcome. It is still possible for us to prove that a great power can be just, friendly and respectful to a small one." [19]

In 1928, Emily was again in Geneva at the Maison Internationale, after some weeks of campaigning in England, Ireland, and Wales for the Kellogg Pact for the renunciation of war. "The dear old rooms were never so attractive as I find them now, nor the garden so lovely with its roses red, white and pink, and its stands of mauve iris and yellow day lilies." Her return coincided with the fiftieth meeting of the Council of The League of Nations. She was asked to present to the Council members the W.I.L.P.F. concern over the importation of munitions into China and in regard to the traffic in arms generally. She used the opportunity of an interview alone with Signor Rosso of Italy and M. Prokope of Finland to discuss the Kellogg proposal as well. "They were more than merely courteous," she reported, "and appeared cordially interested. I also spoke informally of the general situation as regards China, emphasizing the importance of respecting her integrity. I also had an interesting talk with a member of the Information Department in regard to recognizing as a member of the League any Chinese government controlling Pekin."

"There is little change [in Geneva]," she wrote, "but one feels that with the passing of the first flush of early days, the League of Nations is entering a less enthusiastic era with traditions already much more fixed. It is the period of Chamberlain and Poincaré and, except for the fact that Germany is now a member, one feels a certain let-down in the tone of things. It is perhaps most of all the stalemate in regard to disarmament that causes a sense of bafflement and the Kellogg proposal meets too much skepticism in continental Europe to change this." [20]

During this visit we find Emily Balch presiding at a well attended public meeting. The theme was the Kellogg Pact and disarmament; the speakers were Salvador de Madariaga and Professor William Rappard. From her introductory remarks we can perhaps see why, though Emily was not in the conventional sense considered a good public speaker, people thought her chairmanship lent distinction to a meeting and why her quietly voiced remarks invariably commanded complete attention.

"The streets about this hall where we meet tonight" she began, "have historical names: there is the Street of All Souls, Street of Hell, Street of Purgatory. In Calvin's world men looked forward to perfect and eternal bliss or eternal torment. This short life was a melodrama of inconceivable intensity. Every reasonable man's chief concern was his individual salvation.

"When these things became unbelievable, individual lives lost in scale. Individual choices became less important.

"There was gain with this loss. Science and history opened immense vistas. The individual became again important as an active factor, however small, of a vast evolving cosmos. But the common future which history presents to us is uncertain. As the individual Calvinist faced a possible hell or a possible heaven, a fate, whether predestined or shapeable by his own efforts, of infinite weal or infinite woe, so we seem today to face an alternative, as a race. . . . For the first time in all history, our race faces the possibility of suicide.

"To pass from these high matters," she proceeded drily, "I want to say a few words, before I turn to the speakers of the evening, about my own country, not because it is mine but because I believe it is in a degree a useful object of warning and of encouragement. . . .

"If Europeans seem to Americans to find it too difficult to believe, too difficult to act, Americans seem to Europeans too uncritical, too naive, impulsive and idealistic, not to say sentimental, exaggerated, unstable, puzzling, incalculable.

"We are more or less aware of this. We turn with a rather pathetic wistfulness to Europeans with their wide human vision. In all Europe I do not know where we could find finer specimens of all this than in the speakers this evening.[21]

"I wait as you wait to hear what the ripest European thought has to offer us as we face this terrible, this wonderful alternative, a world of wars or a world of peace."

At the end of the decade death began to cause the first break in the ranks of the pioneer leaders and early supporters of the W.I.L.P.F. On August 10, 1929, just before the sixth International Congress at Prague, Dr. Aletta Jacobs died. She was a pioneer suffragist, pioneer woman physician, pioneer worker for peace. More than any other one person, she had been responsible for the convening of The Hague Congress of Women, the maintenance of the International Committee of Women for Permanent Peace in Amsterdam during the war years, and for the founding of the W.I.L.P.F. "Most people," wrote Kathleen Courtney, "do not live to see the success of their work. They live through the crucifixion, but do not see the resurrection. To Dr. Jacobs it was given to see the success of many movements in which she was a pioneer." [22]

In the report of The Hague Congress proceedings is a full-page portrait of Dr. Aletta Jacobs. It reveals a short but stately figure, hair waving in the prevailing pompadour fashion, reflective cast of countenance, a commanding presence with just a touch of the domineering, standing on a richly patterned rug beside a brocaded chair. Her high necked gown with its train sweeping the floor is to modern eyes fearfully and wonderfully made, of various materials, silks, velvets and net, with tiers of appliquéd designs and huge embroidered baskets of flowers at the hem and across the capacious bosom. The portrait is in one way the apotheosis of the Victorian upper middle class at its best, connoting culture, comfort, intelligence. But it is also possible to see in the face a concern with ideal issues, a largeness of vision, a cosmopolitan *Weltanschauung*, the authority of one used to action, as well as lurking humor and vitality.*

From this class, educated, secure economically and socially, were largely recruited the founders and prime movers of the W.I.L.P.F. which formed so much of the texture of the experience of Emily Balch.** They comprised some of the most brilliant and

---

* In 1936, at the height of the Hitler madness, Emily Balch, in a speech describing the small group of women who called together The Hague Congress in 1915, said that "Dr. Aletta Jacobs, a Dutch Jewish physician was the most outstanding figure. I refer to the fact that she was a Jew because I recognize that in her life-long work for peace and internationalism, for humanitarianism and justice, she was engaged in a service markedly characteristic of her people. In what strange ways is that service repaid."
** A knowledge of this "rare comradeship" of Emily Balch's is essential to understanding why she and Jane Addams won the Nobel Peace Prize.

talented women in the America and Europe of their time, though their achievements have not yet been adequately emphasized. But they did not belong to the conventional bourgeoisie. Many, like Dr. Helene Stöcker, were daring innovators in social and civic reform. They were not women of the leisure class but professional women—doctors, lawyers, professors, editors of periodicals, journalists, social workers, reformers, and some public officials. They constituted a veritable International Who's Who—women like Dr. Aletta Jacobs, Jane Addams, Emily Balch, Anita Augspurg, Chrystal Macmillan, Helena Swanwick, Gabrielle Duchêne, Rosika Schwimmer, Clara Ragaz, and Dr. Naima Sahlbom. This background in part explains the complexion and career of the W.I.L.P.F. It began as an organization consisting only of women because the founding feminists in 1915 saw that action impossible to men in time of war might be possible to women—and even welcomed by the men. It never became a mass movement because the moral philosophy underlying the League, that peace is much more then the absence of war, enjoined not only a respect for the sacredness of human life, but associated the pursuit of peace with the pursuit of other ends and ideals necessary to attain a finer and more rational international society. This, involving *changes in the economic order by nonviolent methods,* was a program at once too radical for the right, too restrained for the left, involving too much intellectual discipline to attract the average woman.

Therefore the League remained, to its sorrow, largely a middle-class movement. Its aims, in the words of Emily Balch in 1921, "to mobilize the moral force of the women of the world against war, cruelty and oppression," did not succeed in attracting laboring groups. The German section succeeded in getting some membership among working women, while the French had some labor representation from trade unions. The British section also attracted some working-class membership. The United States section tried valiantly in the 1930's and 1940's to break into labor ranks. But labor was too much engrossed in its own struggles against injustice and preferred to work within the trade-union movement. Second, labor benefited by "preparedness" and "defense." Many unions were dependent on government contracts and contracts with navy shipbuilders. Working women did not wish to take positions against their own unions, or take stands on issues to which their unions were not committed. For similar reasons, in the United States section, attempts to gather Negro women in greater numbers during this period were not successful.

In her first editorial in *Pax et Libertas* in February, 1920, Emily Balch had written: "Reason and love and freedom in human relations—this is all our program. We translate it, as well as we can, into concrete judgments and specific policies according to the demands of the moment. We work for a juster peace, for self-determination for all peoples, for freedom for women, for free exchange of goods everywhere, for industrial justice and cooperation without a taint of exploitation upon it, for education to fit every soul to lead a full and serviceable life." [23] She was to continue to apply her social philosophy, the embodiment of what was best in American thinking, the critical spirit of intelligence in the regulation of human problems, and direct it to the most catastrophic of all social problems—war! To this she added one other ingredient, the spirit of disinterested benevolence and good will, that human reason in the service of charity, or, as she called it, in terms rarely employed by a professor of economics, "an underlying universal love," like the love of Saint Francis of Assisi or the universal love of the Quaker, John Woolman, as a foundation for the actions of nations and for all political activity.

CHAPTER FOURTEEN

Uneasy Interval, 1929-1939

> Miss Emily saw the small things,
> She saw them wonder-hued;
> A linnet in her rocky dell,
> A sunset leaf bedewed.
>
> Miss Emily saw the great things,
> Creation's cosmic plan,
> And, down the corridor of Time,
> The liberty of Man.*

The decade of 1929 to 1939 began with the whimper of world depression and ended with the bang of World War II, once again engulfing the United States. The years of that decade were perhaps the busiest of Emily Balch's life, years of constant activity, years of responsibility, filled with "planetary" concerns but never for a moment without the private services that fill a woman's life.

There was scarcely a Tuesday over a period of many years when Emily's diary did not show the entry "Annie." Annie's illnesses took her to a number of sanatoria, in Wellesley, in South Natick, in Arlington. On Tuesday afternoons Emily would visit

---

* The above verses on Emily Brontë were written by Johnstone G. Patrick.

Annie, bring her sister the books she had carefully selected as desirable, and take back those Annie had read the week before. She felt she could never discharge the long-standing debt she owed her sister. "As I have often said," she had once written to Annie, "you are to me like the four walls and roof of home." Bessie, brilliant, fascinating, gifted with words like her mother, but difficult of temperament, critical of herself and others, completed the close-knit sisterly trio.

In appearance throughout her sixties and indeed through her seventies, Emily was still tall, unstooped, angular, with a fragility that denied her wiry tenacity. Her step was still sprightly "tip-toeing along" as when she was a girl. Her gaze was calm, direct, her grey-blue eyes keen, observant, quizzical, kindly. She had the impersonal air, the gracious aloofness, the dignity of a woman immersed in great affairs. She never gave anyone the impression, invariably suggested by Jane Addams, of being motherly. She herself knew there was nothing maternal about her. Nor was she as "gentle" as Jane Addams. She had more crispness. But in her friendly handclasp, her kindling eyes, her welcoming manner, she had a domestic warmth which was distinctly womanly, even feminine. When she did not like anyone, she gave the impression of being "austere."

She dressed simply and unobtrusively, tending to dark blues, greys, and blacks. The regal Madame Duchêne, who dressed with French distinction, chided her once for wearing a dark blue hat with a black dress. More than once, Emily was known to have put on her hat front side backward. When she was younger, freelancing in social work, her "sense of social compunction" led her to adopt a certain code of dressing "which meant a great deal to me. My ideal was to dress in such a style as would be free from any differentiation of social class. A sister claimed that I said I wanted to dress so that anyone might suppose I was the cook." At any rate she did not want to seem different or out of place in poor streets or among poor people. "I disliked any clothes that suggested ability to afford new styles as they appeared or anything 'select' or 'exclusive' or valued just because not everyone could have the like." At one period when she was tempted to engage in "dress reform" she decided that since she was already a pacifist she had better "economize on queerness."

In Geneva and elsewhere, at public receptions and functions, Emily would slip on over her current best dress a black velvet jacket she had had made at Geneva. Then, with a chain of blue beads or the silver Ischl peasant necklace, and a little black bag, she was in gala dress. The black velvet jacket, a symbol of her concession to formality, was still functioning in America during the second World War.

During this decade when every day brought its preoccupation with explosive issues, Emily managed to live by an inner calendar which gave her infinite leisure. She had leisure for family, for friends, for reading, for exercise ("I worked in the thicket"), for country walking with the light quick step "of one who is both thin and determined," for memorizing poetry, for sketching (it was in 1930 that she began the first of her delicate and sensitive pastels), for meditation, for conversation, wise and salty, and, yes, for losing things. "Bought new fountain pen and then found the lost one." "Lost my purse with $50." "Recovered my grey coat left in train at Lisieux." "Lost my purse with $20." "Lost my diary." When she became too busy to continue her consecutive journals, she kept a record of her activities and readings in daily diaries, occasionally jotting down random reflections and observations on small white pads. Cropping up unexpectedly among her notes for speeches, her outlines for articles, her memoranda for political proposals (which she sometimes kept in a slit envelope labeled "Bright Ideas"), are such bits as:

"I saw something amazing the other day. It was a leaf. I could not understand it at all but I could wonder at it. I never stop being surprised."

"The haze of spring. The frogs' pipings like a peal of small bells in the distance. The strange, sweet, vague, intolerable language of the spring wood, asking one knows not what."

"I am glad that an orange was a rarity when I was little. The soft white leathery layer under the fragrant skin with its pellucid pits of oily fragrance, the delicious transparent lobes of juicy fruit. No wonder one found an orange in one's Christmas stocking."

"Early morning, not yet fully light. The air pulsing with the

song of birds, whistlings and chatterings and flutings intermixed.
The light growing stronger all the time."

The intermittent diary she kept on loose sheets of paper reveals
her moods in the earlier part of the decade, the interactions
between the inner and the outer person:

Jan. 4, 1933—Such beauty of sky and hill view. Good news too
of Annie.

In the Far East ill news and foreboding. Within? Oh, I will
try to rule my inner skies and keep the sun always warm and
bright there.

January 6, 1933—For friends, for evening sky, for sleep, for how
much else, gratefulness.

Jan 7, 1933—Physiological depression such as I have to struggle
with, more or less rationalizes itself as trouble over the Japanese
cruelty in China, W.I.L. finances, family loss of income, especially
Bessie's, Annie's health, Maidie's exhaustion, etc., etc. . . . It would
be nice to know what causes these states ("blues," "cafard") but
at any rate I need not give way to them.

Never had the goals towards which the woman at The Hague
set out in 1915 and at Zürich in 1919—the goals of peace and
freedom—seemed more distant or been more threatened than in the
decade between 1929-1939. It was the period that saw the world-
wide depression, the failure of the Disarmament Conference of
1932, Mussolini's conquest of Ethopia with the breakdown of the
halfhearted attempt to apply sanctions, the civil war in Spain
"with the hypocrisy of nonintervention," the Japanese invasion of
China with the futile Nine Power Conference of February, 1938,
in Brussels, Hitler's systematic persecution of the Jews, the
absorption of Austria by Germany, and the swallowing up of
Czechoslovakia.

From 1929 to 1937 Emily spent a good part of each year in
Europe. In 1929, she took part in the sixth W.I.L.P.F. Congress at
Prague, with its theme—"How to make the Kellogg-Briand Pact a
reality"—and also in the work of the summer school in Hungary
which followed. The year before she had journeyed to Warsaw for
a peace congress, to Geneva for a conference on opium organized
by the W.I.L.P.F. The Prague Congress was the last one presided

over by Jane Addams. She did not wish reelection as international president but continued as honorary international president as long as she lived. Emily Balch, Gertrude Baer of Germany, and Clara Ragaz of Switzerland were chosen as joint international chairmen.

In March and April, 1930, Emily Balch spent three weeks in Palestine studying the situation with its apparently irreconcilable difficulties. She saw for herself the dilemma that Great Britain, the mandatory power, had to face as a result of arousing diametrically opposed expectations, on the one hand by decisions to favor the Zionist movement, on the other by the encouragement given during the war by British spokesmen to Arab nationalist aspirations. Emily Balch had many contacts with Arabs through Frances Hayward, a great admirer of Arabs, who had many Syrian friends. Emily also had contacts with many Jewish groups. She visited Dr. Judah Magnes at the Hebrew University and partook of a Seder at the home of Dr. D. Yellias. She had the unenviable ability, which hardly endeared her to either side, to see the central point in the consciousness of the Zionists and at the same time to enter fully into the feelings of the Arabs. She was not, however, sympathetic to Zionist claims to historic rights in Palestine. She was encouraged to see (1930) that there were "so many," as she thought, both among Jews and Arabs, who like Dr. Magnes, were seeking a workable program.

Like most members of the W.I.L.P.F., Emily regarded the Balfour Declaration as capable of interpretation in two ways, and, therefore, one of the sources of the current troubles, and the narrow nationalistic views among Jews and Arabs, both in Palestine and in other countries, as responsible for much of the unrest. She looked upon Palestine as the home of both Arabs and Jews, and she hoped to see both peoples work together to build up their common home, to secure their own safety, and not endanger world peace. She wanted to bring together groups of Arabs and Jews to work cooperatively towards these ends.

A year later, 1931, at Bryn Mawr College, Jane Addams, who was being honored by the first Carey Thomas Award, said in reply to the citation, that she would use part of the award of $5,000 to support "peace-missions" of the W.I.L.P.F. She had been having conversations recently, she said, with Dr. Magnes, Chancellor of the Hebrew University in Jerusalem, and he had referred to these "commissions" with much appreciation and had said that if anyone in the world could help bring together the Arabs and Jews in Palestine, it was Miss Balch. "Of course," Jane Addams continued, "Miss Thomas knows all about Emily Balch. She was an early Bryn Mawr graduate, the first holder of the European fellowship, and has continued her interest in international work." [1]

The year 1931 was in many ways an eventful one for Emily Balch. As president of the United States section she made an extensive speaking tour in ten states, going as far west as Minnesota, where, to her surprise and pleasure, she was invited to address the state legislature, then in session, on disarmament. She then sailed again to Europe to attend an important executive meeting at Lille, France, and an economic conference in Paris in April 1931, organized mainly by Yella Hertzka.

In the summer of 1931, Emily Balch revisited Germany, mainly to preside at the W.I.L.P.F. summer school at Breslau, on the frontier of Silesia, organized to discuss the bitter differences and grievances of Poles and Germans on both sides of the boundary. "Miss Balch presided and acted as translator, bringing into the discussion her usual spirit of tolerance and understanding," *Pax International* reported. She also visited Hamburg, Munich, and Berlin. It was "a curious and interesting experience," she wrote, "to be again in Berlin where I had been a student thirty-five years ago. The Brandenburger Thor is still there but there is no portal reserved for royalty. The Tiergarten, where I once wrestled with the *Critique of Pure Reason,* is as lovely as of old except for the ugly Siegesallee built since I was there and already überlebt.

"The University is unchanged, but the students who pour out of the gateway seem to be half girls, a great improvement over 1896. Old Adolf Wagner and Gustav Schmoller were friendly to women students, but Professor Treitschke told an acquaintance that a woman should cross the threshold of his classroom only over his dead body. The tone of the students with whom I and an American fellow-student then [1895-1896] discussed the universe was social-democratic or at least near-socialist. To an American in those days this was what Communism would be today [1931], but the contact with it matured and permanently enriched my political-economic views.

"My 'Arbeit' for Professor Wagner was a study of 'Arbeitsver-mittlung Ämter' (Employment Agencies). On this visit, November, 1931, I was taken to visit the present Arbeitsamt in Stuttgart. I shall never forget the faces of the young men, their unseeing hopeless eyes, staring ahead. It was worse than the cold restlessness of the men (and women) who are selling apples on street corners in New York, though these German men were at the moment neither cold nor badly dressed.

"What interests me most as I look back on my impressions of 1896 is my sense of the powerful current of thought and talk (then) which argued that might made right, that a man or nation was free to do anything that it had the power to do. This cynical amoralism, this categorical refusal of all duty and all validity to categories of right and wrong filled me with a Cassandra mood of foreboding. What could, what must happen to a people if this way of looking at life really got the upper hand? It interests me now that I then felt this so keenly." She also remembered that in the university in 1895-1896, anti-Semitism was present. One might see a bench scored with a jacknife, "Juden 'rraus."

In hearing of the nationalist tendencies of so many of the university students, she was deeply disappointed that they had not learned a different lesson from the war. She went to two Hitlerite meetings and did not find them impressive. She felt no sense of a gathering storm, of a reservoir of power, will, energy, or thought or purpose, and certainly of no great enthusiasm for the person of Adolf Hitler. "This is not to say that the situation is not very critical, dangerous and painful. It imperatively demands the most understanding statesmanship. . . . I wish the Germans did not pity themselves so much. It is no wonder they do. I do not criticize them for it—they have suffered and they have been badly treated, but I wish they did not complain so much. Even a *pretense* of courage helps courage to be real. After the war years and the post-war years, and the world crisis of today it is hard to 'whistle' to keep a stiff upper lip [sic] as we say in English, but to do so might lessen the tendency to run into unreason and wild extremes."

Like many informed people, Emily Balch took the Manchurian

incident of 1931 with extreme seriousness. "I was present at the final meeting in Paris of the League of Nations Committee on the subject and heard Briand, already a very sick man, make his tragic and poignant appeal to save the League of Nations as the most precious thing mankind had ever created." In November, 1931, also in Paris, she experienced what she afterwards referred to as one of the "shocks" of her life. She was present at a scandalous and alarming occurrence at a Ressemblement pour la Paix at the Trocadero palace at which Lord Robert Cecil and the American Ambassador Allen B. Houghton, were to speak, Edmond Herriot presiding. A mob of Parisian nationalist roughs of the right invaded the hall, swarmed upon the platform, and with catcalls, shouts, and nationalist songs, prevented every speaker from being heard. "It was horrible to see hand-to-hand fighting going on in the balconies." She sailed home in December, "full of anxiety, as was every thinking person."

For Emily Balch, the issue in Manchuria threw "every other consideration into background." Critical as was the Manchurian situation itself, in which a government was undertaking to secure its way by armed force exercised on foreign territory, she believed that the principle of preserving faith in the usefulness of treaties was of more far-reaching and fundamental significance. The Kellogg Pact, the Covenant of the League of Nations, and the Nine Power Treaty were equivalent to a categorical promise in the face of the world not to seek to settle any disputes by other than peaceful means. "There is a strong feeling that the munitions interests and other economic interests are powerfully at work and making for war. The export of munitions is a very serious matter and one which in each country for itself must be studied, made known and as far as possible controlled." [2]

In America, Emily Balch as national president of the United States section wrote President Hoover on January 18, 1932, urging him, among other things, to give executive support to Congressional action to forbid the shipment of arms to Japan, and to declare loans to Japan as contrary to public policy. She regretted that the United States did not, at the first invasion of Manchuria, protest that Japan had violated both the Kellogg Pact and the Nine Power Treaty, "but we believe that the best service that the

United States can render is *not to pronounce judgment* as a party to the treaties, but to *create an important precedent for the submission of such international issues to judicial decision."*

It was very characteristic of her own pacifist attitude that she thought it would be a misfortune if peace people took sides and felt and talked as partisans. "The people of Japan are as dear to us as those of any country in the world. And we must feel a very special sympathy and admiration for those elements in Japan who see the situation in its wider aspects and are serving the cause of peace and world order under the most difficult conditions. This attitude of friendliness to both sides does not mean that we should be *neutral* on the issues involved."

Emily Balch wrote to Camille Drevet in Geneva that she was against advocating the withdrawal of ambassadors. She thought all channels of communication should be kept wide open for understanding Japan and, above all, for making her understand how much and why her policies were being condemned.[3]

On January 29, 1932, she submitted to the Executive Committee of the W.I.L.P.F. a memorandum on Manchuria on the chance that it might contribute something to the attempt to find a practicable and fruitful solution. A mere return to the previous condition of things would not be a solution. If an administrative authority could be set up in Manchuria for a limited time, say thirty years, to secure order and conditions favorable to economic development, while leaving the rights of China undisturbed, the problem might be on the road to solution. The administration should not be international but made up of a body of paid experts much like the city manager system of some American cities. Since Manchuria was a rich territory with great, only partially developed resources, she advocated loans with conservative interest rate and amortization for productive and developmental purposes, guaranteed against serving as instruments of political penetration or economic exploitation. She hoped that the practical advantages to all concerned, including especially Japan, and the voice of "enlightened self-interest" might recommend some such scheme.[4]

The year 1932 found Emily Balch again in Europe taking part in the seventh Congress of the W.I.L.P.F. in Grenoble, on the subject of "World Disarmament or World Disaster." This slogan was as prophetic as it was timely. The Congress coincided with

the long-delayed League of Nations Conference on Reduction and
Limitation of Armaments in February, 1932, at Geneva. To this
the W.I.L.P.F. made a major contribution of over six out of eight
million signatures for a monster polyglot disarmament petition.*
The W.I.L.P.F. exerted itself to the utmost to support this effort
to stave off the war as one proposal followed another, culminating
in the Russian plan for universal and complete disarmament. "As
every one knows," said Emily Balch, "the world chose disaster."
The conference finally adjourned in 1937, "without result, save
growing chaos. As I sat through session after session of the Geneva
Conference in the special building which the League of Nations
had put up for these meetings, I would watch the gaily dressed
bonnes wheeling perambulators along the quiet *quai* and speculate
how the peaceful scene would be affected if all that oratory led
to nothing as it did. The W.I.L.P.F. demand for *disarmament,
universal and complete,* may have sounded Utopian, but the conference demonstrated the insurmountable difficulties of a partial
and piecemeal solution, and the atomic bomb has been the reductio
ad absurdum of safety through competitive armament."

She thought it may have been putting the cart before the horse
to try to get disarmament before the outstanding causes of dissen-
sion and conflict had been dealt with. But there were positive
reasons for the failure of the latter—the pressure of financial
interests, especially of munition makers and dealers, the rivalries
of power politics "in which none of the Great Powers were
blameless, and above all in the spread of Fascism and Hitlerism
with all that these signified."

In 1934 the W.I.L.P.F. finances, affected by world depression
and restrictions imposed by various governments on sending money
abroad, were at such a low ebb that it could not continue the
salary of Camille Drevet, the invaluable international secretary at

* 180,000 signatures came independently from Japanese women and were
presented to the 1929 Conference on Naval Disarmament in London. Mme.
Andrée Jouve of Paris visited Emily Balch at Wellesley in 1950. She long
afterwards remembered a "brilliant speech" at the college by her 83-year-old
friend on disarmament, and Miss Balch's reference to the thousands of sheets
of signatures preserved, symbolically, under glass, in the League of Nations
Palace with no other meaning save their historic value. "Miss Balch conclut
avec sa tranquille obstination: 'Il nous faut recommencer, sans repit.'" (Miss
Balch concluded with her calm persistence, "We shall have to begin again,
without respite.")

Geneva. Emily Balch came to the rescue by volunteering her services without pay for six months. She sailed in March, 1934, intending to return to Roanoke Road in the autumn, but instead, she remained a year and a half as honorary international secretary.

At the first executive meeting in Geneva after she became honorary international secretary, Emily broached a subject she had been revolving in her mind for some time, the policy to be pursued in case of the outbreak of war. Even ardent believers in the League of Nations machinery for dealing with conflicts had been discouraged. Emily Balch, therefore, proposed to revive the policy of continuous mediation to be offered by nonbelligerent powers. The W.I.L.P.F. members had never forgotten this method advocated so early by Rosika Schwimmer, and so carefully worked out in 1914-1915 by Julia Grace Wales and had turned and were to turn to it again and again. Pacifists always had been reluctant to plan anything in the event of war breaking out, being unwilling to tip the scales even by a hair's breadth towards creating a war psychology. But in 1934 events were forcing them to admit the terribly real possibility of war in the near future and to acquiesce in the necessity of preparing "in a quiet way," as Emily Balch said, "what might be done in that case."

Therefore in December, 1934, Emily Balch wrote from Geneva to Cordell Hull, Secretary of State, urging that the State Department should not wait to improvise something after war and chaos had broken loose, but should give quiet and mature thought to the problem while it was still possible to think things out calmly and thoroughly. Assuming that the civilian policy-making organs of the United States government should plan what to do in different contingencies just as a war staff does, she suggested that among the plans to be critically considered, tested and eventually elaborated should be this plan of early and continuous mediatory activity by nonbelligerents in case of threat or outbreak of war. "Should the Covenant system for restoring peace fail to function," she wrote to Hull, "peace must have ready a second line of defense and it is to be noted that the 'Kellogg Pact' does not furnish any form of procedure. In 1915 the policy of Continuous Mediation by the Neutral Powers was discussed by the Prime Ministers and Foreign Ministers of all the principal belligerent and neutral countries; not one government opposed it and several warmly approved.

President Wilson was so kind as to call first Miss Jane Addams and then me to the White House to report to him on the confidential statements made by the Prime Ministers and Foreign Ministers of the countries. . . . President Wilson took the position as I understood him, that he felt that the proposed joint action of all the neutrals would be cumbrous. In any case his refusal to endorse the plan shattered any hope of carrying it out.

"I am venturing to suggest that under the different circumstances of today the merits of this plan, which in 1915 received such authoritative consideration and, in so many quarters, approval, be studied afresh. . . . There was tragic need [in 1915] of the 'honest broker' and it was essential that this intermediary should be prompt, should be 'always on the job' and should be powerful, especially morally powerful."

Two years later, December, 1936, Emily Balch circulated *Observations on a Mediated Peace in Spain,* drawing up some possible terms of a settlement should a moderate Republican government be in control. These provisions included a political truce for a period of years with agreements about church property, the relation of the church to education, the subjection of the military to the civil government, the preservation of order by an international police force during the period of transition. Like most observers she was disturbed by the progressive suicide of Spain, and by the use of the country as a battleground for the struggle between Fascism and Communism. All hope for any outcome other than either slow exhaustion on the one hand, or an unstable terrorist government on the other, would be through friendly offices from the outside while fighting was in progress. This was only a hope, she thought, as the passionate fury of the combatants excluded all consideration of reason, and the general demoralization of the times made effective mediatory action from the governments, any or all of them, difficult.

From Wellesley she had written to the international chairmen of the W.I.L.P.F. on August 26, 1936: "We believe that nothing can be settled right by the method of fighting nor in the midst of fighting. Everything should be done to secure a truce, at least, so that reason could have a chance to make itself heard. I wish there were a thousand Gertrude Baers in Spain to go out between the lines as she did in Munich.

"It is the tragic fact, as it looks to me, that in this case a Left victory may be much worse, ultimately, for our 'Left' ideals than a temporary victory of the Right. I fear that it will mean a Terror which will further blacken the reputation of 'Communists' and tend to weaken them among 'men of good will.' It will mean, I fear, an internecine feud between anarchists, syndicalists, socialists, communists, and Republicans, instead of a post-war conflict between different groups of Rightists which will tend to disintegrate them. But even if one thinks these things, one cannot take them as basis of action. They are fears, theoretical and uncertain. One can only follow the direct path of favoring those who come nearest to what we believe in. . . .

"I have no patience with the legalistic view that beyond the policy of refusing to send in war supplies (which, important as this policy is, is a purely negative one) friendly governments can do nothing to stop the present horrors without recognizing the rebels and giving them the status of belligerents. 'Friendly offices' conciliation can always be tried. If the Governments had the will to do something they could.

"As it is, with the Governments and especially the great European Powers, lined up in their sympathies behind the two parties and therefore against each other, they are unlikely to act, and we have great cause for thankfulness if only the general explosion is not brought to pass." [5]

In answer to the above, Gertrude Baer replied on September 17, 1936, "I believe the psychological moment for mediation was missed."

In the second spring of her Geneva stay, on May 22, 1935, Emily's diary has the entry: "Learned of the death of Jane Addams on the preceding evening." There is no recorded expression of her grief except an undated scrap of paper on which she wrote: "I am thankful to have known and worked with Jane Addams and that she loved me so much more than I deserved or could repay. Help me not to dwell on my loss. Help me to enjoy her still. To learn from her and be glad of her and do what is in me to do, as she did, living to the full her great soul."

Next to her magnetic, fascinating deeply-loved mother, Ellen Noyes Balch, no one touched Emily Balch's inmost heart, captured her imagination, evoked her intellectual admiration as did Jane Addams. It was probably the greatest personal blow in a life singularly devoid of deep sorrow, illness, or pain. In the early summer Emily worked on a memorial issue of *Pax*, writing an objective article on "Jane Addam's Work For Peace," ending with the words: "Jane Addams' concern for peace was not something that began when the War forced the issue. It was nothing accidental or external. It had nothing to do with compromise or what people mean by 'peace at any price.' It was a state of mind, a method of dealing with contentious problems of all sorts. It was a deep part of herself, at once her philosophy and her life." [6]

Eight years later, in the spring of 1943, under the "disintegrating forces of war-time, with its enforced segregations and moral and physical blockades," during the war Jane Addams had not lived to see, but which her courage and judgment might have lightened for her fellow citizens, Emily Balch was to write to Jane Addams' comrades and her own in the League: "Of all my experiences the greatest and dearest was the being privileged to know Jane Addams. It is as impossible to evoke her for those who did not have the happiness of knowing her as to evoke the fragrance of a ripe strawberry or of a water-lily for someone who has never smelled one. She was so utterly unlike anyone else that I have known—so utterly real and first-hand; so subtle, so simple and direct; so free from any preoccupation with self, as free from asceticism as from self-indulgence; full of compassion without weakness or sentimentality (though she grew up in a sentimental generation), loving merriment while carrying the world's woes in her heart—both the many which pressed upon her in immediate personal shape at Hull-House and those of the nameless, unseen millions whose fates are part of our own personal fate. A great statesman, a great writer, one of the world's rarest spirits, how can I or anyone evoke her?" [7]

The same year, 1935, which was both a year of personal sorrow and of world anguish with the Ethiopian conflict, brought Emily an unexpected grace. In a draft sketch of her "Personal History," written in 1945 in the third person, she has a characteristic sentence, "After her return to America, Wellesley College invited her to give the formal Armistice Day Address, which pleased her." The word "pleased" in Emily's vocabulary has to be magnified

many times to be equated with the feelings it described. Her grati-
fication revealed how deep the wound had been when Wellesley
failed to reengage her. The invitation from Wellesley College was
a lasting satisfaction to Emily and as happens in such cases, the
grace rebounded to the giver. Emily delivered her talk "What of
Peace Today?" while "soldiers are marching and bombs are explod-
ing and the wounded of both sides lie stricken in Ethiopia."

The next International Congress, the ninth, and the last before
World War II, which met under thickly gathering shadows at
Luhacovice, Czechoslovakia, in July, 1937, she was obliged to
forego, because of one of Annie's illnesses. This congress, however,
elected Emily Balch to succeed Jane Addams as honorary international president, an honor, which again, "pleased" her.

In the period of Emily's second Geneva residence, Italian
Fascism and German National Socialism, the very antitheses of
peace and freedom, were capturing millions of adherents. The
words liberty and freedom, which for a hundred years had inspired
men and especially the young, had lost their magic. "There is a
powerful current of feeling," Emily wrote in 1934, "of the duty
and happiness of merging self in the community whether in Fascist
Italy, Soviet Russia or Hitler Germany. It is powerfully stimulated
by government propaganda but apart from this it seems to me clear
that it is a psychological current which has deeper sources than the
self-interest of those who are in power." 8

The rising tide of Fascism made itself felt in some degree even
in Switzerland, Holland, Sweden, and England. The word "freedom," in the name of the W.I.L.P.F., which had caused wonder in
the 1920's, took on a new relevancy. Even in America the concepts
of peace and freedom had drifted under ideological clouds and
took color from the creeds of the waxing dictatorships. As early
as 1927, Emily had written, "How many Americans not only believe, but openly maintain, that fascism is better than democracy,
that unthinking obedience is better than action based on individual
conscience and thought, that patriotism is synonymous with nationalism, that liberty is dangerous, that peace is a dream and not even
a beautiful dream?" 9 This rise of tyranny, in the Greek sense,
Emily looked on as a result and also a cause of widespread dry rot

of belief "in the principles that seem to us among the most precious achievements of the long travail of the human spirit."

"I do not think we could or should attempt," she continued in 1934, "to work against the great social current of the time. On the contrary, I think it is the master current of our era, i. e., fraternal equality. It has a more powerful claim than liberty. But they are not opposed to one another. It is very important that the leaders and masses moving toward a socialized world should be convinced of the values of individual quality and should really understand that forced uniformity is a loss to all, that men must have liberty to make mistakes, to follow false leads, to think honestly as their minds work and not to think as they are told to, or cease from thinking at all. Not only the artist, the poet, the philosopher but the crank, the oddity, the natural heretic and rebel have their place in the social scheme." [10]

As early as 1934 she was advocating a new formulation of "les droits de l'Homme." She regretted that when the Covenant of the League of Nations was drafted it did not include a minimum standard of respect for human rights which states should accept to be eligible to the League. "It would probably have been impossible to agree on such a standard. It is even more probable that if it had been accepted it would not have been satisfactorily observed. Would it not be useful now [1934] if the Ligue des Droits de l'Homme should call an international conference to try to restate a program of human liberties suited to the times?"*

Emily Balch's preoccupation with ideas of liberty and freedom did not remain academic. Like her great great-grandfather Niles, she turned readily from theory to practice, from thought to action. At this time, and for several years to come, a concrete struggle for individual liberty epitomizing the larger issue of peace and

---

* When the subject of equal rights for women came up in 1931 at an international executive meeting, Emily Balch voted for it with the reservation, which she believed also represented the viewpoint of a large number of her colleagues, that she did not accept the interpretation which makes equal rights for women imply identity of laws as regards men and women.

In December, 1939, Gertrude Baer in Geneva had drafted an International Declaration of the Rights of Man. Towards the end of her life, Emily Balch was to write to Gertrude Baer: "I am more than ever conscious, if possible, what an immensity of work and leadership we owe to you."

freedom in the United States was to engage her attention and occupy whatever leisure she had from W.I.L.P.F. responsibilities— the repatriation case of Rebecca Shelley.

Rebecca Shelley's family was of old Pennsylvania Mennonite stock, but she had lost her native citizenship by marrying a German in August, 1922, just before the equal nationality law for women became effective. When she applied for repatriation in 1931, she was denied citizenship in her native country because as a conscientious objector to war, she would not promise to bear arms. Rebecca Shelley, it will be remembered, was the ardent young pacifist girl who had worked with Emily Balch in the Neutral Conference Committee, the Emergency Peace Federation, and the People's Council in 1916-1918. She had been one of the youngest members attending The Hague Congress of Women in 1915 and had sailed on the Ford Peace Ship. Rebecca was now living in Michigan and asked Emily to assume the chairmanship of the Repatriation Committee.

"The Shelley case is very close to my heart," wrote Emily Balch to the treasurer of the Rebecca Shelley Repatriation Committee. "Under the pressure of social and economic problems [in the depression] there is a grave tendency to ignore or minimize the issue of individual liberty." She sympathized with Rebecca Shelley's wish to argue the case on pacifist grounds, eliminating the feminist issue. For several years the case went through long and for Rebecca very trying phases: repeated hearings, recommendations, denials, new decisions, reversals. It was complicated by the necessity of raising funds for the court battle in times of depression, by Rebecca's ill health, and by her individualism asserting itself in ways rather trying to her supporters.

Years afterwards, Rebecca Shelley was to write with gratitude "of Miss Balch's devotion to this struggle which cost her money as well as time and energy she may have felt wasted on so 'difficult' a person as myself. As I re-read her letters of that period more objectively than was possible during my tortuous struggle—I was moved to tears by the purity of her devotion to the cause, her valiant efforts to secure support, the conflict of loyalties, torn as she was between her confidence in the Civil Liberties Union and her conviction that even if the conscientious objector is 'difficult she should not be asked to subscribe to arguments with which she cannot agree." [11]

During this busiest of decades, Emily Balch wrote countless letters from Wellesley and from Geneva, from summer vacations with Bessie in Brooklin, Maine, to Rebecca, to other members of the committee in Detroit, to Roger Baldwin, to Oswald Garrison Villard, to J. Edgar Hoover, and others to enlist their support and interest while the case was being tried and appealed. When in 1937 Rebecca Shelley wrote that she had dismissed her lawyer and decided to conduct her case herself, Emily Balch wrote to a member of the Detroit Committee, "I was very much dismayed. I do not want to act as chairman if the case is carried on in such a way as to be more likely to block future attempts than to do good to the cause. Much as it is my desire to see Rebecca herself reinstated in her American citizenship, the main concern for me, *as for her,* is the cause of getting pacifists specifically recognized, not as heretofore, ineligible for citizenship."

And a little later, to Rebecca herself, whose ardor in pressing her case led her to picturesque but indiscreet actions which boomeranged on her cause, Emily wrote with the exasperated love of a parent: "Your statement about the red flag—I regard the latter as being ill-judged and as making a successful issue of your case more unlikely. It honestly does not seem to me playing the game to let me invest time, effort, and reputation, so to speak, in acting for you and then doing things like that without consulting me when I have said so often and so definitely that I will act only if you consult me before you do things—'things' includes bringing in other organizations, going into print, manifestations and demonstrations of all sorts, writing letters like yours of July 5 to ——, crossing all my wires and tending to undermine a situation I have already helped create as I understood by your wish. All this makes me ready to tear my hair and throw up the sponge. But I am not doing so. My hair is too thin for the one, and my interest in your case too tough for the other.

"You will notice that I have never complained of your dismissing your lawyers (though I think I ought to have been consulted). But that is a bygone.

"Also, I ask no promise or pledge on your part that you will consult me. But I shall feel free to retire at any time when you act without doing so on an issue that seems to me sufficiently vital."

Two closely written pages later she adds: "You may think I am

horrid to be so sharp-spoken but you know I am very fond of you."
Rebecca Shelley finally won her battle for repatriation in September, 1944, by a decision of the Department of Justice to recommend her for citizenship.

During the thirties, Emily Balch wrote and circulated what she described as "various proposals, more or less wise, more or less chimerical." Like Jane Addams, she never had much self-assurance. She put out her ideas in a deprecatory manner, saying, "this isn't much, but I've been thinking about this." But the ideas were fertile and rich in suggestions for other minds to develop them further. Her value as a world citizen was demonstrated in the manner in which she applied her well-trained mind to devising ways and means by which people could become interested in problems of international scope and exert themselves in the treatment and solution of such problems. Though she never held any high public office and made her contributions largely outside government agencies, she managed by her tireless work of writing, travel, organization, and more uniquely by effective and continued letter writing, to achieve a wide hearing and influence. She had a real talent for enlisting the participation of people throughout the world who had not waited for government but had gone ahead under her leadership in the faith that the foundations of peace lie in the hearts of men and women everywhere.

Between 1931 and 1938 Emily had written, published, and circulated proposals on: Disarmament, 1932; Internationalization of Aviation, 1932; Manchuria, 1931, 1932; An Economic Conference (sent to all governments by the League of Nations), 1933; Revision of Treaties, 1933; The Political Situation in Europe, 1935 (an analysis); Reform of the League of Nations, 1936; Economic Reconstruction, 1936; A Mediated Spain, 1937; Internationalization of the Mediterranean, 1937; Neutrality and Collective Security, 1938 (an analysis).

In these proposals occurs again and again her favorite idea of setting up different supranational authorities for coming to an accord on different matters. When the revision of the peace treaties, which she called Banquo's ghost of Europe, came into the foreground, she saw Europe, in holding on to the provisions of the treaties, like the boy in the fable who had the wolf by the ears and dared neither to hold on nor to let go. She advocated the establishment of a commission based on the Lytton Commission* as an excellent precedent as to method. Such a commission would not be asked to effect revision but to work out a plan for revision. It would consist of a small number of highly competent personalities, drawn wholly from countries not directly interested, to consult and advise with all parties.

In such a plan she saw clear advantages; it would provide a body to take the initiative without fear of losing prestige or compromising its case or being resented as a mischief maker. It would provide a friendly consultant to whom each party in interest could expose its views and through which it could discuss matters with the opposite side. Most essential of all, it would consider individual problems—such as for instance, the Polish Corridor—not in isolation but as part of a larger whole, making possibilities of adjustment more elastic. It would be not a return to power politics and the old diplomacy, but a very important step toward the management of world affairs in the interests of all.

In her discussion of the reform of the League of Nations she stressed once more the idea of international authorities to perform specific functions. The part of the League of Nations that had broken down, she wrote in 1936, was the collective guarantee of independence and integrity which President Wilson had decided was the heart of the Covenant. The minds of those who were busy with the problem of adjusting the League to the realities of the day ran to strengthening the League by providing for more coercion, more force. But to Emily Balch much of what she valued was the whole machinery of contact, conference and agreement making, conciliation procedures. The whole complex of activities in the many technical and reform fields with which the League and its organs were active and the importance of which was generally so little understood, and so grossly undervalued, were not necessarily affected.

Even if the device of collective guarantee was scrapped, some

---

* When the Japanese took over Mukden in Manchuria in September, 1931, the League of Nations in order to mediate peace set up in December, 1931, a commission headed by Lord Lytton, made up of nationals of Great Britain, France, Italy, Germany, and the United States to investigate the situation on the spot.

other device for some measure of security might be substituted for
it. She developed at some length the idea of each member state
of the League giving a substantial pledge, or hostage, to respect
the independence and integrity of its fellow members, with provision for organs of implementation. "We are in full Utopia. But
when Utopia is reasonable and not in its nature impracticable, the
obstacles may prove less impregnable than they look.[12]

Early in the Hitler regime, in 1935, she expressed her personal
views in the complex situation presented by Hitler Germany. It
was not a question of whether Hitler's Germany could be trusted.
"It is very evident to me that it cannot be." She thought the
only means of averting the threat of a war breaking out in Europe
was a decision to take the bull by the horns and make every
effort to bring Germany into the European order. She also advocated getting Japan and the United States to work as members of
the League of Nations. This would involve allowing Germany the
right, in fact as well as in an unreal diplomatic declaration, to
equal status in all matters. This meant, to her intense regret,
recognizing some part of the illegal and secret armament already
in process, which seemed to her more dangerous than arming in
public, within agreed limits and under supervision. In reply to
the argument that this policy would strengthen Hitler—"This has
all to be taken in the bitter cup that all of us and especially all
Europeans, have to drink"—she doubted if it would do so in the
long run. "His power, in many of the worst uses that he makes
of it, would on the contrary be undermined. He could no longer
represent Germany as encircled, victimized and in danger of
attack. He could not argue that it is forced, in self-defense, to
militarise its youth, sacrifice all normal liberties and amenities of
life, and pay out of its poverty for a feverish spurt of armament."[13]
The advantages thus offered Germany should be conditional on
her giving explicit and binding guarantees against troubling the
peace. Emily had more than once declared in public that a person
has a perfect right to say to a neighbor, "By your leave, neighbor,
I don't like what you're doing." And so, other countries should
consider it not only a right, but a duty, she wrote, to give frank
expression, both privately and officially, to their attitude toward
terror as a political instrument, the use of torture, especially
deliberate torture of helpless prisoners, racial persecution, abandon-

ment of all safeguards of justice in the accepted legal sense, and contempt for the whole conception of human rights.

Some time later, Emily Balch, writing on American policy in the face of the war in China, and thinking also of Germany, Ethiopia, and Spain, wrote: "Neutrality in the sense of treating the aggressor and his victim alike is morally impossible. . . . I stand emphatically for non-belligerency. I do believe in embargoes on munitions to all parties, at all times and now particularly re Japan and China." She hoped to keep out of war by building up a collective peace system using such non-military forms of pressure, internationally organized, as moral, diplomatic, and if unavoidable, economic, except a food blockade.* "The type of peace people with whom I disagree and whose influence seems to me to have had unfortunate results are those who teach, in effect, that we must do nothing that will make a bully displeased, since if we do he may fight—and then we should have the world in flames again. I do not think we should be scared off from doing what we should otherwise think right to do through fear of how the bully will react. No one can be made to fight who chooses not to. It would be a salutary sight to see a country against which war had been declared refusing to accept that weapon and seeking the solution of the conflict by quite other means.

"Those who believe in force grow the more dangerous when they are led to believe that every one is too much afraid of them to oppose them, and pacifists who avoid war by mere yielding are likely to be the more overwhelmed by it later."** And then she

---

* "I would like to see active aid to China, not only relief but loans, technical aids, not military. Opinion is much divided here. . . . It is a tragic dilemma that the world is in: to acquiesce is moral suicide and perhaps ultimately war; to resist is probably war and is almost impossible, given the political morale or lack of it in England and France, each of them tied to a dying imperialism and divided between capitalist conservatism and an unclear radicalism." E. G. Balch, letter to G. Baer, December 1, 1937.
** The attitude of the International W.I.L.P.F. toward the situation created by the Conference of Munich was briefly expressed by Clara Ragaz: "The 'peace' proclaimed at Munich is not the peace we have always fought for. It is no peace at all. It might at best be called a state of 'non-war' or better still 'deferred war.' It cannot be called peace because it is not founded on justice. It is merely an agreement between four partners, one of whom, the party prosecuting as it were, under threat of war made certain demands which were supported by his second and acquiesced in and granted by the third and fourth partners. The defendant had not been asked to be present: he was

closes: "It is essential to offer effective opposition, but by other methods than those of the violent, or rather to do more than *merely* to *oppose* them. The peace method is, renouncing all idea not merely of revenge, reprisals or punishment, but of 'victory for our side,' and, adopting no 'holier than thou' attitude, to seek out co-operatively a solution that will be beneficial all round. And such a solution is not so Utopian as it sounds. It is even conceivable that such a *via aurea* may be worked out, through mediation, in China and in Spain." [14]

Her absorption in the "great things," in planetary concerns, did not cause her to lose a sense of the importance of the "little things that grow not less." She made a time for the Graces as well as the Muses, for turning inward as well as outward, for the ultimates as well as the ephemeral. Ultimates for her might be "the little friend-linesses" or the aesthetic enjoyment of the "first warm and sweet-breathing day this spring." The ephemeral might be the social-political affairs she was concerned with. Once on a scrap of paper she noted:

> Speak of the great things
> Above Peace, above Freedom
> These are means, not ends.

Her little notations are revealing:
February 3, 1933: Leisure from oneself for others: leisure from details for the whole.
January 19, 1936: I tried today to interrupt my occupiedness, my sense of duties and busyness, to free and open myself—such a creaking and dust choked door to open—I have not succeeded, yet it is something to be beginning once more to try to live not only in the ordinary dimensions but also, in however tiny a degree, in that other dimension which we call God.
September 26, 1937:[Aetat 70] Reasons my spirit has been dark-ened this autumn are perhaps:
1) Unwillingness to face and endure the situation of the world and to think out my own position and to be more than merely passive.

---

not even consulted and was sacrificed in cold blood. The four partners then were acclaimed by the multitude as peace-makers while the victim was going to his death."

2) A growing love of money and concern over it and ill feeling at what I consider injustice to me personally.

3) Lack of resignation to old age and all its incidents and losses and to nearer approach of certain death. [She had twenty-four more years to live.]

4) Indolence in things spiritual; laziness and self-indulgence.

5) Anxiety about Annie.

6) Pressure on my faith in non-violence by the dilemma of Chinese pacifism, a dread of facing the problem, once more, honestly *de novo:*

As the decade drew to its relentless conclusion, Emily could still say publicly; "This is no time for discouragement and we are not discouraged. It is a time to maintain our principles and to use every educational device to make them understood and accepted." [15] To herself she would admit: "It seems as though when things look as bad as possible each day brought some item of news for the worse. My naturally resilient optimism is hard put to it. May I some day look back and think how much I feared unnecessarily. I pick up crumbs of comfort. Frau Seger and her baby have been released from their German concentration camp."

In spite of contemporary trends both in theory and practice towards "an ethic of violence, a cult of tyranny, a narrow nationalism and 'racism,' a scorn of discussion and reasonableness," she saw these movements as an eddy in the swifter currents setting towards the use of men's intelligence and good will in making agreement, consent, and more fruitful cooperation possible. In her own lifetime she had seen relations which rested traditionally on a basis of authority and punishment yield to less coercive solvents, the relations between husbands and their wives, between parents and children, teachers and pupils, employees and employed, penal officials and criminals, the church and its heretics, governments and the governed. It appeared to her that the way of life for which Jane Addams stood and towards which the W.I.L.P.F. aimed, was a value which could never be lost and that the way of oppression and suppression could not in the long run prevail.

In 1937-1938 Emily was considerably occupied in a labor of love, the writing of a short pamphlet history of the W.I.L.P.F. from its earliest beginnings to 1938. She called this little history *A Venture in Internationalism*. It was a work of admirable accuracy and compression. Although it was written in the period of a rapidly "deteriorating" international situation following the complete failure of the Disarmament Conference, she could still say towards the conclusion of the pamphlet: "It is shallow to be so impressed by the blatant victories of violence and unreason as to fail to recognize the more permanent and more significant forces which are constantly working in the contrary direction." Part of her confidence lay in her belief that "we, all the peace forces together," had accomplished a result of first-class historical importance—the spread of the conviction that war must be utterly repudiated. *"This wide-spread determination to put an end to war is a new thing in history."* [16]

All during this decade, the problem of the refugee, political, racial, religious, the flaring up of old fires of intolerance, the cruel lapses from civilized standards, the apathy of those who passed by on the other side either because they were lacking in imagination or because they had become satiated with tales of horror, burned themselves into her consciousness. In an autobiographical fragment she summarized her concern in simple words: "I devoted myself to work for the refugees, members of the W.I.L.P.F. and others, who were then desperately seeking asylum in the United States, securing for them as far as possible the coveted affidavits which were required for entry and carrying on a voluminous correspondence which in the end was too generally futile owing to what seemed to me the narrow-minded and pusillanimous policy of the American State Department." She worked as quietly but as patiently and indefatigably as this description suggests. She filled out so many affidavits for refugees that when her housemate Agnes Perkins asked her how she would support some of them if they became ill, she said "I'll sell apples."

There was almost no one in her ken with a particle of interest, influence or good will who did not at one time or another receive from her a handwritten letter, often, alas, undated, appealing on behalf of a particular case, asking for an affidavit, or a supplementary affidavit, for help in finding a home, in finding work, for money contributions in large or small amounts for transportation from Europe to the United States, or soliciting a friendly visit to some one who had already found asylum in this country. She welcomed, for a time, to the Domichek in Roanoke Road, frail, scholarly little Dr. Elise Dosenheimer who had been deported at an hour's notice from her home in Heidelberg to the cruel bleakness of concentration camp Gurs in southern France.

She wrote a little leaflet, widely circulated and publicized in newspaper columns, *Refugees as Assets,* affirming her belief that this latest immigration movement due to political and racial oppression could be culturally and economically advantageous to the United States. She had to fight the tradition of antiforeignism and contempt for the immigrant historically engendered by certain types of earlier immigration. "There is good reason to be convinced," she said, "that they are bringing to us more than they ask of us. May we ourselves be worthy of the refugee! And to him, may his enforced change of country with all its pain and loss be in the end blessed also!"

In her autobiographical fragment, she underestimates the part she played in urging her fellow Americans to large-scale, practical, and humane action. But in her little day-by-day diary the global tragedy looms more largely and rumbles ominously all through the pages for the year 1939:

Jan. 4–Refugee business

6–Refugee meeting, N.Y.C.

8–Aetat 72

9–Corr. mostly re refugees

Cable that Yella [Hertzka] is safe in England.

14–Worked all day till about 8 P.M. on report of Refugee Committee to National Board

28–Day almost filled with refugee corr. (29 letters and packages mailed).

Feb. 4–Huge mail–new applicants first

March 15–*Hitler enters Prague*

The end of a world

March 17–*Germany swallows Czechoslovakia*

June 24–Two quiet days trying to write more letters than I succeed in doing–tie up loose ends of refugee corr. to date

Beautiful June weather. Garden lovely.

Heart heavy over hopelessness of refugee suffering.

Walked to village by brook to register duplicate aff. for Yella

On this June day in 1939 as she walked, "heart heavy," to the village to register the duplicate affidavit for Yella Hertzka, she preferred, as her diary noted, to take the lovely path by Fuller Brook by whose margin she had sketched the "Dancing Tree." Although beauty in all its forms was to her a constant enrichment, it was not very closely connected with her spiritual experience. But she felt its value as an anodyne. She told a younger friend that as she walked she thought of a letter she had received earlier in the year from Yella Hertzka, newly escaped to England, the bubbling, gallant, irrepressible Viennese Yella Hertzka, lover of animals and gardens and growing things, who sang beside the steps of the charnel house because she had to and because she was afraid:

February 25, 1939

Dearest Emily,

Birds are singing, bulbs are growing and time will come when Emily and Yella will lay down under a big tree planted a hundred years ago, talking about the history of ages and Emily will discover everywhere a small flower showing the miracle of nature. She also will know the name of it, maybe a transplanted one from a country far away brought over simply for joy. What a joy we will have.

Love,

Yours,

Yella

CHAPTER FIFTEEN

World War II, 1939-1945

Many people who were pacifists in the first World War were not pacifists in World War II. An outstanding example was Bertrand Russell. Opinion was much more nearly unanimous concerning the necessity of engaging in the war against Hitler. The opposition in World War I came largely from left-wing liberals, from the Socialist movement and radical youth, from peace denominations, and a handful of ministers. The opposition such as it was, to the second World War, stemmed from the conservative and isolationist element, from a much larger number of clergymen and religious pacifists, and from a core of secular pacifists and humanitarian conscientious objectors who saw no reason to believe that a second world war would not unleash still greater evils than it sought to restrain. But while many earlier pacifists changed their position in World War II, very few pacifists of World War II ever regretted their choice.

Since there was so little opposition to World War II, there was much greater tolerance of dissidence on the part of the United States government, the universities, and the public. Moreover, the lesson of the futility of persecution had been learned from the experience of World War I. The slogan of the first World War, "to make the world safe for democracy," so uncritically accepted by millions of Americans was changed to the subtler, and, to pacifists, equally deceptive slogan, "This is a dirty job that must be done."

Emily Balch was one who shifted her position somewhat. The difference in the characters and causes of the war of 1914 and the war of 1939 made a crucial difference in her attitude. She regarded the first war as largely a power contest which ought to be dealt with in other ways than war. She dreaded a Prussian victory, possibly accompanied by widespread imposition of compulsory militarization in more or less subjugated countries. She also dreaded what actually happened—imitation of militarization and conscription in countries inimical to imperial Germany.

In 1939 her feeling towards the new war then starting was not the same. Hitlerism seemed to her a kind of menace which must be stopped and stopped soon: "The new Allies, which we are too apt to forget included later the new Russia, appeared to me to represent certainly, not an all virtuous body but one infinitely preferable to the cruelty and hatefulness of Hitlerism, not alone exemplified in the concentration camps and the hideous mistreatment of Jews, but in its whole character and purpose." She felt it was such a threat to every human value, that it was imperative to stop it even if there was absolutely no other way possible than by a weapon so hideous as war, which "besides the direct suffering caused, inevitably must have tragic repercussions on the personal and social character of those taking part in it, and more especially on the victorious." She regarded the war as a tragedy made inevitable in a situation created by a tangle of crimes, blunders, and apathy in which all governments and all peoples had a share of responsibility.

Her attitude is best described in her own words: "When the war broke in its full fury in 1939, and especially when, after the disaster at Pearl Harbor, the U.S.A. became a belligerent, I went through a long and painful mental struggle, and never felt that I had reached a clear and consistent conclusion. 'How can you reach inner unity,' I said, 'when in your own mind an irresistible force has collided with an immovable obstacle?' It appeared to me that after the Japanese attack any government would have found it impossible to refuse to fight, impossible that is, given the existing degree of development of mankind and its failure to have ready any effective and generally understood technique for constructive non-violent *action,* such as Gandhi had aimed at. On the one hand, I refused to buy war-bonds; on the other, I contributed, however modestly, to so-called Community War-Funds, a large part of which was devoted to wholly peaceful social aid—which typifies my mixed reaction. I thus lost the respect of my many 'absolutist' pacifist friends. That of the military-minded I neither had nor desired." [1]

In her first letter to Gertrude Baer in Europe after the outbreak of hostilities, she wrote on September 22, 1939, "It is incredible that I have not written all this time but you will know what I have been thinking and feeling. I have the sense of being numb and inert under the blow of war. To the last I hoped it might be averted." [2] And a little later, on October 11, "Of course, I long for mediation by a conference of neutrals such as we are working for but I fear such a conference could effect little actual accomplishment till the situation has matured one way or another. Yet in the period before that occurs they might be affecting the situation psychologically and getting seminal ideas into the minds of the peoples in a way that would be profoundly important.

"The facts of the situation are so largely unknown to us, that one must either be fanatical and naive, or profoundly wise to come to definite and clear cut conclusions. This is an effort to rationalize my own confusion!" [3]

For a second time the women of the W.I.L.P.F. had to face the chaos of a world at war. This time the war threatened to destroy civilization. Brutality and aggression were rampant; freedom in many places was blotted out. Aerial bombardment was to make no distinction between combatant and noncombatant. For a second time the women faced the task of seeking the road towards peace and freedom at a moment when the world knew little of either. They were twenty-four years older and twenty-four years wiser. They had lost their chief spokesman, Jane Addams, with her charismatic personality, but her spirit was alive in a very real sense. Especially, it upheld and sustained Emily Balch. As honorary international president of the League, and as an elder statesman whose function it was to present an undismayed front, to face realities however dreadful without shrinking, to encourage, exhort, and to stand firm in a world in which human values were sinking, she had sent a message in November, 1939, to the International Executive Committee:

"Ringed around by a wall of violence, we draw closer together, more than ever determined that the present method of conducting public business by wars and rumors of wars, must be superseded by reasonable methods as a basis of friendly relations of reciprocal help. Men must outgrow the fatal idea that the way to advantage one's own group is to injure others.—We shall be thinking of Jane Addams and what she gave us. I will not say I am glad she did not live to see this war. Her courage would have been equal to this, too, and we are doing what she would have done when we are able to work with cheerful courage for a good outcome of the widespread and hideous suffering that corrodes our time.[4]

Affly
E.G.B."

As the representatives of the international body met in Geneva, in December, 1939, under many difficulties, they still declared their belief in the essential dignity and sanity of mankind and reaffirmed their conviction that the method of war was impotent to bring into being either justice or the foundation of peace and freedom.

Specifically, they urged the governments of the neutral countries to seek, persistently and patiently, avenues for mediation, and more especially they appealed to President Roosevelt to call a conference of all neutral countries to put forward to the belligerent countries recommendations for ending the conflict on such terms as might secure a just and durable peace.

The women of the W.I.L.P.F. were also fortified by the knowledge that since 1919 their organization had widened and grown, so that a far-flung company of many women in the world were standing with them. Their comrades in Germany and Czechoslovakia were still carrying on under tremendous personal danger to keep up the work embodied in the slogan of Mlle. Mélin of France—"All women against all war." The time Emily had foreseen in 1920 when she had written, "We may have our martyrs," was fast approaching. As early as 1933, Lida Gustava Heymann, and her inseparable companion, Dr. Anita Augspurg, sharer of her work and spirit, had been exiled from Germany, deprived of their considerable wealth, and were living in an attic in Zürich. They refused to call it exile. As truly international personalities they considered themselves world citizens who could never be in exile. For other members—in Germany, Hungary and the conquered or occupied countries—persecution, deportation, concentration camps, death, even torture, were lying in wait.

In May, 1940, Emily was writing to Clara Ragaz in Zürich that she was suffering in face of the question of what the United States ought to do. She was firm that the United States should not join in the slaughter, great as was the temptation to jump in with men and guns: "That is no way to help this poor witch-ridden world even in such a whirlwind crisis as today. If only our people [Americans] would rise to generous and intelligent sacrifice for a peaceful, organized world as well as to relief-giving! We have not been able to conquer restrictive and panicky tendencies in the refugee field though there is much generosity and kindness at work. All this talk of domestic friends of external enemies is having dangerous repercussions here, leading to heresy-hunting and to increased prejudice against foreigners and those of other races. There is a huge work of education to do." [5]

In the United States section, where the always-present trend towards absolute pacifism* had long been causing many of those who did not accept this position to drop away, she firmly urged, in order to promote unity and effectiveness, concentration on work on which all members could agree. They could agree on wishing to keep the United States out of war, on absolute opposition to totalitarian philosophy and practice, on efforts to strengthen American democracy and purify it of race and class prejudice, on friendly constructive help to refugees and conscientious objectors, on loyalty to American traditions of maintaining civil liberties, on

---

* The terms "pacifist" and "peace movement" had undergone clarification since World War I. John Dewey wrote in the introduction to the 1945 edition of Jane Addams' *Peace and Bread,* that the term pacifist had come to assume "a more restricted meaning during recent years. It used to apply to all persons who hoped and worked for a world free from the curse of war. It has now come to stand exclusively for those who are opposed to war under any and all conditions." Then he added, "On the other hand, the significance of the phrase 'peace movement' has deepened. It used to stand for something which upon the whole was negative, for an attitude that made it easy to identify pacifism with passivism. A large measure of credit for producing this latter change must go to Jane Addams."

strengthening the rights of labor, and lastly on pursuing a systematic not a dilettante study of world organization. "All that Geneva stood for is now eclipsed, but the need for it is not less, but greater," she said.

When the United States was finally dragged into the conflict one quiet Sunday afternoon, December 7, 1941, the testing time came for the American section. Understandably the "nearer patriotism" drew many away. But as gaps occurred in the ranks, the remaining members closed them and went forward.

Emily Balch drafted a statement for the guidance of the branches throughout the country. "The problem of the position of peace societies in time of war is not, alas, a new one. Once again it faces us." Since war had been declared by constitutional means, "though it is not the choice we had hoped and worked for," the W.I.L.P.F. must reaffirm its loyalty to the country and the government, and its desire, as a minority group, not to be obstructive. "We believe in a workable democracy wherein decisions can be made and carried out, and yet where there is freedom for variant points of view." The W.I.L.P.F. had important wartime work to do—to supplant wherever possible, hatred with good will, intolerance with understanding. "One hears from time to time, horrifying expressions, unworthy of humanity, of hatred and a desire to make our opponents suffer."

Equally important was the vast amount of active education needed to free fellow Americans from "an unworthy and stupid form of isolationism." With this should go serious and continuous study for a cooperative world organization, political and economic. Wartime dangers of an exaggerated officialism and of overzealous interference with individuals were to be objects of vigilance. The Latin-American program should not be overlooked.[6]

The needs of refugees as victims of war and tyranny were to have an immediate attention in spite of the fact that the primary duty of the W.I.L.P.F. was not to furnish relief, but to fight the underlying causes of which these tragedies were but the symptoms. From the very beginning the W.I.L.P.F. had warned women not to drain off energy and funds from their essential work as an internationally organized body, from what Emily Balch called the "so-bitterly needed work for peace and freedom,"[7] to the work of relief and personal assistance which in all ages has made such an irresistible appeal to women. The members had often been obliged to struggle against the temptation to become absorbed in philanthropic work or in purely national problems shared by other national peace and reform organizations. What gave the W.I.L.P.F. its unique character was that its work lay within a special field of universal concern adhering to a well-rounded and self-consistent body of doctrine.

On January 8, 1942, Emily Balch reached her seventy-fifth birthday. The work to which she had given the best substance of her life, the establishment of better relations between human beings, and of helping to build at Geneva and elsewhere,, year by year, stone by stone, an international organization of friendly cooperating peoples which might make future wars impossible, seemed a failure or a mere dream. The Women's League, however, through which she had mainly chosen to work, and which was as close to her heart as it had been to Jane Addams', was on this war birthday very much alive. As she expressed it in a characteristic simile, "In countries overwhelmed by Nazism, Fascism and war, the League is invisible as are the flowers in winter which will yet fill the fields with color when spring returns."

In May, 1942, the United States section gave a public luncheon in Philadelphia in Emily Balch's honor. After the usual greetings, by cable and letter, from far and near, and the speeches, not so usual, centering, as she had requested, not on herself but on her world-wide interests, there was an expectant hush as Emily Balch, a frail figure, rose to speak. She called what she had to say "Towards a Planetary Civilization," and in a short speech touched on nearly all the strains of her social philosophy.

"In looking back over the years, I have not the feeling that our efforts have been unreasonable," she began. "On the contrary, I have the impression that although the world was not ready to realize them, the trend of development runs obviously and unmistakably toward the end that we have sought—a planetary civilization. Our planetary barbarism, is, I have faith to believe, the forerunner of this.

She then spoke briefly of her personal history and of the definite, conscious purpose which from college days had integrated her life and made it one of continuous and increasing interest.

346 IMPROPER BOSTONIAN: EMILY GREENE BALCH

"When war came in 1914 I felt this at first mainly as a senseless interruption of social-economic progress. I felt that war must be got rid of so that the threat of war might not interrupt and distort the course of this progress. Only gradually I came to understand at least partly how deeply war is intertwined with our whole economic and social system, our scale of values, our ideas of what is right and of supreme importance.

"I see no chance of social progress apart from fundamental changes on both the economic and the political side, replacing national anarchy by organized cooperation of all peoples to further their common interest, and replacing economic anarchy, based on the search for personal profit, by a great development of the cooperative spirit. Peace is too small a word for all this, too negative in its connotations.

"I have a very considerable distrust of government as such, and see no reason to be sure that a world government would be run by men very different in capacity and moral quality from those who govern national states.

"My thoughts run rather to international administration of those matters which are of common interest—to the setting up of international 'authorities' to take charge of interests which concern all peoples. They must act as trustees, in fact. The psychology of a trustee is very different from that of a politician. The record of the trustees is very different from that of the man who is 'not in business for his health.' The trustees of our great hospitals, universities, public service foundations, and so forth, are much nearer to what we need than prime ministers or diplomats or bankers.

"If we are to have a world government I hope that it will not crystallize too early. It may be that it ought to evolve as something very different from the national governments that we know. They are a special historical development with their executive, legislature, powers of taxation, and armed forces.

"My interest tends to concentrate on two fields, which by their very nature transcend national frontiers—the sea and the air. For the first, I dream of an international authority in control of all the seas and great international waterways, including Panama and Suez. No ship should be able to clear from or enter a harbor unless in possession of papers meeting the requirements of this international authority. The policing and safeguarding of the seas would be its province. The existence of such a body would leave little need for an international navy to exercise control.

"As to the air, I dream of an International Air Authority. This should own through appropriate agencies, all aircraft that regularly fly across frontiers; should license and supervise all air pilots, control all airdromes and flight conveniences, weather reports, signals, and so forth. It should control, too, all manufacture of aircraft.

"I wish you would all re-read Kipling's story NIGHT MAIL, with its picture of a personnel disciplined and trained for devoted professional service.

"In a world with no national armies, navies or air forces and with such organized international services as the two proposed, it seems to me that the need for international armed forces would be reduced to a minimum and that these would be hardly more military in purpose and spirit than a London police-man.

"Many of you will live to see developments that I shall not live to see, but my faith is that there will be vast development of international unity and this does not depend upon how fast it comes or in what precise shape. But—and this 'but' is of fundamental importance—international unity is not in itself a solution. *Unless this international unity has a moral quality, unless it accepts the discipline of moral standards and possesses the quality of humanity, it will not be the unity we are interested in.* If it is autocratic and not cooperative in tone, it may be indeed a Frankenstein.

"It is also essential, as I believe, that it should not be rigid, uniform and based on one model, but a natural and many sided fact developing by its own laws.

"It will be imperfect of course. But instead of being largely concerned with so-called political issues and notably with questions of power and prestige its interest will center on human beings in their every day living, with their sufferings and their aspirations and it will be permeated by a warm personal desire to serve the common good." [8]

For a few seconds there was no applause. But there was an unmistakable tightening of throats as though the audience felt this might be seventy-five year old Emily Balch's intellectual last will and testament. Sensing the emotion, she added drily but with a

---

* Italics mine.

gleam in her eye: "But this is not my swan-song. I intend to live quite a while longer. My grandfather used to say, 'An old woman is as tough as a boiled owl.'"

In this birthday speech she made no mention of what was then her anomalous position as a pacifist. A great many of the women in her Philadelphia audience, notably the Quakers, did not take her stand. "I suppose," she often said ruefully at this time, "I should resign from the W.I.L. but I haven't the least intention of doing so." Her ideas on absolutism and relativism in ethics affected her attitude. What is wrong in one context may be right in another. Just as there is no place which is west, but there is always the westward direction, so the "obligation to do right as far as is in our power" was for Emily Balch an absolute obligation with no exceptions. The rejection of physical violence as always evil, the Tolstoian position, she had felt, even as far back as World War I, was not possible to maintain. What seemed to her possible to affirm was the determination to act always in the spirit of good will, in the strongest sense of the word, in the sense of positively and with all one's power willing good.

This position left her without a valid answer to such a complicated question as to what stand she should take in the war against Hitler. She accepted the difficulties involved in this confusion. When questioned after the war as to the exact extent and nature of her pacifism, she replied "The best statement I can make is that embodied in J. H. Randall's too kind biography as to myself."*

He suggests in this fashion the dialectic of her position:

"Emily Balch's reluctant approval of the American war effort would thus appear as the triumph of her realistic intellect over her moral conscience. Or was it rather something else—the inability of even her fine-tempered and fertile mind to see how to implement that deeper and more enduring deliverance of experience, reflection and moral insight that we call 'conscience'? Let him who would give a confident answer search his own heart as deeply as Emily Balch has searched hers. Such profound moral questions men must decide in their own solitariness, face to face with themselves and their God. It is not given to one mortal to pass ultimate

---

* John H. Randall, Jr., booklet on *Emily Greene Balch of New England, Citizen of the World*, 1946, 12 pp.

judgment upon another. Miss Balch herself candidly and disarmingly admits, 'I realize that my position is neither very definite nor very consistent.' How many of us have the sincerity to be as frank?

"Emily Greene Balch remained, and remains, a realistic worker for peace, poles removed from the opportunist who can always find good reason to judge this particular war to be righteous."

Emily agreed in equating this appraisal with the dilemma of the Savoyards:

> Is it weakness of intellect, birdie? I cried,
> Or a rather tough worm in your little inside?

A month after the public luncheon, Emily Balch, heavily oppressed by the daily agony of the war and her continuing unresolved inner struggles, wrote to Clara Ragaz in Switzerland, apparently in great weariness:

"About my attitude toward the war, it is chiefly that on the political plane a state may have to choose between alternative evil possibilities—making war or acquiescing in the progress of the conqueror toward extinguishing liberty everywhere and setting up the policies exemplified in the German treatment of the Jews and in the Gestapo, etc. After Pearl Harbor, I think the U.S.A. had no other practicable course open to her than that she has chosen, and I can only hope that her joining the U.N. may effectively hasten victory. * I am grateful to the C.O.'s; I think they bear useful witness to the supremacy of conscience and the hideous wrong of war. But I am glad there are not enough of them, in the peace-loving countries only, to impede the war. I do not claim that I am consistent. I do not know how to be in the face of irresistible motives pulling in opposite directions. I have no ill will to any one. War seems to me as bad as it has always seemed. Only something even worse seems to me to help hand over helpless victims and to fasten a curse on mankind. . . . I live largely in thoughts of the world after the war for which preparation must begin now. I am trying to work on a book 'After the War.'" [9]

Emily Balch could not have remained uninfluenced in her attitude by some of the European leaders of the W.I.L.P.F. Among the outstanding figures were, besides the Swiss Madame Ragaz, the Germans, Lida Gustava Heymann, honorary international vice-

---

* At that time the U.N. referred to the United Nations Forces.

president, Dr. Anita Augspurg, Gertrude Baer, an early exile; the British K. E. Innes, Barbara Duncan-Harris, and Edith Pye, a Quaker; Yella Hertzka of Austria; fiery Gabrielle Duchêne of France, "chivalrous champion of the under-privileged," as Emily called her; Marie Lous-Mohr of Norway, who was to be imprisoned for two and a half years by the Nazis in Grini Concentration Camp; Eugenie Meller of Hungary who was to be liquidated; and the tragically beautiful Lola Hanouskova of Prague, torn between pacifism, patriotism, and the violently contending factions of her native land.

Many of these, though by no means all, shared the viewpoint of Lida Gustava Heymann, the forthright leader of the German section, the first vice-president of the League under the presidency of Jane Addams. She had never missed attending any of the international congresses, the meetings of the international executive, or the national gatherings of the German section. Wrung by deep anguish, and burning with the conviction that only those people rightly understood "facts" who had a personal experience of them, "as we pacifist women of Europe have had," Lida Heymann voiced a fervent appeal to American women hoping that insight might not come to them too late. It could not have been easy for her to come to the conclusion that it was no longer possible to overcome the violent methods of Fascism and Nazism by pacifist means. When pacifist measures were still possible and the women of the W.I.L.P.F. were demanding their consistent application, the democratic governments had failed, she declared, either because they misunderstood pacifism or neutrality, or for selfish political reasons.

"Today that time has passed and cannot return," she wrote. "A small barking dog cannot stop a dashing train. . . . Fascism and national socialism *today* can be destroyed only through means which are capable of impressing the brutal men of fascism and national socialism. Such means are the means of brute force. From repeated experiences we women pacifists in Europe have come to recognize this . . . without even for a moment, becoming untrue to our pacifist convictions," [10] she concluded with human logic.

Her closest friend, Dr. Anita Augspurg, shared her views; and the British Kathleen Innes, one of the joint chairmen, added that her judgment was the same, although she stated that some in the

British section would not agree.* Gabrielle Duchêne, Clara Ragaz, and Gertrud Baer also concurred in this judgment.

On the other hand Emily Balch was a Quaker and a disciple of Charles Fletcher Dole, a pacifist. Moreover, a good part of the membership and some of the most respected leaders in the United States section of the W.I.L.P.F. happened to be thorough-going pacifists: Dorothy Medders Robinson, who was president all during the war years; Emily Cooper Johnson; Dorothy Detzer; Mildred Scott Olmsted; Elsie Elfenbein; Katherine Arnett; Bertha McNeill; Grace Rhoads; and Helen Marston Beardsley of California, a former student of Emily Balch at Wellesley. Above all in affection and moral persuasiveness stood the supremely lovely personality of the Quaker, Hannah Clothier Hull, of Swarthmore, Pennsylvania, for whom pacifism was not only a philosophy but a way of life. She had been for many years president of the United States section and was one of the most influential Quakers in the country. She left a deep impression on all who met her, not only by her selfless devotion to the cause of peace and internationalism, but by her courteous deference to the personality and viewpoints of others, especially when she was presiding. She had an appealing manner of opening every meeting, and prefixing every speech or remark in discussion, with the gently-spoken word, "Friends." Quaker fashion, she never "demanded." Instead she "urged," "desired," "persuaded." Her ingratiating feminine softness was coupled with the strength of purpose of a St. Theresa.

Emily Balch was often in Hannah Hull's beautiful Swarthmore home, shaded by its three-hundred year old Charter Oak.** Here with her professor-husband, William I. Hull, Hannah Hull made a center and meeting place for peace-minded people from all over the world.

Hannah Hull was one of the finest examplars of the thinking

---

* Lida Gustava Heymann and Kathleen Innes had sincerely convinced themselves that advocating the overthrow of Hitler by force was not inconsistent with their personal pacifism. The apparent contradiction in this position lies in the definition of terms. They did not claim to be what the French members called integral pacifists, or what the Americans called simply pacifists, meaning absolute pacifists. In spite of these differences, there was never any question of their continued working together, and on most practical issues they were able to cooperate.
** An oak old enough to have been standing when William Penn got his charter of Pennsylvania (1682) or made his treaty with the Indians (1683).

of the Society of Friends, which, from its origin in the seventeenth century to the present, has continually held that war and Christianity are incompatible; therefore as Christians, its members cannot under any circumstances support or prepare for war, offensive or defensive. Probably the best statement of the position in regard to war enjoined though not enforced upon Quakers today is the early declaration in 1660 by George Fox and others presented to King Charles II of England. This statement makes clear that members of the Society of Friends must guard against the temptation of engaging in holy wars or righteous crusades as well as in wars of aggression:

> We utterly deny all outward wars and strife, and fightings with outward weapons, for any end, or under any pretence whatever; this is our testimony to the whole world. The Spirit of Christ by which we are guided is *not changeable, so as once to command us from a thing of evil, and again to move us unto it;* and we certainly know, and testify to the world that the Spirit of Christ, which leads us unto all truth, will never move us to fight and war against any man with outward weapons, *neither for the Kingdom of Christ, nor for the kingdoms of this world.** . . . Therefore we can not learn war any more.

All Quakers, however, "exhorted" their members, as did the W.I.L.P.F. and the Fellowship of Reconciliation, and the War Resisters' League, to hold "in respect and sympathetic understanding" all those who in good conscience felt that war preparations and war were necessary or inevitable, to feel with them the sacrifices they might be called upon to make, and to share in their suffering and grief.

On the whole the stronger force contending in the mind of Emily Balch was the conviction and the resulting philosophy of the Quakers, and of that even greater company of men and women—Christians, Jews, agnostics, humanitarians and many others—in Asia as in the West, who through the centuries have found themselves unable to take the lives of their fellowmen either to forward their own advantage, or the advantage of others, or at the command of any external authority. Though they express it in differing vocabularies, they exemplify a way of life based on an acceptance of the idea of the brotherhood of man, on an ethic

---

* Italics mine.

of righteousness, on active, reconciling love or constructive good will, sometimes on the idea of realistically overcoming evil with good. When we acclaim the heroism of the soldier who goes forth to die, they remember that he also goes forth to kill. Their reverence for individual human beings even of "enemy" nations makes it impossible for them to do to others the things that war involves. It does make possible, or releases, a powerful striving for reconciliation instead of revenge and retaliation; a seeking for workable alternatives not yet explored. Instead of relying upon the traditional and primitive instrument of war, they conceive their role as that of precursors, seekers, innovators. They wish to raise human conflicts from the level of combat to the level of a problem. There is neither victory nor defeat to a problem. There is, as the Quakers say, a solution.

All during World Wars I and II, Emily Balch was able to identify herself with such moral conscientious objectors and to support them by pen and action. She could understand their desire to stand up uncompromisingly against war here and now, not when the world should be ready for it,* and their hope that in doing so, their action in bearing the pacifist witness would bring that time a little nearer. "None save those interested in the realization of an idea are in a position to bring it about," [11] said Jane Addams. To be willing to take an absolutist position of this kind needs two qualities rarely combined—human reason added to human charity. When charity—charitableness, universal love, disinterested benevolence—"becomes a dominant trait of the soul, it generates a piety toward being in general and the capacity to 'lie down in peace.'" [12]

In the light of these awarenesses, therefore, pacifists form a

---

* Jane Addams, in an address in Chicago, July 24, 1915, illuminated this: "I am reminded of an old story Tolstoi told me years ago. In Russia there is a sect of Doukhobors, a religious sect who do not believe in going to war. When the young men become of military age and refuse to serve, they are arrested, punished, sometimes exiled or executed. One of the young men was brought before a humane judge who felt sorry for him. The judge told him that he was very foolish to put himself up against a powerful government. The young man gave the judge a homily upon the teachings of Jesus in regard to non-resistance, and the judge, being Orthodox, said: 'Of course, we all believe in that but the time has not come to put it into practice.' The young man answered, 'The time may not have come for you, Your Honor, but the time has come for me.'"

judgment that the "clumsy, uncertain and cruel tools of violence,"* in Emily Balch's words, are not proper instruments for man to use in gaining his ends.

Although it is not generally understood by the public, the act of war refusal entails further positions and consequences for the pacifist, some of which Emily endured, and others expounded and exemplified. The pacifist must be willing to pay the penalty for his convictions, in persecution, obloquy, imprisonment, and even death. When loyalty to God and loyalty to the state conflict, he chooses, like Antigone, to obey the higher laws.

Secondly, the pacifist looks upon his refusal to obey the state as one of the greatest services he can render to the state** and to democracy. While he is opposed to war and conscription, he is willing and anxious to serve the state in its more constructive processes.

Thirdly, it is incumbent upon pacifists to be witnesses, not to a narrow and negative faith, but to positive active service in building a more rational world society. They have long advocated a spirit and program of international and interracial cooperation in political, economic, and other fields, which had it been followed might have prevented much of the strife that has torn the world in the twentieth century.

Nor is the pacifist unwilling to face the intellectual and moral dilemmas and admit the evils which his position entails, just as the supporters of "righteous" war are aware of the hideous dilemmas of their choice. On the contrary, these tragic consequences spur the pacifist to greater efforts to create a more rational society. Emily Balch's letters to Clara Ragaz and many other statements make that clear. Emily Parker Simon, an American Quaker and a friend of Emily Balch, was to speak of this apparent necessity of choice between evils, at the W.I.L.P.F. Congress of Luxembourg in 1946. She had lived and worked with the Spanish people during their tragic struggle in the 1930's when it had seemed to them as

---

* "Fundamental to all else is the need that men should grow to understand and practice patience and tolerance, and come to substitute for the clumsy, uncertain and cruel tools of violence, the methods of reason and cooperation."—Emily Greene Balch, 1933.
** See Chapter 11, Emily Balch's letter to Bishop Cooke, August, 1917, *re* conscientious objectors.

if they had been deserted by all the decent peoples in the world. "Here, if ever," said Emily Simon, "was a real test for the pacifist. Here I discovered that pacifism is so much more than the mere absence of actual fighting, or neutrality, or an attempt to live above the struggle. . . . Working with those hungry homeless children, we could see the violence accomplished by the lies and hypocrisy of a policy called 'non-intervention.' The so-called American neutrality also played its part with violence. We must understand these things. On the other hand, to support the plea to lift the arms embargo would only have increased and extended the violence.

"No, our job as pacifists is not to deny the evil, nor to try to live above it. We must discover and employ those methods, those attitudes, that program which will not deny but which will guarantee our goal of peace and freedom. These new attitudes, methods, programs must be applied not only to our personal way of life but to the political, social, economic and international fields.

"There are many of us who do believe that we must be equally concerned not only with the great ends but also with the means—not only what, but how. In fact, the methods which we use will in the end determine how near or how far we get toward our goal. We can never admit that the choice must be the lesser of two evils. To our limited vision and understanding, it may seem that this is our only choice, but all through history there have been those people who have found a creative third alternative which has led them and all who would follow them into a completely new and freer atmosphere."

To the nonpacifist, refusal to employ military force results in the immediate triumph of "the greater evil." To the pacifist, the resort to socially-sanctioned murder, the killing of the many innocent as well as of the few guilty, is an ultimate wrong that violates the moral conscience and no merely pragmatic arguments in favor of "the lesser evil" can be allowed to prevail.

But the crux of the pacifist case is that the choice of the nonpacifist does not really bring only the "lesser" evil; it perpetuates the "greater" as well. For it leaves both fighter and his opponent unchanged. When the next crisis arises, it will force the same tragic decision. Military force will remain the only method of dealing with evils. Hitler vanquished leaves Communism rampant;

Russia overcome leaves China to fight. China leashed leaves—the
Martians? The "lesser evil" may have been laid low—for a decade
or two. With fighting the only resort, the greater evil will remain,
world without end—or with end. "For what does war but endless
war still breed," on a more diabolical scale? Moral absolutism and
pragmatic intelligence as to war are in complete agreement, thinks
the pacifist.

Strengthened and fortified by her associations and friendships
in America with leading spokesmen of this faith and philosophy—
Quakers and pacifists like Hannah Clothier Hull, Rufus Jones,
Clarence Pickett, Frederick J. Libby; A. J. Muste and Nevin Sayre
of the Fellowship of Reconciliation; Jessie Wallace Hughan, Tracy
Mygatt and Frances Witherspoon of the War Resisters' League—
Emily Balch's position was really not too far removed from theirs.
If she found in the Women's International League an abiding and
congenial home, it was because the League stood, as she conceived
it, not so much for pacifism, absolute or otherwise, as for liberation
from all that divides and separates men, for reaching out to one
another, for building up together.

Emily Balch strongly felt her special responsibility to support
lonely causes or those often neglected by people who had succumbed to the insidious blunting process of war or were engaged
in the grim but alluring process of all-out global fighting. Two
causes at this time called into play the pacifists' sensitivity to the
pain and need of the world and their passionate desire to help—
the Japanese-American evacuation and the need to rescue the
Jewish and other refugees from Nazism.

In the bleak spring of 1942 an event occurred which caused
deep humiliation and profound concern to many Americans, especially to Emily Balch and her colleagues in the W.I.L.P.F., the
forced evacuation without accusation and without trial of more
than 100,000 Japanese-Americans from the Pacific coastal area to
detention camps or barracks in the interior. Old men and women,
the sick and the feeble, farmers, thriving business and professional
men, babies and young children were forced to leave their homes
and most of their possessions. Nearly 2,000 students in universities
and colleges had to leave their studies and live behind barbed

wire in what were little better than concentration camps. Two
thirds of these people were American citizens. One third were
aliens forbidden by our law to become citizens. Most of them were
loyal champions of democratic institutions.

This tragic miscarriage of justice with its denial of every value
in our legal tradition, and its threat to society and to all men, fell
with a heavy blow on the W.I.L.P.F., sensitive to its political
implications throughout Asia and Africa, as well as to its personal,
human tragedies. Emily Balch collaborated with a member of
the W.I.L.P.F. who had a close knowledge of Japan, Gladys
Walser, and with Helen Beardsley of California and Mary Far-
quarson, working for the eventual relocation of all the evacuated
Japanese into friendly communities, for establishing hostels for
their reception, urging compensation for their financial losses, and
ministering to individual needs and cases. From Wellesley Emily
even mailed out jigsaw puzzles and kindergarten materials for the
use of children in the camps.

The end of the year 1942, however, was to reveal still blacker
happenings. Until December 17, 1942, little of what was happening to the Jews in Europe reached the general public in the United
States. On that day the first international action was taken in a
"United Nations" declaration denouncing Hitler's often-repeated
intention to annihilate the Jewish people of Europe. President
Roosevelt for the Americans and Foreign Secretary Anthony Eden
for the British issued a joint statement which gave recognition to
the unique martyrdom endured by the Jews of Europe. The practical measures promised were for punishment and retribution, not
for rescue and immediate aid. The advocates of immediate action
in America were recruited chiefly from the Jewish groups. For
two years our American statesmen made no public mention of
the mounting slaughters in Europe. It was left for a distinguished
delegation of American Jews, in December, 1942, to call the attention of the President of the United States and Secretary Cordell
Hull to the accounts of the massacres in Poland and other places.
Most of the efforts to mitigate Jewish suffering abroad and to urge
acceptance of a substantial number of Hitler's victims upon our
shores were made by Jews themselves. The faith of the great
American Jewish community in the justice, the humanity, and the

essential Christianity of their fellow Americans was deeply wounded.*

A month before these public revelations, on November 27, 1942, out of "boundless horror, sympathy and grief," Emily Balch took it upon herself to write a letter to Rabbi Stephen S. Wise, President of the World Jewish Congress, and through him to all Jewry. It was acclaimed by the Jews as "a voice of true Americanism."

November 27, 1942

Dear Rabbi Wise:

As honorary international President of the Women's International League for Peace and Freedom I am taking it upon myself, unauthorized, to write to you, and through you to all Jews, on behalf of the members of our international family who in every country, from New Zealand to Finland, are suffering from the feelings that I am so inadequately trying to express.

Our boundless horror, sympathy and grief cannot be put into words, as we think of those who are being murdered in masses and of those who while in personal safety are tortured by anxiety and horror over the fate of those near and dear to them.

I want to express also our admiration for the heroic constancy of Jewish endurance and the noble freedom from the futility of hatred and thoughts of revenge, of which Jews have given such noble examples.

We are borne down by the sense of the powerlessness not only of individuals but of the most powerful governments to stop these unexampled cruelties. But most of all those of us who are not Jews are oppressed by a sense of our own responsibility, for we too are guilty. We are all answerable in part for the development of a state of things where the moral insanity of Hitler Germany was possible. And for a state of things where the civilized world can find no better way out than competition in reciprocal slaughter and destruction. We were not ready in time with any other method than this slow and cruel one.

When matters had reached a point where prevention of these wrongs was no longer possible we might still have done far more to alleviate them than we have done, both in the way of welcoming refugees to this country on an adequate scale and by adequate con-

_____
* As a Jewish newspaper dealer in New York City expressed it, with despair in his voice: " The world is so cold and hard; it does not care at all. Christians do not care for us Jews."

tribution to relief. We have been far too un-understanding, cold-hearted and self-regarding.

Neither have we kept ourselves clean of the contagion of the destructive feeling of race prejudice. *Nostra culpa, nostra maxima culpa.*

Even in this dark hour we can believe—or if we cannot believe we can hope—that in spite of everything we are on the way to liberation from race prejudice and that the day is coming when such cruelties. as those now going on in Poland and elsewhere may be unthinkable. And we can not merely hope, we can work actively in many ways to bring that day nearer.

Yours in deepest fellow-feeling
Emily G. Balch[13]

No one can read this letter, in all its Lincoln-like simplicity, without being moved by it, or convinced of Emily Balch's deep personal involvement in the universal anguish of the time. Her W.I.L.P.F. comrades in Europe were giving outstanding proof of their devotion to the principles of peace and freedom, sometimes paying the supreme penalty for their adherence. She was living, in a manner of speaking, on the periphery, physical and spiritual, of events in Europe. She was comparatively safe and sheltered, undergoing no physical hardship or family losses, though in 1944 her brother's son, Robert Balch, was to lose his life in the war.

"How difficult it is," says E. M. Forster in writing about the sensitivities of Goldsworthy Lowes Dickinson to the war of 1914–1918, "to write about the sufferings of any one person under the war! One of the evil things about war is that it provokes a sort of competition in grief. . . . There are two sorts of grief. There is a resentful querulous grief which throws the sufferer in on himself and makes him petty and tedious. There is a grief which expands towards the universal and generates action." [14]

Her years of self-discipline led New England Emily Balch to the latter way. In her quietness of spirit, her calm daily pursuit of the things that must and could be done, her American friends and colleagues in the W.I.L.P.F. found a spring of healing when they turned to her. One younger member and friend to whom the anguish of her fellow humans across the sea had become almost unbearable, had written to Emily Balch enclosing a copy in German of Bertolt Brecht's poem "To Posterity." Emily Balch's letter of reply repeated in another form what she had said many years before: "One must not multiply pain by being too good a *conductor* of it."

"Many thanks for your letter with the original of the Brecht poem which I feel very deeply. So it is; I eat and drink and sleep and dream only occasionally of the horrors of our contemporary life.

"Chesterton says somewhere that antiquity taught the golden mean between extremes but that Christianity teaches to hold, to experience at the same time, opposites in their full intensity, not refusing either, not fusing them but somehow having both. He makes the † with its junction of vertical and horizontal a symbol of this. What I have in mind is how to have at once serenity, quiet, 'accepting the universe'—the ache of compassion, intensest reaction against cruelty, injustice and stupidity, awareness of evil and contact with it, not a tepid point midway between apathy and hate. I do not know how much of my daily comfort is due to old age—the cooling off period of life—how much to personal callousness, and the curious anesthesia of daily activities and interests, and how much to something I am more responsible for.

"I am sure that we ought not to waste our precious store of nervous force (so much needed by our family as well as ourselves) by needless and to-no-purpose brooding on suffering and wrong, that the happiest issue is to sublimate *by doing something to help*, as you *are* doing.

"Also I find it right and helpful to create parks in our crowded and over populated minds—times or occasions in which we seek and find escape. This kind of escape I am sure is *right*, compatible with unflinching realistic knowledge of all that is disturbing.

"Do you remember Robert Louis Stevenson's story of a hard fighting old Huguenot dying in murderous religious warring, saying, 'My mind is like a garden, full of fountains and shelters'? (All this from memory, I think the incident is in *Travels with a Donkey*.)

"So I hope you will find and use enough shelters and fountains to give you what you need. Excuse all this divagating. I am talking to myself too.

Aff'ly,
E.G.Balch" [15]

There was one group of American members of the W.I.L.P.F. who had reason for a deeper and more articulate consciousness of kinship with their European colleagues and who like them, paid a price for their loyalty to the principles and practice of the W.I.L.P.F.—the Jewish members who did not leave the League when the war began—outstanding women like Stella Moos, Elsie Elfenbein, Sarah Lifton, Meta Riseman, later president of the United States section, and Jane Evans.* In particular there was one small band of women led by Ella White, belonging to a branch in Rockaway, New York, consisting largely of Jewish members. Their Christian neighbors in the small community ignored them disdainfully; to their Jewish friends they were an enigma and anathema. Whatever solace, comfort, and pride the other mothers of fighting sons had, was denied to them. In most cases they did not have the cooperation of their husbands, but heart-breaking arguments instead. There was no understanding of why they did not want to participate in war bond drives to supply their fighting sons with needed weapons. This was their costly contribution to the greatness of the cause of peace and freedom. Through such women, Emily Balch—who knew many of them personally, loved them and admired them—constantly renewed her faith.

In January, 1943, President Roosevelt after consultation with Winston Churchill, announced to the world during the Casablanca Conference that the objective of the war was to obtain the unconditional surrender of Germany, Italy, and Japan. At once Emily Balch wrote to Dorothy Detzer in Washington:

"The news of the Casablanca decisions fill me with profound dismay, both for decisions made and decisions that were not made. A decision for unconditional surrender seems to me all wrong, both as a matter of principle and strategically. It presents Hitler and the other dictators with the support of those whose allegiance might be wavering now, or if not yet, later. It tends to make the war longer and bitterer and to make even more complete and

---

* Jane Evans also served as executive director of the National Peace Conference, organized in 1933 to coordinate the program and policies of many American agencies of varied points of view working toward international order and peace. She also, together with Dr. Abraham Cronbach and Rabbi Isidor Hoffman, helped found the Jewish Peace Fellowship in 1941.

irremedial the destruction of physical and human values in all occupied territories, especially throughout Europe—and of the Jews. It would have been so easy to say instead that we demanded surrender *on our terms.* This would have been absolute enough, Heaven knows, but it would have left the peoples that are fighting eager to know our terms and it would have left our side free to offer liberal, constructive and tempting terms." [16]

At that time the extreme opponents of unconditional surrender were using the phrase "negotiated peace" which was greatly in disrepute among many Americans and among influential groups like the Commission to Study the Organization of Peace, led by James T. Shotwell, and the Women's Committee for Victory and a Lasting Peace, initiated by Mrs. Carrie Chapman Catt. The term smacked of appeasement. Emily Balch hoped the W.I.L.P.F. National Board would not take hasty or irrevocable positions on a "negotiated peace." It was not a moment to be wasting the strength of the organization. Again, in accordance with her philosophy of pluralism, she hoped for a strong, wide-based liberal movement forming throughout the country, embracing many shades of opinion, in which the peace people would form a component, cooperative, but distinct part or wing. She did not want the W.I.L.P.F. to proclaim prematurely a position which would prevent collaboration with those who followed different paths to the same goal.

"If we make ourselves an obvious and serious liability," she wrote to Dorothy Detzer and the Board, "to any who stand by our side, we may sacrifice the thing we are working to achieve for the sake of relieving our feelings. So much depends on how a thing is worded. We want to follow our proper techniques, not to defy, alienate or provoke or create misunderstanding in so doing, but to win, persuade and draw to us those who ought to be with us. In all this, I am far from meaning that I want to see us camouflage our position, which is so contrary to the isolationism of which we are accused.

"Love and best wishes in these dark times,

E.G.B." [17]

The W.I.L.P.F. was the congenial instrument through which Emily Balch chose to serve. But, as the above letter shows, in the planning for the kind of peace she wanted, and for the organization of the postwar world, she worked with other peace groups, some of them strongly supporting the war, and with many agencies, organized and unorganized, to all of whom she always gave complete and generous recognition. In the Peaceable Kingdom in which she lived her daily life, there was always a welcome for the lion as well as for the lamb. Though her ways were closest to those of the Christian pacifist,* she never withheld grateful tribute to the Christian warrior, who might be vouchsafed bits of truth and realities of a different order—yet equally needed in the building of a New Jerusalem.

Though she opposed both unconditional surrender and a negotiated peace, she did want President Roosevelt to use all his great influence to hasten the end of the fighting through the offer by the United Nations Forces of peace terms to all belligerents. She united with others, in and outside the W.I.L.P.F., in urging the Allies to state the terms on which they were willing to make peace. On February 12, 1944, the United States section of the League appealed to the President as Commander-in-Chief to postpone the anticipated invasion which would require an enormous sacrifice of young lives—until every possible appeal to the German people over the heads of their Nazi government had been tried and exhausted. The League submitted to the President, and on March 10, 1944, to the State Department, a series of concrete and specific proposals which Emily Balch had been instrumental in drafting. They were meant to be suggestive only, to aim to undo as far as possible some of the wrongs committed in connection with the war, to open the way to cooperation, to avoid vindictiveness and to be offered in the spirit of the Atlantic Charter. They provided for the evacuation of all territory conquered by Axis troops or any belligerent, and of all territory occupied against the will of its inhabitants; the demobilization of all national armed forces; the immediate lifting of all blockades; the liberation of all prisoners of war, and of all persons deprived of their liberty for

---

* Emily Balch would not herself have used the term "Christian pacifist" in describing herself as she did not like exclusiveness of terminology. Her motivation, like Jane Addams', was moral and spiritual rather than religious. In World War I, in her letter to President Pendleton of Wellesley, she had used the term, "the way of Jesus" to present a legal view of her case to the trustees.

political reasons, especially of all persons held in concentration camps and all internees. She stipulated freedom for all refugees and persons who had been removed from their country to return to live and work in their own homes with full legal and political rights. This of course included cessation of all persecution and in particular assurance to Jews of complete legal and political equality. The conditions further included restoration of the rights of labor, and return as far as physically possible, of all loot, including industrial equipment and works of art. Remembering vividly the food blockade of 1919, she wished to include systematic international action to provide needed food and prevent disease. This work was to be carried out on strictly a humanitarian basis, not as a political weapon. And, characteristically, she added that in areas where normal government was temporarily suspended, an administration by international authority should be organized through civilian and neutral agents to prevent disorder and carry on public services.

In 1944, the war not yet over, the Dumbarton Oaks Conference drafted a tentative United Nations Charter for the San Francisco Conference. Though many members of the W.I.L.P.F. in warbound countries could not be reached for political discussion, the consensus of opinion again was to support and help develop a world structure and to put emphasis on the "prevention of aggression and war through active constructive world cooperation." "Once more, as at Zürich," wrote Emily Balch, "the W.I.L.P.F. will be making up its mind as to whether to prefer half a loaf or the risk of no bread, at any rate for an indefinite time. The new body will not be what its paper definition might seem to describe, but what its members actually make of it. The practice of cooperation will be what will give the United Nations organization its chaacter. . . . A plan for international organization if it is to be carried out and not merely put into print must be shaped and agreed on in the press of political realities and not in a vacuum. It is not Utopia that is being planned but the actual world of Europe and Russia and the Americas, and the rest of the countries, with all their conflicting interests and ideas. It is not necessarily even what its authors want but what seems to them the best that there is a chance of getting." [18]

She had often emphasized that the trouble with the League of

Nations was not the faults in the Covenant which the Women's Zürich Congress had analyzed and sharply criticized. The trouble was in the mentalities, the temper, and purposes of the imperialists and trade rivals that sent their representatives to Geneva. So the success of the proposed organization would depend much less on the terms of any covenant or constitution than on how the governments chose to behave. "We have tried the other experiment of an anarchy of armed sovereign states till we have nearly ruined mankind with their slaughter and destruction. The proposal before us is a relatively modest one and therefore it may be that it will be realized." [19]

To Emily Balch and the W.I.L.P.F. members it was a profound regret to see armed forces provided for the use of the new international organization. But they realized that the course of historical development was such that it was inevitable. The choice seemed to lie between force in the hands of the representatives of the peoples and force in the hands of irresponsible and competing nations.

"So long as we can succeed in the elementary task of keeping the peoples from trying to kill one another off, so long will it be possible to develop our common undertakings till we are all so inextricably interwoven that rupture is almost unthinkable. There are long years yet ahead and fresh generations may grow up undistorted by preparations for fighting and therefore freer gradually to develop a juster, more reasonable and kinder world than we have known." [20]

In April, 1945, from Wellesley, Emily Balch, with Gertrude Baer and Kathleen E. Innes, wrote to the president of the United Nations Conference at San Francisco, pressing two points. To meet the problems raised by modern economic and political planning and control, and to reconcile the expansion of this control and standardization with the desire for the freedom, dignity and inviolability of the human personality, there was need in the new charter for a Declaration of Specific International Rights of Individuals and Groups—rights to be recognized within states as well as across frontiers. This was especially important in view of the movements of liberation from imperialist colonialism. Secondly, planned constructive measures of world cooperation to *prevent* aggression seemed to the W.I.L.P.F. a greater safeguard of security and peace than reliance on the military preparedness of individual states. Since modern total war drew into its orbit the modern state in its entirety—its science, industry, technology, its whole civilian population—the whole concept of security was fundamentally changed. To treat security as mainly a matter of military considerations, power and prestige was to make it entirely illusory.

"Modern human cooperative efforts ought to be concerned with *establishing* security rather than with *upholding* a security which does not really exist.'[21]

Emily Balch was profoundly concerned with problems of imperialism in all its forms, but especially in the form of colonialism. She was grateful in 1945 to note the progress in the United Nations. The trusteeship system (she had used the words in her birthday speech of 1942 on planetary civilization) seemed to her in important particulars an advance over the mandate system of the League of Nations. She wished, however, the further improvement that trusteeships should as far as possible be completely international and in the hands of the United Nations instead of in the hands of national governments. The drive for industrialization in underdeveloped territories seemed to her to hold both promise and menace. It was essential that intelligent and humane care must be exercised to prevent loss and suffering caused by the breakdown of native customs through the disintegrating incursions of modern business methods. Naturally she was opposed to any claims for the acquisition of territory by the United States whether in the form of military and naval bases or otherwise.

In one of her earliest messages to the international membership, shortly after Pearl Harbor, Emily Balch had said: "We must be educating ourselves and others, working against intolerance and hysteria, trying to lessen suffering as and where we can, schooling ourselves in endurance and hope and hard thinking, and learning to recognize the little things as little and the great things as great." [22] She never lost sight of what had still remained when Pandora's box of evils was opened. To her New England mind, hope was a discipline as well as a theological virtue. And as the last phrase indicates, she never lost her own sense of the true rhythm of life, even in time of war, and she helped recall it for some of her despairing and over-burdened fellow crusaders. She liked to quote Milton's advice to Cyriack Skinner, written in the turbulent politics of the 1650's, to:

> Let Euclid rest and Archimedes pause
> And what the Swede intend, and what the French . . .
> For other things mild Heaven a time ordains,
> And disapproves that care, though wise in show,
> That with superfluous burden loads the day,
> And, when God sends a cheerful hour, refrains.

After an evening of strenuous committee work, with midnight approaching and no visible end to the piled-up business, she would say, with a smile, "There is so much to do; let's go to bed." "She is a poet in everything she does," said her Viennese friend Helene Scheu-Reiss who had often seen her in action on committees. "Her sense of humor sheds radiance on the driest subject as soon as she touches it. It is such a joy to be with her because she can dress the little details of work with zest and glamor." And no one can tackle with the same distastefulness a certain inevitable chore that comes to almost all desk owners after reading Emily's little note to Dorothy Detzer in 1945: "It takes lots of moral courage to try to clear up a cluttered and confused desk—a small judgment day. Unearthing all this ancient stuff. Excuse me. E.G.B."

The year before America entered the war, in 1941, another grace befell Emily Balch, unexpected, bewildering, as it seemed to her, almost inexcusably gratifying—the publication of a slim volume of verses she had written throughout the years, *The Miracle of Living.* Her friend, Mary K. Simkhovitch wrote the introduction. Gertrude Bussey had been the editor. The verses are interesting, like her sketches and pastels, in showing one facet of a many-gifted woman. Some lines resemble her water colors, as in "Impressions" (of Morocco):

> A stretch of sun-washed wall, cut by an arch,
> At the wall's foot a Moor asleep.

The little book* did not make a dent in literary circles, nor did she expect it would. But it gave pleasure to a good many people, including herself, and to refugee readers who took comfort in the lines:

---

* Emily Greene Balch, *The Miracle of Living,* Island Press, New York, 1941.

Wherever I pass upon the earth I am at home
Wherever cluster the shelters of my kind, I find welcome.

The poems touched on her travels: "Crowding Memories of Egypt," "Mont Blanc Above Combloux," "Girl Painter in Paris." A few dealt obliquely with pacifist themes: "The Flag Speaks," "To a Bedbug" (The Prisoner for Conscience Sake Speaks). There were poems on old age: "The Last Trip of the Old Explorer," "Age No Victor," "Seed"; humorous poems, "Resignation" (The Ass's Misconception), "Over-Extension." There were nature poems, several religious and some semi-mystical poems she had written when she was a student; and a few like "Love Song," "Initiates," "Unmated" which caused her to murmur when the little pale green book appeared in print, "Oh, I feel as if I had undressed in public."

These are some of the many different things Emily Balch tried to do in the years between 1939-1945, when she was seventy-two to seventy-eight years old, and the way she did them. Dorothy Canfield Fisher in 1946 described her as "la bonne intellectuelle," declaring "She was and is proof in moments of distress, increasingly, alas! frequent in our modern society, that human beings can be at the very same time both good and intelligent. We need such proof, almost tragically need it, as a comforting reassurance to all the troubled world." [23] In an earlier letter, in 1941, to Emily herself, Dorothy Canfield Fisher had written of her memory of Emily in the far-away French days of 1890-91 at the boarding school on the rue de Vaugirard in Paris: "I have inside my head such a crystal-clear recollection of you as a little girl saw you— *incarnate intelligence, warmed by selfless goodness.* You probably have never known what a standard you set up, standard and inspiration." [24]

If, in the rough path of her inner life during World War II Emily Balch was beset by doubts, hesitations, self-questionings and reproaches, intellectual and spiritual struggles and torment, reflecting the black abysses and anguish of the times in which she lived, she nevertheless achieved a deeper sense of the tragic destiny of mankind, without which true greatness of spirit is impossible. In the choice Emily Balch was wrestling with, between whole-hearted devotion to peace and necessary allegiance to justice and freedom, the decision for neither side seemed to bring unmixed good. Nor was it possible to pick and choose, to take the best of both alternatives, to grasp at a little peace and a little freedom. Measured by her own high standards, neither decision appeared unalloyedly right. The war years intensified for her the tragic dimension of human living where an individual has to confront choices where there seems to be no right—only two wrongs—and two wrongs that in the last analysis are incommensurable. Before such choices, intelligence was not enough, and conscience itself no sure guide.

Emily could only, in the wisdom of her tradition, confess herself the sinner that all human beings are—and from there go on to work for a future that might eliminate that particular tragic dilemma.

So, at least, in her eighth decade, the world and her Inner Light spoke to Emily Balch. In her pacifism—theory and practice—she bore out the truth of the pleasantly British remark attributed to St. Gregory of Nazianzus that the Kingdom of God is not necessarily made up of fools.

CHAPTER SIXTEEN

Towards a Planetary Civilization

Both before and during World War II, Emily Balch was following events with close attention, and making specific proposals and suggestions, offering them to her friends and colleagues with the recommendation to try them on the appropriate people. Her mind was realistic and concrete; it was committed to two general principles—intelligence and good will. If her thinking often suggested a social philosophy very much like that of John Dewey and Jane Addams, it was due in part at least to the fact that both Dewey and Emily Balch learned much from the intellectual approach of Jane Addams. Jane Addams had a pretty well formulated social philosophy that articulated for her what her heart and mind suggested, though she did not set it forth in her writings, as Merle Curti has remarked, "in a way to please the scholars nowadays who set great store on what is called intellectual sophistication."[1] Emily Balch did not try to state her own social philosophy systematically; she exhibited the fruits of an intellectual attitude and approach which all three kindred minds shared profoundly. They all thought in terms of specific problems and situations; their proposals were not derived from abstract principles, but sprang from a general intellectual temper and attitude that was ingrained, and had become second nature.

Emily was realistic and concrete, but not realistic in the sense that so often means seeing only the darker side of things. "Why do men think it is so much cleverer to believe in evil than in good?" [2] she asked. She was always hopeful, without failing to see the great practical obstacles in the stubbornness, contrariness, and ineptitudes of human nature. Her sense of the limitations of men as they are, always suggested specific and practicable ways of overcoming those limitations sufficiently to get men to take some steps, however short, in the direction her own intelligence indicated. Therefore, she had no great faith in political instruments and governmental action as means of achieving peaceful solution of tensions and problems. But she was fertile in suggesting plans for working together on the economic or practical aspect of difficulties, convinced that such cooperation would in the end bear fruit in establishing habits of political compromise. She did not turn aside from the instruments painfully forged for international cooperation in political terms. She worked manfully for and with the League of Nations, and had the same loyalty to the United Nations organization. But she did not expect too much from them alone, and she hesitated to push them into anything like a world government, or even a cooperative European government, until the groundwork had been far more securely laid. Her approach was always fundamentally pluralistic. Not world government, "but instead a complex inter-weaving of functional arrangements for common interests," [3] was the kind of immediate solution to which her mind naturally turned. Even in her more Utopian moments, she did not propose the abolition of navies or air forces. She tried to analyze what concrete good navies accomplish, and then tried to work out some kind of international agency that could serve the same purpose without being on a nationalistic and competitive basis. This temper of mind, these fruits of what could be formulated as a distinctive social philosophy of international action, are best illustrated by some of the many proposals that crowded upon her mind.

Of the movement for a superstate in the shape of a federal world government, she had strong doubts. She felt it was important in educating people to the need of limiting national sovereignty, of sacrificing national self-will and national self-determination for the will and purpose of the all-inclusive human group. But in so far as it led to depreciation of the United Nations, and desire to scrap it for a world government with executive and legislative organs and a judiciary, on the Swiss or American pattern, she deplored it. She had a deep distrust of the element of coercive power in any human association and was always eager to see it kept as small as possible. Therefore, she had reservations about any form of federal world government "with power to make enforceable laws, in command of adequate military power and other sanctions to back them up, and grounded in an electorate composed not merely of governments but of individual citizens."

She saw "governments" as a historical type of organization, not necessarily the last word in human wisdom. Their record was not a happy one. They were dangerous because people tended to personify and idealize them. They were characterized by having a monopoly of armed force which largely determined their character and their nature. They were steeped in that tradition of militarism, nationalism, and imperialism which it was desirable to outgrow and they were bedeviled by the pursuit of power and prestige.

"For myself I am not in love with governments as such. The sovereign State as we know it is a curious historical growth influenced both by certain by no means infallible political philosophers like Montesquieu and Austin and others, and by accidental occurrences. It is a clumsy irregularly developed instrument for joint action excessively colored by considerations of power and prestige, in some directions meddling excessively with matters that ought to be left to the individual or to non-governmental regulation, and again neglecting to control what needs governmental direction, and withal only reasonably honest or efficient, in spite of the big idealizing terms in which one's 'Country' is conceived.

"The modern European State-Governments in their great variety are far from exhausting the possibilities of political organization as Russia shows today and China may show tomorrow. I am far from wishing to see statecraft frozen at its present point of development and imposed 'as is' on whole converies of peoples." [4]

She did not think therefore that governments were the answer to the problem of organizing the peoples of the world to work together in good comradeship. "While human intelligence has transformed the art of dealing with matter, political science and political art have developed very slowly. As regards the art of

dealing with one another, we are still groping," she said. "Cooperation in practical, technical tasks is one of the best ways of learning
the indispensable art of getting along with one another." [5]

This functional approach to world unity seemed to Emily Balch
to hold a very great promise. It came not as the expression of a
theory but as an answer to felt needs, common interests impelling
unity of action. The list of administrative agencies and special
commissions in the United Nations by 1947 was a already long:
labor, trade, transportation, civil aviation, communications, international law, banking and money, human rights and the status of
women, food and agriculture, health, refugees and displaced persons, education, science and culture, trusteeship, and the enormous
question of population.

To these cooperative organs Emily Balch wished to add consideration of two great planetary areas which by their very nature
would seem to be supranational—the boundless air and the international waterways of the world. A narrower but more immediately
realizable possibility was internationalization of the polar regions—
the Arctic and Antarctic.

In her Geneva years, Emily had hoped that aviation, then in
its infancy, so international by its very nature, could be amenable
to overall planning. She had wished for the establishment for this
purpose of a vast nonprofit air authority. At the League of Nations
Conference on Reduction and Limitation of Armaments which
had opened in Geneva in 1932, bold proposals were made, but the
Disarmament Conference failed miserably. Emily Balch, in the
1940's and 1950's was realistic enough to see that aviation had
evolved too early and too rapidly for it to become the common
business of the peoples of the world. She saw that military aviation
"which made the beautiful art of flight a hideous menace instead
of a blessing" was bound up with two crucial problems, slow and
difficult of settlement—disarmament and international policing. "It
is not necessarily the end of this story however," she said.

As regarded the internationalization of the waters of the world,
the situation seemed to Emily Balch very different. The field, old
as it was, was still relatively open and in need of wide and wise
organization. About the time of the outbreak of the war in 1939,
Emily's mind became concerned with the general idea of naval

internationalization. In a letter to Dorothy Detzer she struck out the sparkles of her idea, admitting that one got into utopia building as soon as one went into details. "All this is moonshine—yes, but beside the intolerable absurdity of national navies, it is realistic common sense." The kernel of her idea was that the control of all those bodies of water which were, through their situation and use, of special international concern should be in the hands of a representative, trusted, competent supernational authority.

In 1947 she drafted a petition to ask the United Nations to appoint a commission to study and report on internationalizing the great waterways of the world and the uninhabited polar regions. It was not her purpose to present a fully elaborated scheme, or urge any particular solution, but she hoped the essence of the plan would be studied without too much attention to minor suggestions. She was conscious that a plan presented by private persons, based on no exhaustive preparatory study, even appearing amateurish, might at first create an unfavorable impression. But she had enough confidence to think her proposal might have value and could be elaborated by competent inquirers. She thought that one way to secure a public authority was through a decision to carry out the study of a specific subject. "This, not to be too cynical," she said, "commits no one to anything, offends no one, and suggests a creditable alertness and openness of mind. If a proposal has real merit, inquiry will at least facilitate its realization."

She suggested the creation of a United Nations Maritime Authority appointed by the General Assembly with wide powers over waterways which were of international interest. She included not only the oceans but also narrow seas like the Mediterranean, straits like the Dardanelles, and canals like Suez and Panama, and possibly international rivers such as the Rhine and Danube, though perhaps they might best be left to a purely European authority.

"The plan is one in which international federalists and those who fear 'world government' can meet," she wrote to Gertrude Bussey on March 16, 1947. "It seems to me a promising approach to disarmament as it would make navies more or less obsolete or without justification at least. . . . The more I mull over it the more the different aspects of it appear to interlock and reinforce one another and not the least the fact that the plan is supposed to pay its own way.* In fact as you see the most insidious infection, pride of authorship, rears its ugly head."

On December 1, 1959, in Washington, D.C., twelve countries signed an historic treaty. The treaty concerned Antarctica, the last unexplored continent on this planet. Antarctica comprises an area about twice the size of the United States, entirely covered with a mantle of ice, containing no vegetation, no wildlife, and no natives. The significance of Antarctica arises from its importance as a possible base for guided missiles, as a possible site for United States and Soviet nuclear weapon testing, and for its influence in affecting weather conditions in the Southern hemisphere.

The treaty was historic for several reasons. For the first time in history, military activity, including the testing of any type of weapons, was banned from an entire continent by international agreement. Secondly, it proved that in spite of lack of progress toward disarmament, areas can be made immune from political and military strife. Third, it proved that the East and West can come to an agreement on the question of inspection, which had hampered other disarmament negotiations.

This was one of Emily Balch's ideas come to fruition. The W.I.L.P.F. was one of the first organizations to urge the peaceful utilization of Antarctica, and since 1947 it had called for some sort of international control under the United Nations. As Gertrude Baer was to write of Emily Balch in 1961: "Her proposals were so practical and practicable. That made her NEW ideas never appear utopian. And many of her proposals for which she worked so hard became a reality."** During the late thirties, Emily had been thinking of the disposition of uninhabited lands, the polar regions,

---

* The expenses of such an establishment would be very heavy, but she suggested that they could largely be met in connection with services rendered without recourse to subventions from nation members of the United Nations. The United Nations Maritime Authority might be given the right to receive fees for clearance papers at ports under control, ad valorem dues on vessels using its conveniences, or other charges for assistance given.

As early as 1924, Emily Balch had urged international control of international waterways: the main straits and the chief canals, like the Dardanelles, the Panama canal, the Suez canal.

** Letter of Gertrude Baer to Marion Balch, January 20, 1961, after Emily Balch's death.

as an opportunity to create some sort of international status, to develop practice in the field of international cooperation, to try experiments, to work out new methods and forms, to test procedures, and above all, to build up mutual confidence. Where, she thought, could such an opportunity for direct international administration be found as in these empty regions where there were no populations to consider, no vested rights, no inherited claims and loyalties, no inflamed concern with prestige? In 1940 she suggested that the United States should propose to other nations a consortium of all, a world trust, to develop whatever the areas had to offer. Later, in 1944, while the war was still on, Emily Balch was dealing further with the idea of the "Polar Regions as a site for an experiment in internationalism." Though the economic values involved in natural resources were problematical, the polar regions were of exceptional importance for meteorological stations and for long-range weather forecasting, a use which is international in all its implications. The Arctic, affording shortcut flying routes of commercial and strategic value with its possibilities of bombing from the air, was of key importance. Here, again, the prime need would seem to be internationally arranged control. Remembering the phenomenal expansion of aviation in the 1920's, she urged administration of "these inclement regions" before conflicting claims and developments became further crystallized and acquisitiveness and prestige further involved. "It might also endow the New World Organization," she wrote, "with an actual material piece of 'real estate' and a territorial foothold."

In May, 1947, she drew up a plan to secure the appointment, by the appropriate authority within the United Nations, of an ad hoc committee to consider and report on the proposal to internationalize the uninhabited polar regions of the globe.* What she hoped for was the control and administration of these areas by

---

* In 1956 Prime Minister Jawaharlal Nehru of India became personally interested in the subject of internationalization of Antarctica (because of rumors and fears that the region would be used for atomic tests), and on October 16, 1956 and again on July 15, 1958, the Indian delegation using materials furnished by the W.I.L., submitted items for the General Assembly agenda to call upon all member states "to agree and affirm that the area will be utilized entirely for peaceful purposes and for the welfare of the whole world." Because of the many crises and problems facing the General Assembly, India indicated that she would not press for immediate action and the item on Antarctica was withdrawn.

commissions under the Trusteeship Council of the United Nations. "Two little animals," said Emily Balch, "have come to hold a special place in the whimsical affections of the American public—the panda and the penguin. It would be sufficiently amusing if the penguin, that pleasing caricature of the professional diplomat, should yet be hailed as, together with the Polar bear, the inhabitant of the first world country." [6]

Preeminent among the things that trouble the relations of peoples with one another, thought Emily Balch, are dogmatism, the state of mind of people who are convinced that they know the right answer, the only right answer; and fear, the state of mind possessed by those who fear that an attempt will be made to impose other people's dogmas on themselves. "When I say this," wrote Emily Balch in 1949, "everyone will naturally think of Russia. May I suggest whether the desire to force one's own point of view on others is only Russian? How many countries are afraid of us and of being Americanized? We are, I think, often quite naive in our unconsciousness that we have a dogma and one that does not seem as self-evident and desirable to everyone as it does to us. I think we are more sure than we ought to be that the accusations brought against us are nonsensical slanders, that there is no basis for the charge that we want to dominate, that we try to force international arrangements that will be profitable for American business, that we intend to see to it that the American way of life makes the tour of the globe. . . .

"I do believe that our dogma is not as crass as Marxism, nor our attitude toward spreading it comparable with the missionary zeal of the Communists but perhaps militant and expansionist Americanism is dangerous because it is so largely unconscious as well as uncritical. Wholly without self-criticism we happily are not. There are more and more voices, especially among those who take their religion seriously, who urge that our civilization is largely based on a distorted sense of values, that we care too much about being comfortable, that self-interest is not a good basis for private and public living, that rivalry and competition are less fundamental than cooperation and mutual aid, that the whole orientation of our economy is far from being in harmony with the principles of Jesus which we profess."

The cold war she saw as two mighty agglomerations of people

facing one another, each obsessed by a fanatical belief in its own ideas and an even more fanatical fear and hatred of the largely misunderstood ideas of the other. When people in America spoke of Communism, they often fused or confused two quite separate ideas—some degree and form of holding goods in common on the one hand, and a totalitarian government such as has developed in Russia and the states that follow her example on the other. "We are obsessed with a fear of communism which naturally evokes a corresponding fear of us and tempts others to the policies and attitudes that feed on fear. Fear and suspicion are powerful corrosives of goodwill and by preventing cool and fair judgment, they make for misunderstanding." [7]

For good international relations, good will *plus* was necessary. Good will* was the fire that made the engine function. "Thank heaven, there does exist in the world a precious substratum of good will on the purely human level. In time of emergency, compassion answers to need and help flows in from the most unexpected quarters." Good will, however, had its weak spots and deficiencies. Prejudices interfered, especially where there were differences of color, or religion or historical background and tradition, differences made more dangerous "by the papers we read, or don't read. How many of us read papers in a foreign language, or published in other places, or even papers that are organs of other ways than our own? How critically do we react to what is fed to us?" [8]

The key conceptions, therefore, for Emily were not coercion and enforcement but reason and good will. "That means that on the side of the intellect," she said, "we try with all our might to understand the problem before us and to understand one another; and, on the side of that essential part of our human makeup, the

---

* Jane Addams, like Emily Balch, was always accustomed to using the term good will not in its ordinary vague meaning, but in the strongest possible sense. See *Peace and Bread*, Appendix, 1922: "The Women's International League for Peace and Freedom is made up of people who believe that we are not obliged to choose between violence and passive acceptance of unjust conditions for ourselves or others; who believe, on the contrary, that courage, determination, moral power, generous indignation, active good-will, can achieve their ends without violence.

"We believe that experience condemns force as a self-defeating weapon . . . and that new methods, free from violence, must be worked out for ending abuses and for undoing wrongs, as well as for achieving positive ends."

power of feeling (a faculty that women perhaps tend to rate relatively higher than do men) we bring to bear a powerful activity of will directed to the good of others, or rather to the good of all. There is no such force as this. It is a creative force that rightly directed has undefinable possibilities. If you really care about a person, or about a people, if you sincerely and strongly wish them good will they will sense it and in time, under halfway normal conditions, they will respond. Attempts to deal with Russia in this spirit have been made I know but not enough. Yes, I remember the old man that sat on the stile and continued to smile to soften the heart of the cow. Smiling does not exhaust our possibilities. I have a saying 'Russia makes it hard for her friends.' She does but this means we must try all the harder.

"We must not be anti-Russian, nor 'anti' any people. We need a new attitude toward Russia, more scientific and more friendly, especially toward the Russian people which is not synonymous with the government, anymore than the American people is fully expressed by what we call Washington. Let us make the most of all non-political ties and contacts, scientific, artistic, philanthropic, and intellectual. I think we ought to read not only more books about Russia, but more books written by Russians, translated novels, poems, treatises. And let us do what we properly can to make ourselves understood, ourselves with all our thoughts and failures as well as our vaunted successes. This is our 'Doctrine' as I see it." [9]

In 1949 she did not think that there should be appeasement of Russia. All proper means, but always international means, should be used to prevent the employment of violence, terror, or chicanery to make any people the satellite of any other against its will. But the alternative to appeasement need not be rearmament and military power. "I am painfully aware how inadequate an alternative to an army or bombing is any concrete plan that we are ready to propose. I believe that we have to accept a real risk. We have to do that in any case. We had better take risks on behalf of a belief that war is no answer at all (but the very opposite of an answer) than to take risks for the belief that threat of war will frighten Russia into acting as we want her to." [10]

Two things she constantly deprecated—fear and cynicism. Fear is a poor counselor, she said over and over again. Fear weakens the nerves and distorts the judgment. "It is not by fear that mankind must exorcise the demon of destruction and cruelty, but by motives more reasonable, more humane and more heroic." And as to sceptics she exclaimed, "It is curious to me how afraid people are of being fooled by believing in the possibility of good. The devil finds ready weapons in scepticism, cynicism and discouragement. He knows well how effective is a little cold water judiciously applied." [11]

In 1949, she sent a message to the Copenhagen W.I.L.P.F. International Congress, alluding to Russia and again voicing her "Doctrine." "The fundamental need is to help men to change their minds. It is to educate ourselves and others, to enlighten the heart as well as the understanding, to open the eyes to see the need of great changes in institutions and in ideas, and to exercise and train our intelligence by trying to understand how we ought to deal with new and excessively complicated problems like the use of atomic power and the correlation of Marxist and non-Marxist democracy." [12] And in 1953, when she was eighty-six years old, she sent a greeting to the twelfth International W.I.L.P.F. Congress at Paris, using a figure of speech as characteristic as it was moving: "Some people are still locked in the ice of totalitarian power or are exploited by colonial masters or landlords. Such tyranny is bound to come to an end. May it go not with violence and explosion but as the ice goes in the spring through resistless thawing." [13]

"Self-interest is not a good basis for private or public living," Emily Balch had boldly asserted, willing, as on many occasions, to risk appearing naïve. She brought to political problems a hard-headed realism combined with adherence to high moral principles. The role of the international statesman, the whole question of ethics in the political field, had been in Emily Balch's mind long before the League of Nations days. She had noted the amoralism in German political life in 1895-1896, as she was to do again on her visit in 1931. She remembered the "sacred egoism" of Salandra in 1915.

She had had, however, many opportunities to hear views of a very different order from Thomas Masaryk during her months of friendship with him in Prague in 1905-1906, and again in 1918, when he was in the United States agitating the cause of Czech

independence, and he and his daughter Olga were guests at the
Balch Prince Street house in Jamaica Plain. These views Masaryk
later expressed in his book *The Making of a State*, in the closing
chapter called "Democracy and Humanity":

> When I took upon myself the obligations of the Presidential
> office, well knowing what my daily administrative tasks would be, it
> was clear to me that no State or policy can prosper unless the ground-
> work be moral. As St. Paul wrote at the beginning of the fourth
> chapter of the Second Epistle to the Corinthians: "Therefore, seeing
> we have this Ministry, as we have received mercy, we faint not; but
> have renounced the hidden things of dishonesty, not walking in
> craftiness nor handling the work of God deceitfully, but by mani-
> festation of the truth commending ourselves to every man's conscience
> in the sight of God." This is the program of the Republic and of
> Democracy *sub specie aeternitatis*. The ethical basis of all politics is
> humanity, and humanity is an international program. It is a new
> word for the old love of our fellow-man.*

Emily Balch was disturbed during the 1930's by the growing
fashion of political writers of asserting that nations are and should
be motivated by self-interest alone. "Such remarks," she wrote,
"are doubtless a wholesome reaction against empty and often
hypocritical claims to lofty and noble motives in national policies.
They may spring from a desire to be realistic, to sound like a man
of sense with no non-sense about him." She realized the Scylla and
Charybdis of the question, the dangers of a Quixotic or crusading
spirit in foreign policies, and the likelihood that if statesmen
assumed popular readiness to underwrite a sacrificial policy, the
people would let them down. She saw the tendency to enlarge,
moralize, and socialize the economic functions of governments and
to narrow their political purpose and meaning. Nevertheless, she
was convinced that "the national group as an enlarged ego should
have many-sided concerns and functions including that of giving

---

* Masaryk went on: "Between morality on a big scale and on a small, there
is no distinction. It is a false notion that political men need take no thought
of ethical principles when the interest of the State is involved. . . . No State,
no society can be managed without general recognition of the ethical basis
of the State and of politics; and no State can long stand if it infringes the
broad rules of human morality. . . . Democracy is not alone a form of State
and of administration. It is a philosophy of life and an outlook upon the
world."

expression to impulses of a generous 'idealistic' and non-self-regarding kind." [14]

In 1938, the issue was serious and timely. In a conversation about the refugee problem with a highly placed member of the State Department in Washington, "from whom I had been led to expect something quite different," Emily Balch heard frankly that it was impractical to expect any country to act on any final motive other than self-interest and that as a matter of fact governments and people "are egoistic and I don't blame them."

Emily had never forgotten the interview she had had in August, 1915, with Secretary of State Robert Lansing about the desirability of shortening the war if possible. As she remembered the conversation in 1938, Lansing had said in substance that no nation cared anything about the length of the war except as far as that affected its own interest. "I said in reply, 'Mr. Lansing, do you really maintain that it is a matter of complete indifference to the United States apart from its own national interest—whether the war ends soon, or the slaughter goes on for years?' His somewhat embarrassed reply was to the effect that of course Americans were different from Europeans and less selfish."*

---

* Typed memorandum August 31, 1915, by Emily Greene Balch, of interview of Dr. Aletta Jacobs and Emily Balch with Secretary Lansing: "Mr. Lansing said nations in their international relations were purely selfish; that they were never disinterested in any degree. Miss Balch demurred, and said it had been her happiness to think all the nations recognized disinterested purposes more than formerly, and that the United States was more advanced in doing so than European nations. The latter point Lansing admitted. Miss Balch instanced disinterested action of the United States in making peace between Japan and Russia. He was very bitter in his condemnation of this settlement; it had done much harm. The United States, he said at one point, had never done anything with regard to European powers except from self-interest. Miss Balch said she hoped that in the East, in returning the Boxer indemnity, we had acted disinterestedly. He said that was a matter of justice, but, bitterly, no other European nation followed our example and returned any money. Miss Balch asked, 'Do you really think that the European neutrals have no desire to see the war end and the bloodshed stop, apart from what may happen to be their self-interest?' No, he did not go so far as this. Of course they did have some unselfish concern to aid it.

"Mr. Lansing spoke of treaties and international agreements. He argued that when the pressure to break such agreements was strong they would be broken. An individual might sacrifice his existence to keep his word, but a person in power, responsible for a nation, would not do this, and he 'did not know that he blamed that decision.'" From Villard papers, by permission of the Harvard College Library.

In February, 1945, Emily Balch wrote to John Foster Dulles asking him whether he would comment publicly upon the words of a United States Senator emphasizing "self-interest" as a "final motive." "If men of authority say publicly and plainly," Emily wrote to him, "that a nation has other things to do besides guarding its own advantage, it would be driving a nail in the coffin of a kind of cynicism which is a menace and a dry rot in public affairs.

"International law cannot require self-sacrifice. International institutions do well not to assume too great readiness for it. But I urge that the possibility of it should never be denied by [political] leaders of political thought and action and that channels should be opened for it. Is it not true that the codes of practice in case of accident or danger at sea are far from being based on self-regard? I know that all this trenches on points of psychology and ethics that argue that no man can act except in what he conceives to be in his own interest. I cannot reconcile this theory with human nature as I observe it and certainly not with any Christian view of suffering. If supersubtle analysis reduces all action to self-regard, in ordinary life we recognize some acts and some persons as 'unselfish.' "[15]

John Foster Dulles replied that he might have the opportunity of commenting publicly on "self-interest." "Certainly the American people," he wrote, "as individuals have a tremendous interest in the welfare of other peoples and a desire to spare them suffering. Whether those in a trustee capacity, as representatives of the American people, have a right to act other than in the national interest is an extremely difficult philosophical and juridical problem."[16]

In 1950, in an article "Decency in International Relations," Emily Balch again pursued the question of the responsibility of a statesman acting not in an individual capacity but in the capacity of a delegate or representative. "My father was a lawyer often making business decisions as a trustee or agent for others, and, (as I recall after all these years) he explained to me, as a girl, the principle on which he acted. He held that he was no more free to do wrong on behalf of a client than on his own. In renting a building, for instance, he considered not only the money return, but the character of the use to which the building was to be put. He considered his principal not merely as an investor but as a person with all a person's responsibilities. The same principle holds in public life.

"In any group, where those taking part consider only the interest of themselves or of some special set of men, there is a lowering of the whole tone of action of the group, whether it be a club, a municipality, a national parliament or whatever. Policies which do not converge in joint efforts for the common advantage are bound to diverge and can secure results only by 'horse-trading' and barter, purchasing compliance in one selfish scheme by agreement to support some other."

With the development of international political life, greater demands were made on human nature. In the early days of the United Nations at Lake Success, New York, at a certain meeting there was a "revealing and disturbing debate" as to whether delegates were to consider themselves as representing their own countries and to act in the interest of these, or whether they should consider themselves as experts, appraising proposals objectively as a scientific man appraises the probable effects of a project, its possible advantages, disadvantages and cost. "But no other attitude," said Emily Balch, "than the *expert* one meets the case. In a court of law opposing advocates set out to make the best they can for one side. This is not the way to fruitful common action. The attitude of complete disinterestedness is a great deal to expect of men warped as we all are, even more or less unconsciously, by nationalistic tradition and atmosphere, but nothing less will suffice."

"Let us note that the need for this devotion to the general interest, this inclusiveness, is something that the international statesman shares with every believer in Christianity or in any other universal or ethical philosophy." [17]

This, like Thomas Masaryk's, was Emily Balch's program for Democracy *sub specie aeternitatis*.

From time to time, in her old age, Emily continued to send annual messages to W.I.L.P.F. international sessions which she could not attend. She always managed to inject a note of freshness, or originality, or hope, and sometimes of humility which struck her listeners with a kind of wonder. Especially in her greetings to the International Executive Committee, she felt free to be more forthright than in her more public pronouncements. In 1951 she addiessed them, setting forth briefly four aims or goals on which she thought all of them could agree, acknowledging that "we have not found the way out of the labyrinth but we know what gate we are looking for."

She ended by saying, "I try to think as a human being and not merely nationally but there is one personal plea that I would like to make to you, my friends, as an American. Please try to forgive America for being so powerful. We cannot help it. We are neither to be praised nor blamed for it. It is the inevitable result of causes, geographical and historical, which just happen to be so. We are not worthy of this power. We have not the experience and wisdom and goodness that it calls for. Condemn our wrong doings, make clear our blunders and do not condone our shortcomings. Help us. We so need help but be realistic and generous in understanding the strange situation in which we find ourselves, like an inexperienced young man who awakes one morning to find himself heir to a large share of an immensely tangled and complicated estate; trying to learn how to adjust himself to work with his senior partners, how not to refuse any responsibilities which it is his duty to undertake nor assume to himself anything that it belongs to the collectivity to decide and carry through. . . .[18]

Affectionately, Emily G. Balch"

In such a moderate and pragmatic fashion Emily Balch hoped that men might work together toward a world civilization. With her dislike for the cliché, she preferred to call it a planetary civilization. But even her whimsical and forward-darting imagination did not anticipate the rivalries in outer space that that phrase was so soon to suggest. When she was eighty-eight, in 1955, a reporter interviewing her on her ideas of internationalization "under the umbrella of the United Nations" asked her about the moon. "My internationalism stops at the stratosphere, young man," she had replied. "Beyond that you can say it's over my head." [19]

As Emily Balch approached the nineties, the circle of her thinking completed its round. She maintained at the end what she had said at the very beginning when she had been one of that first group of women to enter the international political sphere—a domain hitherto preempted by man: "Lovers of our own lands, we are citizens of the world, conscious partakers in the sacrament of all human life or more truly of all sentient life. We do not promulgate phrases, we try to reach actual concrete results in politics and in education." [20] (1922)

In 1957 she could reiterate what she had said in 1919 at the Zürich Congress of Women that it was only by initiative, self-sacrifice, and intelligence in a spirit of honest good will, that a decent world order could emerge from "the ugly, greedy, cruel civilization in which our lifetime has been cast.

"In individual and personal relations, as well as in political and international relations, we must apply the principles which underlie consent and still better, cooperation and struggle of the fruitful and invigorating type. . . . We have made but the merest beginnings in the highest of human arts, that of living and working together on the plane of consent and cooperation without coercion." [21] (1919)

CHAPTER SEVENTEEN

"Inner Life"

In the spring of 1950, when Emily Balch was eighty-three years old, Edith Hamilton, author of *The Greek Way* and other well-known interpretative books on the Greek and Roman classics, gave a lecture at Wellesley College. Since Edith Hamilton was a sister of Dr. Alice Hamilton who had been the close friend of Jane Addams, Emily Balch introduced herself after the lecture. Shortly afterwards, Emily Balch received the following letter from Edith Hamilton:

"I write this with great hesitation, but it is a kind of concern on my spirit. I talked with you for only five minutes, but I shall never forget your face. When I am tempted to be irritable, a very besetting sin, I shall think of how you looked. I don't think one could be irritable when you are around. Nor shall I forget your smile, when you said, 'It doesn't matter.' There is one handwriting on the wall one cannot escape, what the years write upon our faces. It's very clear on your face, so that a stranger in five minutes read it—and got help from it. Please do not answer this. It is only an acknowledgement of a debt." [1]

At the same time, to her sister Alice in Hadlyme, Connecticut, Edith Hamilton wrote: "Emily Balch was there. I had never met her before and I was oh so impressed by her. I thought of that verse 'They took knowledge of them that they had been with Jesus.' She looks like that."[2]

In all the tributes, public and private, which Emily Balch received throughout the years, she was praised for her magnanimity, her courage, her intelligence, her modesty, selfless goodness, humor, and lovingkindness, as well as for her learning and scholarship. Her intelligence, humor, originality, and vitality were gifts of the gods and of her ancestors and parents. Somewhere she had acquired the granite qualities of honesty, courage, firmness of will, and purpose. Perhaps they grew out of the more gossamer qualities of sensitivity, perceptiveness, and imagination with which she seemed also to have been endowed.

In her earliest journals, some passages reveal as do her pen and ink drawings this delicate sensitivity: "It is wonderful," she wrote, "what an effect man sometimes has on man even with scarcely impinging consciousness. I had been in an ill humor from various causes which might have justified it if anything could: in chief a disagreeable errand in a sleeting afternoon necessitated by my own carelessness. As I was passing on, preoccupied, sunless, through slop and chill and common city crowd, one man passed me—a red-faced elderly average sort of man—with such a fund of good temper and cheer in his expression, not aroused by companionship, for he was alone, but which rather seemed the natural spirit and essential temper of the man, that involuntarily the dull lines of my face relaxed, my mouth remade itself. His face reflected itself in mine as promptly as the sudden rift in storm clouds is answered by a gleam over the wet meadows. My mood was altered not to veer again that day."

Not long afterwards, in a Proustian passage, she was trying to describe her consciousness of the fleeting sensations and perceptions of the moment with the unaware and subconscious elements which embroidered the experience. She was returning one evening to her home in Jamaica Plain. "As we swirled round the corner of the house in a hack and the lantern showed the green glistening leaves of the Japonica bush as we passed, I was aware of the motion and the changing light and shade. I did not consciously feel what was yet the very basis of my mood, the loved and accustomed presences, a certain and careless home, approaching light and rest, a continuous daily life satisfied, unanxious and interested in its daily businesses. I only knew all this when I suddenly foresaw that the memory of which perhaps a bush suddenly and partially lit up in all its green complexities and network of sharp leaf shapes by a passing light shall have power to evoke, will mean all this. This it is that makes the aroma, the flavor, the atmosphere of each fact of existence of which we are unconscious at the time but which bitter or sweet is strong in its memory."

The first entry in her journal, November, 1889, couched in a stilted self-conscious style that soon wore itself out, described her inner St. George charging the dragon. She always had a private love of drama: "Today, yesterday, the day before yesterday, the smart of mortification. Alone I had petted and rejoiced in my monster that makes his home within me. Grown bold therefore he stuck out his ugly phiz in public and shamed me. Well for me that I see him in his true aspect and am ashamed. So I may come to get the mastery of him and kill him dead after years of trial." In a note she later inserted "This referred to besetting Egotism."

The next entries show her recognition of the inhibitory and negative aspects of her Puritan inheritance, her somewhat unsure acceptance of the "life of the body," a rejection of dualism perhaps furthered by the Unitarian influence of Mr. Dole: "The Thanksgiving proclamation was read in church this morning. To the alien mood it came in all its true quaintness and beauty, this relic of the godly theocracy of our fathers, in its unique intrusion on another age. . . . May we the descendants of the grim saints not keep their faults and lose their virtues, remaining sour, rigid, restricted, unready in feeling, doubting, self-tormenting, barren of the glad grace of the large spirit of a child of God, and at the same time letting go the fidelity to faith, the purity of motive, the inevitable force of will which made our fathers' very faults a reason for respect. . . . Jammed in a horsecar, in a chilly air my neighbors' warmth and close pressed bodies, whose every motion was felt directly as if my own, gave me a pleasant sense of common animal nature. I felt no squeamishness any more than a puppy snuggling with his brothers in the straw. We so seldom live wholly in our bodies that it is wholesome to sometimes bask, as it were in our physical nature and live a brute. Is there not a loss if we, growing more intellectual, more spiritual, quite forego this which is also a part of ourselves?"

Ten years later she was writing, "My ideal is absolute control of the body, care and respect for it as an instrument, ruthless use of it when the end requires it."

How much was Emily Balch herself responsible for what Edith Hamilton was able to read in the lines of her face? A self-disciplined personality, Mary Kingsbury Simkhovitch and others had called her. Her three journals kept intermittently from 1889—the year she left college—till 1918 when her academic career was terminated, some portfolios which she labeled "Inner Life," and some reflective jottings made during the last, busiest, and most enduring phase of her career, describe the daily battles with her besetting sins of egotism, vanity, ambition, self-consciousness, "paucity of affection," irritability, self-righteousness, lack of method in work, drifting. They reveal the perpetual struggle that went on within her, the resolutions, the failures, the despair, and the fresh attempts to creep to the throne of grace.

Jan. 26, 1890: Again failure after failure to do what I knew to be right, what I had resolved beforehand, knowing the danger of my irresolution, with God in my thoughts. What hope for the next time?

Jan. 29, 1890: I began this journal on the mental condition that it should lead neither to self-consciousness nor afford an outlet for egotism and self-consideration. As a mechanical support to this resolution I meant to banish as far as possible the first personal pronoun from its pages. I make one exception for this entry. *It has always been my desire to be known, a truly vulgar ambition.* I believe it dead and at once it crops up again. As a child I had a habit of fancying a record made of all I did—some posthumous and highly eulogistic biography I imagine. I kept it in my head as I went about whatever I was doing. "Emily now rose and walked quickly across the floor and took her seat by the table." I do not believe I went so far as to think "walked gracefully across the floor" or anything of that sort, neither do I remember any description or attempt to grasp the essence of my situation. It was simply a pernicious habit which once acquired was very difficult to get rid of—I should say I kept it up pretty constantly for a year or two—and which I probably have to thank for much of my miserable self-consciousness.

The dread of a recurrence of this sort of thing and a sense of the unreality of journalistic writing has prevented my ever trying to keep any such record. It seems impossible to quite annihilate a possible reader. If I find this does lead to ill results I will frankly give it up but Amiel* and now DeGuérin have roused the desire in me.

March 24, 1890: The last month has been of slack tide of low inner life, in great contrast to the preceding one in which I lived so much, drinking deep of the poetry of DeGuérin, of the mystical religion of St. Theresa. I always notice this periodicity in my life so that stretches of painful insensibility and oppressive numbness and emptiness seem to posses me after a time of unusual fulness of feeling and keenness of aspiration. I have always hoped to outgrow it and learn to live continuously in that larger air.

May 14, 1890: I took pains to be cross so pleasantly that I hoped I should not notice it but unfortunately I found it out.

April 8, 1900: At Magnolia with Helen, reading Tolstoi's *Resurrection,* talking and keeping silent of many things. A time of great peace.

July 13, 1901: I have been reading Huxley's life. There could hardly be a great life whose lesson I need more. The exact devotion to truth, the scrupulous care, the unremitting industry to secure accuracy, the entire frankness as to everything whatever its personal bearings.

April 24, 1902: Long talk with A.M.K. [Alicia M. Keyes]. If I could learn what she has to teach me—courage and honesty among other things and direct first-hand original study . . . to teach girls to think for themselves, to help them out of their ruts.

Sept. 21, 1902: At home again after my long exciting holiday abroad— too much pleasure to register—to make it easy to buckle down to work. Coming back it is curious to meet again the old thoughts, habits, temptations, opportunities. I hope I may strike in some respects a better level after getting so much out of the rut. To be more effective with less waste of strength, to do or to lay aside as not to be done, and not procrastinate, to act by decision and choice, not by drifting, to plan and foresee, to allow reasonable leisure for friends and recreation and rest and the small friendlinesses.

The new year, January, 1899, came to Emily with a sense of relief, the previous one having brought "such swiftly succeeding, such hard, such perplexing, such moving events, personal and public"—her father's death in February, 1898, when she had been teaching two years at Wellesley College; the Spanish-American

---

* Henri Frédéric Amiel, 1821-1881, a Swiss famous for his widely read *Journal Intime.*

Georges Maurice DeGuérin, 1810-1839, a French poet with a strong and absorbing love for nature.

War; the complex settling of her father's estate and its division among the son and the five daughters; the unauthorized sale by the trustees of the beloved summer home at Cohasset by the sea to the grief and consternation of the whole Balch family. "After fifty years I still feel the scar," wrote Alice.

In August, the month when Francis Vergnies Balch had been accustomed to taking a holiday in the Adirondacks, in New England, or to Nova Scotia with congenial companions like George Chaney or Frank Abbott, Emily wrote to Mr. Abbott: "Wherever you are I know how full your heart will be of Papa, perhaps more at this season than at any other.

"I feel as if I were missing him now so much in the whole tone of my life; it was having the standard pitch (or a human approximation to it) constantly struck so that one kept regaining what one had lost. I constantly find myself below this and it is harder to get right again. I trust I shall not lose even this sense (of correction by his memory I mean). It is very precious. But perhaps I am saying some of those things that hardly can be said so that another person understands. I am thinking most of the smaller matters—kindly interpretation of others and charity in little things."

To the end of her life Emily Balch preserved the packet of all the letters she had ever received from her father, written on small note paper in a fine, legible Victorian hand—letters from 1875 when she was eight years old; letters to Bryn Mawr, Paris, Berlin; his last note from the office in January, 1898. In a letter to Emily in Germany, March 8, 1896, Francis Balch had written a just estimate of his daughter's character and future influence. A propos of the possibility of her studying law in the fall and joining forces with him, he wrote: "It seems to me it would be a mistake to give up what you are doing unless it becomes irksome. I believe you can do a great deal of good. It seems to me that you have a very sane mind on all these questions and that you have a high order of ability and a kindly and equable spirit and that you will always have many and loving friends and a strong influence."

For many years Emily jotted down prayers she was in the habit of composing, half inward petitions, half resolutions. Not long after her father's death she wrote:

June 20, 1898: God help us at all times flood tide and ebb tide, fill us and refresh us and enlighten us.

God help us always lonely and homesick, perplexed and self-bound, tired and unready.

Strengthen us, rebuke us, comfort us, lead us to fortitude, gratitude, readiness, confidence, strength of humility, purpose and love.

A characteristic prayer revealed her fundamental yearning "to be of use" "to be usable" which motivated her throughout her life and which she had caught in her childhood from Charles Fletcher Dole:

May 7, 1911: Father of all those in want, need and pain, use me I pray as a living instrument of service. O may I serve thy ends as far as by my nature and powers I can. Help me, help me, to make myself more fit for use. Help me for this end to remake myself by thy aid. Help me to self-discipline, to insight, to effort, to love, to understanding generous and simple love.

Of thy abounding and infinite grace, grant me grace; make and use me. Make me good that I may be usable. Amen.

As time went on, she abandoned the formal invocation of God by name and her prayers became expressions of aspiration and even more of thanksgiving and the desire to possess in the words she loved by George Herbert, "such a heart whose pulse may be thy praise." And who but Emily Balch and her like could pray to be made more amusing:

December 20, 1933: Handling life with such a heavy hand, with so little merriment, so dull, so unnoticing—lift us and lighten us, bear with us; take us by the hand to go more lightly, to take thy step in harmony with the joys thou dost offer us, to be more fit to live in a world with spring and laughter and children. Make us to be more welcome because gladder, humbler—and more amusing. Sing through us as thou singest through the little birds.

Her theological views were not developed in terms of a consistently thought out philosophy. What she found incontrovertible was a sense of communion with the divine, an aspect of experience not exhausted by purely material explanations or descriptions of it. "I do not believe" she declared, "that man is an orphan in the universe."

Some of her ideas she expressed in a letter to Helen Cheever in 1942. Man is shut in as a material fact inside his own skin and is informed of nothing except through the reports that reach him through his nerve endings. Yet he has "the miraculous power of transcending self and sacrificing self-interest for the most remote and impersonal purposes, ideas or beliefs, as well as for other men, even men he has never seen and of whom he knows nothing in detail, even the men not to be born till generations after his death." These things seemed to her inexplicable unless the universe is a spiritual as well as a material fact, unless men's spiritual capacities and experiences form part of a spiritual world from which they have sprung, in which they are immersed, and in which they are in a constant relation of give and take. With this spiritual source man is in communion, generally drawing from it quite unconsciously in a sense of inner support, above all in a sense of moral obligation, the feeling of "I ought," but in some persons, in some moods, in a more fully realized and deeply satisfied union. "Something like this," she wrote, "is the central point of the Quaker belief, 'the Inner Light,' 'the seed,' 'that which is of God in every man.'"

The question of her religious interests loomed up more largely than most of her friends were to suspect at the beginning of her two years' sabbatical leave of absence from Wellesley College, covering the years 1904 through 1906. The break from teaching seemed to Emily Balch a very serious thing for her as it might serve to give a final and perhaps different direction to her life work. "I shall be forty and some months over when my two years are up. I have only five years then before I am liable to a break in my health. After that, there is a good chance I imagine of nearly twenty years work in the land of Beulah if only I can be ripe and not rigid and superannuated."

There had been for several years in her mind the idea, she was not certain when it began, certainly since the appearance of Mrs. Humphry Ward's novel *Robert Elsmere*, the idea of perhaps "giving herself,' alternately with her teaching, to definite religious work. She felt that to do this as a young woman was unwise because she was too self-conscious and because she was afraid "it would kill the reality of my inner life," to be constantly and rhetorically expressing it, and also because it seemed to her presumptuous to offer herself as a guide or helper when she had herself experienced so little. "Now I think I am steadier and less yeasty at least in some degree and though it is still true that my experience of life especially in the emotional side is singularly slight yet I am at an age where if I were ever to serve in this way I might be fitting myself at once."

The idea had been in part a sort of daydream, a romance, a play. When in church, she allowed herself to fall to planning an "unconventional church" gathered together by herself. "This is partly because I feel Mr. Dole lacking in certain sides which seem to me important, noble and effective as his work is."

At the outset of her sabbatical year she had debated the pros and cons of her idea. Was speaking her best gift? Would a religious profession undermine her inner religious life? "The seed groweth secretly." Yet she believed that the churches might be something more real and alive than they were. She wanted to see a service of worship, training in devotion, training in right social relations, simplicity in living, constant expression of religion in the home, children to be taught at home and to come to the first part of the service only, periods of silence in the service, members of the congregation to speak, no collection, minister to have no salary. In the scale against the idea was the time and money that had already been spent in training for her present profession, her feeling that churches did not attract the live people, the chances against her success in building up an original church, the handicap of being a woman, especially "if I were that woman, and my lack of magnetism."

When the desire or impulse did not fade but became stronger, she did not feel that she dared simply to shut the door on what might really be "a way of service, a vocation." She consulted several of her friends, among them Mr. Dole, "what was not easy," and Helen Cheever, always dear to her heart in spite of pinpricks of disharmony. By the time Emily had their "most kind and sympathetic" advice, her mind, though there was nothing she could actually call a decision, had come to rest in a kind of negative position. "My inner life," wrote Emily in 1904, "has always been one of fluctuations, with a certain rough periodicity, periods of perhaps four or five months of greater and less religious sense alternating with what Fenelon calls 'dryness.' This dryness does not mean unbelief, doubt, distress of mind, only a certain passivity or dullness. All this makes it hard to judge aright."

She came to the wise conclusion to continue her profession and to appreciate the definite limits which that would set on even incidental alternative religious work as a layman. She could not know that ten years later a world catastrophe would deflect her personal course and turn it to the very field of broad moral education that she had dreamed of.

Emily Greene Balch was often called reticent. As a matter of fact she was not really very reticent—though she was given to a wry New England understatement in her speech and writing. Like an earlier Emily from her native Massachusetts, her soul selected its own society, but she did not then shut the door on others and close the valves of her attention. She could talk freely at times and she could write freely of what she called her inner life.

To the privacy of her diary she confided in one brief paragraph what she thought she had missed in being allotted to "the half-life of the unmarried woman."

April, 1904: I have just read a note from a friend who loves me. It is strange that women can love me but a man cannot, and yet the natural complement and the love that would revolutionize life is a man's. I am happy as an unmarried woman (not only unmarried but virgin in my emotions, never having loved or been loved—) but I know that I have only a small part of life. The passion, whether of mother or wife, whether joy or tragedy, is not for me. From the deepest sympathy even I am excluded. Family affection I have, friends I have, objects in life, work and deepest of satisfactions, religion, but the most simply primitively human gift, the deepest reach of life I have not.

The most self-revealing document, an undated fragment probably written about the same time, entitled "Confessions of a Professional Woman," began, "I suppose the impulse to confession comes to all of us at times and most of us have enough of the gossip in our makeup to incline us to be interested in such revelations. . . . I present my case as a human document of some interest for its bearing on a peculiar and important situation—the prevalence of the unmarried." She went on to describe her girlhood in a region where women outnumbered the men, and in a society where behind the polite assumption to the contrary lay the ill-concealed fact that the boy was the more important and, therefore, in a position to be exigent rather than suppliant, in fact, a little the sultan among a crowd of possible recipients of his kind attentions. She described herself as a proud, sensitive, and unattractive girl, awkward in dancing though loving it, prone to talk too much on bookish topics or to run embarrassingly short of small talk, going through "small agonies of shyness, mortification and disappointment," sitting conspicuous and alone in a range of empty seats while her neighbors were "taken out" by those whose turn it was in the German. Her only dances were usually those which fell to her by right when her partner, "alas often hunted up and reluctantly led back to me by the dancing master," took her out. When she was chosen it was too often as a courtesy required by good breeding, and which she felt to be too entirely forced to be any pleasure. This sort of experience, she recounts, made her, not unnaturally, very eager not to seek to desire the notice or attention of young men, and "must have made me, as I now see it, appear both uncordial and uninteresting."

When the way opened to her for further study after college, she gladly entered on it, though not with the idea of giving herself to the life of a celibate scholar. On the other hand what lay before her? Every instinct within her, the pride of the unsought made her averse to be or to appear to be waiting for a possibility which seemed about as imminent as the judgment day.

"Moreover I was as a woman still very immature. I believe that there is a singular tragedy common to a good deal of our old stock, arising from generations that have practiced, as a first precept of both religion and manners, restraint not only of expression of emotion but of emotion itself. They have a very tenacious virginity of nature and the natural instincts which they are afraid and ashamed to think of in their natural springtime, make themselves felt only when they are too late for fruition.

"The intense love of children, the instinct for homemaking, the preference for the companionship of men over that of women—all these made themselves felt only when my path in life had irrevocably fixed itself.

"As a professional woman I am happy in my work, I humbly believe I am useful. I am self-supporting. I have even had the

intimate satisfaction of helping out others. I have escaped the
dangers of unhappy, or only half-happy marriage and the personal
sufferings incident to the most successful marriage.

"But I have missed the fullness of life which I would prefer to
any calm. I would choose high mountain and deep valley, light
and shadow, to the even tenor of the plain, never knowing the
possible glories of sunlit heights. In the midst of the unbroken and
serene content of my life I know that I still have been shut out
except in imagination and sympathy from the most human and
deepest experiences. I doubt if I shall be lonely even as an old
woman. I have a circle of friends and relations and their babies.
I am besides—and this is perhaps the key to the whole story—rather
an impersonal person, quite able to live on what is offered by
books, nature, and since I am confessing the truth here in its
nakedness—on religion which we hold it so indecent to refer to
even if it be the soul of all our life."

In 1927, when Jane Addams was preparing the sequel to her
Twenty Years at Hull-House, she sought, as she had so often done
since the *Noordam* voyages of 1915 and 1919, the help of Emily
Balch. In the chapter describing the social changes in the United
States after the Civil War, Jane Addams dealt with the new
phenomenon of the educated, unmarried woman with a career,
women "selected by the pioneer qualities of character and sometimes at least by the divine urge of intellectual hunger," who were
self-supporting and devoted to their chosen fields of activity. "I
asked one of the finest of them," wrote Jane Addams, "my friend
Emily Greene Balch, who for twenty years had been head of the
Department of Economics at Wellesley College, and who through
periods of study in Europe and as the first secretary of the
Women's International League knew women in many countries to
give me her impression of the situation. I quote the following from
her illuminating reply."

The illuminating reply is given here in full:

Men had normally given hostages to fortune in the shape of
families. Professional women were far freer in general to risk their
jobs for the sake of unpopular principles and tabooed forms of
activity. They had, too, a quite special spur in the desire to prove
incorrect the general belief that they were congenitally incapable.

They found a tingling zest in discovering that it is not true, as women had been brought up to believe, that she was necessarily weaker and more cowardly, incapable of disinterested curiosity, unable to meet life on her own merits. Much good feminine energy went astray in proving that women could do this and that which had been marked taboo, when perhaps this was not the most desirable thing to do. There was also another incentive in the sense of opening the way to others and the sharing of an interesting experiment. Is it compatible with the modern theories about sex that two generations of professionally-trained women lived, without vows or outward safe-guards, completely celibate lives with no sense of its being difficult or of being misunderstood? Some of them later married; most of them did not. Now that they are old or oldish women, how do they feel about it? They are rather a reserved lot, but quite willing to admit that it has been a serious loss, certainly, to have missed what is universally regarded as the highest forms of woman's experience, but there is no evidence that they themselves or those who know them best find in them the abnormality that the Freudian psychoanalysts of life would have one look for. They are strong, resilient and active, they grow old in kindly and mellow fashion; their attitude to life is based upon active interests; they are neither excessively repelled nor excessively attracted to that second-hand intimacy with sexuality which modern science and modern literature so abundantly display. It is, however, strange to them to read interpretations of life, in novels, plays, and psychological treatises, that represent sex as prac-tically the whole content of life; family feeling, religion and art, as mere camouflaged libido, and everything that is not concerned with the play of desire between men and women as without adventure, almost without interest. If the educated unmarried women of the period between the Civil War and the World War represent an unique phase, it is one that has important implications which have not yet been adequately recognized by those who insist upon the imperious claim of sex.[3]

A member of the Norwegian Nobel Institute, August Schou, in appraising the characteristics of peace laureates, both men and women, found that on the whole, their marked tolerance of out-look for individuals, nations, and races was undoubtedly due "to their own harmonious development." In reading the life stories of these people he received the clear impression that "their dissatis-faction with the prevailing state of things is not born of a neurotic reaction against their immediate surroundings, but is rather the result of an excess or superabundance of positive qualities, and an urge to *give* in the widest sense of the word." [4]

In the last analysis Emily Balch and Jane Addams, by their American background and training and their intellectual friendships, did not accept the assumption that there is a fundamental antithesis between the individual and society. Unlike the earlier Darwinian individualistic liberals, they looked upon the social environment not as something historically given to which individuals must adapt themselves, but as a structure capable of being examined, transformed and created anew by will or desire and the intellect—good will and intelligence, according to Emily Balch and Jane Addams. They both belonged to the group of American social scientists who were to be not adjusters but transformers. In this they differed also from those disillusioned "realists" of the mid-twentieth century who believed that human nature had no resources save acceptance of the recurrent patterns of a meaningless and unalterable historical process.

Jane Addams at Hull-House had learned much from what she called those "brilliant men who formed the Department of Philosophy at the new University of Chicago—James Tufts, John Dewey, George Mead, James Angell." Emily Balch also learned from Dewey and Tufts; from Albion W. Small, with whom she had studied at the University of Chicago in 1893; from William James of her native Boston; and from Jane Addams herself. All these emphasized the dynamic character of social organization. For them evolution took on new ethical implications for action.[*]

Through Dewey's influence also both women strengthened their own belief and trust in the slow processes of growth and kept alive their faith in individuality and "what belongs to the internal sources and springs of individuality." [5] They were not impatient,

---

[*] Jane Addams, at a luncheon speech in New York City in October, 1929, in celebration of John Dewey's seventieth birthday, said: "In those [earlier] years when we were told by the scientists, or at least by the so-called scientists, that the world was in the grasp of sub-human forces against which it was absurd to oppose the human will, John Dewey calmly stated that the proper home of intelligence was the world itself and that the true function of intelligence was to act as a critic and regulator of the forces which move the world." *John Dewey, The Man and his Philosophy* (Harvard University Press, 1930), pp. 145, 146.

they were not hurried, they were not fretful. They nourished the roots of life and possessed their own souls. They were living examples of John Dewey's words, spoken as he himself stepped over the threshold to old age: "What we bring to the world in which we live always has and always will, at last, go back to the depths of our own being."

CHAPTER EIGHTEEN

Accolade—the Nobel Peace Prize, 1946

As the Women's International League was celebrating in April-May, 1945, the thirtieth anniversary of its beginnings at The Hague Congress, the German army was surrendering in droves and the world was waiting for the rain of death to cease. A cable to Geneva from Yella Hertzka, exiled in London, ran: "We were pioneers when we began our work. Let us be pioneers as long as it is needed."[*]

In this spirit the women resumed their Sisyphus-like task and began to think of organizing their first postwar international congress. Emily Balch, seventy-eight years old, was looking to the future also. She might be called "an old lady" now, though her forward-springing step denied it. It was almost with an "old lady's"

---

[*] Cable from Yella Hertzka, May, 1945: "In these thirty years our devotion to the ideals of peace and freedom upon which our League is founded has not wavered. We have lived to see these ideals given world-wide expression in the famous charter of 1941. . . . Mankind will demand a higher moral standard in every sphere, a better economic system, insuring security to all, a firmer insistence upon justice and toleration until brutal wars and bloody revolutions cease to be the means whereby change and reform are brought about. Those who plant splendid growing trees, can seldom hope to rest beneath their shade."

tremulous interest that she wondered about the fate of the Women's International League, the organization with which almost all her life since 1915 had been linked, the organization in which her dearly beloved Jane Addams had found a second fulfillment and subject matter for three of her eleven books, and through her labors for which she had become the first American woman to receive the Nobel Peace Prize. "It is to be hoped," wrote Emily Balch, "that we shall find ourselves not only older but with deeper wisdom and that those of us who are not only older but really old may find ourselves vastly outnumbered by those with long years of activity ahead of them." [1] Like Kathleen Innes and Edith Pye of England, Clara Ragaz of Switzerland, Cor Ramondt-Hirschmann of the Netherlands and others, she was planning to step into the background of League activities and, in Emily Simon's words, "pass on the torch generously" to the young generation. She hoped to be useful, a frequent word in her vocabulary, in whatever capacities she could serve the League.

She did not know that the year 1945 was to bring forth an event of revolutionary import. Thereafter, any resort to war as an instrument of national policy became unthinkable. On August 6, 1945, Emily Balch's own country, "these United States of our love," the great, generous, humane United States of America, was to drop the first atomic bomb on Hiroshima, and four days later another one on Nagasaki, on the plea that it would mean the saving of human lives, both American and Japanese. In one split second of time, when the news broke over the world, Emily Balch, the aghast members of the United States section, and sensitive people the world over, realized imaginatively what the consequences of this act were to be day after day, year after year, minute after minute, on every man, woman, child, and nation in the world. Frankenstein's monster was a reality.

It came as a special shock to Emily and her United States colleagues because earlier in the year, in January, 1945, persistent rumors to the effect that the Japanese were seeking peace terms reached the Washington officers of the W.I.L.P.F. In that month the national president, Dorothy Medders Robinson, informed the national board that several attempts were being made to sue for peace. "Feeling keenly that the Japanese war was our war, we pressed on our government in every possible way to explore these

peace advances. No work was more important to us during May,
June, July of 1945 than our attempt to have our government
explore advances made or suggest peace terms themselves to the
Japanese, but we failed, and the atom bomb indicated how great
was our failure."*

As honorary head of the W.I.L.P.F. and a veteran of so many
Congresses, Emily Balch was in constant demand by the European
leaders in matters of League policy and planning and in a position
to sound the spiritual note for the members of the United States
section who were preparing to attend the first postwar congress
in a spirit of deep humility. They had not shared the suffering of
blitz, invasion, and occupation which came as "a natural result
of policies and conditions for which we too were responsible," as
Dorothy Robinson said. "No matter how hard we tried," Emily
Simon was to say at the Congress, in words Emily Balch might
have written, "we could never quite succeed in entering into the
agony and tragedy millions have known. But there are many kinds
of suffering and many ways of coming to greater understanding of
problems. We all need to share whatever light we have. If some
have not suffered through the valley of the shadow, it may be that
they have been spared in order to offer the perspective that can
be so easily lost when one lives so close to tragedy and death." [2]

One of the first questions to be considered at the Congress was
whether there was a place in the postwar world for the W.I.L.P.F.,
a woman's peace organization. This was a question of personal
moment to Emily Balch, for, as she said, "this effort to pool the
intelligence and energy of women for the inseparable ends of peace
and freedom is very much interwoven with my own life." Would
a meeting of minds between former members be easy or even
possible? Would there be an unbridgeable gulf between women
of the "free countries" who had been more or less spared, and
those who had been under dictatorship and occupation and had
taken active part in the resistance movements?

In October, 1945, Emily Balch had written a letter to the
three international chairmen discussing the possible dissolution of
the W.I.L.P.F. as a result of disintegration due to war, the destruc-

* Report of the United States section to the Luxembourg Congress, August,
1946, by Dorothy Detzer and Dorothy M. Robinson.

tion of membership lists and death of leaders, the uncertainty of getting new, young, and vigorous workers, and "ideological" divergences among the members. "These latter were making cooperation increasingly difficult before the war." wrote Emily Balch, "and the proceedings of our Grenoble and last Zürich Congresses were often painful and far from edifying. The divergences will have been accentuated by our different war-time experiences."

The differences seemed to her chiefly of two sorts—the difference in philosophy between "integral" (complete) pacifists and those to whom failure to resist organized political crime—to resist even by force—appeared to imply a degree of complicity that might be worse than war, morally and in practical results; and the differing viewpoints, left and right, in economic questions which in Emily's opinion were hard to bridge and which she saw were complicated and emotionalized by differences in conception of what Russia meant and what attitude to Russia the League should take.

Just before the Congress, in the spring of 1946, the United States section had published a biographical sketch, *Emily Greene Balch of New England, Citizen of the World,* by her philosopher friend, John H. Randall, Jr., of Columbia University. It summarized with great succinctness in twelve pages, her background, motivation, and some of the details of her many faceted career.

Emily Balch, in thanking him, said, "You have made a beautiful thing out of very brittle material.

"It is a more than life-size likeness and I suppose in any portrait the sitter dwarfs the surroundings and accompaniments out of all reasonable perspective. I was particularly pleased with your choice of quotations. I had no idea I had ever said so many sensible things.

"There is however one serious difficulty that I have to raise and I hate so much to propose any operation, any excision in your admirable piece of work that I have let two days go by out of sheer funking of doing what I hated to do. I regret to say that it is not historical, simply not the case, that I influenced statesmen and important people as you have understood that I did. You would I am only too sure not be able to find any evidence in support of what you say on this head.

"Let me add that I thought you handled the difficult question of how I reacted to the recent war and the positions I took and failed to take quite beautifully.

"Believe me, my objection to what you say about my influence referred to above has nothing to do with modesty. It is pretty factual and objective really."

The date of August, 1946, was fixed upon for the meeting of the tenth Congress, and Luxembourg was chosen as the place.

For Emily Balch, that year brought two culminating experiences—her attendance at that Congress with her first air flight across the Atlantic at the age of seventy-nine, and "the amazing event of the Oslo award of the Nobel Prize" in November. The Luxembourg Congress opened a new chapter in the history of the W.I.L.P.F. and also an entirely new chapter in the personal life of Emily Balch. The nine years' interval between the last Congress at Luhacovice in 1937, and the one in Luxembourg was both long and testing. Not one iron curtain but many had divided the women in wartime. "They had been exposed to very different experiences," wrote Emily Balch. "Their information as to what had been happening elsewhere had been screened and colored by the national press of each country. Had their old unity evaporated? I can only say that we found each other again; we tested each other; we were resolved to go on working together." [3]

The lovely old capital of the Grand Duchy of Luxembourg, with its profile of spires and its web of bridges spanning its storied ravines, was an ideal meeting place. In Emily Balch's address of welcome, given in French the evening before the opening of the Congress, she spoke of her first visit to Europe over sixty years before, of her love of Europe though it had been mother of so many wars—wars of religion, dynastic wars, wars of imperialism—and she touched on the very special functions encumbent upon regions like Switzerland, like Alsace-Lorraine, like the country in which they were meeting, Luxembourg, where French and German cultures meet, "une oeuvre d'apaisement, d'entre-aide, de reconciliation," a task of assuagement, of mutual aid, of reconciliation.

The memory of Hitler was still raw and rankling in the minds of her audience as she continued: "Friends, let us forget as far as we can, those things which divide us. . . . There are no superior races. There are no inferior races. Let us learn to think of ourselves as members of that great race which is the human race. Wherever we pass upon the earth, let us be at home. Let us become conscious of the unity which embraces all the children of God.

"Let us try to develop in ourselves a mutual comprehension, a broad tolerance, or better still a universal love which, like the love of St. Francis of Assisi, will include every living creature.

"This quality of love is not all that is needful. Institutions, political machinery, concrete agencies are also indispensable." [4]

There was, however, one drawback to meeting in Luxembourg. The German delegation was missing. Thirteen German members had secured permission from their civil and military governments to leave their country, but public sentiment in Luxembourg, which had been occupied and bombed by the Nazis, was still understandably too inflamed to permit their entering. This became known too late to find another meeting place. It meant losing from the Congress, said Emily Balch, "the loyal and much enduring German women who hold the most strategic position of all, those working to re-educate their fellow-citizens for a new Germany."

"It was to a sick world that I returned after an absence from Europe of ten years," Emily wrote, "years which covered the pivotal chapter of the rise and fall of National Socialism. Midsummer though it was, it reminded me of a March landscape where snow, which hitherto had covered all differences, is gone, when all the ravages of the winter, all the rubbish and detritus under that cold mantle are laid bare; when, also, the green grass is pricking up in sheltered corners and spring is in the air even if the wind is chill.

"This world is full of painful reminders, but it is small details that bite into one's mind. I came upon a street corner in Luxembourg where a 'Tracing Bureau' had filled window after window with pathetic faded pictures of missing men and women, lads and girls, children. Some of the pictures were snapshots, some artificially posed portraits from a photographer's studio. The quaint Luxembourg dialect gave bare data—place and time of birth, status, when and where last heard from. 'Please send news if any!' They hurt me more than the bomb-shattered buildings." [5]

Emily Balch, as honorary international president, opened the Congress with a short greeting. She stood, a frail, thin figure, on the high platform of the large hall in the Municipal Palace. Her speech was characteristically short, classic in its economy of phrasing, strength of feeling and in what she left unsaid, and arresting in its chief figure of speech.

"We cannot come together here today," she began, "without deep feeling. We have gone through a great deal together and a great deal more while separated by the tempest of war. . . .

"Human nature seems to me like the Alps. The depths are profound, black as night and terrifying, but the heights are equally real, uplifted in the sunshine. It is not realistic to concentrate our attention on the recent revelations of the depths of evil to which human beings can descend. To do so leads to stumbling feet, weakness and discouragement.

"The recent years have also brought us amazing revelations of the good and great possibilities of human nature. The instances of sheer physical courage have been innumerable, but this is a very common human quality; it may be very noble and may be a quality we share with many animals. More significant are the revelations we have seen of moral courage, of devotion, self- forgetfulness, of victorious human love and sheer goodness. Many of us have seen these qualities shining forth in Jane Addams."

She closed, as she so often did, with an emphasis on the personal: "We must draw a deep breath and fill ourselves with the fresh air of courage and confidence, of a sober gladness, a love which is universal and all embracing without losing its vivid personal quality." [6]

Both she and Jane Addams in the International, and notably Hannah Hull in the United States, had succeeded in stamping the Women's International League with a quality generally attributed to women, a quality of personal affection, of feeling for the individual. The League, as Emily herself said, though "based on universal, impersonal principles, has been personal as women are naturally personal, warmed by a sense of comradeship and shared affections and admiration." [7] Thus Jane Addams used to sign her letters to her colleagues "Devotedly yours" and Emily Balch ended hers "Affectionately yours"; while Hannah Hull, in her correspondence, drew her fellow workers by addressing them simply as "My dear."

Once again, the Women's League was holding its first postwar

gathering simultaneously with the assembling of a peace conference of the powers at Paris. Following the pattern of 1919, the
Congress sent a message to the representatives of the twenty-one
governments assembled there. They deplored the unhappy delays
in reaching agreement in the peace treaties and urged the statesmen
not to allow national interests, economic advantage, and prestige
to determine the decisions of the conference, but to act as trustees
of the human race as one unit. The women appealed for treaties
based on respect for the dignity of human personality and for a
Charter of Human Rights to be an integral part of every peace
treaty. The text was unanimously voted and signed by Emily Balch
and the three joint chairmen—Ragaz, Innes, and Baer.

Over 200 delegates and alternates from eighteen countries
assembled at the Municipal Palace. The younger delegates saw
deep emotions welling quietly to the surface as old friends and
comrades met after nearly ten years of separation. Many of them
besides Emily Balch were pioneers of 1915, 1919, and 1921. "It is
perhaps not surprising," wrote Emily Balch, "that many of the
participants were women of science like Dr. Gertrude Woker,
professor of chemistry at the University of Berne, and Dr. Naima
Sahlbom, recently decorated by the King of Sweden; or distinguished teachers like Andrée Jouve, professor of history in a Paris
Lycée, Dr. Gertrude C. Bussey, professor of Philosophy at Goucher
College, Maryland, and Marie Lous-Mohr, one of the heroic band
of Norwegian teachers who herself supported twenty-eight months
of Nazi imprisonment with a nobility of spirit for which words
are weak." [8]

There were also a number, including most of the American
delegation, who came for the first time to an international congress, with high expectancy. Emily Balch was pleased to see,
scattered among the delegations at the long tables, so many fresh
and youthful faces. "From the first, the will to continue made
itself felt," she said. "If no other national section wants to go on,
we shall go on alone," said the Danes, with 25,000 members in
their little country.

To have come together in such numbers in spite of innumerable difficulties was in itself an achievement. Over sixty Scandinavian delegates traveled three days and three nights, in chartered
buses, through the frightfully bombed cities of Germany. The

American group, twenty-eight in number, undeterred by shortage of ships, cancellation of passages, steerage conditions when they were obtained, grounding of planes and nerve-racking setbacks in almost every case, arrived intact, on time, and undismayed. In Paris, Emily Balch and her flight companion Eugenie Intemann took turns standing for several hours, battered by crowds, to buy train tickets to Zürich and Luxembourg.

There were no representatives from Italy or Hungary, none from Japan where the national section had done such fine work for peace in a militaristic country, none from Russia. Poland, Belgium, and Brazil sent one each. Yella Hertzka was able to come from Austria, to which she had returned in April, 1946, from her exile in England; "and what a fresh breath her delightful personality brought," [9] said Emily Balch. The most numerous delegations came from Great Britain, the three Scandinavian countries, the United States, France, and Switzerland.

All the younger delegates were familiar with the early history of the W.I.L.P.F., especially with the details of the first two congresses. They were therefore just as moved as the pioneers Emily Balch, Clara Ragaz, Cor Ramondt-Hirschmann, Gabrielle Duchêne, Edith Pye, Audrée Jouve, and Gertrude Baer at the silent tribute to comrades who were missing for the first time. Clara Ragaz, who presided, spoke movingly of Lida Gustava Heymann and the friend whose name was always linked with hers, Dr. Anita Augspurg. The fate of Eugenie Meller, the president, and of Mélanie Vambéry, the secretary of the Hungarian section, presented, she said, a riddle difficult to grasp. Some, like Elsa Kalmus of Czechoslovakia and Rosa Manus of Amsterdam, with whom Emily Balch had worked closely after The Hague Congress in 1915, had died in concentration camps or gas chambers. Marie Schmolkova of Czechoslovakia had died in exile, her death hastened by hardship. Frau Plaminkova of Czechoslovakia, though not so closely linked up with the League but always cooperative, had declined to consider emigration for herself and was handed over to the executioner by the German army of occupation.

The delegates were prepared for a difficult Congress—difficult emotionally and intellectually. Most of the women had gone through experiences of Nazi conquest, occupation, oppression, or blitz. Many had taken active part in the nonviolent resistance movements within their countries. The Czech delegates of whom the blue-eyed, tragic-faced Lola Hanouskova was outstanding, had lived for six years in complete isolation, behind an iron curtain with the illegal radio their only hold on sanity. They had breathed a poisonous atmosphere of lies, corruption, dehumanization of values. "Everything we believed in," wrote Lola Hanouskova in 1945, "rights, laws, moral obligations, conscience, love, sympathy—all that is defiled and ground in the dust.* [10]

The discussions at the Congress—whether the League should continue functioning, and of its future strategy and program of action—threw into relief the main lines of cleavage, as Emily Balch had foreseen. To the Czechoslovakian and French delegations, especially to Mme. Duchêne, "integral pacifism" appeared an enemy of peace, unrealistic and lacking concrete measures. The main causes of war, their experience had taught them, were Nazism and Fascism. Therefore, said Mme. Duchêne, the supreme task was to work against Fascism in all its manifestations, siding in their struggle with people's movements everywhere. The "integral" pacifists, on the other hand, believed themselves equally realistic and concrete in working to create the economic, social, and political conditions that make for peace.

The second difference was in attitudes toward Soviet Russia. These ranged from extreme devotion and repeated pleas "not to divide the world," to extreme suspicion of the totalitarian elements in the Russian regime, and mistrust of its will to peace. All were agreed, however, on the necessity of working to preserve peace with Russia and of drawing Soviet women into the orbit of the W.I.L.P.F. Their hopes on the latter point have not yet been realized.

A third difference was in philosophical and religious outlook, which prevented agreement on political problems—such as the question of war guilt, the disposition of vanquished peoples, the reinstatement of former Nazis into the national life, the attitude towards the court martial for war criminals involving the question of the death penalty, which the women of the League had hitherto definitely rejected. These question divided even those who had shared the common experience of Nazi occupation and oppression;

---

* It is clear from the Congress reports that the Scandinavians, being Nordics, were less cruelly treated than the Czechoslovakians and other non-Nordics.

often the French, Czechoslovaks, Yugoslavs, Belgians, and Poles voted together in opposition to Norway, Denmark, and Austria, as well as to Britain, Sweden, and the United States. Emily Balch, wishing to secure a maximum of real consent and to avoid "majorization" of minority opinion, had proposed that no resolution should be passed which was opposed by a substantial minority of ten or more. The Congress was unwilling to accept a veto in such form. But the same end was reached when certain painful resolutions unacceptable to some delegates, were withdrawn. The Americans withdrew their resolutions on war trials and on treatment of vanquished peoples.

On the last point Emily Balch did not find herself out of sympathy with the attitudes of Yella Hertzka and Marie Lous-Mohr. Yella Hertzka explained that in Austria an official registration had sorted Nazis from non-Nazis. It was difficult to find enough teachers free from Nazism because non-Nazi teachers had been sent to the front, or were dead or had not yet returned to the country. "Education is most necessary," she said, in English, "to counteract eight years of Nazi education. I believe that what the W.I.L.P.F. should do is to forget the past as we Austrians, who have suffered so much under Hitler and had to emigrate, lost our relatives or friends, have made up our minds to forget and look to the future, and help the Austrian people, which is not gifted in politics—but very good in culture, music, handicrafts, etc.

"My opinion is that punishment will have no effect for the creation of a new spirit in Austria. Only a planned re-education can bring Austria again into the state of becoming a democratic country within the union of nations."

Marie Lous-Mohr, speaking in German, also supported the idea of restoring unity among the population. "Belonging to a land which has also suffered under occupation and oppression," she said, "we must consider what to do with the ex-Nazis. We must re-instate them or we will have a dangerous element in our country. We want to help them, so that their ideas will never spread 'nicht nur aus menschlichen sondern aus practischen Grunden.'" ('not only for humane but also for practical reasons.') When another delegate from Norway read a quotation from a Norwegian poet, "Let us not die with the hearts we have today,"

there was considerable emotion and heat among the French delegates." "But on the whole," said Emily Balch, "there was a refresh-
ing absence not only of interruptions for extraneous purposes but,
above all, of eloquence and phrase-making."

An exceptional feature of the Congress was the amount of
time given to the reports of national sections, especially to those
whose countries had suffered occupation by the Nazi forces, "with
the hope" said Emily Balch, "of helping those who had been
spared such an experience to understand what it meant."

The Hungarian section had simply disappeared, as its leading
members had been sent to the gas chambers of Auschwitz and
elsewhere. There was no report.

The reports from Denmark and Norway showed how their
members could put their ideas and principles into practice even
under a remorseless dictatorship. They illustrated how the resistance movements were able to develop techniques of nonviolent
constructive action and how democratic ideas could be maintained
and spread even under the heels of the Nazis. All the accounts
demonstrated the high moral quality of the W.I.L.P.F. in keeping
alive the spirit of tolerance, forbearance and charity without which
comes bitterness, injustice, and the war of all against all.

Many of the first postoccupation reports of what had happened
in Denmark, Norway, France, the Netherlands, and Czechoslovakia
had reached the United States after the liberation in the spring
of 1945. They had appeared in an admirably edited and unique
International Circular Letter which had been issued quarterly all
during the war years by Gertrude Baer from New York City.
Emily Balch had cooperated closely with Gertrude Baer in the
arduous task of editing the *Letter*, making translations and Eng-
lishing the text. It meant two or three days of strenuous concentration, for Gertrude Baer was an exacting editor. Many of Emily's
own political proposals, recommendations, and articles and reviews
had first been circulated in its pages.

Emily Balch was, therefore, in part familiar with what was to
be recounted at the Luxembourg Congress by some of her European fellow delegates who had helped defy Power when it had
seemed most omnipotent. Like her father, Francis Balch, who long
ago had written in "A Layman's Creed," "My creed contains no

explanation of evil,"* Emily Balch had never pretended to arrive at a satisfying theory about the mystery of suffering and evil. She did not have a philosophic cast of mind like her friend Mary W. Calkins of Wellesley or Gertrude Bussey of Goucher College and the W.I.L.P.F. She had had to come to grips personally with the problem of undeserved suffering in the destiny of her sister Annie, "in some ways the nicest of all the Balches." At the Congress of Zürich in 1919, Emily Balch, as well as Jane Addams, Dr. Alice Hamilton, and Florence Kelley, who were only too well acquainted with the evils in the social fabric they dealt with, had listened with incredulous horror to the story of starvation and its attendant demoralizations as told by the Austrian Leopoldine Kulka. They did not realize that their century was yet young in crime. Emily had seen degradation of the most sordid kind in her Denison House Settlement days in Boston, in the slums of London in 1896, and in the open sewers of Glasgow during her first trip to Europe in 1885. She had had the first intimation, the first glimmerings of evil, none the less terrifying because not understood, when as a little girl, tripping to Miss Chase's School, through the Boston Public Gardens, "a man exposed himself to me."

But in her Luxembourg speech Emily had also said realistically enough, "The recent years have also brought us amazing revelations of the good and great possibilities of human nature." She listened on the second day of the Congress to reports of many representatives of national sections, accounts factual, sometimes stark, devoid of self-pity, illustrating what she called "revelations of moral courage, of devotion, of self-forgetfulness, of victorious human love."

On April 9, 1940, both Denmark and Norway were taken wholly by surprise by the Nazis and overrun by German soldiers. For five years both countries were occupied. "The Danish section of the W.I.L.P.F.," said Else Zeuthen,** the chairman, "tried throughout to stick to our beliefs and usual actions. We succeeded in getting through the war with our membership undiminished [25,000]. With a large number of other cultural, political and

---

* Francis V. Balch, "A Layman's Creed," *The Christian Register*, May 12, 1898.
** Else Zeuthen in 1956 was elected international president of the W.I.L.P.F. In 1958 she was her country's delegate to the United Nations Assembly in New York City.

youth organizations, we made an effort to preserve the democratic
ideals of the people, and especially to preserve the young people
against Nazi influence. Between 1941 and 1943 we had 1,000 meetings, and in the autumn of 1940 we had our usual peace-day selling
little white flags, which were, by the way, bought with great
eagerness by promenading German soldiers who placed them on
the backs of their lapels, not daring to wear them openly. Otherwise, the leading motto was not to have anything to do with the
intruders."*

"One thing" said Else Zeuthen, "helped us to keep what we
stood for alive in the eyes of our members. Before the outbreak
of the war, we had obtained permission to receive three hundred
Jewish children from Central Europe. We did this, of course, first
and foremost to help, but also to show in action our abomination
of the inhuman treatment to which German Jews were exposed.
The first group came on the day when the war broke out. They
came with terror and despair in their hearts having that same
morning said good bye to parents, sisters and brothers, perhaps
for the last time. After a year in Danish homes, they were to go
on to Palestine. Most of them, however, had to stay in Denmark,
though forty-three were deported to Theresienstadt. Working to
help these young people under very difficult circumstances helped
us to feel that in the face of Nazi oppressors we were faithful to
our League's ideal of tolerance and compassion.

"As the German measures became more cruel, hatred and feelings of revenge towards the Germans of course increased violently.
From the start, we took the view that whatever the deeds of Hitler
and his gang, it would not be an ennobling experience for the
people to be ruled by these feelings with regard to the German
people as a whole. So we took every opportunity to speak against
hatred and revenge, and to explain that no nation ought to be
judged as a whole, but that there were good and bad people in

---

* In the summer of 1943, as the Allies progressed, and Danish sabotage
increased, the Germans decided to assume fuller control. A wave of terror
set in, beginning in October, with the persecution of the Danish Jews. Of
the 7,000 Jews in the country, the Danish people, with the backing of the
Swedish government and people, helped nearly all to flee secretly and by
night across the sound separating Denmark from Sweden. The physicist, Niels
Bohr, Nobel Prize winner, was one of the Danish Jews who escaped to
Sweden in a rowboat.

any nation, and that revenge and hatred would only breed revenge and hatred. Of course, many people at that time disagreed with us, but still we found many adherents.

"We, as an organization containing many absolute pacifists, took no part in the so-called active resistance; that was left to each individual according to her nature and conscience. If we did not actually help in defeating the physical power of the Hitlerites, we were very active in keeping alive the democratic and humane spirit of our own country. Many people at home and abroad will think this was only a slight contribution in the face of the threatening blackout of civilization, but we ourselves think that our job was worth doing. For what was the use of bringing about the downfall of Hitler, if the victors themselves afterwards turned Hitlerites?" [12]

In Norway, the invasion of the German troops paralyzed all usual peace activity except relief work. "What should be a peaceworker's attitude to the aliens who had invaded our country? What could be done to prevent bitterness and hatred to conquer our hearts?" asked a circular letter that was sent out to the chairmen of the W.I.L.P.F. committees urging them to remember the ideals of the women's first Congress at The Hague in 1915 when enemy women "held out their hands to each other across the barbed wires of the world war."

For the first three and a half years the Norwegian resistance was nonviolent in method, not because the Norwegians were pacifists but because of the ideological character of the struggle. In this weaponless war, the Germans were not able to conquer Norwegian justice nor nazify the heroic Norwegian school teachers, nor coerce the Norwegian church.

In August, 1940, Marie Lous-Mohr, an Oslo teacher, the president of the Norwegian W.I.L.P.F. had to accompany a Gestapo official to the office of the League and give an account of its history, organization, and activity. Fortunately, all membership lists and compromising papers had been disposed of earlier. Orders were given: "The League is now dissolved," said Commissar Fehmer. In spite of this, small groups continued to meet privately in Oslo and other towns during the whole occupation. In January, 1943, Marie Lous-Mohr was arrested and sent to Grini Concentration Camp near Oslo, where she was imprisoned for twenty-eight months until the liberation of May, 1945.[13]

Emily Balch was deeply impressed by the serenity, calm simplicity and sense of perspective of Marie Lous-Mohr. The day before the Congress opened, Marie Lous-Mohr had been invited as a guest of honor to luncheon with the American delegation. She related some of her prison experiences in her excellent English with the circumspection, and understatement as of the born New Englander. She was in a locked cell for the first one and a half years; after that she was allowed to join the "free prisoners" in washing and mending duties. She apparently was a leader, sustaining the others, singing her folk-songs and giving "small lectures." Her cell was only a few feet from wall to wall. There was a window, but it was too high to look out of unless one climbed on the radiator. The Nazi women guards "were not too bad on the whole, though their morals left much to be desired." The women prisoners were let out of their cells twice a day to attend to their bodily needs. "It was a hard time," Marie Lous-Mohr said, "but a rich time because of the growth of fellowship among the prisoners. The things we could do illegally for one another gave a little sport to life—a smuggled newspaper sent to one another by a string." At Christmas there was a little program when the guards were off for dinner. Communication was through holes in the doors. Marie Lous-Mohr led in singing the Christmas carols and told the Christmas story. Each prisoner was allowed two packages and a little dinner. At nine o'clock they were permitted to sing carols out of the window into the starry sky. A German soldier on guard in the courtyard stood motionless and listened. "It was a wonderful Christmas," she concluded simply.*

---

* From some men prisoners who had a smuggled radio, the women learned by finger language of the Danish liberation and made ready for theirs. "It was hard," said Marie Lous-Mohr, "to think that our liberation depended on the death of so many other people. They all said they would be glad to stay in prison another year if Norway were not invaded."

In July, 1945, after her liberation, Marie Lous-Mohr attended the combined first meeting of the Scandinavian sections in beautiful Dalekarlia, Sweden. She gave an account of her imprisonment which a Swedish member reported as "calm, full of warm humor and without bitterness." She ended her speech with the words: "We have learned that no sacrifice is too great or great enough in building an enduring peace."

At the end of the Congress Marie Lous-Mohr was elected one of the two international chairmen. The other was an American, Gertrude Carman Bussey, Professor of Philosophy at Goucher College, Maryland. Emily Balch had always found in this colleague twenty years younger than herself, a kindred spirit, kindred in her broad range of sensitivities, with a poise, balance and realism equal to her own, one of the few people with whom Emily could discuss religion as freely as she could books and politics.

Emily Greene Balch, with acclaim, was again voted honorary international president. The whole Congress rose to its feet. Emily was almost eighty, nearing the end of her life, as she thought. Her face seemed to the spectators an impassive mask but it might not be too far amiss to conjecture that Jane Addams was in her mind, and that to be thus held a successor to Jane Addams was as great a glory and honor as she could bear.

The evening meeting which closed the Congress was open to the public. The final speaker was Lola Hanouskova of Prague, who spoke in German, saying, in touching apology, that it was "the language of Goethe, of my friends Lida Gustava Heymann, Anita Augspurg and of my Swiss friend, Mme. Ragaz." At the end she paid tribute to Luxembourg and to the national hero of Luxembourg, Jean L'Aveugle, who was also king of her own country, Bohemia, as Johann der Blinde. The motto found on his coat-of-arms was "Ich Dien" or "I serve." This motto, beneath the three plumes, the English Black Prince was to adopt at the battle of Crécy as his own—as the obligation and end of nobility.* "Wir müssen alle dienen," Lola Hanouskova ended, "We must all serve." [14]

For Emily Balch, however, the most stirring word uttered was the final cry of a member, "And now to work!"

When the radios one mid-November afternoon in 1946 announced the award of the Nobel Peace Prize jointly to Emily Balch and Dr. John R. Mott, Emily Balch was lying ill with a bronchial infection in the Wellesley-Newton Hospital. Most people were caught unawares. They had never heard of Emily Balch. Suddenly she was in all the headlines all over the world at once.

---

* This charming legend, unfortunately, is not historically accurate.

There was much curiosity and interest, much pleasure, and in some quarters wonderment. For Emily Balch came from the ranks of plain private citizens. She had never held any political office. She had no official connection with the United Nations. The only body she represented, the Women's International League for Peace and Freedom, through which she mainly worked, was a private organization. As her friend, Professor Brand Blanshard wrote at the time, "It was as if searchlights from all over the world turned their light simultaneously on the tired, frail figure on a hospital bed. She woke up one morning to find herself in 'the fierce light that beats upon a throne.'"

"When this happens," he added, "it is just as well to have lived a life that will stand such light. Miss Balch's will." [15]

The Nobel Prizes are bestowed "for the greatest services to mankind," without regard to nationality, "so that in every case the prize may go to the worthiest." The Peace Prize is directed to be given to the person "who has done the most or best work for the brotherhood of nations, the abolition and reduction of standing armies, and for the formation or popularization of peace congresses." Emily Balch was one of the few laureates who had fulfilled the requirements in all three categories. At times the prize is given to a statesman for a specific achievement, as in the case of Dr. Ralph Johnson Bunche in 1950.* This award was a particular source of pleasure to Emily Balch, as Ralph Bunche was the first Negro to receive the prize.

In honoring people like Emily Balch, Jane Addams, Bertha von Suttner, Norman Angell, and Dr. Alfred Fried, the Nobel Committee was giving recognition to what unofficial citizens can contribute to the conditions for international peace. Emily Balch was doubtless chosen as a practical scholar of the peace movement, as a symbol for all the unofficial and voluntary workers for peace throughout the world, and as an outstanding spokesman for the plain everyday peoples of the world. In her recognition, they all received honor and encouragement.

It was characteristic that two days after the announcement of

---

* After the assassination in 1948 of Count Folke-Bernadotte, the United Nations mediator in Palestine, Dr. Bunche, became acting mediator and a large share of the credit for the truce agreements that ended the Palestine conflicts in 1949 was due to him.

the award, Emily Balch summoned up enough strength from her hospital bed to send a message to the New York *Neue Volkzeitung,* which was commemorating the tenth anniversary of the award of the Nobel Peace Prize to Carl von Ossietsky in 1936:

"In remembering Carl von Ossietsky today," wrote Emily Balch, "we are remembering a man of heroic courage and devotion. He defied the Nazi power at its height and paid a bitter penalty. He was, I think, never allowed to profit in any degree by the Nobel Award. We can but hope that the recognition may have been some consolation in his suffering. It is a sobering thing to follow him and Jane Addams and so many other noble and rich person-alities in the list of those who due to Nobel's generous thought have received the honor of this peace award." [16]

Emily Balch's name had been placed early in 1946 before the Nobel Committee of the Norwegian parliament by a group of dis-tinguished American and foreign sponsors. She was awarded the prize the very first time that her name was proposed. In the United States, Manley G. Hudson, Judge of the Permanent Court of International Justice, who had known Emily Balch well at Geneva; the philosopher John Dewey, who had influenced Jane Addams and been influenced by her; and Joseph P. Chamberlain, were the first to give their warmly generous encouragement. Joseph P. Chamberlain of the Columbia University Law School had first admired Emily Balch in her Wellesley years as an influence in immigration problems, and he was deeply aware of the extent of her labors in rescuing European victims of Nazi tyranny.

The sponsor whose support received the most publicity was President Mildred McAfee Horton of Wellesley College, who had been Commander of the Waves during World War II. It was partly that a high-ranking naval officer was proposing a well-known pacifist for the Nobel Award; it was partly that in this way Wellesley College seemed to make restitution for "what may have been an unjust decision" years before.

Towards the end of January, 1946, at the Domichek, Emily braced herself to spend an evening reading for the first time the letters of sponsors and supporters and the biographical sketch that accompanied them. "The sketch," she wrote to two close friends in New York City, "represents me as more of a supporter of the war than I can admit that I am but I realize that my position is neither very definite nor very consistent. How can one be when an irresistible force meets an immovable obstacle in one's own mind? One is lucky not to be as disintegrated as Hiroshima!

"As for the letters I am of course both flattered and abased by them. It is as good as going to one's own funeral without having to die first (which I don't at all want to do, till I am more played out than I am already). The touching thing is that so many busy people took the trouble to write these letters and in many cases with such great personal kindness. . . . If, as I expect, nothing else comes of it, I have had a great experience such as I should not have thought possible." [17]

While Emily Balch was still in the hospital after the Nobel award, improving but still low in strength, guarded from undue exertions by her brother Francis, her sisters, and faithful Agnes Perkins, she eluded their vigilance by writing an anniversary greeting on November 30 to Paul U. Kellogg and friends of *The Survey*, "through which my most ambitious piece of work, *Our Slavic Fellow Citizens*, first found readers." She tried to voice her faith in the promise of the United Nations and in eventual world peace. Her brother sent it on to Paul Kellogg in New York, saying "her undimmed enthusiasm and faith shone out as clear as the noonday sun."

"I do not want to be a Pollyanna," wrote Emily Balch, "or refuse to face squarely all the realities—as well as the hobgoblin fears—but I feel a great hope that world history is passing a critical point; that the age-old dream of a world peace, instead of proving an iridescent Utopia is beginning to be seen as the hardest kind of common sense; both practicable and an absolute necessity unless we choose bloody chaos and atomic and bacterial war.

"I hope that we are not going to try a federal world state, but instead a complex interweaving of functional arrangements for common interests. What is needed is exactly the sort of thing the Economic and Social Council, and the UNESCO stand for— namely: human, tolerant, elastic cooperation in which the threat of war is as inappropriate as it is in any civilized undertaking.

"It is curious to me how afraid people are of being fooled by believing in the possibilities of good, when it is just as bad, and even easier, to be fooled by *refusing* to believe." She ended by saying, "Let us work for the things the *Survey* has always worked for—for a world in which every man, woman and child shall have a fair chance to grow to full human stature." [18]

Being very human, it was with reluctance that Emily Balch had to abandon the plan of going to Oslo in December to receive the award in person at the usual ceremonies. An English W.I.L.P.F. member, Myrtle Wright, a Quaker, who had been in Norway during most of the war, wrote a little account of the ceremony to friends in England. "Though Emily Balch was not able herself to come to receive the Nobel Peace Prize, her spirit was with us and her name honored during the celebrations in Oslo yesterday. In the morning we gathered in the small and crowded Nobelsal with its four great chandeliers overcoming the darkness of a dull and wet winter's day outside. The Diplomatic corps filled the right-hand aisle and promptly at one o'clock we rose as the King, Crown Prince and Princess arrived and took their places in the front row, followed by another little procession of John Mott and members of the Nobel Committee. The proceedings opened with a hidden orchestra playing a *Mozart* Overture.

"Gunnar Jahn, the chairman of the Nobel Committee, made an excellent speech in honor of Emily Balch giving a sense of her amazing activity. He ended with the words, 'She has shown us that the reality we seek must be won through hard work in the world in which we live, but she has shown us more than this; that one does not become exhausted and that defeat gives new courage for the struggle to those who have within them the holy fire.' The heading of one of the evening papers was 'she has within her the holy fire.' A representative from the American Embassy received the Prize on Emily Balch's behalf." [19]

Gunnar Jahn, moreover, in the course of this speech divulged in no uncertain terms at least one reason why Emily Balch had been given the Nobel Prize—her work for peace in and through the Women's International League. He spoke of the origins of the League at The Hague in 1915, and of the women's proposals which had received the commendation of President Woodrow Wilson as the best that had been formulated up to that time. "For the program was practicable," said Gunnar Jahn. "The proposals were the work of the Congress, but Emily Balch contributed a great deal to giving them practical and concrete form, thanks to her scholarship and her sense of reality." Then he proceeded to speak of the second Women's Congress of Zürich in 1919. Marie Lous-Mohr long afterward remembered that at his words, the members of the Women's League who were present at the ceremony sat up, electrified. "I will simply say," Gunnar Jahn was declaring with emphasis, "that it would have been wise to listen to what the women had to say. But there were few who paid any attention. That is hardly surprising, if one recalls the general state of mind at that time. In any case, the proposals were made by women! In our male society, the proposals of women are rarely taken very seriously. From time to time men might do better than to respond merely with a sardonic smile."[20]

Myrtle Wright further described the small dinner held in the evening for the Nobel Prize recipients. Most of the eight women present, including Marie Lous-Mohr, represented the W.I.L.P.F. Three of her table neighbors, wrote Myrtle Wright, were jailbirds. One of them was Christian Oftedahl, a member of the Nobel Committee who later was to go to Wellesley to honor Emily Balch there in person. He had been the editor of a liberal newspaper in Stavanger, Norway. In 1940 he had been condemned to death, was later sent to Germany, and spent practically the whole of the war in a German prison at hard labor.

After her recovery from what was diagnosed as virus bronchitis, Emily was taken by her ever-loving sister Maidie for a few weeks at a rest home in South Natick. There on January 16, 1947, she wrote:

"Last night there was a snowfall, not deep, very dry and light. The pine and especially the spruce boughs with their pendants are adorned with soft masses, cushioned or outlined. The sun shines on the white quilt, lying in folds like those Dürer loved. It is just fourteen weeks since I got home to Wellesley (October 12, 1946) after twelve weeks in Europe: Luxembourg, Zürich, Geneva, and two weeks in Paris. Two walks along the Seine in dreaming October weather were memorable.

"On Christmas Day I went home [to Prince Street] for a singularly happy celebration.

"I have been reading, writing some letters, playing the Old Sea Captain, knitting, pacing the hallway, doing cross-word puzzles prepared for me by Bessie, and thinking. Reading mostly not of consequence except for the Excursion and Palgrave's *Arabian*

Travels, lent me by Alice, which I enjoyed very much. I have refreshed *Ode on Intimations of Immortality, Duty* and *March.*

"We have lost this year Margaret Whiting and Cora Bowditch."

Like Jane Addams, Emily Balch turned over most of the prize money to the Women's International League, which she considered the true recipient. Her share amounted to a little over $17,000. She gave $10,000 to the international body to be used without restrictions, put $5,000 in a bank for a European colleague who had worked sacrificially for the international for many years, and kept $2,000 for the trip to Oslo and for secretarial assistance in future work for peace.

The year 1947 brought Emily a huge correspondence and many honors. "Shall I someday turn out to be somebody?" she had asked wistfully in her childish diary. Her carefully disciplined sense of humility had long ago made room side by side with a naturalistic enjoyment of what this earth had to offer. It was not till the end of March, 1948, that Emily Balch, accompanied by her niece, Ellen Stone, Alice's daughter, sailed for Scandinavia to deliver in Oslo the lecture that was expected of Nobel laureates. She was especially eager to use the European trip to visit Germany where she had not been allowed to go by the authorities after the Luxembourg Congress.

On April 6, she was received by King Haakon of Norway, with whom, over thirty years before, she had had an interview of almost two hours on neutral mediation. Her niece Ellen described the visit to the Palace. "We were shown into a waiting room, with a minimum of ceremony and questions. Before long we were ushered upstairs and into the king's office. He and Aunt Emily greeted each other as old acquaintances and they had a most interesting conversation. The tall thin king with his lined face had a very pleasant manner, easy and direct. After we left the king, we were shown to the Crown Prince's study where we had an interview with him. What I especially remember about this was that Aunt Emily decided we shouldn't use up any more of his time and got up to take our leave. The Crown Prince took this perfectly graciously but we were told afterwards that you should always wait for royalty to terminate an interview. If Aunt Emily had known this it wouldn't have made any difference. If she thought it was time to go, go she would." [21]

The day after these audiences, Emily Balch delivered her Nobel address, "Toward Human Unity or Beyond Nationalism." She also spoke, generally a number of times, in Oslo, Stockholm, Helsinki, Copenhagen, and Odense. In Germany she went to Hamburg, Bremen, Hanover, Heidelberg, Stuttgart and Frankfurt. A highlight was seeing in Mannheim an exhibition of Käthe Kollwitz's "strong and compassionate art." Käthe Kollwitz had been a W.I.L.P.F. member. In Heidelberg, Emily was much touched by a public address given by the rector of the University, in which he acknowledged the collective guilt of Germany "in a spirit of manly and self-respecting responsibility."

"Everywhere," she wrote, "I was overwhelmed with friendliness and very frequently I was honored officially in a way that surprised me." Representatives of the State Department of her own country, city officials, and authorities of the American and British occupation forces "received me" as she put it, "as an officially credited mouthpiece of the universal determination, or at least, the longing to secure a peaceful world. . . . In Germany, amid hunger, humiliation and deep confusion, great forces are at work. It is too early to see what the new Germany will be. . . . We must help with our sympathy and active cooperation, that mighty work in which women, now so greatly in the majority, must seek to play a worthy part." [22]

The last weeks she spent in England, seeing for the first time the ruins of the bombing there and experiencing the indomitable spirit of the British people.. There was profound concern among her friends over the situation in Palestine and the British part in it. Barbara Duncan-Harris, a prominent member of the Women's International League, said that Emily Balch "fulfilled a program of engagements which would have tried far younger folk. She was claimed by the B.B.C. for a delightful broadcast; her press conference was a marked success, and she was entertained by a group of members of Parliament in the House of Commons. A special occasion was a luncheon given in her honor within the gracious tapestried walls of Crosby Hall, attended by many friends, old and new: Margaret Backhouse, Lord and Lady Pethick-Lawrence, Florence Paton, Edith Pye and Lady Astor." [23]

At the end of the trip, in June, Emily's old friend, Yella Hertzka, accompanied Emily and her niece from London to Southampton to wave good-bye as they sailed for home. Emily, like Jane Addams, Clara Ragaz and so many others, had always been captivated by Yella Hertzka's charm, high spirits, and humor. They had also been quick to admire her for her keen intelligence and to sense the depth of her compassion for suffering and injustice which her Viennese gaiety and nonchalance could not hide. Emily knew that Yella Hertzka's health had been more or less undermined by her hard work earning her living as a gardener in England, but she did not foresee the heart attack which was to "put a sudden and instantaneous end to her valiant and lovely life in November, 1948."

It was with Yella Hertzka in mind that Emily Balch, in December "in the season of affectionate remembrance and hope, when we are aware with a stab of pain how far we are from realizing either good will or peace," wrote her annual message to the international membership: "Each one of us," she said, "has her own calendar of saints and heroes. In their name, we in our different ways, bring our little gifts and offerings."

It was in remembering Yella Hertzka's boundless love for all breathing things, her faith burning even in the darkest hour of night, that Emily Balch could close her message with the plea and the hope, *that the good that is so small, so undeveloped, so disregarded may grow to be the light of the world.*[24]

"Then he showed four lights when he wished them to to set full sail and follow in his wake." Magellan

CHAPTER NINETEEN

Lapland Night

> And an old age serene and bright
> And lovely as a Lapland night
> Shall lead thee to the grave.

"To live to be old is a strange and deeply interesting experience," wrote Emily Balch when she was eighty-six years old. "In some ways I find it the best part of life. Perhaps I exploit it unduly. One's personal life seems to fall into perspective in which public and private interact."

Emily Balch had several times attempted to write her autobiography. It seemed to her a pity to be the only one of her associates who had not shared with the public autobiographical facts and memories, "the two not being always the same," she said. Jane Addams had written *Twenty Years at Hull-House* in 1910, *Peace and Bread in Time of War* in 1922, and *The Second Twenty Years at Hull-House* in 1930—all three autobiographical. Emily Balch's other friends, English and American, had written autobiographies which were contributions to the social and political history of the period from the turn of the century to World

War II—Dr. Alice Hamilton, Vida Dutton Scudder, Mary Kingsbury Simkhovitch, Lillian Wald, Emmeline Pethick-Lawrence, Helena Swanwick, Mrs. Philip Snowden, and Sarah Cleghorn. Their narratives were the product of varied and intense experiences acting upon richly endowed and sensitive natures, keenly alive to the menace to civilization of international conflict. Several of these books dealt at some length with the impact on their lives of the Women's International League.

But Emily Balch was always sociable. After the "amazing event of the Oslo award," she thoroughly enjoyed the mild degree of canonization that went with it. She liked to remain "in circulation," as she said. And so her autobiography never was written except for isolated fragments and some haphazard jottings. She had made two or three abortive beginnings. One of them ran: "I believe an honest biography of any person who has lived has value and is its own reason for being. It is, in every case, both of two things—the history of an experience which is unique because every personal experience is unique, and a chart of the course of one of the ultimate units of the society of a given period, the resultant of the social forces playing upon its special qualities. If an autobiography, it ought to be frankly egotistical but without conceit. *Ought* is a great word."

The Nobel Prize, however, proved to be a great intellectual stimulus in other ways, and an incentive to continue working toward peace under the trying conditions of her ninth decade. "She has lived in most difficult times for any one interested in the cause of peace," said her friend Brand Blanshard of Yale University, "working without embitterment, with unflagging courage, and with her kindliness and sense of justice unimpaired. She has never held high office in any government, but this makes it all the more remarkable that she has achieved so wide a hearing and influence."

On January 8, 1952, on her eighty-fifth birthday, Emily Balch found herself, like the Roman god Janus, of her birth month, facing forward and backward. It was not inappropriate that this tutelary spirit of hers, represented as two-faced, was the god of doors, of openings, of new glimpses—the god of beginnings—especially good beginnings which insure good endings, with the end partaking of the quality and substance of the beginning.

That winter day brought morning hours of quietness and reflection, and at night a modestly splendid dinner tendered by her beloved League at the Hotel Puritan in Boston with the novelist Pearl Buck as the main speaker. All those closest to Emily in kin and friendship were there, her brother Francis and his wife Polly; her sisters Marian, Alice, and Bessie; the friends of her girlhood, Helen Cheever and Frances Hayward. Her colleagues in the League came from New York, Washington, Philadelphia, Baltimore, and elsewhere to participate in the jubilee. Emily Balch took home with her the birthday book, with its red leather, gold embossed cover, containing the letters of tribute. The most moving letters perhaps were from colleagues who touched on personal memories or shared experiences. Helen Beardsley, a former Wellesley student wrote:

"I remember an evening at Wellesley early in the war of 1914 when you talked to a small meeting, putting into words your pain that day after day young men were killing each other. I remember our pride when you went to Europe to work for peace."

Else Zeuthen of Denmark, later to be international president of the W.I.L.P.F., remembered a visit of Emily Balch to her house in Rungsted Kyst, Denmark: "I shall never forget your pleasure when you saw a spray of early cherries on my wall. You must have had a wonderfully full life."

And Vida Scudder of Wellesley, a neighbor only a hedge or two away, wrote: "Anyone who has walked with Emily Balch through spring woods when the trillium is blossoming, as I have often done, knows how discerning, exquisite and varied are her joys. They must have afforded her much relief from her sharp relations with the menacing human situation."

A friend and colleague who could not come to the dinner in Boston wrote Emily Balch a line from Sappho in the Greek Emily loved and knew so well: "O Evening that bringeth together all that bright morning has scattered."

Though Emily Balch generally looked to the future, which, as she once wrote to Tano Jodai of Japan, "is longer than the historic past," on her eighty-fifth birthday she decided to indulge in the luxury of reminiscing. "Even though I have never hunted LIONS nor collected distinguished acquaintances," she wrote*, "as I look

---

* In an autobiographical fragment. Swarthmore College Peace Collection.

back I recall so many interesting people that I have known or at least met." Some of the most interesting she met during her years of teaching at Wellesley—Prince Kropotkin, Thomas Masaryk, H. G. Wells, Morris Hillquit, Florence Kelley. "Many I owe to my brief service with *The Nation* in 1917-1918, when Mr. Villard, like the knight-errant that he was, put me on the staff when my Wellesley appointment came to a premature end as a result of my too notorious effort to try to prevent the U.S. entering the first world war. There I met Hendrick Van Loon, who was kindness itself to me, and John Reed, Randolph Bourne, Crystal and Max Eastman. Freda Kirchwey [recently out of college] was one of the staff but I was not farsighted enough to foresee her future editorship.

At Geneva Emily Balch met Fridtjof Nansen, Romain Rolland, "whose steel-blue eyes had a quality such as I have never felt," and his sister Madeline Rolland. She also met Gandhi, Gandhi's friend Madeleine Slade, Maud Gonne of Ireland, Yeats who had immortalized Maud Gonne, Gilbert Murray, Pierre Ceresole, and many others.

A literary event of the year 1953 was the publication of the first critical biography of the novelist Willa Cather,* that consummate artist whose temperament led her to portray and exalt the past, especially the pioneer past of America. When Emily Balch's book *Our Slavic Fellow Citizens* appeared in 1910, Willa Cather asked Emily Balch to luncheon in Boston to find out more about the Bohemian immigrant farmers she was to portray in her Nebraska novel *My Antonia*. Emily Balch, therefore, was deeply interested in E. K. Brown's sympathetic revelation of Willa Cather's painful malaise that developed as she reached middle age, her nostalgia for the values of pioneer society and of the past, her gradual withdrawal as her pessimism grew, and her bitter refusal to accept change—even the changes caused by the deaths of those she had loved personally.

"I don't feel at all like that," Emily observed in a conversation, with a briskness amounting to disapproval. "One must continue to be in living relation with the period we live in. The thing to do is to avoid condemnation of new things. The past is restful. You

---

* E. K. Brown (completed by Leon Edel), *Willa Cather, a Critical Biography*, 1953.

can't do anything about it; you are not responsible for it. But the future is more malleable. We must be more respectful of the future, and of the present which is bubbling over with vitality and urge." However, she added in honesty, as you grow older you often can't understand the new generation. "We understand least the scene we are immersed in!" She quoted her "brilliant, humorous, affectionate" grandfather, Dr. Noyes: "An old person looks at a young person through an opera glass and brings him close to hand. A young person looks at an older person through the reverse end of the opera glasses and sees him as very remote."

In an outline for a speech at this time, Emily Balch has the notation, "We must realize how little we can do, and learn to admire and trust our successors." But while admiring she could also briskly challenge the exponents of what she called the modern creed. "Many of them are hard to bear, shallow, unreal, self-centered, without tenderness or the finer humor, without the thoughts that lie too deep for tears, without more than a skin-deep sympathy, sense of beauty, power of self-devotion. The next generation need to learn more, not less self-discipline, to be steadier and more purposeful than we have been." Like Willa Cather she, too, could sometimes grow exasperated with the temper of the age she lived in. "The art of contrast has replaced the cult of the delicate nuance. Art seems to me to seek esthetic experience largely in terms of shock. Relative callousness replaces sensitivity. Poetry has become in part a special form of word-puzzle."

"Old people have a rare treasure in their keeping. It is not used enough. Younger people do not know what they are losing in letting what the old could give them slip through their young fingers." In her review of two companion volumes, her friend Vida Scudder's autobiography *On Journey* and Mary K. Simkhovitch's autobiographical *Neighborhood—My Story of Greenwich House*, Emily Balch wrote, "The younger generation will make and is making notable contributions which it is too early to assess. They will not be and ought not to be in any degree trammelled by their forerunners but if, in their busy and specialized lives they find time to get into touch with the experiences inner and outer of those who preceded them in trying to trace ways through the social jungle they will find that this expands and enriches their understanding of this difficult field of human endeavor."

Even before she was eighty-five and working on a considerably shortened tether, Emily Balch, just as she had faced in her youth her shortcomings of egotism, ambition, irritability, and inefficiency, now faced squarely the problem of the shrinkage of individual capacity as age began to change the character of her mental operations. "The sense that I have something to contribute," she wrote in 1954, "is less than it used to be, perhaps, but I have a growing sense of how much I need to receive from others, of how much my inner springs need to be fed by the comradeship and inspiration of others." But in the same letter, in writing of the current wave of reaction in America, she repudiated one of the attitudes usually attributed to older people. "I do not know how it may be with you, but I have been taken by surprise by the cult of fear and suspicion, of which the grotesque phenomenon of McCarthyism is a symptom, and most of all by the hostility to thought lest it lead to change—as if change were not the very essence of life!" [1]

There is a certain greatness of spirit in Emily Balch and her fellow pioneers that even in old age they could dispute the sacredness of the status quo, and hail and welcome:

> All, all that speaks of change,
> Of Life's sacred communion, of process.*

The concluding sentence of Emmeline Pethick-Lawrence's autobiography, *My Part in a Changing World*, comes with a cumulative impact on the reader. It is moving in its summing up—that the varied experiences of her adventurous years had taught her that the essence of the quality of life is change. While Willa Cather, in humanly understandable homesickness for the precious, the irrecoverable past, wrote in *Not Under Forty*, "The world broke in two in 1922 or thereabouts," Jane Addams, in that self-same fateful year of 1922, was writing, "The world was bent on change," and declaring that the real denial and surrender of life lay not in "physical death and decay, but in acquiescence in hampered conditions and unsolved problems." [2] And Emily Balch in 1948, in her Nobel lecture in Oslo, "Toward Human Unity or Beyond Nationalism," said, "We must remember that nothing can be woven out of threads that all run the same way. An *unchallenged* belief or

---

* Emily Greene Balch, "Beside an Egyptian Mummy," in *Miracle of Living*.

idea is on the way to death and meaninglessness." In commenting on the character of her epoch as one of plastic change she observed: "Such a time is hard on those who lack resilience and capacity to readjust themselves, and on those who depend for their inner stability on accustomed conditions and old habits. On the other hand it has an immense appeal for the adventurous. Those who are rooted in the depths that are eternal and unchangeable, and who rely on unshakable principles, face change full of courage, courage based on faith."*

On one occasion, in a reversal of roles, Emily Balch's quiet leadership helped her much younger colleagues in the United States section of the League to adjust to an unexpected and rather drastic personal change. Dorothy Detzer, the national executive secretary, had announced to the Board her resignation after twenty-two years of brilliant and unique service. In the prolonged shock of silence which followed her announcement, Emily Balch rose to say: "It is a constantly recurring experience in every life, in every body of people, that the irreplaceable, the indispensable person has to be dispensed with. The change is often due to death. This change is not so tragic but hard enough to meet. A family, a church, a business organization goes on even when it suddenly confronts a change. The quality of a group which loses its pivotal personality is measured by how it meets the challenge. Neither the death of Jane Addams, nor the disruptive explosion of war broke us up. We do not propose to be disrupted by having to find a successor to Dorothy Detzer in her high national office."

When Emily was twenty-four years old, in the fullness of the moment, she had written on a scrap of paper, "Now I am at the apex." She did not know then that even in the tranquil plateau of her extreme old age, there were to rise other peaks of fulfillment. Shortly after her eighty-eighth birthday, Emily Balch wrote to Gertrude Baer from Wellesley that she had written a *Letter to the Chinese People*,[3] that the *Christian Science Monitor,* the paper which was flung daily on the doorstep of the Domichek, had printed it, that Pearl Buck wanted one hundred copies to send to China and elsewhere, and that the W.I.L.P.F. was sending a

* Emily Greene Balch's Nobel address, "Toward Human Unity or Beyond Nationalism," Oslo, April 7, 1948.

reprint to its members. "Of course it is 'silly,'" wrote Emily Balch, "but I think such have also their role, you know."

Dear People of China:

This is a letter of love that I am sending you.

Men and women with your patient faces,
Little children with your bright eyes,
How could I not love you?

I am an American, and what you perhaps call a capitalist.
Need that be a barrier to love?
It does not hold back mine.

Of course there are many differences between us.
The traditions of our countries are different.
There are differences even in our features,
And in our languages and religions.
But how much more we are alike!
Alike we are born to suffer.
We laugh and we cry as only men can do.

Shall fellow-men be divided by ideologies?
No. No. They shall not be so.
Of course, "coexistence" has great difficulties.
Even men who have a common country,
Who speak the same language, profess the same religion—
Even such do not find mutual understanding, mutual trust too easy.
Yet the greatest barriers are not insuperable.
Let us strive to learn to live together.

You may know bad Americans. There are such.
But there are also here friendly, right-meaning people
Who want to help make the world better for everyone.
There are bad people and good people, I suppose,
In every country.

Let us be patient with one another,
And even patient with ourselves.
We have a long, long way to go.
So let us hasten along the road,
The road of human tenderness and generosity.
Groping, we may find one another's hands in the dark.

Emily Balch, U.S.A.

The message reached the people of China through various channels and was translated into Chinese, appearing in the *Ta Kung Pao,* an old established newspaper with a national circulation. Emily Balch was extending the hand of friendship "in the dark," and to her surprise, there were hands in China that reached out to grasp hers. The Minister of Health, who was also chairman of the Chinese Red Cross, Mme. Li Teh-Chuan (Mme. Feng Yulisiang) was deeply moved by the message and invited Emily Balch to spend some time in China as her personal guest. Emily replied on November 8, 1955, to the correspondent through whom the invitation had been issued: "It is a surprise and happiness that what I tried to say in my so-called poem found its mark and met such understanding and response. . . . It is hard to bring myself to close the door to what would have given me profound satisfaction to see. But I must do so.

"It is not because I am too old to take the journey. It is, alas, far more that I am too old to be of use if I went. I hate to confess this but it is so. It is not merely that deafness would make personal contacts difficult nor that my speaking voice would not be effective in public addresses if I were to have opportunity for such, but that my nearly ninety years have too far depleted such effectiveness as I ever had along the line. It is hard to lose the capacity to be of service while my desire to do so is as keen as ever."

In November of the same year, from the easy chair in her friendly green and brown living room with its two faded rugs, Emily Balch took another step along "the road of human tenderness and generosity," this time directed to a region on which her thoughts could only rest in pain. Concerning Palestine, where there was an Israel section of the W.I.L.P.F., she wrote to Marie Lous-Mohr of Norway,[4] "It would seem to me that anything that the W.I.L. women in Palestine could do to help would be on Gandhi principles and on the level of high magnanimity, though I fear the Arabs' chivalrous vein cannot be counted on to respond, and I fear it would be very painful to our Jewish friends to have our suggestions take this shape.

"Still it is what I find it in my heart to suggest. For the only possible steps to a way out for the Jewish women to whom the ethical aspect is always of supreme importance, seems to invent ways of rising above the conflict.

"P.S. An effort to put into words what I conceive Jewish W.I.L. women might possibly want to be saying:

> As women, as human beings,
> violence is odious to us.
> So too are all hate and ill will.

> We long to rise above the conflict
> and to find ways to work, alone
> and also with Arab women, for a
> better future for all.

> Every sane person knows that there
> are things which once done cannot
> be undone. The creation of Israel
> is such a fait accompli. But Jews
> and Arabs must continue to live as
> neighbors. Let us as Jewish women
> learn somehow to do so in dignity and forbearance
> and mutual helpfulness.

> We wish not merely to meet Arabs
> halfway but to go all the way
> begging them to believe in our good will
> which we will try to prove in
> practical ways.

E.G.B."

In a letter to Marion Balch, Gertrude Bussey recalled: "Emily once said in her humility, that one cannot rightly accept too much admiration, but that one could not have too much love." But all her life Emily Balch had received both admiration and love without stint. Jane Addams at a meeting had once introduced Emily Balch as being "the good-est person" she had ever known. Whereupon Emily, with an answering gleam replied:

"When I was young I wanted to be beautiful. But I soon realized that the Lord didn't intend me to be beautiful. Then I wanted to be clever. But I soon found out that the Lord didn't intend me to be clever.

"So I decided to be good."

But praise in fulsome ways was always to be fended off. "Don't let Helen Cheever glut you with admiration," Alice Gould had

written scornfully to Emily in their younger days. In 1919 Helen
Cheever, honest in her humility but not overly sensitive to reactions, had copied out a private tribute which she had written
"years ago of E.G.B.:" "I often feel fettered by my own limitations"
wrote Helen Cheever, "and you give me a glimpse of greater freedom. I admire your fine mind and the way you are always taking
in something new. I think you are very generous of those fruits
you have gathered and share them with clever and simple alike.
I suppose I cannot appreciate your knowledge nor talk with you
as your intellectual equals can, but I doubt if many people in the
world estimate your good points so fully. . . . Your self-discipline
is all for use of others. . . . I call yours a consecrated life. It
increases my faith in the sort of human society we might build
up if we all strove for these things."

A more tempered admiration came from Margaret Whiting. In
1895, from Deerfield, just before Emily went to Germany, she had
written, "I would be touched in a quick place if you liked me as
well as I like you, but the thought that you are there in the flesh
and that once in a while I may hear of you or even see you is a
more delightful thought to me than you have ever guessed. Probably you have never speculated on the size of the little niche
where I trim a well-burning wick for Emily, perhaps you have
never caught a glimpse of its flame, but there it hangs, year in and
year out, and the oil holds out well, too."

But Emily could also evoke opposite and droll reactions. Back
in 1901, Mary Tappan Wright of Cambridge, a perceptive novelist
and writer, had invited Emily Balch, their mutual friend Alicia
M. Keyes, and others to spend a few days at her country home at
Castine, Maine. In her Line-a-Day on July 30, Mrs. Wright notes:
"Wet day spent in making baskets and embroidering. *Intensely
tiresome!* Miss Balch a little cross. Rolls her left eye like a rocking
horse." July 31: "M. Thomas and Miss Balch left. Miss Balch
crosser in the morning, intensely irritable at noon and positively
disagreeable on going away."* However, earlier in the same year

---

* Mary Tappan Wright, wife of John Henry Wright, Professor of Greek at
Harvard and Dean of the Harvard Graduate School, mother of Austin Tappan
Wright, later to be the author of *Islandia,* which Emily admired, and of John
Kirtland Wright, distinguished geographer. Perhaps this reaction should be
taken with a grain of salt as an entry the day before Emily's visit admitted:
"I am worn out with other people's moods. I am also not well. I am never
quite well in Castine."

she had invited Emily Balch, Alicia Keyes, and Reginald A. Daly, the geologist, to dinner at her Cambridge home to meet Prince Kropotkin and had recorded: "The dinner was delightful. Alicia and Miss Balch were just the right people. Everyone stayed till half-past five."

And once at Zürich, in 1934 at a meeting of the International Executive, Emily Balch had drawn an avalanche of wrath and indignation upon herself from some French and German members. Madame Duchêne afterwards called her "conspiratorial" and Lida Gustava Heymann and Anita Augspurg had refused to shake hands with her.* The episode, especially the word conspiratorial caused a pain which rankled in Emily's mind in spite of herself. "I tried to be honest," she had later explained, "but *conspiracy* was not my way of doing things." The minutes, which make lively reading, record that Emily Balch said "that Edith Pye with characteristic generosity has taken responsibility for an unfortunate situation for which she feels herself partly responsible. When Gabrielle Duchêne had asked her point-blank whether she (E.G.B.) thought the League would be better without the French section, she had replied that she had arrived, with great pain, at the conclusion that G. Duchêne was hampered in her work by her connection with the W.I.L.P.F. and that the W.I.L.P.F. often found its work made difficult by G. Duchêne." Whereupon, the minutes continue, Lida Gustava Heymann "protested vehemently against the attack made on G. Duchêne and said she was sure the Germans would secede if the French Section were excluded. Many of our troubles have arisen because there is too much 'Quakerism' in our executive. I have the greatest admiration for the work done by Quakers in the social and humanitarian sphere . . . but the W.I.L.P.F. is a political organization. . . ." The ensuing discussion in which Emily naturally took no part veered from heat to light and finally ended with the chairman, the irenic Mme. Ragaz, concluding, "We may therefore count on the further cooperation of Mme. Duchêne." [5]

---

* The episode occurred at a meeting following the second Zürich Congress. The French delegation had voted against the clause in the new statement of aims, repudiating the use of violence under any circumstances. It was the British Quaker, Edith Pye, who had raised the question of being chairman of an executive committee divided on a fundamental point. She had found out in a conversation with Mme. Duchêne that the latter had never been in favor of the Zürich formula.

When Emily was ninety-two, she wrote, "I have had a long and happy and I should like to think not wholly useless life to look back on. I think few people can have gone through nine decades with so little suffering, physical or non-physical. I dare say one ought to choose, if one had the choice, an experience richer in contrasts, but one is not given the choice. This is the way my life has worked out and I should be ungrateful indeed if I were not thankful for it."

The traumatic experiences in contrast that the two World Wars had brought to so many of her European fellow workers she did not know except in her own vivid imagination. But the contrasts and losses that penalize the glory of a rich and vital old age she met with very little outward comment on the whole. In February, 1948, quiet Etta Herr, one of the three members of "the family on the other side" in 15 Roanoke Road, died. The daily routine at the Domichek, the even tenor of her "busyness" at Wellesley, no longer to be broken by her frequent trips to Europe, began to take on a precarious fragile beauty. There were not many springs left in which to hear the New England Spring Peepers on the Dover Road, "like a peal of small bells in the distance," or to see the "tulips begin to push up small hard leaf-points through the soil." The ordered domestic life with "the other family" became more precious, each hour to be held and loved: the 8 o'clock breakfasts and quiet conversation in the sunny chintz-curtained dining-room, the deep embrasure of the window full of carefully tended African violets; the hour of reading aloud after dinner in the evening, in the warm-toned, book-lined living room at No. 15, with Agnes Perkins listening, head bent to one side, and Mabel Cummings placidly knitting, and an occasional overnight guest enjoying the quiet musical tones of Emily's voice. Adventures were not lacking in the almost daily errands to the college campus or to the village, past Little Birch Road, a glory of pale green in the spring, and in the fall, like all of Wellesley, "one of the ones that Midas touched." Odysseus had found his way home at last. Yet one evening when some one read aloud to her in the Domichek, Gerald Manley Hopkins' poem "Heaven-Haven":

> I have desired to go
> Where spring not fail,
> To fields where flies no sharp and sided hail. . . .

> And I have asked to be
> Where no storms come. . . .

she listened in grim attention and on being asked whether she liked it, remarked drily, "No, it's much too static for me." Her Marco Polo nature much preferred the spirit of one of her girlhood favorites, "Wanderschaft" by von Eichendorff, which she had marked in the little book of German lyrics Cousin Agnes Balch had given her so long ago:

> Wem Gott will rechte Gunst erweisen,
> Den schickt er in die weite Welt;
> Dem will er seine Wunder weisen
> In Berg und Wald und Strom und Feld.

There were still the annual August visits to Bessie's summer home in Brooklin on the coast of Maine; the partings in early September, eloquent with a mute question as they looked at each other's eyes; the trips to Frances Hayward's at Vinal Haven; or to the home of Mary Simkhovitch and her husband Vladimir at North Perry. The frequent fogs of Maine were bloom to Emily and the salt tang of the sea the breath of life. "Morning fog," she described in a letter. "I look out into a world of grey frustration behind the clear definite spruce spires in the foreground. The islands begin to make themselves felt." June or July was generally sacred to a three weeks' holiday inland; sometimes to New Hampshire, sometimes to Vermont, with Helen Cheever, all the old irritations long since worn off. At Peacham, Vermont, not very far from the Fairlee once settled by her enterprising pioneer ancestor Nathaniel Niles, the village people would see two sprightly, devoted old ladies sally forth each morning after the New England 8 o'clock breafast with sketching and painting materials in hand. Emily added to her collection of pastels one of the old red brick blacksmith shop at Peacham Corner, and of the abandoned grist mill, fringed with luxurious masses of phlox, overhanging the little river at South Peacham.

In 1950, when Emily was eighty-three years old came the first break in the Balch family since the death of the much-loved father, Francis Balch, in 1898, and of Auntie in 1924. Emily Balch wrote to Gertrude Bussey, "Annie died, Wednesday, May 17, after thirty years of intermittent mental suffering with depression. She died of cancer but did not suffer." This was the decade when Emily's oldest friends, friends from her childhood in Jamaica Plain, from her Louisburg Square school days, from her youth and student time were to drop away—the laughter-loving Lena Fabens, Alice Bache Gould, Mary Kingsbury Simkhovitch, Vida Dutton Scudder and last of all, at the ages of 94 and 92, the devoted all-around-the-clock friend, Helen Cheever, who had shared Emily Balch's convictions, and the dynamic life-loving Frances Hayward who did not. When Alice Bache Gould died in Simancas, Spain, after almost a lifetime of separation from her native New England, broken only by correspondence and occasional visits home, Emily murmured "I did not think I should feel it so much." The solid fabric of her days had become transparent gauze. The death of Frances Hayward punctured it. "Frances Hayward brought her a joy of life," said Emily's sister Alice, "and optimistic love of adventure and the sense that nothing was impossible, which matched Emily's own spirit and which no other friend brought her. She was so full of energy that she exhausted many people but she refreshed, amused and exasperated Emily." [6] Emily would say, "Frances approves of me so much in general and disapproves so much in detail."

Among the first of the founding members of Emily Balch's "goodly fellowship" to die was the indomitable Lida Gustava Heymann in July, 1943 at the age of seventy-five. Even in death she was not divided from her friend and companion Dr. Anita Augspurg, eleven years older, who followed a scant five months later. "I wish I had the gift of portraiture," said Emily Balch, "and could sketch these brilliant and devoted women. The ashes of 'Lida Gustava' and Dr. Augspurg are buried in the garden of the Maison Internationale in Geneva. I shall never forget the superb pride with which they bore the loss of their home and personal cherished treasures, their very considerable means and their exile. As exile they refused to consider it. Their internationalism was intensely real and practical." To their British and American colleagues their bluntness and their extreme feminism amounting to a suspicion and dislike of men, sometimes gave rise to an amusement which did not detract from very real appreciation of their great qualities. Dr. Alice Hamilton recounted that in their favorite sport of country bicycling, Lida Gustava Heymann had declared that if they had to choose between running over a man or a dog, they wouldn't hesitate to run over the man. Emily Balch said: "I try to be as candid as I can in this complicated world, but when Lida Gustava Heymann got up and said she was going to be 'aufrichtig' it was devastating."

Though Emily Balch did not have the gift of portraiture, as she admitted, she often used a telling phrase or paragraph in summing up a life. "Knight-errant" she had called Oswald Garrison Villard, describing in that phrase the selfless generosity of his lifetime of crusading and the unquestioned ideas animating it. On the death in 1951 of Amy Woods, an able, original farsighted worker and organizer for peace in the United States section of the League, Emily Balch wrote: "The role of Cassandra endowed with tragic insight which she could not get others to share and suffering the ensuing loneliness and frustration is one of the strange and painful ways in which God is served and surely not in vain."

When in 1948, Yella Hertzka went out like a flame, brightness fell from the air for Emily. In 1952 and 1954 two British comrades died, Lady Marion Emily Parmoor, head of the British section and often Emily Balch's hostess on her English visits, and Lady Emmeline Pethick-Lawrence. The words from Bunyan read at the short cremation service for Emily Parmoor epitomize the qualities both of her own career and those of her colleague, Emmeline Pethick-Lawrence: "My Sword I give to him that shall succeed me in my pilgrimage, and my Courage and Skill, to him that can get it." It is certain that the trumpets sounded for them on the other side. The year 1957, when Emily was ninety years old, brought the loss of Clara Ragaz, for many years an International chairman, a gentle, beautiful, harmonious personality, close to Emily in affection, often similar in political and spiritual outlook, and like Emily gifted with the ability of reconciling contending viewpoints.

Four more years of life were left to Emily Balch. "Never lonely, never unoccupied, never bored" she had written on a scrap of paper in her last home, the Vernon Nursing Home in Dana Street, Cambridge, which she entered in December, 1956, when her increasing frailties made life in the Domichek no longer possible. It was the only home which circumstance and her always inadequate pittance allowed. "I am happy now but if one day I am not happy, that is all right too," she wrote. She admitted as she wrote to Mildred Olmsted, that life in a nursing home was sometimes "duller than ditch-water." "I have had too many birthdays" she remarked to her doctor, "but the alternative is grim too." She continued to receive many visitors, to sign statements, sometimes to formulate messages, to write letters which grew shorter and shorter, and always to read. "My inner life has of course been enriched by persons, but I think more by reading," she wrote. She always regretted that being unmusical "one whole aspect, one whole kind of expression of spiritual feeling has been closed to me." But her constant pleasure in beauty remained alive to the end, "beauty both in its august manifestations and in its smallest and quaintest and most amusing aspects."

"My life has been considerably enriched by dreams, my own and those of other people," she remarked unexpectedly to a visitor in Dana Street who was a bit startled by such an admission in a Freudian age. Emily's diaries and jottings had occasionally described the substance of dreams, some of them having strong political tinges. "I am so grateful for my dreams," she had once written. "Through them I have experience of emotions and states otherwise not open to me and these like all wider experiences extend the reach of my sympathies and my understanding. . . . It is the actual experience of miracle."

Although she had once written of the callousness due to old age, the cooling-off period of life, her sympathies continued keen and imaginative almost to the end. The warmly passionate and loving nature of Ellen Noyes Balch still lived on in her daughter. To a friend in the clutches of an illness of indefinite duration, Emily had sent a card depicting the swirling beauty of the spiral nebula of Ursula, with the caption: "Out of chaos, order; out of darkness, light." In one of her letters to Annalee Stewart who in 1946 had succeeded Dorothy Detzer in her legislative work on Capitol Hill in Washington, D.C., and who considered herself expendable, Emily Balch wrote: "One final word—do *please spare yourself* more. You are not made, after all of steel and rubber, but of flesh and blood—fortunately." And to Alger Hiss and his wife Priscilla, at a low ebb in their history, she had sent a Christmas card portraying a blond little angel sitting on the banks of a frozen river, letting down a line to catch the reflection of the Christmas star. Underneath she had written "Fishing for a star in icy waters."

She had said of herself in her youth, "I am not classic." But her last years had a certain Mediterranean clarity and were enveloped in a luminous atmosphere. One blur of uncertainty obtruded, a wishfulness, a longing, a probing into questions of immortality. She read the books of her friend and contemporary, W. Ernest Hocking; she questioned her younger philosopher friends. It found expression in one of the poems she wrote in the onset of age:

> Ready almost to fall, its wrinkled skin
> Discolored and its flesh unsound within,
> The rotting fruit deep in its shelter hides
> The ripening seed in which its life abides.
>
> And is an aging body now as well
> Making its soul? Is this likewise the shell
> Of life resurgent though invisible?

The one book by Jane Addams she did not care for was *The Excellent Becomes the Permanent,** a collection of obituary talks delivered at Hull-House by Jane Addams over a period of years. They were perhaps too humanistic in tone to satisfy Emily. When Hannah Clothier Hull, that creature of light and airy fineness, died rather suddenly in 1958, a member of the Cambridge Quaker meeting, Florence Selleck, was asked to break the news to Emily at Dana Street that she might not learn of it through the newspapers. The two Friends sat together and recited "The Eternal Goodness." Emily, like the New England Quaker poet, had known what it was to "put the scholar's promise by," and taking up a "weapon in the war with wrong" had been content "to turn the crank of an opinion-mill," and hold her way, like Whittier: "against the public frown, / The ban of Church and State, the fierce mob's hounding down."

As the low sun shone fainter for Emily Balch, she could, however, echo the crescendo note of hope in Whittier's "My Triumph," forereaching the good to be, never doubting with the poet that others would right the wrong, finish what he began—"What matter, I or they?" And she could voice the same quiet faith as his:

---

* Jane Addams, *The Excellent Becomes the Permanent*, Macmillan, 1932.

> And for the things I see
> I trust the things to be.

When her niece, Katherine Balch Shurcliff, visited Emily early in January, she found her looking "peaceful, serene, unlined, and ready to gently go." A week later, on January 9, 1961 the day after her ninety-fourth birthday, Emily Balch died.

"I am bringing my days to a close in a world still hag-ridden by the thought of war," Emily had written in one of her last auto-biographical fragments, "and it is not given to us in this new atomic world to know how things will turn out. But when I reflect on the enormous changes that I have seen myself and the amazing resiliency and resourcefulness of mankind, how can I fail to be of good courage?"

Although the last forty years of her life were lived in an era of injustice, unspeakable brutality and war, she never lost that courage, never faced the world with fear. In the depths of the "boundless horror, sympathy and grief" she shared with the world in 1942, she was able to write, "Even in this dark hour we can believe—or if we cannot believe we can hope—that in spite of everything we are on the way to liberation from all such prejudices, and that the day is coming when such cruelties as those now going on in Poland and elsewhere may be unthinkable. And we can not merely hope, we can work actively in many ways to bring that day nearer." She did not indulge in shallow optimism but she never ceased to believe in the possibility of a more rational international order. This faith she infused into the thinking of all who came in contact with her. She was like the "Darkling Thrush," of Thomas Hardy's poem which he wrote the last month of the old century in spectre-grey frost and oncoming night:

> At once a voice arose among
>   The bleak twigs overhead
> In a full-hearted evensong
>   Of joy illimited;
> An agèd thrush, frail, gaunt, and small,
>   In blast-beruffled plume,
> Had chosen thus to fling his soul
>   Upon the growing gloom.

So little cause for carolings
    Of such ecstatic sound
Was written on terrestrial things
    Afar or nigh around,
That I could think there trembled through
    His happy good-night air
Some blessed Hope, whereof he knew
    And I was unaware.

References

Chapter One

1. Charles Francis Adams, *Three Episodes of Massachusetts History* (Cambridge, Mass., 1896), I. 143.
2. *Ibid.*, p. 153.
3. Henry Cabot Lodge, *Boston* (New York, 1892), pp. 6, 12.
4. Alice G. Lapham, *The Old Planters of Beverly in Massachusetts and the Thousand Acre Grant of 1635* (Cambridge, Mass., 1930), p. 94.
5. Edward L. Pierce, *Memoir and Letters of Charles Sumner* (Boston, 1893), III, 1 ff.
6. Article on William Bartlett (1748-1841), *Dictionary of American Biography* (New York, 1943), Vol. II, p. 3, Claude M. Fuess.
7. *Proceedings* at Bar Meeting Held at Boston, March 26, 1898, upon the death of Francis Vergnies Balch (Boston, 1898), pp, 6, 18 ff.
8. *Ibid.*, pp. 8, 10.
9. The Rev. George L. Cheney, Boston Evening Transcript newspaper clipping, Feb. 17, 1898.
10. Speech by F. V. Balch, April 7, 1888, at a Sumner Memorial Meeting in Boston. Also E. L. Pierce, *op. cit.*, IV, 343-44.
11. *Proceedings* at Bar Meeting, *op. cit.*, p. 25 (Mr. Barker).
12. *Ibid.*, pp. 18 ff.
13. Alice Balch Stone, "Memoir" (ms).

Chapter Two

1. Jane Addams, *Twenty Years at Hull-House* (New York, 1910), p. 45.
2. Florence Kelley, "Notes of Sixty Years," *The Survey*, Feb. 1, 1927, pp. 557 ff.
3. Edith Finch, *Carey Thomas of Bryn Mawr* (New York, 1947), pp. 54, 87.
4. Vida Dutton Scudder, "The Relation of College Women to Social Need," a speech made Oct. 24, 1890, quoted by Arthur Mann, *Yankee Reformers in the Urban Age* (Cambridge, Mass., 1954), p. 223.

5. Emily G. Balch, ed., *Catharine Innes Ireland, A Memorial* (Boston, 1929).
6. Alice Balch Stone, "Memoir" (ms).
7. Emily James Smith Putnam, "Paul Shorey," *Atlantic Monthly*, June, 1938, p. 798.
8. Vida Dutton Scudder, *op. cit.*

Chapter Three

1. Dorothy Canfield Fisher, "A Young Woman in Paris," *Four Lights*, Vol. VI, No. 6, Jan., 1947.
2. Florence Kelley, "Notes of Sixty Years," *The Survey*, Feb. 1, 1927, p. 557.
3. Emily G. Balch, "International Social Workers' and Trade Union Congress," *Lincoln House Review* (no date), pp. 111-12.
4. *Ibid.*, p. 112.
5. *Ibid.*, p. 113.
6. *Ibid.*, p. 114.
7. *Ibid.* p. 114.

Chapter Four

1. Ruth Sapin Hurwitz, "Coming of Age at Wellesley," *The Menorah Journal*, Vol. 38, No. 2 (Autumn, 1950). P. 226.
2. Vida Dutton Scudder, *On Journey* (New York, 1937), p. 184.
3. Jane Addams, *Twenty Years at Hull-House* (New York, 1910), p. 262.
4. *Ibid.*, p. 274.
5. Emily G. Balch, *The Wellsley Magazine*, Vol. XV, No. 4 (Jan., 1907).

Chapter Five

1. Jane Addams, *Peace and Bread in Time of War* (New York, 1945), pp. 30-31.
2. Jane Addams, *The Second Twenty Years at Hull-House* (New York, 1930), pp. 118-19.
3. Emily G. Balch, "Working for Peace," *Bryn Mawr Alumnae Bulletin*, Vol. 13, No. 5, May, 1933, p. 12.

4. E. M. Forster, *Goldsworthy Lowes Dickinson* (New York, 1934), p. 135.
5. K. D. Courtney, *Extracts from a Diary during the War* (privately printed, 1927), pp. 16-17.
6. Jane Addams, *Peace and Bread* (1945), p. 112.
7. Emily G. Balch, *Bryn Mawr Bulletin, op. cit.*, p. 12.
8. Helena M. Swanwick, *Builders of Peace, Being Ten Years History of the Union of Democratic Control* (London, 1924), pp. 37, 48.
9. Marie Louise Degen, *The History of the Woman's Peace Party* (Baltimore, 1939), p. 11.
10. Jane Addams, *Peace and Bread*, p. 8.
11. Theodore Roosevelt, quoted in "Is the Woman's Peace Movement 'Silly and Base'?" *Literary Digest*, May 1, 1915, pp. 1020, 1023. (Unsigned article).
12. Jane Addams, *Chicago Record-Herald*, April 13, 1915.
13. Emily G. Balch, *Women at The Hague* (New York, 1915), pp. 1-2.
14. *Ibid.*, pp. 3-4.
15. Alice Thatcher Post, *The Public*, May 21, 1915, pp. 494-96.
16. Emily G. Balch, *Women at The Hague*, pp. 4-6.
17. Jane Addams, *Peace and Bread*, p. 13.
18. Emily G. Balch, ms Journal kept on *Noordam* (Swarthmore College Peace Collection).
19. *Towards Permanent Peace*, Report of the British Committee of the Women's International Congress, June, 1915, pp. 5 ff. (S.C.P.C.)

Chapter Six

1. Jane Addams, Presidential Address, *Report of the International Congress of Women* (The Hague, 1915), p. 18.
2. *Ibid.*, p. 18.
3. Dr. Aletta Jacobs, Address of Welcome, *ibid.*, pp. 5-6, 8.
4. *Ibid.*, p. 314. See also Alice Thatcher Post, "Diary of Hague Congress" (ms), pp. 118-23. Files of M. M. Randall.
5. Mary Chamberlain, "Women at The Hague," *The Survey*, June 5, 1915, pp. 219-22.
6. Emily G. Balch, *Women at The Hague*, p. 15.
7. Elizabeth Glendower Evans, "The International Congress of Women" (ms in files of Woman's Peace Party in S.C.P.C.)
8. Emily G. Balch, *Women at The Hague*, pp. 14-15.
9. *Ibid.*, pp. 9, 15-17.
10. Julia Grace Wales, letters to M. M. Randall, Sept. 14, 1950, Dec. 27, 1950.

11. Emily G. Balch, *A Venture in Internationalism* (Geneva, 1938), p. 6.
12. *Ibid.*, p. 6.
13. K. D. Courtney, prefatory note to English ed. of J. G. Wales' pamphlet on *Neutral Mediation without Armistice* (1915).
14. K. D. Courtney, *Report* of Hague Congress (1915), p. 173.
15. Jane Addams, *Report* of Hague Congress, p. 179.

Chapter Seven

1. Emily G. Balch, *Four Lights*, Vol. III, No. 2, June, 1943. p. 1.
2. Emily G. Balch, *Women at The Hague*, p. 99.
3. Catherine Marshall, *Towards Permant Peace* (June, 1915), p. 25; in S.C.P.C.
4. Emily G. Balch, *ibid.*, p. 26.
5. Emily G. Balch, letter to Marie Louise Degen, quoted in Degen, *History of The Woman's Peace Party* (Baltimore, 1939), p. 93.
6. Emily G. Balch, *Women at The Hague*, pp. 109-10.
7. Jane Addams, *Peace and Bread*, p. 16.
8. *Ibid.*, p. 82.
9. Mark Sullivan, *Our Times, the United States, 1900-1925*, (N.Y., 1927-1935), Vol. V, 162.
10. Jane Addams, *Women at The Hague*, p. 83.
11. James W. Gerard, *My Four Years in Germany* (New York, 1917), pp. 412-13.
12. Alice Hamilton, *Women at The Hague*, pp. 43-44.
13. *Ibid.*, p. 50.
14. Jane Addams, *Women at The Hague*, pp. 97-98.

Chapter Eight

1. Emily G. Balch, *Women at The Hague*, p. 100.
2. Emily G. Balch to Louis Lochner, June 1, 1915, in S.C.P.C.
3. Selma Lagerlöf, quoted in *Report of Zürich Congress, 1919* (Geneva 1919), p. 158.
4. Emily G. Balch, *Women at The Hague*, p. 103.
5. *Ibid.*, p. 104.
6. Emily G. Balch, letter to Jane Addams, Amsterdam, July 3, 1915, in S.C.P.C.
7. Emily G. Balch, *Women at The Hague*, p. 106.
8: *Ibid.*, p. 109.

Chapter Nine

1. Merle E. Curti, *Peace or War: The American Struggle, 1636-1936* (New York, 1936), p. 243.
2. R. S. Baker, *Life and Letters of Woodrow Wilson* (Garden City, N.Y., 1937), Vol. VI, 122.
3. *Ibid.*, p. 122.
4. *Ibid.*, pp. 122-23.
5. *Ibid.*, p. 123, 123n, 124. See also Charles Seymour, *The Intimate Papers of Colonel House*, (Boston, 1926), Vol. II, 22.
6. Charles Seymour, *op. cit.*, II, 61.
7. Letter of Bryce to House, Nov. 26, 1915, in Charles Seymour, II, 111.
8. *Ibid.*, pp. 88-89. See also R. S. Baker, VI, 124.
9. Emily G. Balch, letter to Jane Addams, Aug. 19, 1915, in S.C.P.C.
10. Aletta Jacobs to Jane Addams, Aug. 26, 1915, in S.C.P.C.
11. C. Seymour, *op. cit.*, II, 94.
12. Aletta Jacobs to Jane Addams, Sept. 15, 1915, in S.C.P.C.
13. Louis P. Lochner, *Henry Ford, America's Don Quixote* (New York, 1925), pp. 8-9.
14. Charles Seymour, *op. cit.*, II, 96-97.
15. L. P. Lochner, *op. cit.*, pp. 20-21.
16. Jane Addams, *Peace and Bread*, p. 27.
17. Charles Seymour, *op. cit.*, II, 84-85.
18. Mrs. Philip Snowden, *A Political Pilgrim in Europe* (London, 1921), pp. 45-46.
19. Jane Addams, *Peace and Bread*, p. 28.
20. *Ibid.*, p. 36.
21. *Ibid.*, p. 35.
22. *Ibid.*, pp. 36, 39.
23. *Ibid.*, p. 37.
24. Walter Millis, *The Road to War* (New York, 1935), p. 243.
25. Sarah Cleghorn, *Threescore* (New York, 1936), p. 188.
26. Jane Addams, *Peace and Bread*, pp. 19-20.
27. Jane Addams, *Hearing before House Committee on Foreign Affairs on H.R. 6921 and H.J.R. 32*, 64 Congress, 1st Session, Jan. 11, 1916, pp. 13-17.
28. Alice Hamilton, *Exploring the Dangerous Trades* (Boston, 1943), pp. 165, 179.
29. W. Millis, *Road to War*, p. 308.

Chapter Ten

1. Emily G. Balch, "Miss Balch on the Ford Peace Conference," *The Survey*, July 29, 1916, p. 444.
2. Emily G. Balch, "The Stockholm Conference," New Republic, Sept. 9, 1916, pp. 141-42.
3. *Ibid.*, p. 142.
4. Rebecca Shelley, letter to M. M. Randall, Feb. 27, 1954. In S.C.P.C.
5. Lella Faye Secor, *We Did Not Fight, 1914-1918* (London, 1935), pp. 115 ff.
6. Marian Tilden Burritt, *Year Book of The Woman's Peace Party* (1916), p. 25.
7. Emily G. Balch, letter to *New York Tribune*, July, 1917.
8. Morris Hillquit, *Loose Leaves From a Busy Life* (New York, 1934), p. 178.
9. R. S. Baker, *Life and Letters of Wilson*, Vol. VI, 461: Wilson to Tumulty, Feb., 1917.
10. Paul U. Kellogg, letter to Jane Addams, Feb. 9, 1917, in S.C.P.C.
11. Jane Addams, *Peace and Bread*, pp. 61-62.
12. E. M. Forster, *Goldsworthy Lowes Dickinson* (New York, 1934), p. 162.
13. Randolph Bourne, *History of a Literary Radical* (New York, 1956), p. 205.
14. *Ibid.*, p. 218.
15. *New York Times*, Feb. 2, 1917.
16. Jane Addams, *Peace and Bread*, p. 64.
17. *Ibid.*, 66.
18. John Haynes Holmes, Sermon, April 1, 1917 (Church of the Messiah, New York City, 1917)
19. *Report* of Zürich Congress, 1919, p. 155.
20. Joseph P. Tumulty, *Woodrow Wilson as I Know Him* (Garden City, N.Y., 1921), pp. 256, 259.
21. John L. Heaton, *Cobb of "The World"* (N.Y., 1924), pp. 267 ff. (The book reports recollections of Maxwell Anderson and Laurence Stallings.)
22. Claude Kitchin, *Congressional Record*, 65 Congress, Part I (Vol. 55), 1st Session and Special Session of Senate, April 5, 1917, p. 332.
23. *Ibid.*, p. 317.
24. Frances Witherspoon, letters to M. M. Randall, Oct. 12, 1956; Oct. 25, 1958.
25. Emily G. Balch, in *Congressional Record*, 65 Congress, Vol. 55, April 5, 1917, p. 338.

Chapter Eleven

1. David Starr Jordan, statement sent to *San Francisco Bulletin,* April 8, 1917; in his *The Days of Man* (World Book Co., 1922), Vol. II, 734.
2. Morris Hillquit, *Loose Leaves From a Busy Life,* p. 170.
3. Emily G. Balch, *Holy Cross Magazine,* Dec., 1937, p. 370.
4. Nicholas Murray Butler, Commencement Day Address to Alumni, June 6, 1917. Columbia Alumni News, Vol. 8, No. 36, p. 883.
5. *Report of Woman's Peace Party,* 3rd Annual Meeting, Phil., Dec. 6, 7, 1917 (U.S. Section of International Com. of Women for Permanent Peace), in S.C.P.C.
6. Minutes of the Trustees of Columbia University, Vol. 37, March 5, 1917.
7. Jane Addams, *Peace and Bread,* p. 140.
8. Quoted by Randolph Bourne in "A Letter to the Editor of the *New Republic,*" Oct. 1917, in *The History of a Literary Radical,* pp. 185-86.
9. Jane Addams, *Peace and Bread,* pp. 139 ff.
10. Emily G. Balch, "Working for Peace," *Bryn Mawr Alumnae Bulletin,* Vol. 13, No. 5, May, 1933, pp. 13-14.
11. *A Program During War Time,* leaflet of Woman's Peace Party, in S.C.P.C.
12. *Statement of the Executive Board of Woman's Peace Party,* Oct. 25, 1917, pamphlet, in S.C.P.C.
13. Jane Addams, *Peace and Bread,* pp. 111-12.
14. Woman's Peace Party, *Statement, op. cit.,* in S.C.P.C.
15. Jane Addams, *Peace and Bread,* p. 121.
16. Emily G. Balch, letter to Bishop Cooke, *The Christian Advocate,* Aug. 20, 1917.
17. Emily G. Balch, "Working for Peace," *Bryn Mawr Al. Bull.,* Vol. 13, No. 5, May, 1933, p. 13.
18. Vida Scudder, letter to Emily G. Balch, April 25, 1918, in S.C.P.C.
19. Mary Whiton Calkins, letter to Emily G. Balch, April 23, 1918, in S.C.P.C.
20. M. W. Calkins to Emily G. Balch, in S.C.P.C.
21. Accounts related by Wellesley professors to M. M. Randall.
22. Vida Scudder to Emily G. Balch, May 11, 1918, in S.C.P.C.
23. K. L. Bates to Emily G. Balch, April 2, 1919, in S.C.P.C.
24. Ellen Pendleton to Emily G. Balch, May 8, 1919, in S.C.P.C.
25. K. L. Bates to Emily G. Balch, Sept. 1, 1919, in S.C.P.C.

26. Alice Payne Hackett, *Wellesley, Part of the American Story* (New York, 1949), pp. 189-90.

Chapter Twelve

1. Interview of M. M. Randall with Oswald Garrison Villard. May, 1949.
2. Jane Addams, *Peace and Bread*, pp. 152-53.
3. John Maynard Keynes, *Economic Consequences of the Peace* (New York, 1920), p. 297.
4. Alice Hamilton, letter to Mary Rozet Smith, May 12, 1919, in S.C.P.C.
5. Alice Hamilton, *Exploring the Dangerous Trades*, (Boston, 1943) p. 228.
6. J. Addams, *Second Twenty Years*, pp. 148-49.
7. *Ibid.*, p. 149.
8. Florence Kelley, letter to M. R. Smith, May 22, 1919, in S.C.P.C.
9. E. G. Balch, *A Venture in Internationalism* (Geneva, 1938), p. 9.
10. J. Addams, *Peace and Bread*, p. 159.
11. Alice Hamilton to M. R. Smith, May 12, 1919, in S.C.P.C.
12. Reply from Wilson, in *Report of Int. Congress of Women, Zürich, 1919*, p. 162.
13. Jane Addams, *Peace and Bread*, pp. 161-62.
14. *Report of Int. Cong. of Women, Zürich, 1919*, pp. 242-43.
15. *Ibid.*, p. 198.
16. Quoted by Jane Addams, *Peace and Bread*, pp. 163-64.
17. John M. Keynes, *op. cit.*, pp. 145-46.
18. Emily G. Balch, "Impressions of the Zürich Congress," typescript in Archives of W.I.L.P.F. International Headquarters, Geneva.
19. *Ibid.*
20. Emily G. Balch, "Why Peace and Freedom," leaflet, undated (c. 1927).
21. Emily G. Balch, *Venture in Internationalism* (1938), p. 32.
22. Emily G. Balch, leaflet, undated, no title (c. 1926).
23. Jane Addams, President's Address, *Report of Int. Congress of Women, Prague*, Aug. 1929, p. 14.
24. Emily G. Balch, *Report* of Zürich Congress, p. 110.
25. Helena Swanwick, *I Have Been Young* (London, 1935), p. 318.
26. Emily G. Balch, "Impressions of the Zürich Congress," *op. cit.*
27. Jane Addams, *Report* of Zürich Congress, 1919, pp. 237, 238.
28. Helena Swanwick, Memorial Issue of *Pax International*, Vol. 10, Nos. 3-4, May-June, 1935, (Quoted on cover).

Chapter Thirteen

1. Emily G. Balch, editorial in *Pax et Libertas,* Vol. I, No. 1, Feb., 1920. p. 1.
2. Emily G. Balch, *Four Lights,* Vol. 3, No. 2, June, 1943. p. 1.
3. Emily G. Balch, *International Circular Letter,* No. 4, 1944, Nov., 1944.
4. Catherine Marshall, *Report* of Int. Cong. of Women, Vienna, 1921, pp. 65-66.
5. Emily G. Balch, *Report* on Activities Relating to the League of Nations, Nov., 1920–March, 1921 in S.C.P.C.).
6. *Ibid.*
7. Emily G. Balch, quotations from "Impressions of the First Assembly of the League of Nations," *Women's Int. League Monthly News Sheet,* Vol. 6, No. 4, Feb., 1921, in S.C.P.C.
8. Emily G. Balch to Jane Addams, Feb., 1921, in S.C.P.C.
9. Jane Addams, *Peace and Bread,* p. 224.
10. *Ibid.,* pp. 226-27.
11. Emily G. Balch, letter to Anna Garlin Spencer, Dec. 31, 1919, in S.C.P.C.
12. Emily G. Balch, letter to Annie, Oct. 11, 1922.
13. Emily G. Balch to Mary Sheepshanks, Nov. 17, 1927, in Archives of W.I.L.P.F., Geneva.
14. Emily G. Balch to Madeleine Doty, Nov. 22, 1925, in Archives of W.I.L.P.F., Geneva.
15. Emily G. Balch to V. Glücklich, March 29, 1923, in Archives of W.I.L.P.F., Geneva.
16. Emily G. Balch to Annie, from Cairo, March 9, 1923, in S.C.P.C.
17. Emily G. Balch to Mary Sheepshanks, Jan. 16, 1928, in Archives of W.I.L.P.F., Geneva.
18. Emily G. Balch to V. Glücklich, Jan. 30, 1925, in Archives of W.I.L.P.F., Geneva.
19. Emily G. Balch, files on Haiti, in S.C.P.C.
20. Quotations from Emily G. Balch, "Back in Geneva," *Pax International,* Vol. 3, No. 8, July, 1928.
21. Speech by Emily G. Balch, in Geneva, Sept. 14, 1928, typescript in S.C.P.C.
22. Kathleen Courtney, *Pax International,* Vol. 4, No. 10, Sept., 1929, p. 5.
23. Emily G. Balch, *Pax et Libertas,* Feb., 1920, p. 1.

Chapter Fourteen

1. Letter from Hannah C. Hull, *Pax International*, Vol. 6, No. 7, June, 1931.
2. Emily G. Balch, ms in S.C.P.C.
3. Emily G. Balch to Camille Drevet, Jan. 31, 1932, in Archives of W.I.L.P.F., Geneva.
4. Emily G. Balch, memorandum on Manchuria, Jan. 29, 1932, in S.C.P.C.
5. Emily G. Balch, "Observations on a Mediated Peace in Spain," Dec., 1936, S.C.P.C.
6. Emily G. Balch, "Jane Addams," *Pax International*, Vol. 10, Nos. 3-4, May-June, 1935.
7. Emily G. Balch, *Four Lights*, Vol. 3, No. 2, June, 1943.
8. Emily G. Balch, ms of 1934, in S.C.P.C.
9. Emily G. Balch, "Why Peace and Freedom," pamphlet (c. 1927).
10. Emily G. Balch, ms *re* "Liberty," 1934, in S.C.P.C.
11. Rebecca Shelley, letter to M. M. Randall, Feb. 27, 1954.
12. Emily G. Balch, "Reform of League of Nations," typescript in S.C.P.C.
13. Emily G. Balch, "The Present Political Situation," *Pax International*, Vol. 10, No. 1, Feb., 1935.
14. Emily G. Balch, "What We Are Facing," *Pax International*, Vol. 13, No. 1, Feb. 1, 1938.
15. Emily G. Balch, Introduction to *Report* of Int. Cong. of Women, Luhacovice, Czechoslovakia, 1937, p. 7.
16. Emily G. Balch, *Venture in Internationalism* (1938), p. 33.

Chapter Fifteen

1. Emily G. Balch, draft of *Personal History* (1945), in S.C.P.C.
2. Emily G. Balch to Gertrude Baer, Sept. 22, 1939, in Archives of W.I.L.P.F., Geneva.
3. Emily G. Balch to Gertrude Baer, Oct. 11, 1939, in Archives of W.I.L.P.F., Geneva.
4. Emily G. Balch, Message to Int. Executive Committee at Geneva, Dec. 1939, in S.C.P.C.
5. Emily Balch to Clara Ragaz, May 1940, in Archives of W.I.L.P.F., Geneva.
6. Emily G. Balch, "The W.I.L. in Wartime," *Four Lights*, Vol. 1, No. 7, Jan., 1942.

References   457

7. Emily G. Balch, Report of Com. on Refugees to National Board, Jan., 1939, in S.C.P.C.
8. Emily G. Balch, "Towards a Planetary Civilization," *Four Lights*, Vol. 2, No. 2, June, 1942, ms in S.C.P.C.
9. Emily G. Balch to Clara Ragaz, June 18, in Archives of W.I.L.P.F., Geneva.
10. Lida Gustava Heymann in *Int. Circular Letter*, No. 4, Dec., 1941.
11. Jane Addams, *Peace and Bread*, p. 147.
12. Herbert W. Schneider, *Meditations in Season* (New York, 1938), pp. 82-83.
13. Emily G. Balch, Letter to Rabbi Wise and All Jews, Nov. 27, 1942, printed in *Congress Weekly*, Dec. 11, 1942, p. 16.
14. E. M. Forster, *Goldsworthy Lowes Dickinson*, p. 156.
15. Emily G. Balch, letter to M. M. Randall, undated (c. 1943).
16. Emily G. Balch to Dorothy Detzer and the National Board, Jan. 27, 1943, in S.C.P.C.
17. *Ibid.*
18. Emily G. Balch, *Four Lights*, Vol. 5, No. 1, May, 1945.
19. *Ibid.*
20. Emily G. Balch, *Int. Circular Letter*, No. 4, 1944, Nov., 1944.
21. Emily G. Balch, K. Innes, G. Baer, letter to President of U.N. Conference in San Francisco, from Wellesley, Mass., April, 1945, in S.C.P.C.
22. Emily G. Balch, New Year's Message to International Membership, *Int. Circular Letter*, No. 4, 1941, Dec., 1941.
23. Dorothy Canfield Fisher, *Four Lights*, Vol. 6, No. 6, Jan., 1947.
24. D. C. Fisher, letter to Emily G. Balch, July 7, 1941.

Chapter Sixteen

1. Merle Curti, "Jane Addams on Human Nature," *Journal of the History of Ideas*, Vol. 22 (1961), 240-53.
2. Emily G. Balch, Greetings to the Copenhagen Congress of the W.I.L.P.F., 1949, in S.C.P.C.
3. Emily G. Balch, letter to Paul U. Kellogg, Nov. 30, 1946, in S.C.P.C.
4. Emily G. Balch, *Int. Circ. Letter*, No. 4, 1944, Nov., 1944.
5. Emily G. Balch, "The United Nations: What It Is and What It May Be," address at Seventh Anniversary Nobel Peace Dinner, New York, Dec. 10, 1947. Printed in *Four Lights*, Vol. 7, No. 7, Jan., 1948.

6. Emily G. Balch, "Polar Regions as a Site for an Experiment in Internationalism," *Int. Circ. Letter*, No. 1, 1945, pp. 18-19. See also Emily G. Balch, letter to *New York Times*, "A Consortium of All, Rules for Waste Space," March 31, 1940; and "Polar Regions as Part of One World," *Survey Graphic*, Sept., 1948.

7. Emily G. Balch, "What Are We Moving Toward?" speech at Hartford, Conn., May 7, 1949, in S.C.P.C.

8. Emily G. Balch, notes for speech, "Do We Desire Peace?" undated, in S.C.P.C.

9. Emily G. Balch, speech, "What Are We Moving Toward?" (1949), and speech at Philadelphia, April 26, 1947, in S.C.P.C.

10. Emily G. Balch, "What Are We Moving Toward?" (1949).

11. Emily G. Balch, "Do We Desire Peace?"

12. Emily G. Balch, Message to Copenhagen Int. Congress, 1949, in S.C.P.C.

13. Emily G. Balch, Message to Paris Int. Congress, 1953, in S.C.P.C.

14. Emily G. Balch, "Decency in International Relations," *Pax et Libertas*, Vol. 16, No. 5, Nov.-Dec. 1950, p. 10.

15. Emily G. Balch, letter to John Foster Dulles, Feb. 5, 1945.

16. John Foster Dulles, reply to Emily G. Balch, Feb. 8, 1945.

17. Emily G. Balch, "Decency in International Relations," *Pax et Libertas*, Vol. 16, No. 5, Nov.-Dec., 1950, p. 10.

18. Emily G. Balch, Greetings to Int. Executive Committee, May, 4, 1951, in S.C.P.C.

19. Interview with Emily G. Balch in *The Nation*, May 14, 1955, p. 418.

20. Emily G. Balch, "Our Call," *Bulletin of W.I.L.P.F.*, Geneva. Feb., 1922.

21. Emily G. Balch, *Report of Zürich Congress, 1919*, pp. 109-10.

Chapter Seventeen

1. Edith Hamilton, letter to Emily G. Balch, March 24, 1950, in S.C.P.C.

2. Edith Hamilton, letter to Alice Hamilton. March, 1950, in S.C.P.C.

3. Jane Addams, *Second Twenty Years at Hull-House*, pp. 197-98.

4. August Schou, *Nobel, The Man and His Prizes* (Stockholm, 1950), p. 573.

5. *John Dewey: The Man and His Philosophy* (Cambridge, Mass., 1930), p. 181. Addresses Delivered in New York in Celebration of His Seventieth Birthday.

Chapter Eighteen

1. Emily G. Balch, ms, "Statement for the Next Chapter," in S.C.P.C.
2. Emily P. Simon, *Report of Luxembourg Congress, 1946,* p. 160.
3. Emily G. Balch, "Women for Peace and Freedom," *Survey Graphic,* Vol. 35, No. 10, Oct., 1946, p. 358.
4. Emily G. Balch, Address in French, Luxembourg, 1946, in *Four Lights,* Vol. 6, No. 6; tr. by M. M. Randall.
5. Emily G. Balch, "Women for Peace and Freedom," *Survey Graphic, op. cit.,* p. 358.
6. Emily G. Balch, Speech of Greeting, *Report of Luxembourg Congress, 1946,* p. 11.
7. Emily G. Balch, "Pursuit of Peace," leaflet, W.I.L.P.F. (U.S.), Jan., 1950, in S.C.P.C.
8. Emily G. Balch, "Women for Peace and Freedom," *Survey Graphic, op. cit.,* p. 360.
9. *Ibid.,* p. 359.
10. *Int. Circ. Letter,* No. 3, 1945, Sept., 1945.
11. Yella Hertzka, Marie Lous-Mohr, notes taken at Congress by M. M. Randall, in S.C.P.C.
12. Else Zeuthen, Report, in *Int. Circ. Letter,* No. 4, 1945, Dec., 1945; also in *Report of Luxembourg Cong.,* Report on Denmark, pp. 70 ff.
13. Norwegian Report, *Int. Circ. Letter,* No. 4, 1945, Dec., 1945; also in *Report of Lux. Cong.,* pp. 95 ff.
14. From notes taken at Luxembourg Congress by M. M. Randall, in S.C.P.C.
15. Brand Blanshard, *Four Lights,* Vol. 6, No. 6, Jan., 1947.
16. New York *Neue Volkszeitung,* Nov. 23, 1946.
17. Emily G. Balch, letter to J. H. and M. M. Randall, Jan., 1946, in files of M. M. Randall.
18. Emily G. Balch, to Paul U. Kellogg, Nov. 30, 1946, in S.C.P.C.
19. Myrtle Wright, letter, Oslo, Dec. 11, 1946, in *Int. Circ. Letter,* No. 4, 1947, Jan., 1947.
20. Speech of Gunnar Jahn, Dec. 10, 1946, Oslo, in S.C.P.C.
21. Ellen Stone (Eppelsheimer) to M. M. Randall, Feb. 9, 1961, in files of M. M. Randall.
22. Emily G. Balch, "W.I.L. Revisited," *Monthly News Sheet* of British Section of W.I.L., July, 1948; also *Int. Circ. Let.,* No. 10, 1948, pp.1-2.
23. Barbara Duncan-Harris, *Int. Circ. Let.,* No. 10, 1948, p. 6.
24. Emily G. Balch, Christmas Message to International Membership, Dec., 1948, in *Int. Circ. Letter,* No. 12, 1948, p. 1.

Chapter Nineteen

1. Emily G. Balch, Message to Meeting at Kalamazoo, Michigan, June, 1954, in S.C.P.C.
2. Jane Addams, *Peace and Bread*, p. 51.
3. Emily G. Balch, "Letter to the Chinese People," *The Nation,* May 14, 1955, p. 418.
4. Emily G. Balch, letter to Marie Lous-Mohr, Nov. 21, 1955; also in *Pax et Libertas*, Vol. 22, No. 1, Jan.-March, 1956.
5. *Minutes* of International Executive Committee, Zürich, Sept., 1934, pp. 12-15, in S.C.P.C.
6. Alice Balch Stone, letter to M. M. Randall, Feb. 8, 1962, in files of M. M. Randall.

Index

461

Elder, Louise, 66
Elfenbein, Elsie, 351, 361
Eliot, Charles W., 119, 197
Embargoes, 333
Emergency Peace Federation, 220, 227 ff., 230, 231
Emerson, Ralph Waldo, 37
Employment Agencies, Germany, 318
Envoys to Northern Capitals, 180 ff.
Envoys to War Capitals, 166 ff.
"Equal rights" for women, 327n.
Equality, fraternal, concept of, 327
"Erin Go Bragh," 55
Ervine, Julia, President of Wellesley College, 106
Evans, Mrs. Glendower, 149, 156
Evans, Jane, 361, 361n.

Fabens, Lena, 56, 60, 70, 72, 76, 441
Factory Inspection Commission, 114
Fan Noli, Father, 290
Farquharson, Mary, 357
Fascism, 321, 326 ff.
Fisher, Dorothy Canfield, 78-80, 368
Fisher, H. A. L., 287, 290
Fisher, Mary, "The Quakeress," 167
Fear, 377, 379
Fellowship of Reconciliation, 260, 352
Ferri, Enrico, 98
Fichte, Johann Gottlieb, 90
Fine, Jean (Mrs. Charles Spahr), 67
Fiske, Helen, *see* Jackson, Helen Hunt
Fiske, John, 119
Flynt, Josiah, 94
"Food Blockades," 266, 267, 333
Forchammer, Henni, 286
Ford, Henry, 202, 211, 225
Ford, Mrs. Henry, 205
Ford Peace Expedition, 141, 162, 206 ff., 213
Foreign Policy Association, 136
Forster, E. M., 15, 22, 36, 135, 359
Fosdick, Harry Emerson, 236
Fourier, Charles, 77
Four Lights, 217

"Fourteen Points," 141, 159, 159n., 259n.
Foville, Alfred de, 74, 75
Fox, George, Declaration of, 352
Francis, Saint, 126, 311
Fraser, Leon, 238n.
"Freedom of Association" in 1917, 249
Freedom, concept of, 326 ff.
Freud, Sigmund, 19, 443
Fried, Alfred, 419
"Frothinghams," 41
Fry, Joan, 291
Functional approach to world unity, 373

Gale, Zona, 218
Gandhi, Mohandas K., 126, 430
Garrison, William Lloyd, 37
Gasparri, Pietro (Cardinal), Secretary of State, 168, 175, 175n.
Geneva and internationalism, 282, 283
Genoni, Rosa, 155, 166
Gerard, James W., 171
Germany, amoralism in, 318, 380; anti-semitism, 318
Giddings, Franklin H., 69, 70, 72, 82, 119
Gillespie, Mabel, 112
Gilman, Charlotte Perkins, 219
Gladden, Washington, 219
Glücklich, Vilma, 155, 297, 299
Gnauck-Kühne, Elisabeth, 92
Gobat, Marguerite, 282, 286
Gonne, Maude, 430
Good will and reason, 378
Gorges, Captain Robert, 25
Gould, Alice, 50, 51, 56, 62, 66 ff., 436, 441
Gould, Mrs. Ayrton, 262
Gould, Benjamin Apthrop, 51, 66
Gregory, Saint, of Nazianzus, 369
Grenoble Congress of Women, 1932, 320, 321, 405
Grey, Sir Edward, 164, 168, 170, 177, 186, 187, 191, 196, 204, 205
Grey, John, 33
Gronna, Asle J., 233
Gurs Concentration Camp, 337

474 IMPROPER BOSTONIAN: EMILY GREENE BALCH

Sonnino, Baron Sidney Constantine, 168, 174, 175
Soviet Union, attitude of W.I.L.P.F. toward, 411
Spain, 323, 334, 354
Sparling, Mrs. H. A., 99
Spencer, Anna Garlin, 140, 294
Stallings, Laurence, 232n.
Standard Oil Company, 106
Stevenson, Archibald, 263
Stevenson List: *Who's Who in Pacifism*, 263
Stevenson, Robert Louis, 360
Stewart, Annalee, 443
Stöcker, Dr. Helene, 155, 279, 310
Stockholm Conference on neutral mediation, 107n., 213, 225
Stone, Mrs. Robert Bowditch, see Balch, Alice
Stone, Ellen, 424, 426
Stone, Lucy, 66
Stone, William J., 230, 233
Stürgkh, Count K., 168, 172
Suez Canal, 374
Summer School of Applied Ethics, 1892, 82, 105
Sumner, Charles, 23, 34, 35, 38
Survey, The, 136
Suttner, Bertha von, 133, 419
Swanwick, Helena, 139n., 156n., 262, 276; on Jane Addams, 280; 286, 310, 428
Sylvain family, 306
Sylvain, Dr. Normil, 306

"Tainted money," 106
Tarbell, Ida, 106
Tennyson, Alfred Lord, 70
Theresa, Saint, 391
Thomas, Dr. James Carey, 52
Thomas, Mrs. James Carey, 52
Thomas, M[artha] Carey, 52, 53, 62-65
Thomas, Norman, 236, 252
Thompson, William Hale ("Big Bill"), 223, 249
Thoreau, Henry David, 37, 229
Ticknor, Caroline, 39, 39n., 45, 47
Tisza, Count, Stephan, 168, 173, 174, 174n.
Tolstoi, Leo, 126, 391
Totalitarianism, 380

Towards a Planetary Civilization, 345
Towards the Peace that Shall Last, 136
Traherne, Thomas, 38
Trask, William, "Old Planter," 27
Treaty of Versailles, 267, 268
Treitschke, Heinrich von, 317
Trevelyan, Charles, 139n.
Trevelyan, George M. (the younger), 135
Trusteeship system, 366, 383
Tufts, James H., 400
Tumulty, Joseph P., 212, 332
Tymkevich, Father Paul, 121

"Unconditional surrender," 361
Union of Democratic Control, 139, 140, 214
"L'Union pour le Suffrage des Femmes," 156
United Nations, 364, 371; and self-interest, 384
Usteri, Paul, 287

Vambéry, Mélanie, 410
Van Loon, Hendrick, 430
Vardaman, James K., 230, 233
Varese-Lugano Summer School, 295
Venture in Internationalism, 335, 336
Versailles, Treaty of, 261
Vienna Congress of Women, 1921, 292 ff.
Villard, Fanny Garrison, 134, 144, 216, 218, 224, 293
Villard, Oswald Garrison, 193, 194n., 199, 212, 216, 218, 224, 226, 257, 260, 329, 430, 442
Viviani, René, 168, 176

Waffen Nieder, Die, by Bertha von Suttner, 133
Wagner, Adolf, 90, 92, 96, 317
Wald, Lillian D., 134, 136, 193, 201, 216, 226, 262, 428
Wales, Julia Grace, 145, 150, 158, 161-63, 167, 180, 207n., 322
Walker and Seegar School, 53
Wallas, Graham, 189
Wallenberg, Knut A., 168, 181-86
Walling, William English, 112